I0269425

Welsh Guardsman
by
Augustus John, O.M.

WELSH GUARDS AT WAR

MAJOR L. F. ELLIS
C. V. O., C. B. E., D. S. O., M. C.
Welsh Guards

LONDON STAMP EXCHANGE LTD
1989

FOREWORD

As an old Guardsman I shall always be proud that the Welsh Guards played such a gallant and distinguished role under my command in the Second World War. In 1940, the 1st Battalion fought with me on the beaches of Dunkirk whilst the 2nd Battalion was fighting beside the 2nd Battalion of my own old Regiment, the Irish Guards, at Boulogne.

Later, the 3rd Battalion of the Welsh Guards took an active part in the North African campaign which was brought to a final and victorious conclusion by the Battle of Tunis, resulting in the complete annihilation of the German-Italian forces under General Oberst Von Arnim and the capture of 248,000 prisoners. From then onwards this splendid Guards Battalion was to remain under my command all through that hard and bitter struggle of the Italian campaign, which starting in Sicily ended in the Alps with the mass surrender of a million German soldiers and the entry of the Allied Armies into Austria. Throughout the many battles fought and won during the long years of the war, this young Battalion not only worthily upheld, but added fresh lustre to the proud traditions of the Brigade of Guards.

Elsewhere in North-West Europe the 1st and 2nd Battalions of the Regiment were winning fresh laurels for themselves in the Battle of Normandy, and shortly afterwards led the Guards Armoured Division in its historic advance to Brussels and struck into the heart of Germany.

In recording the great deeds of the Welsh Guards on the battlefields of Europe we are not unmindful that individual Welsh Guardsmen served with distinction in nearly all theatres of operations where His Majesty's Forces were fighting the common enemy.

In this book is outlined the story of those campaigns in so far as they affect the Regiment. In a work of this sort it is not possible to record all the gallant and heroic deeds performed in the fight for freedom. Many, such as Lieutenant the Honourable Christopher Furness, V.C., laid down their lives in the cause for which we all fought; many others died and suffered in the struggle. Although their devotion and heroism is not mentioned here, Wales and their families can be justly proud of them.

I hope that this book will be widely read by present and future generations as it shows how young and old, from all walks of life were welded together into a great team by common ideals, discipline and respect for our age-old traditions ; and by their individual and collective efforts triumphed over a hard fighting and bitter enemy.

Thus, the United Nations at War were able to vanquish fear and oppression and once again be free men and Welshmen in particular, by the gallantry of their sons can justly claim the right to say :—"*Cymru am byth*——Wales for ever."

Alexander of Tunis

CANADA,
September 18*th*, 1946.

CONTENTS

Part I THE STORY OF THE REGIMENT

CHAPTER I PREVIOUS SERVICE 1

THE SECOND WORLD WAR
    II FIRST ROUND—"A GRIM START" 5
    III SECOND ROUND—"A GOOD RECOVERY" . . 17
    IV THIRD ROUND—"THE END OF THE BEGINNING" . 24
    V FOURTH ROUND—"THE BEGINNING OF THE END" . 41
    VI FIFTH ROUND—"THE END" 74

Part II BATTALIONS IN ACTION

FRANCE, 1940
    ARRAS 89
    BOULOGNE 96
    VYFWEG AND WEST CAPPEL 107

TUNISIA, 1943
    FONDOUK 114
    HAMMAM LIF 123

ITALY, 1944
    CERASOLA 129
    CASSINO 140
    PICCOLO AND ARCE 147
    PERUGIA AND SAN MARCO 155
    THE ARNO VALLEY 164

FRANCE AND BELGIUM, 1944
    CAGNY AND LE POIRIER 173
    FIGHTING IN THE "BOCAGE" 181
    RECONNAISSANCE TO ESTRY 182
    ST. PIERRE TARENTAINE 187
    MONTCHAMP 189
    LE BAS PERRIER 193
    ADVANCE TO BRUSSELS 202
    WAVRE 212
    BEERINGEN, HELCHTEREN AND HECHTEL . . 216
    NIJMEGEN AND "THE ISLAND" 227
    VEULEN AND SITTARD 235

ITALY, 1944-45
    CONSUMA AND POMINO 241
    BATTAGLIA AND VERRO 245
    THE PO AND THE ADIGE 259

GERMANY, 1945
    THE RHINELAND BATTLE—HASSUM AND BONNINGHARDT . 266
    NORDHORN TO LINGEN 274
    VISSELHOVEDE 281
    WESTERTIMKE 285

EPILOGUE AND ACKNOWLEDGMENTS 289
ROLL OF HONOUR 293
HONOURS AND AWARDS 300
ILLUSTRATIONS 311
CAMPAIGN MAPS 375
INDEX 381

LIST OF ILLUSTRATIONS

Plates

WELSH GUARDSMAN—*by Augustus John, O.M.* . . . . *Frontispiece*

DAWN AT DUNKIRK—*by Sergeant C. Murrell* . . . *facing page* 14
    This drawing was made on the spot while men of the 1st Battalion were waiting in the sand dunes for ships to bring them home.

WELSH GUARDS OFFICER—*by Lieutenant Rex Whistler* . *facing page* 38
    The portrait is of Lieutenant R. G. Whiskard, who like Rex Whistler was killed in action while commanding a troop of the 2nd Battalion's tanks in the Battle of Normandy. He is wearing the distinctive overalls worn by Officers of the 2nd Battalion during training for tank warfare.

WINTER IN HOLLAND—*by Sergeant C. Murrell* . . *facing page* 70
    Cromwell tanks of the 2nd Battalion in the winter of 1944.

CASSINO—*by the Author* . . . . . . *facing page* 142
    The ruins of the gaol where the 3rd Battalion had their Headquarters when they were in Cassino; and beyond the Castle which No. 3 Company held. The Monastery is on the hilltop to the extreme left of the sketch.

PICCOLO AND ARCE—*by the Author* . . . . *facing page* 152
    From this point of view it is easy to see how the road to Arce was dominated by Piccolo on the left, and Monte Orio on the right, Arce looking down the road and Rocca d'Arce on the mountain above.

MONTCHAMP—*by the Author* . . . . . . *facing page* 190
    This is typical "Bocage" country. In the first phase of the attack by the 1st Battalion, on August the 4th, 1944, seven Germans were captured in the cottage seen in the foreground. Away behind Montchamp lies the ground near Estry which was occupied by the 2nd Battalion.

ON THE ROAD TO BRUSSELS—*by Sergeant C. Murrell* . *facing page* 206
    From the driving cab of one of the 1st Battalion's 15 cwt. trucks.

IN "THE ISLAND"—*by the Author* . . . . *facing page* 230
    The scene of the fighting near Aam, showing the partly constructed road, and in the distance Arnhem. The tree-lined ditch across the centre of the picture was the furthest point reached.

IN THE RHINELAND BATTLE—*by Sergeant C. Murrell* . *facing page* 270
    A jeep of the 1st Battalion is passing the Divisional Advanced Dressing Station near Kevelaer.

"JEEP" PASSING
BOGGED-DOWN "SHERMAN."

Diagrams

THE CASSINO POSITION	42
THE BATTAGLIA RIDGE	250

Illustrations of Arms and Equipment

By SERGEANT C. MURRELL

BRITISH

1	FIGHTING ORDER AND NO. 18 WIRELESS SET	xv
2	BREN GUN, STEN GUN AND HAND GRENADES	23
3	2-IN. MORTAR	244
4	P.I.A.T. (PROJECTOR, INFANTRY, ANTI-TANK)	154
5	BREN GUN CARRIER	16
6	BREN GUN CARRIER	95
7	No. 38 WIRELESS SET	128
8	FIELD TELEPHONE	87
9	MINE DETECTOR	172
10	DESPATCH RIDER AND 6-POUNDER ANTI-TANK GUN . . .	163
11	CROMWELL TANK	40
12	CROMWELL TANK	211
13	CHALLENGER TANK	311

LIST OF ILLUSTRATIONS—*contd.*

ILLUSTRATIONS OF ARMS AND EQUIPMENT
BY SERGEANT C. MURRELL

BRITISH—*contd.*

		page
14	HONEY TANK	288
15	CHURCHILL TANK	72
16	JEEP AND SHERMAN TANK	ix
17	25-POUNDER SELF-PROPELLED GUN	292
18	STRETCHER-BEARERS	106

GERMAN

19	TIGER TANK	180
20	PANTHER TANK	xiii, 273
21	MARK IV TANK	113
22	PANZERFAUST ("BAZOOKA")	284
23	SPANDAU, SCHMEISER AND HAND GRENADES	139
24	FIVE-BARRELLED MORTAR ("MOANING MINNIE")	226
25	88 mm. DUAL-PURPOSE GUN	85

Maps

1 CAMPAIGNS (OPERATIONAL ROUTES)

FRANCE, 1940—ROUTE OF THE 1ST BATTALION *Inset map facing* 378-379

TUNISIA, 1943—ROUTE OF THE 3RD BATTALION . . . 376

ITALY, 1944-1945—ROUTE OF THE 3RD BATTALION . . . 377

THE WESTERN FRONT—

    ROUTE OF THE 1ST AND 2ND BATTALIONS—NORMANDY TO BRUSSELS 378

    ROUTE OF THE 1ST AND 2ND BATTALIONS—BRUSSELS TO CUXHAVEN 379

2 SITUATIONS

BRITISH EXPEDITIONARY FORCE, 24TH MAY, 1940 . . . 13

BRITISH EXPEDITIONARY FORCE, 27TH MAY, 1940 . . . 15

ALLIED ARMIES IN TUNISIA, 6TH APRIL AND 15TH MAY, 1943 . 33

LIST OF ILLUSTRATIONS—*contd.*

MAPS

2 SITUATIONS—*contd.*   *page*

ALLIED FRONT, ITALY, MAY AND JUNE, 1944	49
ADVANCE TOWARDS ARNHEM, SEPTEMBER, 1944	69
ALLIED FRONT IN ITALY, WINTER OF 1944-1945	64
A YEAR'S PROGRESS	73

3 ACTIONS

PLAN OF BOULOGNE	98
VYFWEG AND WEST CAPPEL	108
FONDOUK	116
CERASOLA	130
PERUGIA AND SAN MARCO	156
THE ARNO VALLEY	60
APPROACH TO THE GOTHIC LINE	62
CAGNY AND LE POIRIER	174
FIGHTING IN THE "BOCAGE"	184
WAVRE	214
BEERINGEN TO HECHTEL	218
ROUTE TO "THE ISLAND"	66
THE RHINELAND BATTLE	268
BATTAGLIA AND VERRO	246
ADVANCE TO THE PO	260
THE PO TO THE ADIGE	264
THE FINAL BATTLE IN ITALY	78
ADVANCE INTO GERMANY	81
LAST FIGHTS IN GERMANY	83

4 PLAN

THE CASTLE POSITION AT CASSINO	145

Illustrations and Notes

	page
HIS MAJESTY THE KING AND THE COLONEL OF THE REGIMENT	312
LIEUTENANT THE HON. CHRISTOPHER FURNESS, V.C.	314
BOULOGNE	316
THE CHATEAU AT WEST CAPPEL	316
THE FONDOUK BATTLEGROUND	318
GERMAN POST ON "THE RAZOR-BACK"	318
HAMMAN LIF—TWO VIEWS OF EL ROROUF	320
MONTE CERASOLA—THREE VIEWS	322
CASSINO FROM THE AIR	324
CASSINO DURING BOMBING	326
CASSINO SHOWING CASTLE HILL	326
CASSINO LOOKING BACK TOWARDS MONTE TROCCHIO	328
THE LIRI VALLEY	330
THE FIRST MEN INTO ARCE	332
AREZZO—WELSH GUARDS RESTING	332
SAN MARCO	334
THE POMINO RIDGE	334
VIEW FROM TORRE A MONTE	336
MONTE BATTAGLIA—TWO VIEWS	338
MONTE DEL VERRO—TWO VIEWS	340
GREVE FROM BATTALION HEADQUARTERS	340
MR. CHURCHILL WITH THE 2ND BATTALION	342
THE TRAINING BATTALION ON PARADE	342
LANDING IN NORMANDY	344
SCENE NEAR LANDING BEACH	344
CAEN	346
1ST AND 2ND BATTALIONS MOVING UP	348
2ND BATTALION GOING INTO BATTLE	350
1ST BATTALION GOING INTO BATTLE	350
1ST BATTALION ATTACK NEAR CAGNY	352
2ND BATTALION TANKS IN "THE BOCAGE"	354
A PATROL OF THE 1ST BATTALION REPORTING	354

LIST OF ILLUSTRATIONS—*contd.*

ILLUSTRATIONS AND NOTES

	page
Burning Enemy Transport	356
Advance to Brussels	358
Into Belgium	360
The liberation of Brussels—two views	362
Two views of Hechtel	364
Prisoners of war	366
Salvage	366
Valkenswaad	368
Nijmegen bridge	368
In Germany—"Magnum"	370
Near Westertimke	370
After the War	
The second entry into Brussels	372
Farewell to armour	372
1st Battalion in Scotland	374

GERMAN "PANTHER" KNOCKED OUT.

Part I

A GENERAL SURVEY OF THE REGIMENT'S PART IN THE WAR OF 1939 TO 1945, SHOWING WHERE AND WHY AND WITH WHAT RESULTS THE BATTALIONS FOUGHT

Detailed accounts of the principal actions are given in Part II

GUARDSMAN OF RIFLE COMPANY AND SIGNALLER USING 18 WIRELESS SET.

CHAPTER ONE

PREVIOUS SERVICE

Hwy clod na hoedl
Fame lasts longer than life
Welsh Guards Company Motto

THE Welsh Regiment of Foot Guards was formed on the 26th of February, 1915, and three days afterwards, on St. David's Day, mounted Guard at Buckingham Palace for the first time. The Regiment is thus one of the youngest in the British Army.

But it is a member of a very old family of Regiments—the Brigade of Guards—which has been mounting the King's Guard and fighting the King's enemies since 1660. Through nearly three hundred years Regiments of the Brigade have maintained the highest standards of training and discipline and have served with distinction in almost every campaign and continent where British infantry have fought. When the Welsh Guards went to war for the first time, less than six months after they were formed, their strength was derived not only from a foundation of officers, warrant officers, non-commissioned officers and men— mostly Welshmen—who had transferred voluntarily from the older Guards Regiments, but also from the inheritance of a great tradition into which they had entered. The following pages give some account of how they have striven to maintain that tradition and to justify their proud place in the Brigade of Guards.

The Welsh Guards were formed after the Great War had been in progress for six months. Six battalions of the Brigade had gone to France with the original Expeditionary Force in August, 1914. Grenadier, Coldstream, Scots and Irish Guards had helped to stem the German "race to the sea" and to save the Channel ports. They had fought in the retreat from Mons to the Marne and in the advance across the Aisne : they had fought in the first battle of Ypres and in the battles of Neuve Chapelle and Festubert : and they had fought in the trench warfare which followed the stabilisation of the front. In August, 1915, these battalions, with others sent out from England, were formed into a Guards Division. In this Division was the 1st Battalion Welsh Guards.

A month later the Welsh Guards went into action for the first time in the battle of Loos and their bearing was held to have been "up to the best Brigade of Guards standard." "Loos" is the first Battle Honour borne on the Colours of the Regiment.

During the winter of 1915-1916 the Battalion was occupied with the rest of the Guards Division in trench warfare. In the summer of 1916 they fought in the battle of the Somme, taking part in actions at Ginchy, Flers-Courcelette and Morval, all three of which were awarded to the Regiment as further Battle Honours. There followed another winter of trench warfare.

In July of the following year (1917) the Guards Division fought in the third battle of Ypres. Sergeant R. Bye, Welsh Guards, won the Victoria Cross "for most conspicuous bravery" on the first day of the action and the Battalion captured all of its objectives. The battle begun that day continued through the summer and early autumn, and the Battalion took part in further attacks at Poelcappelle and Passchendaele in October. A month later, following a break-through at Cambrai by British tanks which was inadequately followed up, the Germans counter-attacked and threatened, in turn, to break through the British front. The Guards Division was hastily moved up and, in a series of actions which included an attack by the Welsh Guards at Gouzeaucourt, helped to save an ugly situation.

The collapse of Russia about this time made it possible for the Germans to transfer large reinforcements to the Western front, and on the 21st of March, 1918, sixty-four German divisions attacked the line held by the 3rd and 5th British Armies. The Guards Division had been holding and strongly fortifying a line east of Arras and had just been relieved. The line they had left held, but they were at once moved up to the front which was being pressed back south of Arras. They shared in the fighting which continued through the early summer, till the enemy were exhausted and firmly held, and in August they joined in the Allied advance which was to end only with Armistice Day and the final defeat of the German army. Their main actions were at St. Leger, the crossing of the Canal du Nord and the breaking of the Hindenburg Line, the capture of St. Vaast, the crossing of the

Selle and the final attack at Bavai five days before the Armistice.

The 1st Battalion Welsh Guards had gone into action at Loos seven months after the day on which the Regiment was formed. From that day till the Armistice it had served continuously at a cost of over two thousand casualties in killed and wounded. It had won the right to bear on its Colours : "Loos," "Ginchy," "Flers-Courcelette," "Morval," "Pilckem," "Poelcappelle," "Cambrai, 1917, 1918," "Bapaume, 1918," "Canal du Nord," and "Sambre," with the following additional Battle Honours shown in the Army List : "Somme, 1916, 1918," "Ypres, 1917," "Passchendaele," "Arras, 1918," "Albert, 1918," "Drocourt-Quéant," "Hindenburg Line," "Havrincourt," "Selle," "France and Flanders, 1915-1918." It had been awarded a V.C., a C.B., two C.M.Gs., twelve D.S.Os. and one Bar, thirty-five M.Cs. and two Bars, twenty-two D.C.Ms. and two Bars, one hundred and forty-six M.Ms. and nine Bars.

The new Regiment had added to the inherited tradition of the Brigade of Guards a Welsh Guards tradition.

With the rest of the Guards Division the 1st Battalion marched into Germany after the Armistice, occupied Cologne and remained there till the following March, when the Division was brought home. As the Battalion sailed proudly from Dunkirk on March the 11th, 1919, nobody thought that it would embark there again under sadly different conditions in May, 1940.

Shortly after returning home the Guards Division, as a Division, ceased to exist. In a farewell message it was called by His Majesty King George V—"A Division which knew no defeat." Its official historian summed up its story in these words :

> "Whatever their leaders demanded of them the troops of the Guards Division did manfully and well. They gave an example of unflinching courage and endurance to the whole Army and on more than one occasion . . . their discipline and unyielding steadfastness saved a critical situation."

* * * * *

There followed for the Welsh Guards ten years of service at home spent in the normal routine of training and Public Duties, after which, in 1929, the Battalion embarked for its first tour of foreign service in Egypt. It returned at the end of 1930 for another ten years' home service. As that decade drew to its close the likelihood of war with Germany grew daily more apparent, and in 1939 two steps were taken which affected Welsh Guardsmen. The 1st Battalion was ordered to reinforce the Garrison at Gibraltar and embarked on the 22nd of April. Four days later the King signed a special Order of the Day approving the creation of a second regular Battalion. The 2nd Battalion was formed on the 18th of May and when war was declared in September, 1939, it was stationed at the Tower of London. The 1st Battalion was still in Gibraltar.

CHAPTER TWO

THE SECOND WORLD WAR
FIRST ROUND—A GRIM START
(1939-40)

Gwell y wialen a blygo na'r hon a dorro
Better to bend than to break
Old Welsh Saying

WAR was declared on Germany on the 3rd of September, 1939. The 1st Battalion at Gibraltar was not at once greatly affected; drafts arrived and the Battalion was put on to a war footing, duties were somewhat increased, guards had to be found for prize-ships brought into harbour by the Royal Navy and there was work on the strengthening of some of the defences. Apart from these abnormal tasks and a very temporary shortage of some ration foods, life on the Rock was but little disturbed. The only fact which the War Diary thought worthy of record on the 25th of September was "liver and sausages arrived at Gibraltar."

War came with greater urgency to the 2nd Battalion, only recently formed and not yet trained for war. They moved at once to camp in the grounds of a fun fair at Theydon Bois, Epping Forest, and there, where the booths and roundabouts stood shrouded and silent, the fun of the Cockney and the aimless movement of holiday crowds gave place to ordered drill and the irrepressible humour of Welshmen preparing for battle—and no soldiers are gayer when off parade. Reservists rejoined, both officers and men, recruits came from the Guards Depot, and the first batch of officers with Emergency Commissions arrived. And here, at the outset of this story, it is most fitting to acknowledge the Regiment's great indebtedness to the men of very varying ages and of almost every calling (except that of a soldier) who gave their talents, their experience and in many cases their lives in its service. Without them the half of what is recorded in these pages could not have been achieved.

Early in September a large draft was sent away to make the

1st Battalion up to war strength, and those who rose early to see them leave Theydon Bois wondered sadly how many more must go before there could be peace again. Numbers rapidly increased as more men were called to the Colours, and, having completed the organisation of the 2nd Battalion and the nucleus of what was to be the Training Battalion, Lieutenant-Colonel Sir Alexander Stanier, Bart., M.C., who commanded, moved the 2nd Battalion back to the Tower of London and the Training Battalion under Major H. T. Rice struck the tents at Theydon Bois and moved to Roman Way Camp, Colchester. There Lieutenant-Colonel Lord Glanusk, D.S.O., took command and Major Rice went to command the Welsh Guards Company at the Depot. Like Lieutenant-Colonel Stanier, he had fought with the 1st Battalion in the last war and had had long service with the Regiment in "the years between."

The Tower of London is at the best of times a bad station so far as training is concerned, but now the number of war-time duties and defence measures which the 2nd Battalion was required to perform made any consecutive training impossible. Men learnt the drill and discipline required to mount King's Guard and to find other Public Duties, and the 2nd Battalion mounted King's Guard for the first time on the 16th of October. It was the first time in history that the King's Guard had been mounted from the Tower of London. Lieutenant-Colonel Stanier continued to press for the opportunity to train for war, but during this first winter his Battalion was retained in London —an insurance against risks which did not in fact mature.

On the fine but bitterly cold morning of February the 14th, 1940, His Majesty the King, Colonel-in-Chief of the Regiment, visited the Tower and after inspecting the 2nd Battalion presented their first Colours. It was a proud day for the new Battalion and for Colonel W. Murray Threipland, D.S.O., who had commanded the 1st Battalion when the Regiment was formed, had been Captain of the first King's Guard mounted by the Welsh Guards, on St. David's Day, 1915, had led them in their first battle, and was now Colonel of the Regiment he had done so much to mould in the early days.

So the winter passed, and it was not until April, 1940, that the 2nd Battalion was relieved of London duties, brigaded with

A Grim Start—1939-40

the 2nd Battalion Irish Guards under Brigadier Sir Oliver Leese, Bart., D.S.O. and moved to Camberley for training.

While these events were taking place in England, the 1st Battalion was transferred from Gibraltar to France, sailing for Marseilles on the 7th of November and spending a night in Paris (where they did a ceremonial march-past and had a great reception) before going to the front. To understand the part which they and the 2nd Battalion played in subsequent events it will be well to look at what was happening in France during this first winter of the war.

On the day after war was declared a British Expeditionary Force, under General The Viscount Gort, V.C., began to move overseas. Its first task was to collaborate with the forces of France in defence of the frontiers, and the sector allotted to the B.E.F. was the salient formed by the frontier between France and Belgium, north and east of Lille. Its right was at Maulde and its left at Halluin, across the River Lys from Menin, with a defensive flank along that river to Armentières. Most of the winter was spent in the organisation of this position in depth and in "work projects of great magnitude" on bases and lines of communication. Because of the possibility of attack by sea and air troops were landed at Cherbourg, while stores and vehicles were despatched via Nantes, St. Nazaire and Brest. The decision not to risk the use of Channel ports thus involved the development and maintenance of very long lines of communication and had important bearings on what happened when fighting began. It is a first fact to be borne in mind if subsequent operations are to be understood.

The second is the comparatively small size of the fighting force under Lord Gort's command. By mid-December he was able to report that a quarter of a million men, 45,000 vehicles and a monthly total of 60,000 to 100,000 tons of stores and equipment had been landed. But these considerable figures are likely to mislead unless it is realised that at the end of January, 1940, out of this large total the *fighting* force at his disposal consisted only of six divisions, with Corps and Army troops—a smaller fighting force than the "contemptible little Army" which had landed in France in August, 1914. By May, 1940, when the fighting began, Lord Gort had still but nine fighting divisions, and even so he reported that the situation in regard to equipment caused him "serious misgivings"; in particular there was shortage of guns, ammunition, technical apparatus and, above all, of armoured troops.

Finally, it must be remembered that Lord Gort was not acting independently, but under the orders of the French Command.

During this winter of preparation the role of the 1st Battalion was to provide protection for General Headquarters, then in and around Habarcq, eight miles west of Arras. The Battalion was based at Izel-les-Hameau about three miles away with Companies widely dispersed in villages and the northern outskirts of Arras. Officers and men quickly adapted themselves to their new life and made friends with their French neighbours. It was a hard winter, wet and stormy, with long periods of frost and snow varied by others of thaw and mud, but spirits were high and health good and such training as was possible was carried on. There were a few exercises, many fatigues and as much of games and concerts as could be arranged in spare time. His Majesty the King, Colonel-in-Chief of the Regiment, visited the Battalion on the 7th of December, one of the few really fine days, and on other occasions H.R.H. the Duke of Windsor and the Presidents of the French and Polish Republics paid them visits. So passed their first winter in France.

* * * * *

On the 10th of May the whole situation changed with dramatic suddenness. At daybreak on that morning the enemy started bombing key towns and aerodromes, British Headquarters being among their targets. The same day their armies entered Holland and Belgium. The "phoney war" gave place to a *blitzkrieg* which was to end with the conquest of Holland, Belgium, Luxembourg and France, in less than four weeks.

To give an account of the whole campaign would be outside the scope of this story, but the part played by the Welsh Guards can only be understood if the outline of events which led to a catastrophic collapse of opposition to the enemy is known.

Norway and Denmark had been overrun in April, but Holland and Belgium had persisted in their belief that if they remained

A Grim Start—1939-40

neutral they would be left alone. Holland was the first to learn of the futility of their policy. On May the 11th, unheralded by any warning, German forces crossed the Dutch frontier at many points and landed both by sea and air near Rotterdam and The Hague. With a small and ill-equipped army, Holland could do little to stem the advance of German troops which followed, and Britain was in no position to take on more than she was already committed to in France. The Government decided, however, to send a small force over to assist the Dutch in dealing with the local situation, on the understanding that if the Netherlands Government evacuated The Hague this force would be withdrawn to England. The 11th of May was the Saturday before Whitsun. The 2nd Battalion Welsh Guards and the 2nd Battalion Irish Guards had completed a period of training at Camberley and, having had little previous leave, were sent away on that morning by special trains. At ten o'clock on the same morning their immediate recall was ordered by the War Office and some of the special trains were stopped *en route*. It was clear, however, that a day or two must elapse before the full strength of either Battalion could get back, and orders were accordingly given that a composite battalion of Irish and Welsh Guards should be formed from the first men to return. Lieutenant-Colonel J. C. Haydon, O.B.E., Irish Guards, was to command, with Major G. St. V. J. Vigor, Welsh Guards, as Second-in-Command. Eventually the contingent which the Welsh Guards contributed to this composite battalion consisted of a company 201 strong, under Captain C. H. R. Heber-Percy, out of the total of 651. Lieutenant-Colonel Stanier was to form a second composite battalion as soon as the remainder of the men who had gone on leave got back to Camberley; but as it turned out this second composite battalion was not required, for the battalion which sailed on the 12th fulfilled the function for which both had been intended. Landing on the Hook of Holland on Whit Monday, May the 13th, they took up positions covering the port and dug in. There was some heavy bombing (involving casualties to men and stores) and paratroops were seen coming down for the first time. Next day, though no ground attack materialised, the general situation in the country deteriorated rapidly and after the Queen and her Ministers had crossed to England the Battalion was ordered home again. Before leaving by the destroyers sent to fetch them, they set fire to as many petrol stores as possible to prevent these from falling into German hands. On the same afternoon the main Dutch forces laid down their arms.

On the morning when this Company of the 2nd Battalion Welsh Guards left England for Holland, the enemy invaded Belgium, preceding their attack by the bombing of key towns and aerodromes in Belgium and France. Belgium's disastrous refusal to prepare for just such a situation had compelled the French and British armies to organise defences behind the Belgian frontier, but they promptly went to her aid. Leaving the positions which they had spent nine months in fortifying they now moved forward to meet the enemy on an unprepared line. The British army took up positions to the east of Brussels with French and Belgium troops on their left and the French on their right. On the 14th of May, the day on which Holland surrendered, the German forces in Belgium broke through on the Albert Canal and turned the Belgian defence in the north, while twenty miles to the south of the British sector they overran undefended Luxembourg and strong armoured columns pushed through the Ardennes into Belgium. On May the 15th they crossed the Meuse and struck deep into France.

With these penetrations to the north and south of the British positions, it was clear that Lord Gort's forces must be withdrawn if they were not to be left in a dangerous salient. On the orders of the French Generalissimo they fell back, fighting, till their old positions on the Franco-Belgian frontier were reached. Meanwhile the enemy's drive westwards through the French positions to the south reached Abbeville on the coast and turned north towards the Channel ports. Not only were our long lines of communication cut and Lord Gort's forces separated from their reserves and supply bases, but there was danger now that they might be attacked from the rear. Accordingly Territorial troops which had been brought to France for labour duties, with some Artillery and Engineers, were used to form a second line running from the sea near Gravelines and facing south-west. To the corridor thus formed Arras was the southern door.

And Arras was held by the 1st Battalion Welsh Guards. They had been stationed there twenty-two years before in the first

A Grim Start—1939-40

Great War. Now some Engineers, part of an Overseas Defence Battalion (9th Battalion West Yorkshire Regiment) and various details, including an improvised tank squadron, were also there. Lieutenant-Colonel F. A. V. Copland-Griffiths, M.C., the Commanding Officer of the 1st Battalion was appointed to command the garrison and Major W. D. C. Greenacre, M.V.O., took temporary command of the Battalion. Later on, the 6th Battalion Northumberland Fusiliers, the 8th Battalion The Green Howards and a battery of 25-pounders joined the garrison. Arras was held from the 17th of May, when the Battalion moved in, until the 24th of May, when they were ordered to withdraw. During that time the town was repeatedly bombed and shelled and a number of tank attacks were beaten off; the enemy had nearly surrounded Arras before the garrison left. The story of Arras, 1940, is told more fully in the second part of this book. Two sentences from Lord Gort's despatches are its best summary :

> "Thus concluded the defence of Arras, which had been carried out by a small garrison, hastily assembled, but well commanded, and determined to fight. It had imposed a valuable delay on a greatly superior enemy force against which it had blocked a vital road centre."

Meanwhile the 2nd Battalion, brought out from England after their share in the excursion to Holland, had also "imposed a valuable delay" at another critical point. On the morning of May the 21st, while out on an exercise at Camberley, they were ordered by telephone to proceed overseas the same afternoon, with the 2nd Battalion Irish Guards, now both under Brigadier W. A. F. L. Fox-Pitt, M.V.O., M.C., a Welsh Guardsman who had recently succeeded Brigadier Sir Oliver Leese, Bart., in command of the 20th Guards Brigade. It was a happy turn of fortune which sent Lieutenant-Colonel Stanier's Battalion into their first action under a fellow Welsh Guardsman.

On reaching Dover the Battalion learnt that they were to cross that night to Boulogne, already closely threatened by German forces. Their true role was not as clear to them at the time as it was afterwards, namely to hold German forces round Boulogne while the miscellaneous troops collected there were evacuated and to delay, by that much, the enemy's full concentration against the main British forces farther north.

The detailed story of their fight is told elsewhere (see page 96). For two days they held the German armour at bay, and though forced back from their original positions they never let the enemy through. As many as possible were withdrawn to England on the 24th of May by orders from the Government, having done what they were required to do—but at a high cost. All the wounded who had been sent to hospital fell into enemy hands and a large proportion of two companies (over 300) who failed to reach the ships in time to be evacuated and tried to break out of the town were surrounded and captured in the streets on succeeding days. When the last ship left, Major J. C. Windsor Lewis (No. 3 Company) with a remnant of his Company was still holding a road block. Next morning he withdrew to the harbour and continued to hold one arm of the docks for nearly two more days though by then the enemy held all the rest of the town and harbour. He was badly wounded but only when food and ammunition were exhausted did he surrender, to be taken on an ambulance to hospital. How he escaped and returned to England six months later, how he commanded the 2nd Battalion when it returned to France in 1944, how he led them into Belgium, Holland and over the Rhine into Germany, must be told later.

On this same day, the 24th of May, the 1st Battalion marched out of Arras. They were ordered to proceed via Douai—but the direct road to that place was being heavily shelled. They tried the nearest alternative road—to find it blocked by the enemy. If a section of the Carrier Platoon had not promptly and stubbornly attacked, while the column behind them was turned round, there might well have been a catastrophe. Lieutenant the Hon. C. Furness and several of his men lost their lives in the fight, but their gallantry was not in vain, for those behind moved safely to another road. They would have been glad to know that day that the 1st Battalion would return to Arras in triumph four years later. Furness was subsequently awarded the Victoria Cross for "his magnificent act of self-sacrifice against hopeless odds." The full story is told on page 93.

The accompanying map shows the position at this time :

A Grim Start—1939-40

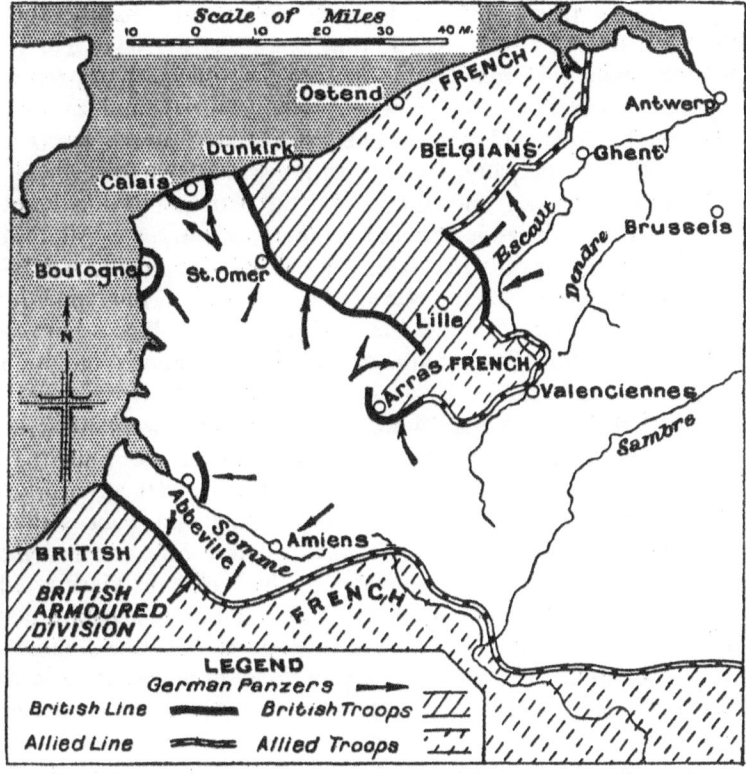

Through the next three days the Battalion retired, getting a short rest at Waziers and a longer one (the last they were to get in France) at Premesque, now Lord Gort's Headquarters. Here for the first time since they came to France the whole Battalion was in one place.

From Premesque they were ordered to Cassel, where General Headquarters was to be stationed; but when they reached Steenvoorde, four miles short of their destination, Cassel was already closely invested by the enemy. They were at once ordered to go to its defence and were soon in position and under fire, but the enemy's attempts to penetrate their line were stopped for the time being and shortly after the Battalion were ordered to withdraw to Houtkerque. They had hardly arrived, however, when they were ordered back to Cassel which was again being attacked. There they held their former positions till the following afternoon; then they were transferred north to hold another threatened flank position, south of Bergues, at Vyfweg and West Cappel. Here they had a quiet night, but were attacked by tanks and infantry next day. The brunt of the attack fell on No. 2 Company, whose position was surrounded. They had heavy casualties, and when finally the Battalion were ordered to withdraw only about twenty of the Company succeeded in fighting their way out after dark. Part of Headquarter Company was also overrun, but the rest of the Battalion was successfully withdrawn. The stand of the Battalion had helped to cover the 1st Guards Brigade while they took up a defensive position behind them, on the banks of a canal. Had the enemy succeeded in breaking through here there might well have been dire consequences for the troops retiring to the beaches.

After this fight near Bergues the Battalion were ordered to withdraw to the coast for evacuation. Much has been written elsewhere of the scene on the beaches near Dunkirk—of the wonderful part played by the Navy, by the Merchant Marine and by the hundreds of little ships which between them brought food and water to the waiting men and took more than three hundred thousand home to England. The experience of the Welsh Guards on the beaches was not so distinctive that it need be described here. The 1st Battalion was at that time in three groups. First there were the Prince of Wales Company, No. 2, No. 3 and Headquarter Companies with the Commanding Officer. Of this group Lieutenant-Colonel Copland-Griffiths was one of the last to embark. "My turn came at last. I waded up to the chest, got into the boat and seized an oar. We rowed off to a tug about half a mile out at sea . . . eventually she moved alongside a paddle steamer and we transferred . . . I am told that we were bombed on the way over, but I was too tired to notice."

Next there were the personnel of "B" Echelon transport which Major Greenacre had been detailed to bring home. On their way to the coast they were deflected and used to fill a gap in the defence of the canal which formed the boundary of the ground behind the beaches which was held to the last. On being relieved they too marched to the seashore. With them was Lieutenant J. C. Buckland, the Quartermaster and, true to form, he went

Dawn at Dunkirk, *drawn at the time by Sergeant C. Murrell*

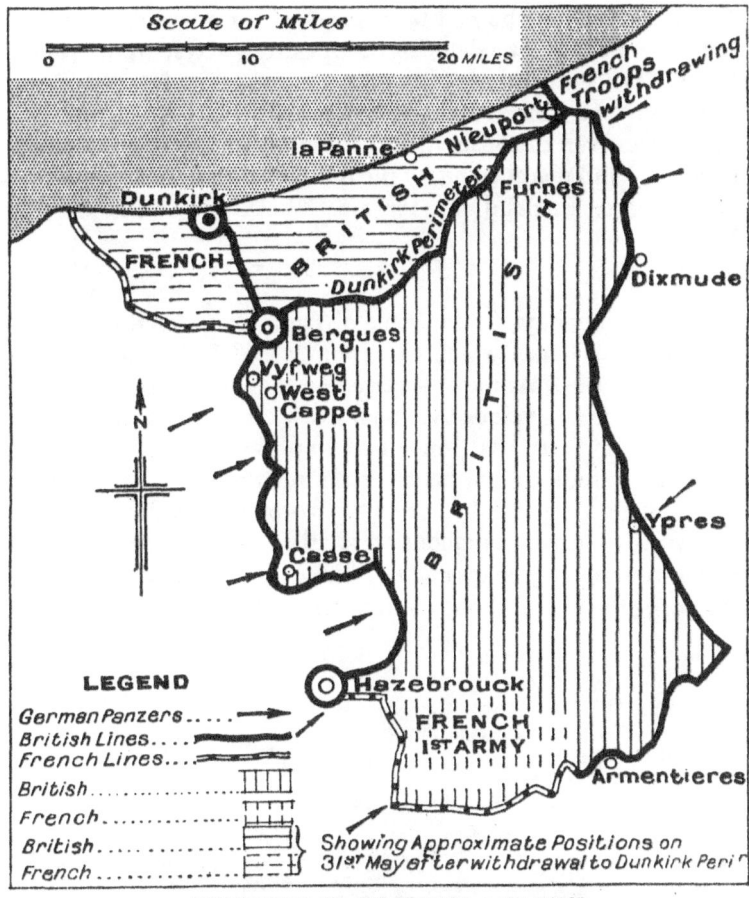

WITHDRAWAL TO THE BEACHES—LAST PHASE.

"scrounging" for his men to Lord Gort's cook at General Headquarters in La Panne while the men waited their turn to embark. When he returned with two dixies of hot tea the queue of waiting men had moved forward and the Welsh Guardsmen near the head of the queue were standing waist deep and more in the sea. So the Quartermaster waded in beside them and while two men held the dixies "above sea level" he gave every one in the party a mess-tin full of hot tea to start the journey on.

Finally, after the Commander-in-Chief had left for England,

No. 4 Company, who had been attached for guard duties to his personal Headquarters during the past few days, were ordered home. The Company fell in as for a normal parade, the roll was called and the Company inspected; then with arms at the slope they were given the order "Advance in column of route from the right . . ." and marched off by the route along the sands which for many led to England but for most Welsh Guardsmen led to Wales.

* * * * *

Thankfulness for "the miracle of Dunkirk"—for that evacuation of 337,094 men which Mr. John Masefield has justly called "The Nine Days Wonder"—has somewhat obscured the miracle of endurance and valour by which a few divisions of the Regular Army, with Territorial units and improvised forces from the lines of communication, held the German army at bay to make those nine days possible. Seventy-two officers and men of the two Welsh Guards Battalions were killed and only eighty-eight of the wounded were evacuated. Four hundred and fifty-three, including the rest of the wounded, remained in enemy hands.

BREN GUN CARRIER OF TYPE USED IN 1940.

CHAPTER THREE

SECOND ROUND—A GOOD RECOVERY
(1941-42)

Nid ar redeg y mae aredig
One does not plough at the double
Old Welsh Proverb

FOUR years were to pass before the 1st and 2nd Battalions of the Welsh Guards went into action again. After their return from France they were refitted and made up to strength by drafts from the Training Battalion and they were stationed respectively at Wimbledon and Byfleet. Lieutenant-Colonel Copland-Griffiths and Lieutenant-Colonel Sir Alexander Stanier left them, on promotion to the command of the 1st Guards Brigade and the 223rd Infantry Brigade, and Lieutenant-Colonel J. Jefferson and Lieutenant-Colonel G. St. V. J. Vigor took command of the Battalions. These remained at Wimbledon and Byfleet for a year, training strenuously and practising anti-invasion roles. It is hardly possible to exaggerate the peril in which the country stood at that time. The thought of invasion and what it would involve haunted men's minds, for preparations to meet invasion made the reality of the impending danger obvious to all. The raising of the Home Guard; the building of road blocks, pill-boxes and tank obstacles; the guarding of waterworks, lighting plants and other vulnerable points; and the disappearance of place-names from road-signs and railway stations, streets and shops, were constant reminders of the danger which confronted the nation. What was less obvious to the general public was the fearful poverty of our defence. Immediately after Dunkirk there were practically no fully trained and equipped divisions with which to oppose a landing or repel an invader.

The position was forcibly brought home to the Regiment when in June, 1940, four hundred men of the Training Battalion, mostly young half-trained recruits, were hurriedly sent to defend

Harwich, a port and a naval station on the North Sea coast. The conditions they met there revealed a state of unpreparedness and naked peril which is still appalling to contemplate. Lieutenant-Colonel Lord Glanusk, in command of the Welsh Guards contingent, was appointed to command the Harwich garrison—but apart from his own recruits "the garrison" comprised only a few Royal Air Force personnel employed on barrage-balloon sites and for the most part unarmed : a few partly trained Territorial gunners with some obsolete guns mounted in a conspicuously dangerous place and unable to range on the open beaches : and a unit of oldish men with service in the last war who were being re-employed on the protection of the naval installation. Barbed wire for defences was practically unobtainable, ammunition in adequate quantities was hard to get, and there were not even enough rifles to arm everyone in this token garrison. For a hectic fortnight the Welsh Guards worked hard on the construction of improvised defence works ; then they were relieved so that they might resume their imperative task of training.

The short campaign in France had taught us something of modern, mechanised warfare. We were to learn more from campaigns which occupied the next few years and enabled us to study the equipment of an enemy who had dedicated the science, industry and man-power of a whole nation to the purposes of war. Above all they gave us *time*—time to mobilise the resources of our own nation and the British Commonwealth of Nations ; time to explore and experiment, to perfect new methods and new weapons of our own ; time to train and equip. And not only ourselves but the United States had time in these years to prepare the vast forces which played so important a part in the Allies' ultimate victory. But in 1940, when we stood alone, we did not know we were to be given so long and training was a matter of terrible urgency. Not only had we to make good a heavy loss of trained men ; not only had we to replace the arms, ammunition and equipment which had been accumulated in France during the first nine months of the campaign and lost in the last nine days. Much more must be done, for the character of war had changed.

Aircraft, armour, wireless, mechanised transport, these were to make this war radically different from any other. All four had been used in a limited degree, but their potentialities in combination were not yet fully developed. Modern aircraft make it possible to attack the enemy from his factories to his front line and to land troops and supplies behind his defences. Armour makes it possible to push forward the attack at a speed and to a depth never before approached. Wireless overcomes all difficulties of communication and control in large-scale operations and quick-moving battles. And the mechanisation of transport makes it possible to maintain an advance to almost any distance, makes even infantry more mobile than the fleetest cavalry of former days. Add to these a conspicuous advance in the employment of engineering science and equipment, and the whole conduct of war is revolutionised.

The old mastery of himself and his rifle which made the Guardsman of other days famous and is expressed in the discipline and tradition of the Brigade of Guards must still be acquired, and it can only be acquired through long and patient training. But it is not enough for the Guardsman of today to learn what his father learnt, for now he must be master not only of himself and of a rifle but also of the Bren gun, Piat, Sten and "Tommy" guns, of several sorts of grenades, of mines and 2-inch mortars; he must learn not only the drills of movement on parade and in several sorts of transport, but also battle drills to be applied in action. He must learn to co-operate with armour and with other arms, and if he be a specialist, as very many are, he must become as well a considerable technician and learn the intricate mysteries of wireless and other means of signalling, of 3-inch mortars, carriers, medium machine-guns, anti-tank guns or motor transport. All these require standards of craftsmanship and fieldcraft which take many additional months to perfect. The recruit's first four months were spent in a Welsh Guards Company at the Guards Depot, Caterham. Even for the non-specialist at least four more followed in the Training Battalion, which moved to Sandown Park, Esher, soon after leaving Harwich. There he went through a comprehensive course of training before being drafted to a regular Battalion where he could take part in schemes and large-scale exercises and realise in the field the significance of earlier lessons and their application to the new ways of war. The Battalions owed much of their success to the high standard of discipline and skill maintained at both training centres throughout the war, and the zeal and example of officers, warrant officers and non-commissioned officers employed there on inconspicuous but invaluable duties should not go unnoticed. These were the men who taught the miner, the farmer, the shop assistant and the clerk how to become Guardsmen.

Throughout the winter of 1940-41 recruits came into the Regiment in large numbers. The 1st and 2nd Battalions were now up to strength again, the Depot was full to capacity and the Training Battalion overflowed. Men who had completed their preliminary courses were formed into Holding Companies, and on April the 1st, 1941, these were comprised in a Holding Battalion, under Lieutenant-Colonel W. D. C. Greenacre, M.V.O., and stationed at Hounslow. Later in the year (October the 24th) it was reconstituted as the 3rd Battalion Welsh Guards, Lieutenant-Colonel A. M. Bankier, D.S.O., O.B.E., M.C., being then in command.

Earlier that year the momentous decision was taken to form a Guards Armoured Division. Knowing now the part played by this famous Division in the final defeat of Germany, it is a sobering reminder of the country's position in 1941 to recall the considerations which led to its formation.

During the late spring of 1941, the Commander-in-Chief, Home Forces, was told that *he should be ready the following spring to meet invasion* by a large number of enemy divisions, including a serious proportion of armoured divisions and a considerable proportion of airborne divisions. To meet such a threat he had a very limited number of armoured divisions, and he decided that he must as speedily as possible convert two infantry divisions to armour. After various deliberations and after the Major-General Commanding the Brigade of Guards had consulted His Majesty the King, approval was given for the formation of the Guards Armoured Division—to meet the threat of *an invasion still to be expected in* 1942 !

Divisional Headquarters was formed on June the 19th, and the Division assembled on the 15th of September, 1941. Both the 1st and 2nd Battalions of the Welsh Guards were included in the new Division and they moved at once to the area in which it was assembling. The 1st Battalion went to Midsomer Norton and the 2nd Battalion to Codford St. Mary. The former was to provide part of the infantry of the Division; the latter to be converted to the 2nd Armoured Battalion. There were other consequent moves. Lieutenant-Colonel Vigor changed over to the command of the 1st Battalion and Lieutenant-Colonel Jefferson to the 2nd Armoured Battalion, and, with his matchless judgment of officers and other ranks, Colonel R. E. K. Leatham, D.S.O., Lieutenant-Colonel Commanding the Regiment, made a number of other transfers as between the various Battalions.

Those selected for the 2nd Armoured Battalion had almost everything to learn. They had to learn first of all how a tank works and how to maintain it in working order, and how to drive it not only on the road but across rough country—in other words to learn Driving and Maintenance, "that unfathomable mystery known to tank lovers as D. and M." Also they had now to learn to shoot, not with a rifle but a gun (and different sorts of guns at that), and not only when they were stationary and could take careful aim but on the move. And they must learn to use wireless constantly, both to receive orders from outside and to pass orders to each other through the noise inside a tank. They began learning, that summer, long before they had any tanks. Almost eighty per cent. of the Battalion went away on courses to various training centres, and for the rest they had a contraption used by the Navy and known as a RYPA from the initial letters of the movements it performed. For in this ingenious skeleton gun-turret they could practise gunnery while an amused assistant saw to it that as they tried to hit the target the turret **R**olled, **Y**awed, **P**itched and **A**ltered course. In November Lieutenant-Colonel Jefferson was promoted to command the 33rd Guards Brigade (which included the 3rd Battalion Welsh Guards) and Lieutenant-Colonel Greenacre succeeded him in command of the 2nd Armoured Battalion.

The expected invasion was not attempted, and by the end of 1941 it was clear that the enemy's air attack on Britain had failed. 43,000 civilians had been killed and over 50,000 seriously injured and widespread material damage had been done; but little else had been achieved. The rapid and continuous expansion of our war industries had never been seriously hampered and production had increased by leaps and bounds. So through 1942 the Battalions continued their training. The 1st Battalion practised new roles in an armoured division. The 2nd Battalion developed new skills, first on a collection of old Covenanter Tanks which broke down on the smallest provocation or on none at all, later on Crusaders and Centaurs. In September the Battalions moved to Fonthill Gifford and Heytesbury near Salisbury and about the same time the 3rd Battalion, now commanded by Lieutenant-Colonel G. W. Browning, moved from Uxbridge, where it had been training, into billets at Hampstead.

There had been other changes earlier in the year. Colonel Leatham had retired and Colonel Bankier had become Lieutenant-Colonel Commanding the Regiment. Lieutenant-Colonel Lord Glanusk had left the Training Battalion at the same time on promotion to take up a special appointment, and Lieutenant-Colonel T. A. Oakshott was appointed to succeed him.

Meanwhile even in 1941, while we had hardly recovered from the damage suffered in the first round of the fight and when invasion still threatened, we had begun to hit back under Mr. Churchill's courageous leadership. But it was a ding-dong fight. General Sir Archibald Wavell brilliantly defeated the Italian army in North Africa, killing many and taking 130,000 prisoners. But then Greece was conquered by Germany after Roumania and Bulgaria had joined the Axis forces and Jugo-Slavia had been divided, bombed and broken through. The Abyssinian campaign was successfully concluded, but only by a subtraction of forces from General Wavell's army which left little more than a screen on the North African front; and when Rommel took charge of the remaining Italian forces and attacked with German armour and a large air force we were driven back to Egypt.

Germany turned on Russia, Japan bombed Pearl Harbour, and the United States of America and Russia became our allies; but Japan captured Hong Kong and Singapore, overran Burma and Siam, French Indo-China, the Dutch East Indies, the Philippines and most of the islands of the Pacific. A renewed British advance in North Africa early in 1942 started well but was turned to defeat and we were driven back into Egypt; Russia lost the Crimea and the Germans reached the Volga and besieged Stalingrad. So the first nine months of 1942 passed and, although we were steadily growing stronger, points mounted against us.

Then at last the tide of battle turned. At the end of October Rommel was decisively beaten at El Alamein and the 8th Army began to drive him westwards. Early in November British and American forces began landing in Morocco and Algeria to open a new North African front. In the same month Russia started a counter-offensive which captured the forces besieging Stalingrad and began the reconquest of Russian soil. Recovery had been slow and painful, but at last the Allies had the initiative; as this round ended they were scoring heavily.

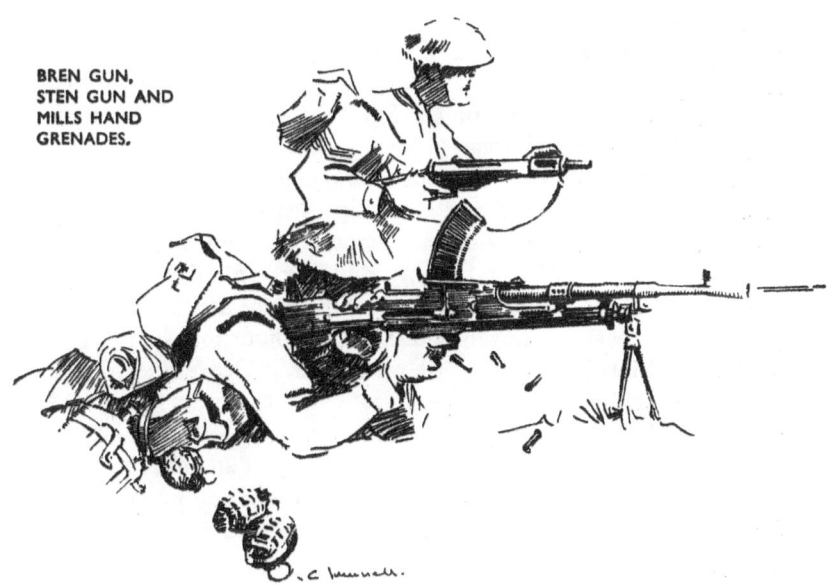

BREN GUN, STEN GUN AND MILLS HAND GRENADES.

CHAPTER FOUR

THIRD ROUND—"THE END OF THE BEGINNING" (1943)

> Oni heuir ni fedir
> *Unless one sows one shall not reap*
> Old Welsh Saying

WHEN 1943 opened the Guards Armoured Division was training in the Salisbury Plain area, the 1st Battalion Welsh Guards being at Heytesbury and the 2nd Battalion at Fonthill Gifford. The 3rd Battalion was stationed at Hampstead; its role was to find reinforcements for the regular Battalions. Lieutenant-Colonel Browning had just gone to the Staff College and Lieutenant-Colonel D. E. P. Hodgson had been appointed to succeed him in command of the Battalion when its role was changed. On January the 8th an order to mobilise for service overseas was received and on the 5th February the 3rd Battalion embarked for North Africa.

The opening of the Tunisian campaign had been full of promise. Eight hundred and fifty ships had borne forces under General Eisenhower's supreme command from Britain and America. The British 1st Army and the United States 2nd Corps had passed safely through the dangers of the Atlantic and the Western Mediterranean and almost without loss had begun landing in Morocco and Algeria on the 8th of November, 1942. Weak and ineffective opposition from French forces there had been quickly overcome, and advanced units on assault scales of equipment had been pushed rapidly forward in an effort to seize Tunis and Bizerta and so deny the Axis use of the ports which face Sicily across the Mediterranean at its narrowest channel. But the attempt was frustrated, and the reasons are not difficult to discover.

First, the initial delay imposed by the uncertainties of the French attitude, the vagaries of French policy and the distinct loyalties of separate French Commanders enabled the Axis to seize Tunis and Bizerta and the Tunisian airfields before we could reach them, and from their nearby bases in Sicily and Italy to reinforce their hold on Tunisia more rapidly than we could advance in force from the distant Algerian ports. Sicily is but a hundred and fifty miles from Bizerta, Algiers is four hundred ; moreover it is several thousand miles from America and from Britain by the routes which transports had to follow at that time. The British 1st Army then consisted of only two infantry divisions and the 6th Armoured Division, and not only in ground forces but especially in the air the enemy had an initial advantage which it took three months to overcome.

The nature of the country gave a second advantage to the enemy. Tunisia is a land of rugged mountains and rocky hills with few and well-defined plains, all on the eastward or enemy side. The mountains are precipitous and the rock-broken hills are largely clothed in cork forests and thick breast-high scrub. On their commanding heights a few cleverly placed defenders can watch and hold up an attacking force of far greater numbers. Only in the Medjerda valley in the north, with the central plain which stretches from Tebourba and Goubellat to Pont du Fahs, and in the Kairouan plain extending southwards between the central mountains and the sea can armoured forces operate with any freedom ; and access to these areas is through passes which were dominated by the enemy. The roads over these passes often run through long defiles, easy to block with mine-fields and to cover by fire from the surrounding heights. In such country, command of the air, which the enemy had for the first three months, enables the possessor to slow up advancing armies by making movement in daylight virtually impossible and a tedious and inconvenient dispersion necessary at all times.

The gateway to Tunis is the Medjerda valley with Medjez el Bab at its western entrance. Medjez itself is an ancient settlement with Arab and French houses, a domed marabout, a little station and a venerable bridge over the Medjerda. It is overlooked from the hills to the north ; from "Longstop Hill" on the northeast, where river and railway run towards Tebourba ; and from "Grenadier Hill" and "Banana Ridge," its southern door-post. Coming to it from Beja, the last of the mountains are left behind and the road through Oued Zarga tips gently over the edge of the hills and falls slowly to the river, the last major tank obstacle before Tunis, thirty-seven miles away. At the beginning of the campaign units of the assault force penetrated to the outskirts of Tunis, but after bloody fighting were forced back. In the early contests for command of the Medjerda valley which followed, the 1st Guards Brigade, under Brigadier F. A. V. Copland-Griffiths, D.S.O., M.C., had much hard fighting. The Brigade consisted at first of the 3rd Battalion Grenadier Guards, the 2nd Battalion Coldstream Guards and the 2nd Battalion Hampshire Regiment—to whom six Welsh Guards officers had been lent. Four days after landing in Africa—on the 26th of November, 1942—this Hampshire Battalion was detached from the 1st Guards Brigade and hurried into battle at Tebourba (eighteen miles west of Tunis). From that battle—in which all the Welsh Guards officers who were serving with the Battalion were either killed or wounded—the Hampshires emerged with only three officers and a hundred and seventy men, having fought with a steadfast courage which will rank high in the annals of the British Army. But the Guards Battalions had also had heavy casualties, and at the beginning of February the 3rd Battalion Welsh Guards were ordered from England to reinforce the Brigade.

The Battalion landed in Algiers at about four o'clock in the afternoon of February the 16th, 1943, after an uneventful passage. They had been told on board ship that they were to do a three-mile march through the town on landing "to show the flag" and were then to go to a camp a few miles away. After unloading stores and equipment, the first part of this programme was carried out, and having completed the march through the town they fell out for the normal hourly halt—and learnt that their camp was about *fourteen* miles further on ! "Coming on top of an idle voyage when they had been drinking tea and eating cakes and chocolate as hard as they could, not knowing when such things would be so plentiful again, this was enough to damp even Welsh Guardsmen's spirits. . . . We had our choirs in various parts of the column, and walking up and down the line you could see some of the troops fairly sweating rock-cakes and tea." But the longest march comes to an end and having covered seventeen miles they reached camp about midnight. As companies dispersed it started to rain heavily. ". . . we there experienced our first North African mud—such a loving type of mud; it first clings to your boots and then works its way up to your arm-pits."

The Battalion stayed there till the 24th of February, when they left to join the 1st Guards Brigade at the front. For three days the companies travelled by train—in the trucks marked "Hommes 30—Chevaux 12" so well known to those who have soldiered in France—upholstered with a supply of straw which, according to Regimental Sergeant-Major A. C. Barter "worked out at three straws between two men." Meanwhile the transport and the carriers moved by roads which ran for several hundred miles through gorges and over mountains—a strenuous test of the drivers' training, passed with flying colours and the loss of one van which rolled over a precipice, luckily shedding its occupants at the outset. The transport met the rest of the Battalion at Guardimaou on the 28th and carried them a further fifty miles to El Aroussa, twenty miles south-east of Medjez el Bab, where they joined the 1st Guards Brigade on 1st of March.

They had sailed for Africa when the first three months of somewhat inconclusive fighting was drawing to a close, and while they were crossing from England and moving up to the front the whole position radically changed. First, the 8th Army, which had driven Rommel out of Egypt and had hustled him back through Cyrenaica and Tripolitania, arrived at the southern boundary of Tunisia and invested the Mareth line; the Axis forces were thus contained between General Eisenhower's growing army in the north and the 8th Army in the south. The second momentous change followed. General the Hon. Sir Harold Alexander, under whose supreme command General Sir Bernard Montgomery and the 8th Army had fought their way from Egypt, was made Deputy Theatre Commander to General Eisenhower, and all the forces in Tunisia (including both the 1st Army in the north and the 8th Army in the south) passed under his command. From then onwards the action of the Allied armies was closely co-ordinated and General Alexander was able to vary the grouping of his forces with a freedom which would not have been possible had they remained under separate commanders.

As the 3rd Battalion Welsh Guards moved up to the front he was setting out the board for the final stages of the campaign.

Allied troops consisted of the British 1st and 8th Armies, the United States 2nd Corps and the French 19th Corps. For many Frenchmen had refused to subordinate liberty and honour to German convenience, and a "Free French" movement, headed by General de Gaulle and embodied at first in French soldiers evacuated from Dunkirk, had developed a considerable underground organisation in French territories. Free French forces had already fought bravely with the British armies in Cyrenaica and elsewhere and there were many who were eager to help in the liberation of French North Africa. It was not surprising, therefore, that opposition to Allied landings ordered by the Vichy Government proved as feeble as Vichy policy elsewhere, and that once it had been overcome large numbers of French troops were ready to turn from recent masters to old friends and to renew their fight against Germany and Italy side by side with the British and American armies. Considerable air reinforcements were also arriving and during March air supremacy passed to the Allies. On the other hand, the Axis forces in Tunisia were strengthened by the arrival of six divisions which had been falling back before the 8th Army's advance; and during February the enemy launched a series of armoured attacks in an attempt to strengthen his hold on the all-important passes through the southern mountains and the high ground which guards Bizerta in the north and commands the Medjerda valley.

The enemy's most successful attack was directed against the United States 2nd Corps. The American positions near the Kasserine pass were broken and German armour, sweeping over the pass, turned northwards towards Thala. Here they were held by the 6th Armoured Division, in which was the 1st Guards Brigade. Next he attacked in the north and the 1st Guards Brigade were switched back to that front. They arrived at El Aroussa and helped to restore the position at Medjez el Bab a few days before the 3rd Battalion Welsh Guards joined them on St. David's Day. On the 2nd of March the Brigade was again moved north to the Beja area, where the front was reported to be in a critical position, but although the Welsh

Guards were there for five days they were not involved in any serious fighting. No. 4 Company was the first company of the Battalion to go into the line. They were sent off in a hurry to hold the nearby Djebel Bou Ouden, where enemy patrols were reported to be through the British forward positions, but after occupying the hill for twenty-four hours without seeing anything of the enemy they were withdrawn, wet but cheerful.

On the 8th March the Battalion were sent to relieve the 1st/4th Hampshires, who were holding positions just west of Oued Zarga, half-way between Beja and Medjez el Bab. They were there for a week. At one time the enemy seemed to be working forward slowly and there was a good deal of shelling on both sides, but no attack developed and active patrolling kept the ground in front of our position clear. The Battalion met mules for the first time when twelve "reported for duty," and the first issue of the Battalion paper *The Daily Leak* spread some good jokes and some highly unreliable "information"; otherwise little happened.

On the night of the 14th the whole Brigade went back to Medjez el Bab, moving by a roundabout route as the enemy was astride the direct road from Oued Zarga to Medjez. They remained at Medjez for ten days. At first the Welsh Guards had two companies in the line under command of the 3rd Battalion Grenadier Guards, and afterwards they held the forward positions on "Grenadier Hill" and in Medjez el Bab. Again neither side attacked, but there was much active patrolling and a few minor clashes. On the 26th of March the 1st Guards Brigade was relieved and moved back to Sakiet Sidi Youssef on the Algerian frontier.

The positions held by the Allied forces at the beginning of April are shown on the map on page 33. The moves that followed are not difficult to appreciate.

The 8th Army coming up from the south turned the flank of the Mareth line, when an American attack near El Guettar and Macknassy had pinned down the German 10th Panzer Division and some native formations. Rommel then withdrew to the north and, after a stiff rearguard action had been fought at Wadi Akarit, the 8th Army made contact with the United States 2nd Corps, now advancing east from El Guettar and Macknassy. The ring round the enemy was complete.

While the enemy was withdrawing from Wadi Akarit the 6th Armoured Division in which was the 1st Guards Brigade, attacked the Fondouk gap with the object of cutting into the flank of the enemy retreating through Kairouan. The gap is about a thousand yards wide and is flanked by rugged hills on either side. The capture of those to the south was entrusted to United States troops; the 1st Guards Brigade was ordered to take those to the north and the 3rd Battalion Welsh Guards were detailed for the opening attack. They had left Sidi Youssef on the 4th of April after a stay of nine days, in which some training had been carried out. They moved by way of Maktar to El Ala and lay there under cover of olive groves. On the 8th they moved up after dark to within a mile of the Djebel ain el Rhorab (the hill feature which had to be captured), and in the early morning of the 9th they attacked.

All went well at first, but the attacking companies had severe casualties and were pinned down before reaching the hills. So the co-operation of artillery and armour was enlisted and while tanks of the Lothians and Border Horse worked round the northern flank and the Gunners shelled the position the attack went forward again and the companies climbed steeply to storm the final objective. By three-thirty in the afternoon the northern bastion commanding the gap was securely in our hands. The full story of this action is told on page 114. The 3rd Battalion had heavy losses that day, but they won high praise for the steadiness and courage with which they fought their first battle; and once El Rhorab was captured the 6th Armoured Division broke through the gap and, advancing by Kairouan, made contact with the 8th Army two days later. The main body of the enemy managed to escape to the north, but the noose was tightening and General Alexander was able to make fresh dispositions for the next move. The 6th Armoured Division went back to the Majerda valley, the Welsh Guards going to El Aroussa on April the 16th.

* * * * *

Shortly after the fight at Fondouk, Brigadier Copland-Griffiths handed over his command of the 1st Guards Brigade to Brigadier S. A. Forster and left for England to be sent on a long mission to America. He had commanded the Brigade for over two years. By the Welsh Guards and especially by those who had served under him when he commanded the 1st Battalion in 1940 his departure was keenly felt.

* * * * *

As the 8th Army approached Enfidaville the French 19th Corps swung north to keep touch with them and the United States 2nd Corps was transferred from the south of our line to the extreme north. (See map on page 33.) At the same time the British 1st Army concentrated in the central position and was strengthened by the addition of an armoured division, withdrawn for the purpose from the 8th Army.

Attacks were now launched all along the line. In the north 1st Army troops fought for the high ground north and south of Medjez and, after breaking an armoured counter-attack, took Longstop Hill at their third attempt and made progress on both banks of the Medjerda river. Other troops attacked in the centre and early on the 22nd of April captured the hills east of the Bou Arada–Goubellat road. The 6th Armoured Division then went through in an effort to force a passage between the mountains which lie to the east of Goubellat plain. The Armoured Brigade made good progress along the shore of the salt lake which lies to the north-west of Pont du Fahs, but were brought to a halt by tanks and artillery strongly placed in the rocky hills. Meanwhile the 1st Guards Brigade was deployed, but only the Coldstream Guards were seriously engaged. The Welsh Guards held positions in which they were bombed repeatedly and shelled from time to time, but they were not involved in fighting. The battle had become mainly an armoured contest and, when some ground had been gained and the enemy's armour severely crippled, General Alexander decided to break off the fight and to concentrate all his available force on a final and decisive attempt to take Tunis from the direction of Medjez el Bab. So the 1st Guards Brigade moved northwards again to the Medjerda valley with the rest of the 6th Armoured Division.

General Alexander's plan for what was to prove the final battle in Africa was simple as it was effective. Leaving the 8th Army and the French in the south to exert pressure strong enough to hold the enemy on the Enfidaville line, and ordering the United States Corps in the north to continue pressing towards Bizerta, he further strengthened the 1st Army by a number of divisions secretly transferred from the 8th Army. By now we had complete mastery of the air and could prevent enemy interference with troop movements, and in making these dispositions General Alexander took steps to deceive the enemy so as to leave him in the belief that the final thrust would come from the 8th Army at Enfidaville.

Then on the 6th of May his reinforced 1st Army struck on a three thousand yard front up the Medjerda valley. The formation was as follows :

7th Armoured Division.   4th Indian Division ⎱
6th Armoured Division.   4th Mixed Division ⎰ line of attack→

The 1st Guards Brigade, including the 3rd Battalion Welsh Guards, was still in the 6th Armoured Division.

The leading divisions attacked in bright starlight at three o'clock in the morning of May the 6th and before noon they had pierced the enemy's defences and the armoured divisions were launched through the gap. These spent the afternoon in mopping up and pushing forward and by the evening were on a line abreast of Massicault, where the 3rd Battalion spent that night. On the following morning, the 7th of May, armoured cars of the 6th and 7th Armoured Divisions entered Tunis, closely followed by the remainder of the 7th, which then swung north towards Bizerta, while the 6th turned south-east towards the neck of the Cape Bon peninsula. Meanwhile the United States 2nd Corps in the north overcame strong resistance and captured Bizerta and Ferryville.

On the 8th of May, the 6th Armoured Division continued south-eastwards and by the afternoon reached the approaches to Hammam Lif. At this point the hinterland ends in precipitous hills, which less than a mile from the sea, overshadow the town which corks the bottle-neck. Hammam Lif is thus a very awkward position to capture. On the heights which command the town the enemy was strongly placed. Approach to the town itself was covered by over thirty guns of various calibres ; the beach is intersected by a wadi impassable for tanks. The first step was clearly to capture the heights, and at half-past three that afternoon the 3rd Battalion Welsh Guards were given this task.

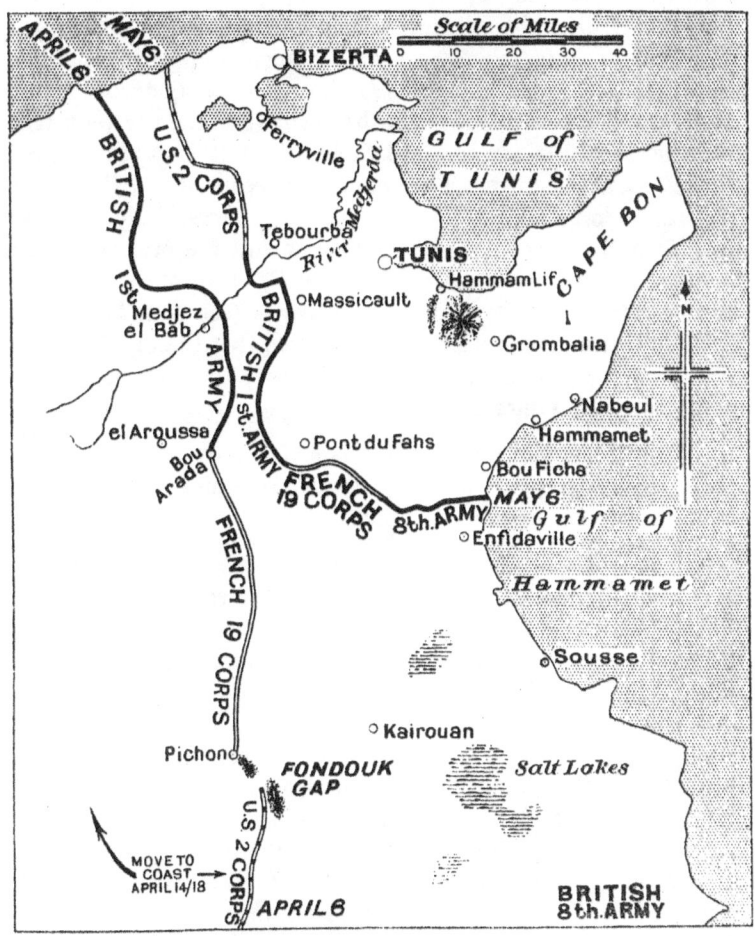

TUNISIAN CAMPAIGN—LAST PHASES.

The Grenadier Guards, attacking farther inland, encountered comparatively light opposition (400 Italians surrendering), but the Welsh Guards' objective, a jagged ridge of hills flanking the town, was strongly held by German troops and was only taken after hard fighting in which seventy-four Welsh Guardsmen were killed or wounded. Then the Coldstream Guards came up the hill in the night and completed the mopping up of the seaward end of the ridge.

Next morning the armoured Brigade attacked frontally, but were held by guns which covered the narrow approaches to the town; but with great enterprise and courage a squadron moved across the beach, passed round the point at which the wadi falls into the margin of the sea, and though heavily engaged reached the far side of the town. The enemy then realised that Hammam Lif was no longer tenable and as the tanks successfully renewed their frontal attack he hastily withdrew and the 6th Armoured Division took up the chase. The full story of the Welsh Guards' part in the action is told in later pages (see page 123). The German Commander afterwards admitted that the rapid forcing of this strong position took him completely by surprise; in the words of a War Office report :—

> "This victory at Hammam Lif was undoubtedly a major factor in bringing about the quick disintegration of further enemy resistance."

Certainly it dispelled any hope the enemy may have had of a final stand in the Cape Bon peninsula, for the next night the Welsh Guards passed through Grombalia and dug in across the escape route. Early on the 11th they entered Nabeul on the south of the Cape Bon peninsula. No. 1 Company occupied the town and the remainder of the Battalion covered it from the nearby hill and collected prisoners : three thousand passed through the Battalion's hands that day. The town was in a state of hysteria and No. 1 Company had a strenuous time before order was restored. They moved again that evening and on the day following, May the 12th, the battle finally ended while the Battalion was dug-in on the coast near Bou Ficha, watching the hills on which the remnants of the German Afrika Korps and the 1st Italian Army were making their last stand. "We saw our Artillery ring the hills with the smoke of shell bursts, and the R.A.F. zoom over to drop their bombs in the target area. Long columns of lost Italian platoons came winding along to surrender, carrying their enormous packs of kit ; and eventually the Second-in-Command sent a message to say that the campaign was officially considered over. The companies remained in their areas that night, and next morning we shifted down to the beach by Battalion Headquarters—for once without having to dig in ! After Hammam Lif it was a triumphal progress—the French offering us wine and bunches of flowers, cheering crowds, white-washed mosques among the lemon trees—a terrific change after weeks up in the bare hills, short of water, unwashed, unshaven and covered with dust. Thousands of prisoners were wandering about trying to give themselves up ; everywhere were abandoned enemy equipment, guns, lorries, machine-guns, bundles of clothes, boxes of food, barrels of wine, suitcases, cooking pots, water bottles, papers. The Italians laughing and joking and offering us cigarettes and wine and treating the whole thing like a Sunday School picnic ; the Germans sullen, arrogant and a bit bewildered. The whole thing happened so quickly, it is difficult to realise it is over. We are now camped in an olive grove near the sea and are able to bathe in the beautiful blue Mediterranean—white crisp sand, tiny breakers and a lovely hot sun. I don't know what happens next, but I hope we stay around this place for a bit—it's O.K."

They got the official "Cease fire" at five o'clock that night, the 12th May, 1943, for finding himself squeezed between the 6th Armoured Division and the 8th Army, shelled from both sides and heavily bombed from the air, the enemy's last isolated resistance ceased.

During the rest of that year the 3rd Battalion remained in North Africa training, sampling the rather limited amusements of their various stations, and encountering weather which varied from a sand-storm with the thermometer at 100 degrees in the shade ("the doors of hell opened and a wind blew, for about twelve hours, straight off the furnace"), to snow drifts which threatened to cut off the Battalion from the rest of the world, or rain and the "loving type" of mud which they had met when they first landed. They were stationed near Sousse till August, and from then until the end of the year outside Constantine back in Algeria.

If in the first three months of the campaign progress had been disappointingly slow, the last three brought victory which was as rapid and complete as could be desired; 267,000 prisoners were taken and it is estimated that another 50,000 were killed or seriously wounded. The German 10th, 15th, 21st and Hermann Goering Panzer Divisions; the 90th and 164th Light Divisions; the 334th and 999th Infantry Divisions; the Manteuffel Air Force Division; and the 19th and 20th Anti-Aircraft Divisions had been defeated and largely eliminated, while twenty-five Divisions and six Regiments of the Italian Army had been similarly defeated in the fighting in Egypt, Libya and Tunisia.

The first campaign of the 3rd Battalion Welsh Guards was ended. They had fully maintained the high traditions of the Brigade of Guards and had added a new chapter to the proud story of the Regiment. Both the battles in which they had made the opening attack, Fondouk and Hammam Lif, were important, and in both they did thoroughly and well all that was required of them. On the heights of El Rhorab, looking out through the Fondouk gap, and on the rocky hill that stands over Hammam Lif facing blue distances across the sea, two marble stones were raised later bearing the names of those who fell in battle, with the Regimental crest and motto "Cymru am byth." Rupert Brook wrote that where he fell would be "for ever England." So to the 3rd Battalion the hill tops by Fondouk and Hammam Lif are marked as "Wales for ever."

* * * * *

In England, meanwhile, the Guards Armoured Division continued assiduously to prepare for battle. They knew now that they were to take part in the projected invasion of western Europe. The 2nd Battalion had become masters of their tanks and both they and the 1st Battalion learnt much this year of the new mobile warfare. There had been various changes in the command and organisation of the Division and the roles of both Battalions had been altered more than once; but this was probably to their advantage, for by switching from one tank to another, one role to another, one formation to another, they gained much valuable experience. When the Guards Armoured Division eventually went to France it consisted of two Brigades, namely, the 5th Armoured Guards Brigade and the 32nd Guards

Brigade, with Reconnaissance Units, Divisional troops, Artillery, Engineers, etc., and Headquarters.

The 5TH ARMOURED GUARDS BRIGADE comprised the main Armoured force, namely :—

    1st (Motorised) Battalion Grenadier Guards, in Armoured Half-Tracks.
    1st (Armoured) Battalion Coldstream Guards, in Sherman Tanks.
    2nd (Armoured) Battalion Grenadier Guards, in Sherman Tanks.
    2nd (Armoured) Battalion Irish Guards, in Sherman Tanks.

The 32ND GUARDS BRIGADE consisted of the Infantry of the Division :—

    1st Battalion Welsh Guards.
    5th Battalion Coldstream Guards.
    3rd Battalion Irish Guards.
    No. 1 Company Royal Northumberland Fusiliers with machine guns and 4.2-inch mortars.

DIVISIONAL RECONNAISSANCE UNITS.

    2nd Battalion Household Cavalry in Armoured Scout Cars.
    2nd (Armoured Reconnaissance) Battalion, Welsh Guards in Cromwell tanks.

This was now the 2nd Battalion's official name, but it will be referred to simply as "the 2nd Battalion" in the pages which follow.

The Cromwell, which was the tank in which the 2nd Battalion fought, has been called the thoroughbred among tanks. Its first characteristic is its remarkable speed. It weighs thirty tons, yet it can move at thirty-seven miles an hour (on occasions it did more), and speed is an important asset in mobile warfare. Its second characteristic is reliability : the Cromwell seldom gave any mechanical trouble. Its third characteristic, noise, is less desirable. It is driven by a six-hundred horse-power Rolls-Royce engine, *unsilenced*; add to the roar of this huge engine the squeal of steel tracks on the road, and the noise of a column of Cromwells moving can be heard a long way off. It has a compact, business-like and rather low hull, carries a hundred and ten gallons of petrol, and has a range of about a hundred miles.

The crew of a Cromwell is five men. Two sit in front side by side, the driver and the hull gunner. The latter is a spare driver and has charge of the Besa machine-gun. There are three men in the turret and when it revolves it takes them with it. There is first the tank commander, who normally has his head and shoulders out for better observation. Then there is the gunner, who sits between the commander's legs and fires the 75 mm. high velocity gun, using either solid armour-piercing shot, high explosive or smoke shells. Mounted alongside the gun and moving with it is a second Besa machine-gun, and by moving a simple lever the gunner can fire the weapon of his choice. He has at his disposal seventy-five rounds of ammunition for the gun and fifty-six machine-gun belts. Opposite him sits the wireless operator, in touch with the tank commander on one set and with the outside world on two others. He has also to load the guns in action, and as shells for the gun are heavy and the machine-gun belts very awkward to handle in a confined space he must be both strong and active.

The Cromwell tank is not comfortable to live in. For one thing hardly any movement is possible inside it, and for another it is nearly always very cold, as air for the engine is drawn through the turret and a gale comes in at the driver's open visor. But it did its work magnificently. It carried not only discomfort for the enemy, but rations and bedding of those whose home it was for so long, and many became greatly attached to their tanks by the end of the war.

There were three fighting squadrons in the 2nd Battalion, each consisting of squadron Headquarters and five troops; and since there were four tanks in each Headquarters and three in each troop there were nineteen in each squadron, or fifty-seven in the three. There was also a reconnaissance troop of twelve tanks (at first Honeys but later Cromwells) and Battalion Headquarters with four. Thus the Battalion had seventy-three tanks in all. Two Cromwells in each squadron Headquarters had larger (95 mm.) guns, and one of the three tanks in each troop was a Challenger, mounting a seventeen-pounder gun.

Welsh Guards Officer
by
Rex Whistler

Lieutenant A. Whiskard, like Rex Whistler was killed in action in Normandy while commanding a troop of tanks of the 2nd Battalion—Dark overalls were worn by officers of the 2nd Battalion during training

So then the fire power included in this one armoured Battalion was seventy guns (from 75 mm. to seventeen-pounders) and one hundred and forty-six machine-guns. And this formidable armament could move at over thirty miles an hour and cover a hundred miles in a day. How far removed from the armament with which the 2nd Battalion had fought against German tanks at Boulogne in 1940 !

At the end of February, 1943 (as the 3rd Battalion in Africa were moving up to the front for the first time), the 1st and 2nd Battalions in England went on the biggest exercise that had yet been organised. Exercise "Spartan" took them over half England, lasted ten days, and left them at King's Lynn and Thetford. In July of that year they went to Scarborough and Pickering for training on the Yorkshire wolds, exercise "Blackcock," "Eagle" and many more. They only moved south to Eastbourne and Brighton in May, 1944, for their last weeks in England ; and only after they had finally waterproofed their vehicles and reached a sealed concentration area did their training finish.

* * * * *

In December, 1943, Lieutenant-Colonel Greenacre had been promoted to be Second-in-Command of the 5th Guards Armoured Brigade, and Lieutenant-Colonel J. C. Windsor Lewis, D.S.O., M.C., now commanded the 2nd Battalion Welsh Guards ; at the end of March, 1944, Lieutenant-Colonel Vigor left to command the Westminster Garrison Battalion and Lieutenant-Colonel Browning was appointed to command the 1st Battalion.

* * * * *

Seldom have this country's armies been so well prepared for battle. Many men of the 1st and 2nd Battalions had been serving soldiers when the war broke out, some with considerable service already behind them. Many others were reservists who had not only completed their time with the colours but had had valuable experience in responsible civilian employment (such as the police) before they were recalled. Even recruits who had joined since the outbreak of war had, when they sailed, anything up to five years of intensive war-time training. A considerable number had seen some fighting in 1940; all had lived and worked together through times when national danger drew men closer and called out the best that was in them. There can never have been two happier Battalions. The average age was nearly twenty-five and their average service six years. In physique, strength and power of endurance they were in their prime, and they were equipped with the most up-to-date weapons yet devised and trained to the last ounce. All they waited for was the word "GO". But before they got that word the 3rd Battalion, having already seen the completion of the African campaign, were to be fighting in Italy.

THE FAMOUS "CROMWELL" (30 TONS)

CHAPTER FIVE

FOURTH ROUND. THE BEGINNING OF THE END (1944)

> Deuparth gwaith ei ddechrau
> *Well begun is half done*
> Old Welsh Proverb

FOR the Welsh Guards this momentous year opened quietly with the 1st and 2nd Battalions training in England and the 3rd Battalion in Algeria; but before the end of January the 3rd Battalion, with the rest of the 1st Guards Brigade, were ordered to move from North Africa to the Italian front.

By that time General Alexander's forces had conquered the southern half of the Italian peninsula and held a line stretching roughly north and south from Ortona on the Adriatic coast to the mouth of the Garigliano river on the Mediterranean Sea. Moreover, during January Allied troops had landed fifty miles up this coast at Anzio and were fighting hard to establish and extend their bridgehead. Rome lay thirty miles to their north and eighty miles from the Allies' main front.

The German winter line, at which our forces had been battering for several months, was skilfully chosen. Commanding heights in the centre threw off formidable rivers to protect the lower ground on either flank between the mountains and the sea. A poor system of roads and rough tracks, which must in any case have hampered an advance, was rendered almost unusable by bad weather. Heavy rain impeded operations; snow and ice interrupted movement; and mud—the soldier's bane—seriously influenced tactics and greatly hampered administration in the mountain districts. Yet in spite of the weather's reinforcement of a naturally strong defence, our pressure on the enemy had never relaxed; slowly but steadily our positions had been improved and the enemy's hold on his "Gustav Line" had correspondingly weakened.

General Alexander's aim at this time was to break through in the south and, pushing up the Liri Valley, to join with our forces in the Anzio bridgehead in an advance on Rome which would turn the German line. But the key to the Liri Valley is Cassino, closely guarded by the almost unscaleable Monastery Hill, "two hundred feet higher than Gibraltar and just as steep," supported by Monte Cairo and a range of closely surrounding mountains; and the whole position is moated on the east and south by the Garigliano and its tributaries.

The Allies' first attack on the immensely strong position was still in progress when the 1st Guards Brigade sailed for Italy.

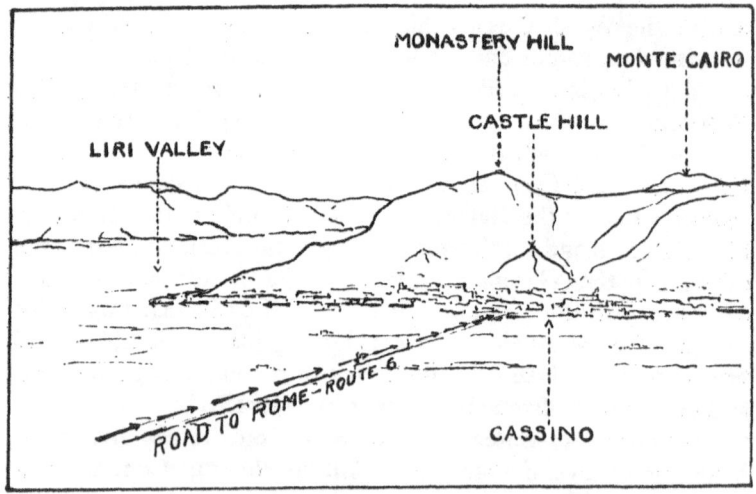

THE CASSINO POSITION.

The 3rd Battalion Welsh Guards, now commanded by Lieutenant-Colonel Sir William Makins, Bart., embarked at Philippeville on February the 3rd and landed at Naples on the 5th. By then the American attack on Monastery Hill had failed, but to the south-east of Cassino British forces had won a foothold across the Garigliano and had captured a series of mountain heights, forming a salient over the river which was later to prove of great value. The 1st Guards Brigade was required for the exploitation of this success while a second attack on Monastery Hill was being prepared; and immediately on landing the 3rd

Battalion Welsh Guards were moved forward. They went in cattle trucks by train to Capua, and after one day in billets, relayed in troop-carriers through a cold, wet night and at three o'clock in the morning transferred into three-ton lorries and drove to Ponte, north of Sessa. From there they marched to "Skipton Dump" where Sappers had bridged the Garigliano behind a newly captured salient. Wheeled transport could go no farther, and as the supply of mules and native porters was inadequate the marching companies took up additional loads of stores and ammunition to carry up the mountains. They were to rest for twenty-four hours on a shoulder of Monte Furlito, a thousand feet above the river, while reconnaissances for their impending operations were carried out; but next morning the proposed operations were abandoned and they were ordered to relieve the 5th Battalion of the Hampshire Regiment on Monte Cerasola.

As it turned out they had little rest either on the night spent on Furlito or on the ten which followed, while they held Cerasola against German attacks and lived in a misery of snow and ice, of blinding rain and biting wind, and endured bombardment from other peaks which overlooked their positions. A German attack on the Hampshires was in progress when their advance party climbed the mountain : twice in the dawn of their first day on Cerasola they drove the Germans back with bayonet and grenade ; and at daybreak on their last day there they and the Coldstream Guards on neighbouring Monte Ornito not only killed and wounded large numbers in repelling a determined enemy assault but captured many prisoners. At the end of that day the Welsh Guards were relieved. They had kept their charge intact, but only at the cost of heavy casualties. Lieutenant-Colonel Sir William Makins was ordered to hospital half-way through the action and Major D. G. Davies-Scourfield then took command ; on February 19th, he brought the Battalion out to rest, battered but unbowed.

At that date the Anzio bridgehead was still closely contained by the enemy ; Cassino, Monastery Hill and Monte Cairo were still in German hands ; and it still rained with cold persistence, so that swollen rivers, flooded ground and sodden tracks combined to delay the capture of those mutually supporting heights. It was the end of February.

On St. David's day the 3rd Battalion Welsh Guards went back into the line after ten days' rest at Cascano. This time they were on the right of their former position and on the easier slopes of Monte Purgatorio. They had to guard a front of nearly four thousand yards which involved much active patrolling; but they were separated from the enemy by a considerable valley and apart from shelling and mortar fire they had a comparatively uneventful time and fewer casualties.

During their stay on Purgatorio a third attempt was made by Allied forces to capture Cassino and Monastery Hill. It had better results than the two earlier attacks, but even so was only partially successful. For although over a thousand tons of bombs reduced the town to rubble, infantry and tanks trying to penetrate the sodden ruins found their advance still stiffly contested; and after several days of bitter fighting only Castle Hill, the station area and about half of the town had been captured. The remainder of the town, with Monastery Hill, and Monte Cairo were still held by the enemy when the battle died down towards the end of March.

On the 29th of March, having had a short rest in Sessa after their sojourn on Monte Purgatorio, the Welsh Guards took over from the New Zealand troops ground that had recently been won to the south of Cassino railway station. They held this ground for a week and on the night of April the 5th they moved out to harbour near San Pietro. On the night of April the 7th they went into Cassino.

Cassino was unique in the Italian campaign, and the life of the Welsh Guards while they helped to garrison its ruins was unlike anything they experienced either before or after. They had learned to live in the blaze of an African sun and in the stormy gloom of Cerasola's crest. Now they were to live by lamplight, burrowing in the rubble of a shattered town. The story of their life in Cassino is more fully told in later pages. They were in the northern sector of the town from April the 7th to April the 23rd and again from May 5th to May the 18th.

Yet at long last this hard and dreary winter's fighting ended. Just before midnight on May the 11th, whilst the Welsh Guards and other troops of the Cassino garrison kept watch among the ruins, the unheralded roar of a thousand guns announced the opening of a new battle—the fourth attempt to break the German line and open the road to Rome. This time it succeeded.

At the end of seven days' heavy fighting Polish forces had captured Monastery Hill and the heights immediately beyond; British and Dominion divisions had crossed the Rapido (a tributary of the Garigliano) south of Cassino and had then turned north-west to meet the Poles on Route 6 beyond the town; and French troops, using the Cerasola-Ornito salient as a fulcrum to loosen the enemy's hold in the south, began a momentous drive through the mountain range which marches with the Liri Valley on the Mediterranean side and separates it from the coastal belt; there American units attacking up the coast also made rapid progress.

On May the 18th the Welsh Guardsmen in Cassino left their positions in daylight for the first time and for the first time saw clearly the full devastation in which they had lived so long. Then they marched out to bivouac among the orchards and vineyards beyond the town, and to enjoy the sunshine on the first stage of their journey northwards.

The fall of the Cassino position compelled the Germans to retire, but they extricated their forces with great skill and battle on a big scale was still in full and noisy progress. Dominion, Polish and Indian divisions were fighting forward in the mountains north of the Liri Valley. In the valley itself British and Dominion troops were steadily driving the enemy from that fertile ground. The French were winning height after height in the southern mountains, and beyond them in the coastal belt American forces, aided by naval bombardment from the sea, more than kept pace in their conquest of the coast towns and Route 7, the old Appian Way from Naples to Rome. On May the 23rd, the Canadians, after bloody fighting, broke through the Adolf Hitler line between Aquino and Pontecorvo, and at six o'clock on the same morning British and American troops broke out of the Anzio bridgehead—held with grim suffering since January—and started to fight their way towards Rome.

As this great battle-line moved forward the Welsh Guards followed, with the other Battalions of the 1st Guards Brigade. They passed through lanes and orchards torn by shell fire, ploughed and patterned by tanks and bulldozers and the numberless wheels of a modern army. The dust and smoke of battle hung heavily in the hot air and congestion on the few available routes delayed long lines of crawling vehicles (on one day it took eighteen hours to cover thirteen miles), so the Welsh Guards had time to note the debris of the battle-field—the burnt out guns and tanks; used shell-cases and unfired ammunition; abandoned stores and equipment; broken weapons of many sorts and steel helmets of many shapes; recent graves and bodies yet unburied, marked only by a bayoneted rifle, stuck gauntly in the uncomplaining soil.

The 1st Guards Brigade had rejoined the 6th Armoured Division, the division (whose sign is a mailed fist) in which they had fought in North Africa. It was now ordered to lead the advance up Route 6 and on May the 24th passed through the Adolf Hitler line where the Canadians had broken it and reached the point where the Melfa river is crossed by the main road. On the night of May the 25th as they harboured nearby, a Welsh Guards officer wrote home, "I am writing this in our Company office tent. Outside hundreds of fire-flies are swimming about in the warm air just above the corn and the poppies and the cornflowers. Someone has a wireless in among the trees. A bulldozed track leads through our harbour area and an extraordinary selection of army vehicles passes by along it: when they halt we give them mugs of tea from our cookhouse. There are crickets chirping and in the distance a pond somewhere with a bull-frog." But shortly after midnight, when they (if not the bull-frog) had gone to sleep, the Luftwaffe made their one and only raid. A neighbouring unit's ammunition trucks were hit and some of the Welsh Guards' vehicles. Far more serious was the loss to the Battalion of three killed and twenty wounded.

Seven miles ahead of the Melfa river lies the town of Arce. It is a place of some significance, for Route 6 turns sharply south at the town where another road bends northwards through the mountains. It was necessary for the Allies not only to secure the continued passage of Route 6, but also to deny the enemy use of the northern road as an escape route for his withdrawing army. It was also important to capture Arce quickly. But the plans of a commander are liable to be upset by the various and vexing uncertainties of war, and on the morning after this rudely disturbed night, tanks of the Armoured Brigade were held up by shell fire on the road and the Grenadiers went forward on foot through the orchard country on the south side and reached Coldragone. There in turn they also were stopped by mortar and machine-gun fire.

To the north of Coldragone, near the hamlet of Le Cese, the road tops a small rise and then runs forward into Arce through a bottle-neck pass between steep hills which form a crescent of defence. Stone-built, on a rocky spur which lifts it well above the intervening ground, the town looks squarely through the pass and down the long straight road. Anyone breasting the rise near Le Cese, where our advance was halted, is instantly in full view, while for a still greater distance the ground is overlooked from the sister town of Rocca d'Arce, whose gleaming walls cling precariously to the peak a thousand feet above. How strongly the town and the hills were held was not yet known.

The Grenadiers had reached the neighbourhood of Coldragone at about three in the afternoon, and the Welsh Guards, then some way behind, were told to move up shortly after; but it was not until half-past eight that night that they received orders to advance on foot through the pass and to seize Arce, a mile and a half beyond. They started soon afterwards, but made little progress in the darkness. Next morning the two leading companies were detailed to secure the flanking hills. The company on the right succeeded in establishing itself on the high ground after a patrol had located the enemy, but the second company were unable to secure Monte Piccolo on the left and had heavy casualties in a valiant attempt to do so. In the end it required all three Battalions of the 1st Guards Brigade, assisted by the fire-power of the 26th Armoured Brigade and the Divisional mortars and artillery, to capture the position; and it was not until the morning of May the 29th that a company of the Welsh Guards, riding on the tanks of the 2nd Lothian and Border Horse, entered Arce almost unopposed. A more detailed account of this costly action is given in Part II.

After this untimely delay the 6th Armoured Division moved forward again, the 26th Armoured Brigade leading with tanks driving "like the driving of Jehu," and the 1st Guards Brigade following, with infantry ready to be called on immediately should their assistance be needed. Leaving Route 6 to other troops and taking a road which runs through the foothills and hill-towns, they by-passed Rome and turned northwards up the Tiber valley.

The reason for this change of direction can easily be understood by reference to the accompanying map. As our forces advanced after breaking the southern half of the Gustav Line the exposed German flank correspondingly lengthened. The mountainous nature of the country on which he rested enabled the enemy to maintain this exposed flank while his forces withdrew; but north of Rome we reached more open country and were able to crowd the enemy towards the Adriatic and to reduce the number of his escape routes. The road up the Tiber valley towards Terni which the 6th Armoured Division now took was one of these.

As the Welsh Guards moved forward in the divisional column, with the dome of St. Peter's clearly visible, tremendous events were taking place.

On the 5th of June American troops entered Rome, the first European capital to be liberated. On the 6th of June (D Day on the western front) Allied forces began landing in Normandy and the 1st and 2nd Battalions of the Regiment waited impatiently to recross the Channel and renew the fight which had seemed to end four years before in the dunes near Dunkirk and the harbour of Boulogne. Other news was hardly less inspiring. The Russian armies were advancing rapidly on a three hundred mile front and almost all Russian soil was already freed. In the Far East there were signs that the tide of war was turning in our favour. "The beginning of the end" had been reached, though another year's hard fighting was needed before the end came.

Heartened by the news from other fronts and by their own progress, the armies in Italy pressed forward. The 6th Armoured Division was already fifteen miles beyond Rome when, on June the 8th leading tanks were held up by shell fire and demolitions and the Welsh Guards were ordered to continue the advance on foot while Sappers made a way for the armour.

The Tiber, hereabouts, winds its way near the left of the road (Route 4) which is separated from the river only by water-

The Beginning of the End—1944

meadows and an occasional copse of willows; on the right is undulating grass-land, scored deeply at intervals by streams hurrying to the Tiber from the hills five miles away. It was where the road crosses these streams that the bridges had been blown.

The Welsh Guards advance, planned in three bounds—"Tom," "Dick" and "Harry"—was made in darkness and accomplished without much opposition; but the sunken streams

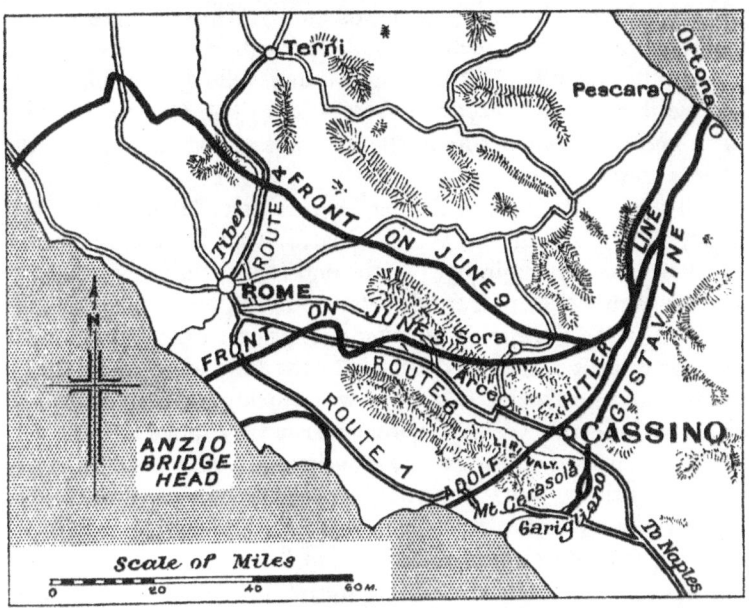

PROGRESS AFTER THE FALL OF CASSINO.

and blown bridges were well registered by the German gunners, and two were killed and seventeen wounded before their final objective was reached. Lieutenant-Colonel D. G. Davies-Scourfield was among those wounded and Lieutenant-Colonel J. E. Gurney, M.C., was appointed to command the Battalion.

The tanks continued the advance next day till they were again stopped by a blown bridge over the River Farfa, when the Coldstream Guards crossed the river on foot and cleared a further mile in face of considerable opposition. The Grenadier

Guards and the Welsh Guards then passed through them and made a long advance across country in darkness, the bounds for the operation being named "Jack," "Hulbert," "Cecily," and "Courtneidge." After this the tanks forged ahead again and in the next ten days covered seventy-five miles, reaching the hills before Perugia without calling on the infantry.

The country through which the Battalion passed is some of the most lovely in Italy and it had been almost untouched by war. "The fields are full of vigorous green maize, sturdy corn, now a golden yellow, and orchards and fruit trees connected by garlands of bright green vines. Through all this luxuriance winds the unruffled Tiber, sluggish and yellow, but mighty in its indifference to everything around it." The passing Guardsmen had been whispering in the darkness of Cassino's ruins less than a month before.

All three Battalions of the 1st Guards Brigade were deployed before Perugia, but the Welsh Guards were in reserve during the first two days' fighting. At the end of that time key positions on the approaches to Perugia from the west and south were in our hands and the enemy, to avoid being surrounded, abandoned the town itself and moved back into the hills which overlooked it from the north and east. He was quickly pursued. On the 20th of June the Welsh Guards, assisted by tanks of 16th/5th Lancers, passed through the southern outskirts of Perugia, delayed little by a few remaining snipers and rather more by an uproarious welcome from the townsfolk, and in face of heavy shelling and mortar and machine-gun fire overcame all opposition, occupied San Marco two miles beyond the town and established a company on Montione, a hill which rises steeply to seventeen hundred feet about a mile away to the north-west.

Like Piccolo, the hill is half clothed in olives and other trees and is crowned with a tumble of loose rocks and scrub which easily conceal a waiting foe. And like most of these mountains and hills, its top is neither obvious when reached nor limited to a single hump. The company which took the hill reached the highest point and formed a strong position of slit trenches where the ground was soft and of stone sangars where it was hard; but there was still room for the enemy to hide behind other rocks on the summits and slopes and the Welsh Guards were counter-attacked that night. They fought off the attack and maintained their own position, but they were not strong enough to clear the enemy off the hill and they were nearly surrounded before they were withdrawn next night. In the following few days all three Battalions carried out attacks on this or other neighbouring heights which drove the enemy further and finally from Perugia.

Having now lost both Perugia and the hills beyond, the enemy retired again and all three Battalions of the 1st Guards Brigade sent out fighting patrols to follow them up. The Welsh Guards force (detachments of riflemen, mortars, anti-tank guns and carriers) pushed vigorously north and, brushing aside weak opposition at Compresso, harboured that night (June the 30th) at Canneto. Next day they renewed the chase, outflanked Monte Tezzio and reached San Giovanni, where they regained contact with the enemy. They had advanced "eight miles as the crow flies and about fifteen as hounds ran" when they were relieved by troops of another division and rejoined the Battalion to rest and prepare for the next task.

It was now the end of June. Since the fall of Cassino on May the 17th a notable feat of arms had been achieved; the enemy had been driven back over two hundred miles and had lost heavily in killed, wounded and prisoners. But the effort to cut off the German divisions which had been forced to retire when their winter line was broken had been unsuccessful. The exposed flank had been pulled back and the German armies were now aligned, east and west through the "calf" of Italy, with Lake Trasimene strengthening their centre; the Gothic Line was stretched across the Apennines only fifty miles behind them. The accompanying map gives the approximate front on various dates and shows how, by holding our advance in the central mountains and on the Adriatic coast as long as was necessary for the withdrawal of his own troops, Kesselring had been able to extricate most of the forces which were outflanked when Cassino fell and the Allies drove forward up the western side to Rome and beyond.

* * * * *

At the beginning of June the prospect seemed brighter than ever before to the people at home. News from the Italian front was splendid and there seemed to be no stopping the Russian

Armies' advance. Yet the man-in-the-street waited wistfully for our assault on the western front, knowing that without this the board was not set for final victory. Now, when success on other fronts seemed assured; when spring had turned to summer and men and military stores evidently accumulated in southern England, the time seemed ripe. A keen sense of expectancy, a feeling that the great event was at last impending, filled men's minds. And if for the more thoughtful hope was tempered by an element of dread, this was not from doubt of the ultimate result but from fear of the immediate cost. The very fact that such prolonged and mighty preparation had been called for seemed to underline the perils which men must face before a fortified and defended coast could be conquered and held.

So it was with a double sense of relief that the great news of D Day—June the 6th, 1944—was received. The long-awaited landings in France had been effected and the cost in casualties had been less than was anticipated. More than six thousand aeroplanes, over four thousand ships and thousands of smaller craft were employed that day, and among the troops who made the first assault was the 231st Infantry Brigade, commanded by Brigadier Sir Alexander Stanier, who had fought at Boulogne in 1940 in command of the 2nd Battalion Welsh Guards.

In the days that followed, despite untimely storms in the Channel, the build-up of Allied forces continued uninterruptedly. The 1st and 2nd Battalions of the Welsh Guards crossed in various detachments between the 18th and the 29th of June and landed at Arromanches in the shelter of an artificial harbour formed by grounded block-ships and specially constructed "Mulberry" units. They disembarked on a sandy beach and went by steeply rising bulldozed ramps to the trampled marshalling area in the fields above. Thousands of vehicles and the multiplying personnel of a swelling army moved there, but the apparent confusion was resolved continually as unit after unit collected its component parts and moved to its appointed place.

The 1st Battalion went to St. Martin les Entrees, a little east of Bayeux; the 2nd Battalion concentrated in fields nearby, and both made themselves ready for whatever might be required of them. Where and to what purpose they were employed is best understood if the plan of the High Command is known. In simplest outline it was this.

Phase I. Initial landings to be made in Normandy, the ground won to be extended as rapidly as possible till it included Cherbourg on the west and Caen and the Orne estuary on the east.

Phase II. Once firmly established, to threaten to break out of the Caen or eastern sector, so as to draw the main enemy reserves to that side.

Phase III. Having thus got the main enemy forces committed on the eastern flank, to break out on the western flank and, first driving southwards to the Loire, to turn east and sweep up to the Seine about Paris.

At the end of June *Phase I* had not been completed, for the ground won did not yet include either Cherbourg or Caen.

On the 28th June the 1st Battalion took over a quiet sector of the line near Bretteville l'Orgueilleuse, but south of their position the fight for Caen and the nearby Carpiquet airfield raged fiercely, and on the following day they and the other battalions of the 32nd Guards Brigade were detached from the Guards Division and sent forward to take up a defensive position behind a point where newly won ground was not yet secure. Till then they had seen little evidence of war damage. Bayeux itself was practically untouched and its picturesque *pavé* streets and grey, stone buildings gave them a pleasant introduction to the Normandy setting in which their first battles were to be fought. The neighbouring country is mostly cultivated land, rising gradually towards the east till it falls again to the valley of the Orne. The enemy were in this valley and British forces were fighting beyond the crest line. The 1st Battalion took up their positions behind it round Cheux, a little stone-built hamlet eight miles west of Caen. Here for the first time they were in the battle area. Cheux had been half destroyed by shell fire and the hot and dusty air was foul with the smell of death. Dead cows and horses shared with Battalion Headquarters a large field behind the village. The companies dug in on the reverse slopes of the rising ground in front, from which the spires of Caen and the buildings on Carpiquet airfield could be seen half hidden by the smoke of battle.

The element of chance in warfare was never more clearly illustrated than on their first evening there. The companies were hardly in position and the men of Battalion Headquarters were still digging-in in their field when they were heavily mortared. The Commanding officer, the Second-in-Command, the Anti-tank Gun Officer, the Signals Officer, a Company Sergeant-Major and a number of Guardsmen were wounded and had to be evacuated to England. And this was not the end of their misfortune. Major J. E. Fass, who took command, was killed on the following evening almost in the same place and in the same way. In Lieutenant-Colonel G. W. Browning, Major M. E. C. Smart and Major Fass the Battalion thus lost its three senior officers before they ever saw the enemy. Major C. H. R. Heber-Percy, M.C., was now promoted to command the Battalion.

They held the Cheux position for twelve days, but the line in front of them was secured without their being called on and on the 11th of July they were withdrawn to rejoin the Guards Armoured Division at St. Martin les Entrees near Bayeux. The 2nd Battalion lay a few fields away.

On the 27th of June Cherbourg was taken by American troops, and by the 8th of July British and Canadian troops had captured all of Caen that lay north of the Orne and had enlarged their bridgehead across the northern reaches of the river. *Phase I* had been achieved ; the time to open *Phase II* had come, namely to threaten to break out on the eastern flank.

At dawn on the 18th of July Field-Marshal Montgomery attacked with strong forces of armour and infantry east of Caen, the assault being preceded by the heaviest and most concentrated bombing hitherto used to support a military operation. British and American bombers blasted a "lane" between Caen and the hills to the east, and the Guards Armoured Division, including both Welsh Guards Battalions, moved slowly into the north of this "lane." The battle that followed is described in Part II. The 1st Battalion were engaged at Cagny and Le Poirier ; the 2nd Battalion took part in the heavy armoured fighting of the first two days and were then employed on the eastern flank till the Division was withdrawn on July the 22nd. Their orders took them to most uncomfortable positions on the outskirts of Caen. The 2nd Battalion lay at Collombelles on rising ground in full view of the enemy, "providing Aunt

Sallies for the German gunners," as the Commanding Officer said with some bitterness. They were in fact held there as part of the "display of armoured force" which was designed to impress upon the German Command the seriousness of our threat to this flank, and when eventually the Welsh Guards were released from their uncomfortable positions the battle had already achieved this purpose. Believing that our threat was serious, the German commander had decided to commit the major part of his reserves and these were being held and badly mauled.

The time for *Phase III* had now come, for while this bitter fight in the east was still raging American troops had conquered the remainder of the Cherbourg peninsula and were ready to break out on the west. British forces (which included the Guards Armoured Division) were now transferred from the east of Caen to the west of Bayeux to co-operate in the breakout, and the two Welsh Guards Battalions re-crossed the Orne on the night of July the 30th. The Americans had attacked on the 25th of July and, overcoming the enemy's resistance, had broken out west of St. Lo and were spreading rapidly southwards. On the 30th of July British armour and infantry launched a major attack on the left of the Americans, striking south through Caumont.

Here was the rich, close, "Bocage" country—difficult fighting ground, especially for armour. Yet the difficulty and determined opposition by the enemy were alike overcome and after a fortnight's fighting the Guards Armoured Division was astride the Vire-Vassy road, thirty-five miles from the coast where they had landed. The 1st Battalion Welsh Guards had their initial actions at St. Denis Maisoncelles and St. Pierre Tarentaine, which they captured on August the 2nd. Two days later they began a gruelling battle for Montchamp. Having taken the village, they were heavily counter-attacked and German tanks overran some of the positions of the leading companies; it was not until the next day that the place was wholly in our hands. Welsh Guards casualties were heavy and among the wounded was Lieutenant-Colonel Heber-Percy, already their third Commanding Officer in Normandy. Major J. F. Gresham from Prince of Wales Company then took command and four days later fought a difficult and successful action near Le Bas Perrier, in which the whole of the 32nd Guards Brigade and some of the armour of the Division were also involved. By the end of that day, August the 9th, they had captured the high ground north of the Vire-Vassy road, and on the 16th the 1st Battalion Welsh Guards crossed the road and occupied positions based on Boulay Aux Chats. A map of the country is given in Part II where the fighting is described more fully.

During these operations the 2nd Battalion had also been engaged at a number of points—fighting enemy armour and self-propelled guns, cunningly dispersed in the thick Bocage country ; doing flank guards ; covering infantry ; or probing into the enemy's positions well ahead of the infantry in their role of Divisional Reconnaissance troops.

The 1st Battalion were not at once able to replace their heavy casualties from available reinforcements, so No. 2 Company was temporarily disbanded and a company of Scots Guards became an integral part of the 1st Battalion and served in all subsequent actions with gallantry and distinction.

The stubbornness of the enemy's efforts to hold the high ground north of the Vire-Vassy road was soon explained, for while we were engaged in taking it the Germans launched a strong counter-attack across our front, striking westwards on the other side of the road. It had been ordered by Hitler himself. "The Fuehrer has ordered the execution of a break-through to the coast in order to create the basis for decisive operations against the Allied invasion front. For this purpose further forces are being brought up to the army." So ran an army order issued by the German Commander on the 8th of August. It added prophetically, "On the successful execution of the operation the Fuehrer has ordered, depends the decision of the war in the west and with it perhaps the decision of war itself."

And this is what happened.

On August the 9th the Germans attacked with six armoured divisions in an attempt to cut the American forces in half and reach the coast at Avranches. They got as far west as Mortain, twenty miles from the coast, but the American forces not only stood firm and held the enemy in battle but swept round them, moving eastwards towards Paris. Field-Marshal Montgomery seized the opportunity thus presented and started to enclose the enemy forces. Canadians struck south and captured Falaise on the 16th of August; part of the American columns *en route* for Paris turned north and captured Argentan. The "Falaise pocket" was closed and the enemy's forces, trying desperately to escape, were practically annihilated.

After resting for a week, the Guards Armoured Division moved towards the Seine and the Welsh Guards went through this "killing area." "Round here the scene is indescribable. The remnants of a shattered army lie on the roads, in the fields and in the woods. Everywhere destroyed vehicles, dead Germans, dead horses—terrible to behold and worse to smell." But on August the 30th, after a seventy-mile drive that day, they reached the cleaner atmosphere of the Seine, which they crossed near Vernon that evening. British and Canadian forces had won crossings on August the 24th and 25th; American troops had reached the river south of Paris on August the 19th; the capital itself had been liberated and finally cleared of the enemy by August the 26th, mainly by Maquis and a French Armoured Division, but with help from American infantry.

The battle of Normandy had been won. In the preliminary plan, made months before D Day, ninety days had been allowed for the advance from the beaches to the Seine. In fact it only took seventy-five. With this one variation the plan was fully executed and in the process forty-three German Divisions were either eliminated or severely mauled. The Guards, fighting as an Armoured Division for the first time, had won high praise, and both Welsh Guards Battalions in the Division had fought well: the story of their part in this battle is told in detail in Part II.

* * * * *

While these stirring events were taking place on the western front, the 3rd Battalion had been busy in Italy. After the loss of Perugia and the ground to the north, the German armies were aligned across Italy with Lake Trasimene in their centre; but before a week was out they had been forced to give ground and were pushed back well to the north of the lake.

After the Welsh Guards had rested for two days on the shores of Lake Trasimene, the whole of the 1st Guards

Brigade concentrated round Cortona to prepare for further operations. They were there from the 7th to the 14th of July and in that time two steps of importance to the 3rd Battalion were taken. The first concerned its general well-being. Lieutenant-Colonel Gurney realised that, although the fighting had been spasmodic, the journeying since Cassino had been wellnigh continuous and very fatiguing; in the peace and beauty of the country round Lake Trasimene he saw an opportunity to relieve tired bodies and strained nerves. With great enterprise he secured the use of a large villa, looking from the foothills on the north of the lake, down a mile-long drive of cypress trees, to the unruffled waters and the far-away blue hills. To give it a more homely sound it was renamed by the Welshmen "The Cardiff Arms," and during the summer most members of the Battalion profited by a stay there at one time or another.

The second step taken at this time concerned the Battalion's strength. Since the fighting for Monte Piccolo at Arce the Battalion had only three rifle companies, for No. 2 had lost so heavily in that fight that there were not enough left to carry on as a company. Now this loss of strength was made good temporarily by the addition to the Battalion of a company of Grenadier Guards, whose arrival at "The Cardiff Arms" was warmly welcomed.

Heavy fighting was in progress farther north. The enemy now seemed determined to retire no farther, but to stand on a line based on Ancona to the east, Arezzo in the centre and Leghorn in the west. Field-Marshal Alexander was equally determined not to let him and attacked all three positions. As part of these operations the 6th Armoured Division was ordered to capture Arezzo. The 26th Armoured Brigade had been pursuing the enemy while the infantry were at Cortona, and they were already within sight of the hills guarding the town when the 1st Guards Brigade were ordered up. Leaving their concentration area on the night of the 14th of July, the infantry went into action next morning.

The operation was well conceived, well prepared, well executed and completely successful. The enemy had deployed the equivalent of a division along the ridge of hills which forms a six-mile barrier to the south of Arezzo. Any direct approach up the valley brought immediate response from the enemy, so an outflanking movement was planned. New Zealand troops captured the highest hill at the south-eastern end of the ridge (Monte Lignino) on July the 14th, and on the 15th the 1st Guards Brigade continued the attack along it towards the twin hills which form the gateway to Arezzo. The Grenadiers began the attack in the darkness and after some sharp fighting broke into the enemy's flank. The Coldstream next carried the fight forward and took a further sector of the ridge. Then the Welsh Guards climbed the hills in the heat of the day and passed through the remainder of the Brigade to capture two strong hill-positions on either side of a gap through which the road from Rome runs up to Arezzo. They had some casualties from shelling, but by the time they had reached their objectives the enemy had gone. His deployment along the ridge had been turned to his disadvantage by the direction of our attack, and once his line began to be rolled up from the flank his position was untenable. By five o'clock in the morning of July the 16th the whole ridge was in our hands, and that morning patrols which were pushed forward reported that Arezzo was abandoned: after extensive demolitions and mines had been cleared, the Armoured Brigade entered the city. Three days later both Ancona on the Adriatic coast and Leghorn on the Mediterranean were also captured by Allied troops; the German front across Italy had been broken and Florence now became the next objective.

Little more than a mile to the north of Arezzo the River Arno turns north-west towards Florence, sixty miles away. On its western side are the Chianti mountains flanking the road from Arezzo to Florence (Route 69). Across the river, a mile or so to the east, secondary roads connect the little towns and villages in the foothills of the Prato Magna massif, encircled by the great loop of the Arno and still in enemy hands. When the 6th Armoured Division renewed their advance, three days after the capture of Arezzo, they moved up Route 69 while other troops converged on Florence. The 1st Guards Brigade were used to clear the right flank of the divisional front by occupying in turn key places on the secondary road and by patrolling actively in the foothills of the Prato Magna. The

Welsh Guards moved successively to positions based on Quarata, with companies at Ponti Burriano and Castiglion Fibrocchi; on Renacci, with companies at Faella, Vaggio and Castel Franco; at Torre a Monte; and Sant' Ellero. Then they seized the Altomena ridge and liberated Pelago. They had now reached

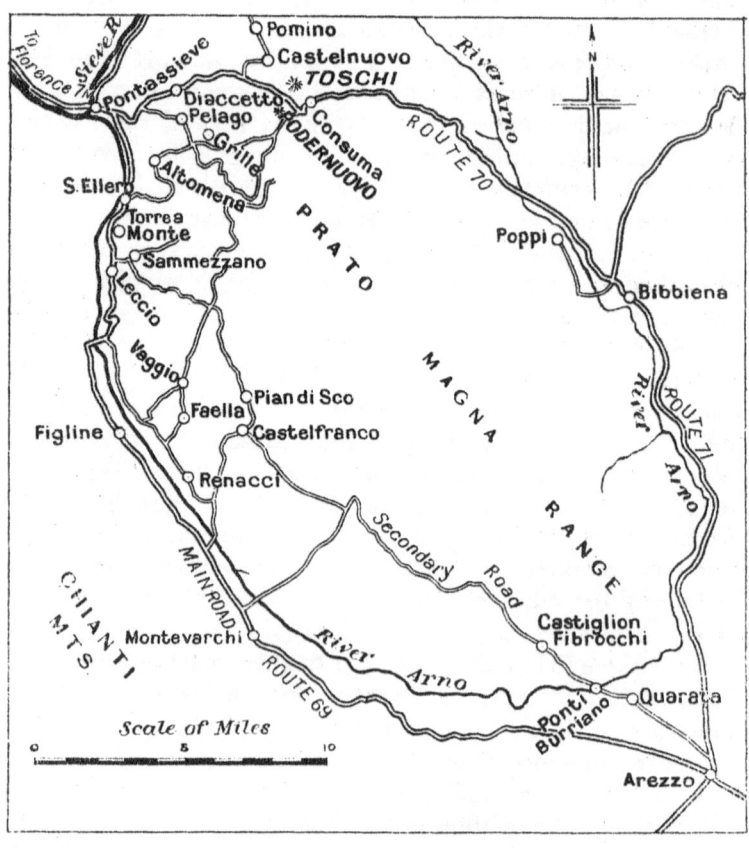

THE ARNO VALLEY.

the head of the valley. Here at Pontassieve the Arno turns west to Florence, while Route 70 starts eastwards over the northern spurs of the Prato Magna range to join the upper Arno and Route 71 at Bibbiena. Another division was advancing up the latter road and the 1st Guards Brigade spread out to hold Route

70 till their arrival. The Welsh Guards occupied the central position based on Podernuovo and they worked gradually forward over the long finger of high ground running up past Castelnuovo. It was the end of the Arno valley chapter of their story, which is told more fully in Part II. Immediately before them was the much advertised Gothic Line.

Allied troops reached the southern outskirts of Florence on the 4th of August, but the enemy had demolished the bridges and held the main town on the north bank of the river; and the Arno here is a sizeable obstacle. Numerous attempts to force a crossing failed, and it was not until the 24th August that the enemy abandoned the city. And even as he suffered the loss of this important town he received a severe blow elsewhere. For while the fight for Florence was still going on Field-Marshal Alexander secretly regrouped his forces and, concentrating them strongly behind the Adriatic sector, attacked the eastern end of the Gothic Line. On August the 26th, after very bitter fighting, the enemy's defences there were smashed, and by the 2nd of September they had been breached to a distance of twenty miles in face of opposition which showed no sign of weakening.

By the middle of September, when our troops were within a few miles of Rimini, the German commander so far succeeded in strengthening his defence that the Allies' threat was halted. Yet the breach which had been made in the eastern sector of the Gothic Line, coupled with the loss of Florence, compelled the enemy to withdraw in the centre, and on September the 10th the 1st Guards Brigade went after him along the road which runs up through the Apennines from Pontassieve. Here was an end of open vales and spreading vineyards. The loneliness of the road up the narrow valley of the Sieve river is only relieved by an occasional village in the shadow of the mountains and by the fringe of hill-side farms, where peasants cultivate their tilted plots or terrace southern slopes for olives. Dicomano, eleven miles up the road from Pontassieve, had been found to be deserted; and when the Welsh Guards arrived there on September the 12th Sappers were busy bridging demolitions, while the Grenadiers and Coldstream occupied covering positions on the neighbouring high ground. Less than three miles away at San

Bavello were the first fortified positions of the Gothic Line, and
a Welsh Guards patrol which went forward in daylight "found
all the defences as advertised—the barbed wire and the concrete,
the felled trees and the cottages converted into strong points—
and they were suffered to inspect all this with impunity. The
Gothic Line had been abandoned." Unable to man the continuous defences of these forward slopes, the enemy had decided

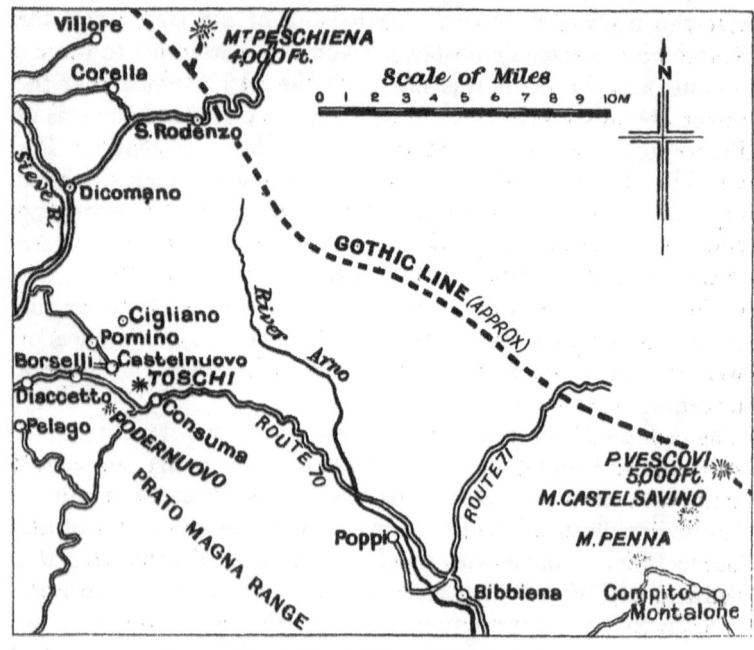

APPROACH TO THE GOTHIC LINE.

to concentrate on holding the main peaks of the mountains
behind.

Two days later the 1st Guards Brigade moved forward and
penetrated further "Gothic" defences round Villore, and on the
16th of September a company of the Welsh Guards were sent
through to probe the defences of the northern spur of Monte
Peschiena, rising to over four thousand feet a little to the north-
east. They climbed to within a few hundred feet of the crest,
taking a prisoner *en route*, but a patrol which reached the summit

found the Germans in strength. Next day a battalion attack was put in by the Grenadier Guards and, moving up the southern spur (where there were better opportunities for deployment), reached the summit; but the mountain top was not cleared of the enemy when the Brigade was relieved and moved at short notice to another part of the front.

Leaving the 6th Armoured Division in the mountain country north of Florence, they retraced their journey through the Arno valley by Route 69 and turning north again by Arezzo took Route 71, where the upper Arno encircles the Prato Magna mountains on the east. Five miles short of Bibbiena they left this road and moved out on to the forward slopes of Monte Penna facing another sector of the Gothic defences, and one which up till then had been held by the enemy. But here again our penetrations elsewhere were compelling the enemy to retire, and, on September the 22nd, three days after their arrival a Welsh Guards' patrol climbed four thousand feet to the top of Monte Vescovi unmolested. The enemy had gone.

The 1st Guards Brigade were moved back to Arezzo, for they were not required to follow the retreating enemy here but to face him elsewhere—back in the mountains north of Florence. The Allies' advance there had made good progress in face of stiff opposition and all the handicaps of natural conditions and artificial contrivance. But it was slow going. The mountains had to be captured ridge after ridge and the demolitions overcome by bridge after bridge. (Surely the Bailey bridge made the winning of the war possible—with the jeep as a very close runner-up!) In particular American troops had fought their way up the Santerno valley road towards Imola and had captured the dominating peak of Monte Battaglia. The enemy, however, seemed determined to recover this important height and was making repeated counter-attacks when the 1st Guards Brigade went to relieve the Americans, who were needed elsewhere.

The Welsh Guards went on to Battaglia on October the 2nd and the detailed story of what happened to them there and in the months that followed is told elsewhere (in Part II). For they remained in this sector till the middle of the following February (with short intervals out of the line between their tours of duty),

first on Battaglia and later on Verro and Penzola, on the other
side of the Santerno valley road. Unlike the armies of bygone
days, which at this time of year would have sensibly retired to
winter quarters, they continued to man what must surely be one
of the most fantastic winter lines ever devised for the discomfort of the troops. On Battaglia they were two thousand
five hundred feet up on a narrow ridge only reached after a six
hours' climb, and on Verro the approach was but little less
arduous. At first the rainfall was abnormally heavy for an

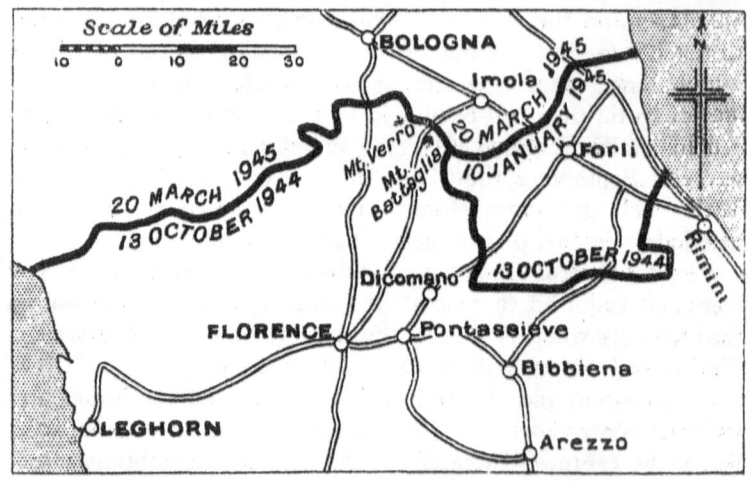

THE WINTER LINE IN ITALY.

Italian autumn; later the conditions were exactly those to be
expected on the top of the Apennines in winter ! Occasionally
the enemy tried to recapture some feature but failed, and
occasionally an attempt was made to improve our positions and
succeeded, but these affairs, though serious enough for those
who took part in them, had only local importance; the line
in this area remained substantially unchanged all through the
winter. To the east, between the mountains and the Adriatic,
it was at first pushed slowly northwards, but even there the
combination of geography, weather and German resistance
brought operations to a standstill till early in January. From
then till March the *War Office Weekly Intelligence Review*

The Beginning of the End—1944

either ignored the Italian Campaign or repeated firmly, "There is nothing to report." They might have been saying it since October of all but the Adriatic sector.

* * * * *

The 1st and 2nd Battalions had reached the Seine when we left them after the battle of Normandy had been won. On their right two American armies were starting advances which were eventually to lead them to the Rhine, and a third, which had begun landing on the Mediterranean coast near Marseilles in August, had already driven a two hundred mile wedge northwards up the Rhône valley.

Field-Marshal Montgomery's next objectives were the clearance of Northern France with its V bomb sites and the capture of airfields in Belgium and the port of Antwerp. The former task was entrusted to the 1st Canadian Army. All through the Battle of Normandy V bombs had been falling on southern England. Some 5,500 people were killed and over 16,000 seriously injured. On the 28th of June one had dropped among the Welsh Guards Training Battalion at Esher, killing nineteen and injuring one hundred and seven, a grievous blow for the Regiment.

The second objective was given to the 2nd British Army, with the 30th Corps as its spearhead. With this Corps the Guards Armoured Division crossed the Seine on August the 30th. In the next four days they gave a historic demonstration of what an armoured division can do where favourable circumstances and the necessary drive are present. On the first day (August the 31st) they advanced over eighty miles, to harbour that night near the Somme. On the second day they reached Arras and, while the 1st Battalion re-entered triumphantly the town they had been the last to leave in 1940, the 2nd Battalion occupied the nearby Vimy Ridge, taking many prisoners *en route*. Both moved to Douai on September the 2nd and the Division was reorganised into Regimental Battle Groups, each consisting of one armoured battalion and one infantry battalion from the same regiment. And on the fourth day they started early, with the Welsh Guards Group leading on one route, and maintaining a record-breaking pace and overcoming all opposition, they

liberated Brussels as night was falling. It was described in the
War Office Weekly Intelligence Review as "an armoured dash
unequalled for speed in this or any other war." The whole
Division lay in or about Brussels that night, including the 231st
Infantry Brigade Group, and the Belgian Brigade Group both
under command of a Welsh Guardsman, Brigadier Sir Alexander

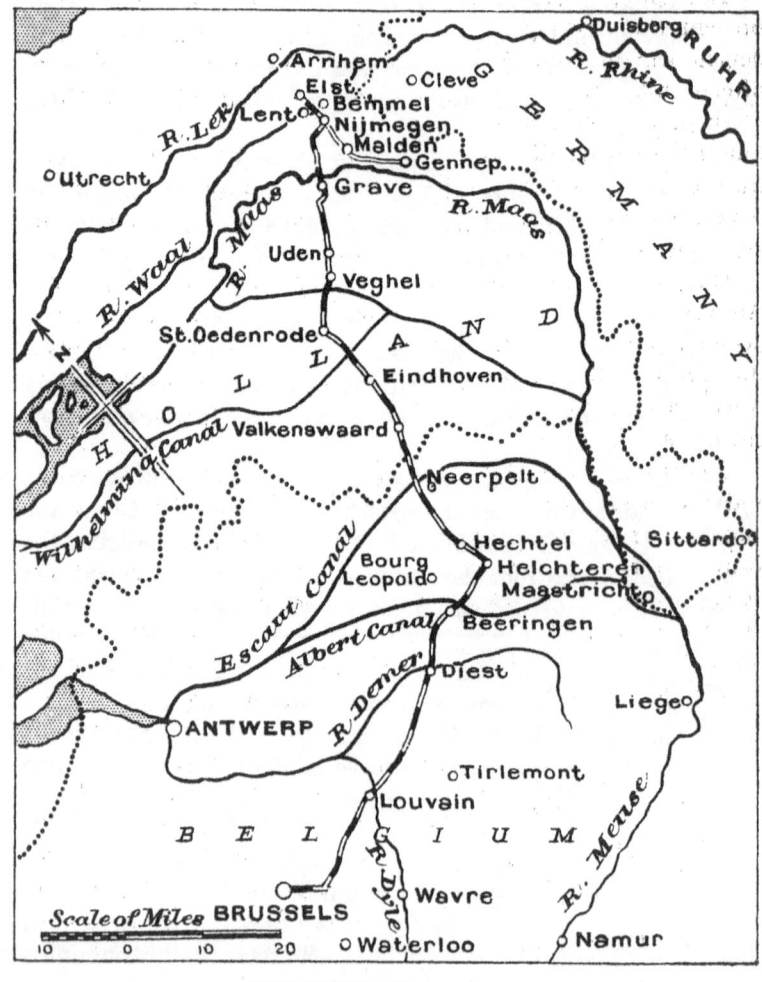

FROM BRUSSELS TO "THE ISLAND."

The Beginning of the End—1944

Stanier, who was able to welcome the first Belgian troops to return to their own country since 1940.

The Division remained at Brussels through the 4th and 5th of September, the 1st Battalion Welsh Guards on the outskirts of the city, the 2nd Battalion at the golf course near Quatre Bras on the road to the old battlefield of Waterloo.

On the 4th tanks of the 2nd Battalion helped to clear the road to Louvain which the Grenadier Group captured in time to prevent the blowing up of the Dyle bridge. On the 5th a detachment of both Welsh Guards Battalions went to Wavre, fifteen miles south-east of Brussels, on a report that some German armoured troops there wished to surrender. They found the troops but no readiness to capitulate, so they fought till the town was clear and in the evening handed it over to an American unit from the corps coming up on the right, before rejoining the Division.

Allied troops had captured Antwerp the day before, and with Antwerp and Brussels in our hands Field-Marshal Montgomery decided to push forward again in an effort to secure a bridge over the northern Rhine before the winter set in. It was a daring aim. Antwerp was ours but could not yet be used as a port, for the enemy still held the approaches through the Scheldt estuary. The northern coast of France and Belgium were not ours yet and the armies had to be maintained with supplies coming, mostly by road, from bases in Normandy four hundred miles away. Moreover, starting from Brussels, ten waterways must be crossed before a bridgehead over the Rhine can be won, and as yet only the Dyle bridge at Louvain was ours. But weather was still favourable and the enemy largely disorganised, though he was beginning to recover his balance. So the advance was renewed.

"Reconnaissance reported on the 6th September that all bridges over the Albert Canal had been blown, but during the next day our troops forced a bridgehead over this waterway in face of intense enemy opposition and extended it in violent engagements. The enemy evidently intended this canal to be one of his main lines of defence."

War Office Weekly Intelligence Review.

The bridge over the Albert Canal at Beeringen had been blown, though not wholly destroyed, when the Welsh Guards Group reached it on the 6th of September. They had to fight for a foothold on the far bank to cover the Sappers while they worked on repairs to the bridge, and these were not finished till dawn next day. By then enemy reinforcements had reached the town and there was stiff fighting all day. The town was only partially cleared when the Irish Guards took on the fight so that the Welsh Guards could go forward.

The enemy clearly intended to hold not only the canal but also the road system behind it, and for the next five days there was hard fighting, with the tide of battle gradually receding from Beeringen, Helchteren, and Bourg Leopold till only Hechtel remained. The Welsh Guards, after being engaged at Beeringen and Helchteren, attacked Hechtel on September the 7th, and, not succeeding then, they attacked again and again on subsequent days; but they only captured it finally on the 12th, having by then accounted for over eight hundred of the enemy in killed, wounded and prisoners, and captured and destroyed a large amount of war material. (See Part II.)

Meanwhile the Irish Guards Group bypassed Hechtel and captured intact the bridge over the next obstacle—the Escaut canal; and the Division remained there until the 17th of September. On that day began the attempt to turn the German north flank, by capturing a bridgehead across the lower Rhine beyond the main fortifications of the Siegfried Line. Airborne divisions were to seize the vital bridges at Grave on the Maas, Nijmegen on the Waal, and Arnhem on the Rhine : in rapid support of the airborne troops, armour and infantry were to advance along the route through St. Oedenrode, Veghel, Uden, Grave, Nijmegen and Arnhem.

At this point the weather broke. From the start adverse conditions seriously affected the operation. On only two of the eight days through which it lasted did weather permit even a reasonable scale of offensive air support and transportation. Airborne formations could not be landed at full strength and re-supply missions had to be cancelled or reduced. Nevertheless over thirty-four thousand men, five thousand tons of equipment and supplies, nearly two thousand vehicles and five

The Beginning of the End—1944

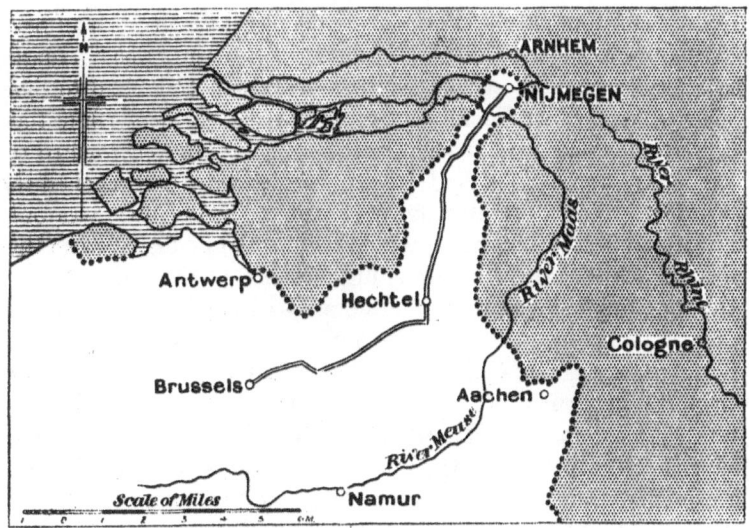

THE ADVANCE TOWARDS ARNHEM.

hundred pieces of artillery were transported by air in the course of the operation. A fifty-mile penetration of the enemy's position was made and bridgeheads were secured over the Maas and Waal. Only the final objective—the Arnhem bridge over the Rhine—was not secured.

On the morning of the 17th of September the Welsh Guards watched the planes going over from their positions near the Escaut canal and made ready to follow up. It was not their turn to lead, and when they reached Nijmegen on the 19th American airborne forces and the Grenadier Guards had captured the bridges intact. The Welsh Guards had only a small flank action near Valkenswaard on the way. The story of the part they played in subsequent efforts to reach Arnhem and to enlarge the bridgehead over the Waal are told in Part II. They were involved in fighting near Fort Lent, at Bemmel and at Amm, where they pushed our line to the most forward position reached. They remained in "the Island"—as the country between the Waal and the Rhine was called—until October the 6th, occupying a number of positions in support of other units. By then the attempt to reach Arnhem had been abandoned, but the bridges at Nijmegen and the bridgehead beyond were firmly and finally ours.

The Guards Armoured Division was then relieved and the Welsh Guards Battalions went back to Malden, four miles south of Nijmegen, where they cleaned themselves up, practised their drill, did some training, played Rugby football and were generally refreshed. And reinforcements arriving, the 1st Battalion re-formed No. 4 Company, which had had to be disbanded after the casualties at Helchteren and Hechtel. On the 12th of October some few of both Battalions had the honour of being present at a visit of their Colonel-in-Chief, His Majesty the King. On the 31st October the 1st Battalion took over for four days the responsibility for guarding the Nijmegen bridges, a task with several unusual features. After that, they went to hold Veulen, twenty miles to the south. It is a bleak little hamlet and the 1st Battalion, with a squadron of the 2nd Battalion to support them, had a most uncomfortable time there. It rained incessantly and movement in the deep mud which developed became almost impossible, but no attack took place and apart from physical hardship the week they spent there was chiefly memorable for patrol activity and minor incidents. On the 11th of November they were relieved and, with one night at Deurne *en route*, they then went into the Sittard sector, another forty miles south of Veulen. Sittard itself, on which they were based, is a small Dutch market town ; Millen and Tuddern, where the companies held the front, are German villages just over the frontier. They had a comparatively uneventful time there for twelve days and then side-stepped to Galeen, two miles farther south. They were there for twelve days more and on the 17th of December at last came out to rest. Staging once on the way, they reached the country south of Tirlemont on December the 21st, the 1st Battalion going into billets at Hougaerde and nearby villages and the 2nd Battalion to the little township of Jodoigne. Here they were only fifteen miles from Louvain and, more important, only twenty-five from Brussels, and they prepared to make themselves comfortable and to celebrate Christmas. Alas ! for their plans. Five days before, the enemy had begun the most serious counter-offensive of the whole campaign—a final and desperate effort into which every available reserve was

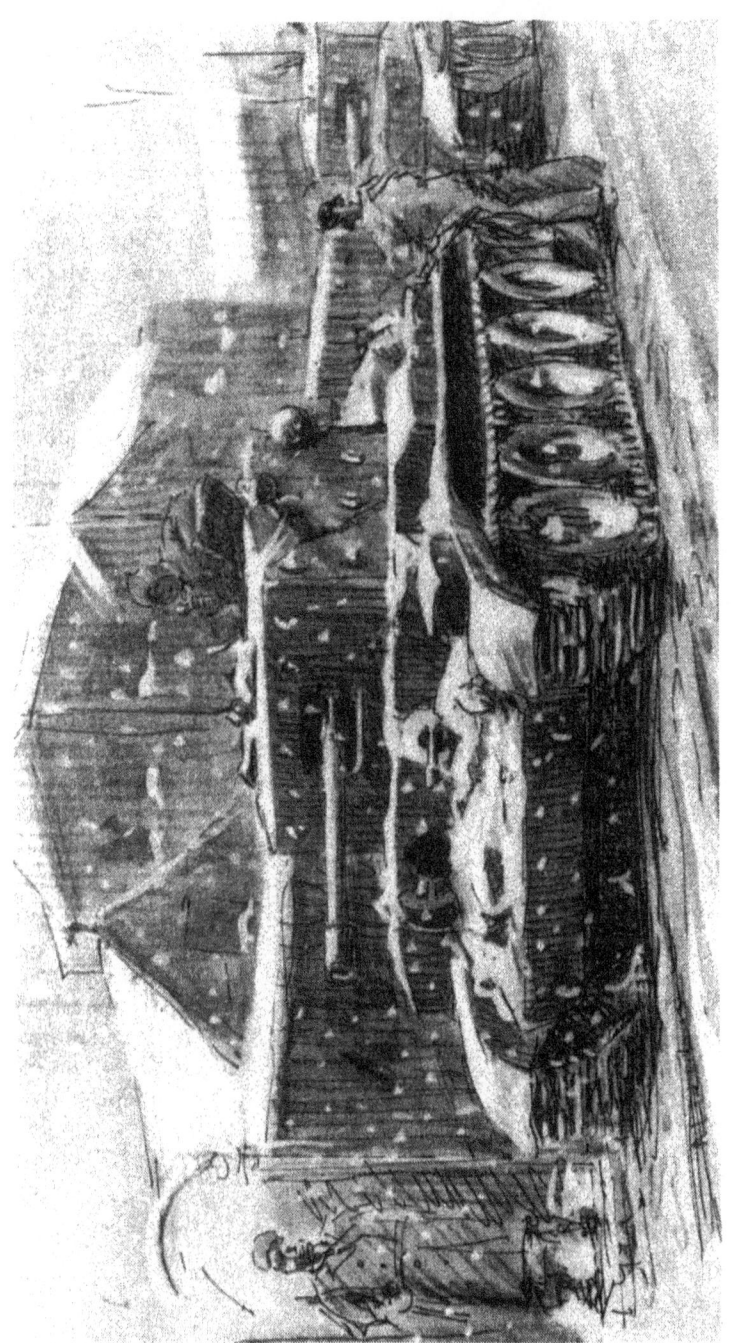

Winter in Holland, by Sergeant C. Murrell
Cromwell tanks of the 2nd Battalion, Welsh Guards

thrown. In addition to the main striking force of fourteen infantry and ten panzer or panzer grenadier divisions, Field-Marshal Von Rundstedt employed one panzer brigade which fought in American uniforms and equipment in the hope of causing panic and confusion; German paratroops were also dropped in parties throughout the battle area, and while small groups attempted sabotage of key bridges and headquarters as far to the rear as Paris, the Luftwaffe gave the ground forces active support for the first time since our landings in Normandy.

To describe fully what happened would be out of place here, for it is not part of the Welsh Guards' story. The enemy breached a forty-five mile gap in the Allies' front and penetrated over sixty miles westwards, nearly reaching the Meuse to the south of Namur. But he failed to secure any really important objective; he lost something like a hundred and twenty thousand serious casualties and six hundred tanks and guns; and disillusionment spread through the German army and in Germany when it was realised that nothing decisive had been attained.

When the offensive was at its height the Guards Armoured Division was moved to the Namur sector as a precautionary measure. The Welsh Guards were in the town and on high ground nearby, but the German penetration did not reach their positions and they were relieved and returned to eat their Christmas dinners in Hougaerde and Jodoigne on the 29th of December.

* * * * *

The 3rd Battalion, in Italy, had gone on to the snow-clad heights at Monte Verro in the Apennines on Christmas Day.

* * * * *

So ended this crowded year. The 3rd Battalion in Italy had helped to push the Germans back from the Gustav Line to the mountains which enclose the Po valley. After holding Cerasola and Cassino, they had fought him up the valleys of the Liri river, the Tiber and the Arno, capturing Arce, Perugia, Arezzo and many smaller places.

Meanwhile on the western front the 1st and 2nd Battalions had played their part in battles which drove the German armies from Normandy to Nijmegen and beyond—the battle of Normandy, the drive through northern France to Brussels, the fighting before the Escaut canal and in "the Island"—and had held the front at Veulen and Sittard.

The achievement of the Allied armies as a whole is graphically set out on the accompanying maps.

"CHURCHILL" INFANTRY TANK.

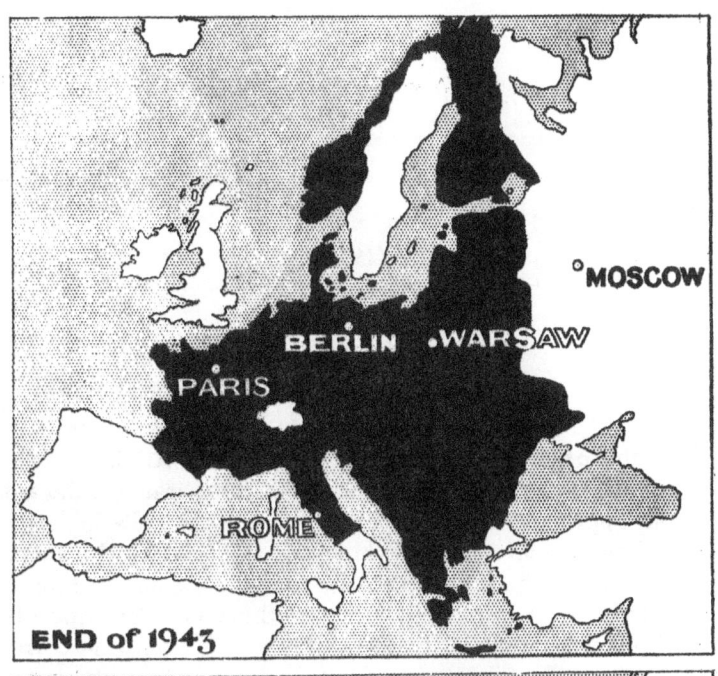
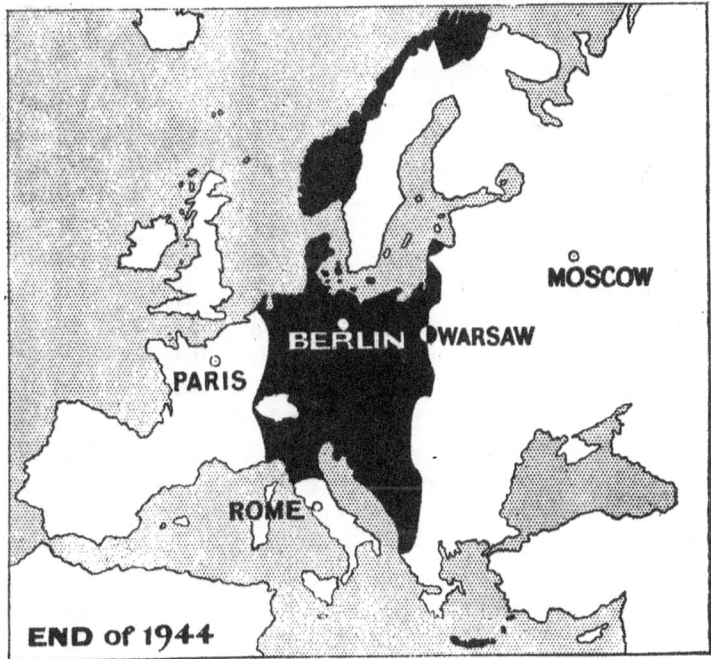

A YEAR'S PROGRESS.

CHAPTER SIX

FIFTH ROUND—THE END
(1945)

Ar y diwedd y mae barnu
It is at the end that one passes judgment
Old Welsh Saying

AT the beginning of 1945 the Allied front still lay between Nijmegen and Arnhem and from there ran southwards, roughly approximating the German frontier-line to Basle ; almost all of Germany west of the Rhine was still held by the enemy. Three tasks lay before General Eisenhower's armies. First, to destroy the enemy forces west of the Rhine and close up to the river ; second, to seize bridgeheads beyond the Rhine from which to develop operations into Germany ; third, to destroy the enemy forces which remained east of the Rhine and advance into the heart of the Reich.

While the Welsh Guards rested at Jodoigne and nearby villages, the enemy was eliminated from the salient west of the Roer where the Welsh Guards had held a sector, at Veulen, in November. There remained to be cleared the Rhineland territory lying south of Nijmegen between the Roer and the Rhine. The Rhineland battle opened on the 8th of February when the 1st Canadian Army struck south-east from the Nijmegen bridgehead. It had been intended that the 9th United States Army should simultaneously strike north-east so that the enemy's troops would be crushed between two converging assaults. This indeed is what happened in the end, but at the outset the enemy succeeded in delaying the American assault for a fortnight by opening some of the Roer dams and flooding large areas of country. The whole battle was characterised by appalling weather conditions and the opening stages were largely carried out in a variety of amphibious vehicles. The mud and slush were indescribable and greatly hampered

The End—1945

the movement of troops and supplies through heavily wooded areas markedly lacking in roads. The battle was also characterised by the enemy's intense and fanatical opposition. Behind them across the Rhine lay the Ruhr, the great industrial heart of Germany, and no doubt the German command realised as clearly as did General Eisenhower that if this were lost to them Germany's capacity to continue the struggle must quickly peter out.

In the opening phase of the battle the Guards Armoured Division was one of the reserve divisions of the 30th Corps and the Welsh Guards had had a grand rest before they were needed. They had been received on arrival at Jodoigne and Hougaerde as honoured guests; they left as warm personal friends, and the Regiment will not forget the kindness they received in Belgium. When they moved out and were concentrated round Malden on the 13th of February, most of the country to the north of the Reichwald had already been won. Thereafter the Welsh Guards Battalions, or detachments from them, took part in actions at Haversum, Kassel, Hassum, Mull and Bonninghardt, and both of them had amazing good fortune throughout. Field-Marshal Montgomery described the Rhineland operation as "a battle which in intensity and fierceness equalled any which our troops experienced in this war. The Germans quickly built up to about eleven equivalent divisions. . . . in particular their paratroops fought magnificently." Yet the Welsh Guards, although they had some hard fighting, never met anything like the resistance they had known at Hechtel or in Normandy and did not themselves have heavy casualties.

Owing to the situation in regard to reinforcements it had been decided that the 1st Battalion would be relieved, and when the battle ended they had fought their last fight of the war and their long and fruitful partnership with the 2nd Battalion was broken. Both Battalions moved back to the Malden area. "X" Company Scots Guards, who had fought with them so long, said good-bye and joined the 2nd Battalion Scots Guards, who were now to be associated with the 2nd Battalion Welsh Guards as a Battle Group.

The 1st Battalion were inspected by Major-General Alan Adair in Nijmegen stadium, and after he had thanked them for their work in the Guards Armoured Division he added, "As the senior Guardsman out here I say that the 1st Battalion Welsh Guards during the last few months has added lustre to the great history of your Regiment." Then they saluted him as their Divisional Commander for the last time in a march past. They sailed from Ostend on March 23rd, and on that night Field-Marshal Montgomery began operations to secure crossings of the Rhine and a bridgehead on the eastern bank.

On all fronts the Allied forces were ready for the final battles. On the western front Cologne had fallen to American formations and others were already across the Rhine further to the south. The Russian Armies were in Germany and coming up rapidly from the east. And in Italy, where the war was to end first, Field-Marshal Alexander's armies lined up for their final and victorious fight.

The End in Italy.

Along the frozen front which stretched across Italy, Field-Marshal Alexander's army remained all winter, persistently harassing the enemy's forward troops while our air forces bombed his back areas with unremitting thoroughness. To the German Commander his hold on the fertile Po valley became more and more important as his slender communications with Germany were progressively disrupted, for he had to maintain thirty divisions there to check our further progress. These thirty divisions Field-Marshal Alexander was now planning to destroy.

The task was a formidable one. The enemy had his right flank firmly planted in the rugged western mountains; on the east he was entrenched behind the Senio, Santerno, Sillaro and Idice rivers. A maze of dykes, ditches and flooded fields strengthened his positions, and beyond them to the north stretched the Po and the Adige and successive lines of mountains and rivers all the way to Austria. But we had complete mastery of the air; he could do little to defend his roads or his railways, and Field-Marshal Alexander planned to destroy his main forces before they could escape.

The 15th Army Group, under the command of General Mark W. Clark, destined for this task, was an army of many creeds and colours, for it included not only British and American troops but also New Zealand and South African, Polish and Palestinian, Indian, Italian and Brazilian formations. These were grouped in two Armies—the 8th under Lieutenant-General Sir R. L. McCreery and the 5th under Lieutenant-General L. K. Truscott. The 6th Armoured Division was part of the 8th Army and now consisted of the 26th Armoured Brigade, the 1st Guards Brigade and the 61st Infantry Brigade; and during the spring units were given opportunity to rest and prepare for the coming battle. The 3rd Battalion Welsh Guards left the mountains in which they had spent the winter on February the 17th and, after spending five days at Greve outside Florence, they joined the 1st Guards Brigade at Spoletto, away back to the south of Perugia. They were there for nearly three weeks and moved to Port San Georgio on the Adriatic coast on March the 6th. In the sunshine of a perfect Italian spring they bathed and boated and did some training; the 1st Battalion Welch Regiment took the place of the Coldstream Guards in the 1st Guards Brigade and many old friendships were renewed.

On the 2nd of April, after the Battalion had been at San Georgio for nearly a month, troops of the 8th Army made a preliminary thrust to win a bridgehead over the River Senio, at the southern end of Lake Comacchio; a week later—on April the 8th—the main battle opened. The 8th Army on the right was to force the Santerno river and the Argenta Gap (five miles of usable ground between large flooded areas) and strike up to the Po at Ferrara and Bondeno. The 5th Army on the left was to debouch into the Po valley, seize or isolate Bologna and strike north. Between these two armies the main enemy forces south of the Po were to be caught and crushed.

Everything went according to plan. The Senio defence line was broken on April the 9th, and the following day the 6th Armoured Division, who were in Army Reserve during this first phase of the battle, moved up to Forlimpopoli behind the assaulting divisions. On April the 16th they moved again and they were at Bognacavello, just north of Argenta, from the 16th to the 19th. By that time the doorway to Ferrara, the Argenta gap, had been forced ajar, and on the 19th of April the 6th

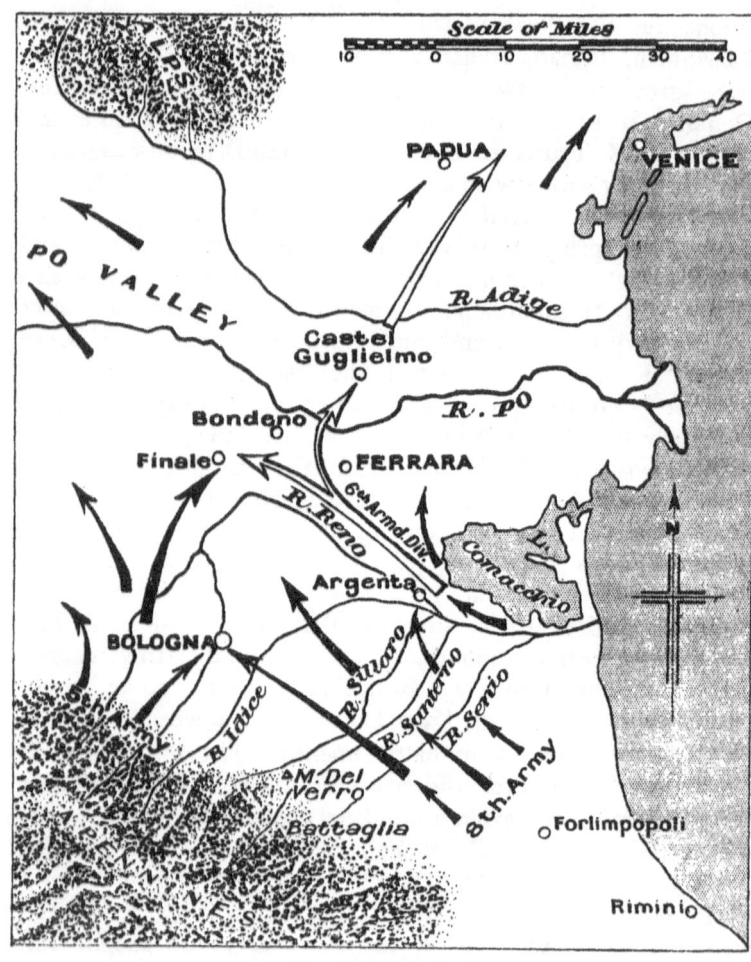

FINAL BATTLE IN ITALY.

Armoured Division burst it wide open and struck out into the country beyond. They met stiff opposition and at first progress was slow, but by the 20th they were well away, with the Armoured Brigade leading and the infantry backing up. Overcoming all opposition, they cut the railway between Ferrara and Bologna, which was one of the enemy's vital lines of communication, and bypassing Ferrara captured Bondeno, reached

Finale, drove seven thousand prisoners of war into the arms of the 5th Army coming up on the left, and reached the Po by April the 23rd. The next night the Grenadier Guards crossed the Po, with the Welsh Guards following them. Only weak opposition was met, for the Allies' attack had been so rapid and so overwhelming that the enemy had lost all grip on the situation. In particular the pace of the 6th Armoured Division's advance and the speed with which the Po crossing was effected left the enemy no time to prepare a coherent defence of the river position—and his troubles did not end there. For after the Grenadiers and the Welsh Guards had secured a substantial bridgehead and swept the surrounding country, Lieutenant-Colonel R. C. R. Price, D.S.O., who had succeeded to the command of the 3rd Battalion, led a spectacular attempt to seize the bridge over the Bianco Canal at Castel Guglielmo before it could be destroyed and only failed by a short head. Even so the canal was crossed next day, and on the 27th, after opposition at Lendinara had been overcome, the Welsh Guards reached the Adige, firing their last shots of the Italian campaign on the river bank.

All along the front the 5th and 8th Armies had triumphed. "The blows that knocked out the Germans in Italy began as slow deliberate punches with heavy fists. Within two weeks the enemy was staggering; the fists became wide-stretched hands, with fingers probing, then grasping vast numbers of Germans and all Italy's north. After a campaign lasting only twenty-three days the remnants of the foe surrendered; he had been destroyed south of the Po."

The story of the Welsh Guards' part in this great battle is told in later pages.

No formal "Cease fire" ever reached them, but this did not matter, for as they drove north beyond the Adige they no longer found anyone to fire at. The Germans, beaten and bemused, were only anxious to lay their arms down and to put their hands up. The Battalion was near Udine on May the 2nd, 1945, when the German Command in Italy surrendered unconditionally, adding 230,000 prisoners of war to the hundreds of thousands already taken.

From Udine on May the 5th Major-General H. Murray,

D.S.O., Commanding, addressed a special order of the day to the 6th Armoured Division, in the course of which he said :

> "Seldom in a campaign of the magnitude of the Italian campaign has one formation contributed in such great measure to final victory."

In this Division, both in Africa and Italy, the 3rd Battalion Welsh Guards had the honour to serve.

The End in Germany.

The 2nd Battalion Welsh Guards crossed the Rhine by pontoon bridges at Rees on the 30th of March and they harboured that night in a wood near Dinxperlo. It was hoped that a quick break-through would be made and that they would have another chance to show their paces. But what happened was something very different. The German troops on this section of the front included their old foes of the Parachute Divisions, and other of the best units withdrawing from the front in Holland which they had held so stubbornly. There was no large force to block our advance, and what troops there were were short of tanks and guns, short of transport, of petrol and indeed of all equipment; but they were skilled in delaying tactics which at times turned an armoured advance into a nightmare. Bridges were blown, roads were blocked, verges were mined. And though they had a few of the self-propelled guns which did such damage in Normandy, their long dual-purpose anti-aircraft guns were skilfully sited at awkward corners and, firing low airbursts over the tanks, they could do much damage. But they relied chiefly on demolitions, obstructions and mines and on the rifle, the light machine gun and the *panzerfaust* or bazooka. These in the hands of well-trained troops can delay armour most effectively in country where abundant woods, plantations and hedges afford ample cover from which to fire them at close quarters. Instead of the rapid advance which the Guards Armoured Division had hoped for, they seldom had a clear run for many miles and they lost more tanks than in many of the earlier large-scale battles. Nevertheless in the first ten days of April they advanced over a hundred miles.

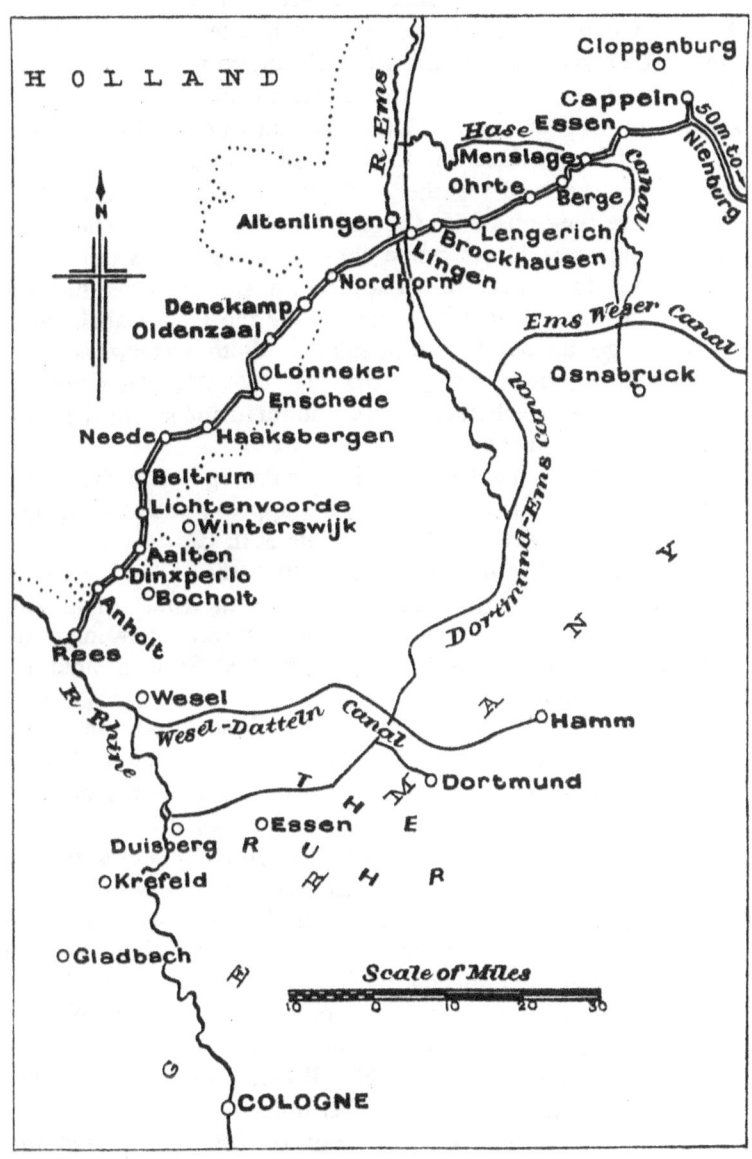

ADVANCE INTO GERMANY.

The Scots-Welsh Group met their first opposition at Enschede; then after other troops of the Division had led into Oldenzaal, they made a spectacular dash from Nordhorn to Lingen, to the dismay and destruction of the Germans unprepared to find armour moving at night. After reaching the Dortmund-Ems Canal they fought their way to Nordholt and later to Lengerich, which they captured together. They reached Berge next day. From there they pushed on to the Menslage Canal, where the main bridge was blown while they were dealing with a road block built to protect it. They found another crossing and raced forward to seize a bridgehead over the Hase Canal—only to see it go up as they approached. Both waterways were bridged in the night and next day they took Menslage and the nearby village of Herbergen—with a hundred and sixty prisoners. This was on April the 10th.

A lot of their tanks had been lost or damaged and they were given a few days for maintenance at Cappeln; and at first light on the 17th of April the Division left 30th Corps and moved east to country beyond the Weser and the Aller. After a ninety-mile drive they reached Walsrode the same night and joined 12th Corps. They were to strike northwards now in a wide turning movement designed to loosen the German hold on Bremen and Hamburg.

Next day (April the 19th) the Scots-Welsh Group advanced and after a series of fights at intermediate villages took Visselhovede. They had hardly had time to consolidate the position when Group Headquarters were counter-attacked by the enemy with bazookas, grenades and machine guns, ably assisted by snipers. Fighting went on for nearly two hours before the attack was finally beaten off. Four hundred and forty prisoners were taken, mostly German Marines; among them were a Brigade Commander and his staff.

After this, they went on again, clearing the road to Neuenkirchen and held up at Hemslingen while they covered the rebuilding of a blown bridge; taking Brockel (and a large number of prisoners); and joining with other units of the Division in the attack on Rotenburg, which they captured (with a hundred and fifty prisoners) on the 22nd of April.

For three days then they remained in the Sittensen area, glad

of a chance to refit before they were launched in a westerly
direction as part of the movement towards Bremen. Their
objective was the stretch of rising ground between Zeven and
Tarmstedt where they would meet the 15th Panzer Grenadier
Division and would come into the formidable gun area which
defended Bremen.

The next two days' fighting was as hard as any they had in
Germany. On the 26th they reached Ostertimke only after the
Grenadier and Coldstream Groups had overcome stiff opposition
at Zeven. On the 27th the Group captured Kirchtimke, losing
seven tanks in the process, and got a squadron into Westertimke,
freeing a series of large prisoner-of-war camps which the

Germans were preparing to evacuate. And there on April the
27th their fighting ended. On May the 1st they entered Stade
unopposed and they were there when on the 5th of May, 1945,
at eight o'clock in the morning the "Cease fire" was ordered on
the 21st Army Group Front. On the previous day Field-
Marshal Montgomery had received the unconditional surrender
of all German land, sea, and air forces in north-west Germany,
Holland and Denmark. On May the 7th the 2nd Battalion
Welsh Guards entered Cuxhaven and there they had the
satisfaction of seeing what was left of the Parachute Division
they had encountered from Hechtel onwards lay down their arms
in unconditional surrender. On May the 7th at twenty minutes
to three in the morning the representatives of Admiral Doenitz,
on whom Hitler's mantle had fallen, agreed to capitulate to the
Allies on all fronts, and the final act of surrender was signed in
Berlin on the night of May the 9th.

* * * * *

The war was ended. The most powerful army ever prepared
for war by a single nation had suffered defeat on every front, had
indeed been totally destroyed as an effective fighting force.
Nemesis had overtaken the German nation. Their economy
was wrecked, their industry in ruins, their country ravaged,
their honour forfeit. But the United Nations had purchased
victory at a fearful cost and the cost will be higher before the
world has peace.

Four hundred and sixty-nine Welsh Guardsmen paid with
their lives; one thousand four hundred and four suffered wounds,
and many more who served at home or abroad during the war
years paid in other ways. Yet in helping to defeat the enemy
they had won great renown. Battle honours to mark the
Regiment's achievements had not been announced when this
record was compiled, but a hundred and seventy personal
Honours had been awarded to Welsh Guardsmen and a hundred
and thirty-three were mentioned in Despatches for distinguished
service.

Through six years of war all Battalions of the Regiment
sustained honourably and loyally the charge laid on them by

The End—1945

His Majesty the King when he presented Colours which he described, in memorable words, as "the outward symbol of a threefold tradition—the tradition of your Regiment; the tradition of the Brigade of Guards; and the tradition of Wales, which goes back to the dawn of our history."

Hwy clod na hoedl
Fame lasts longer than life

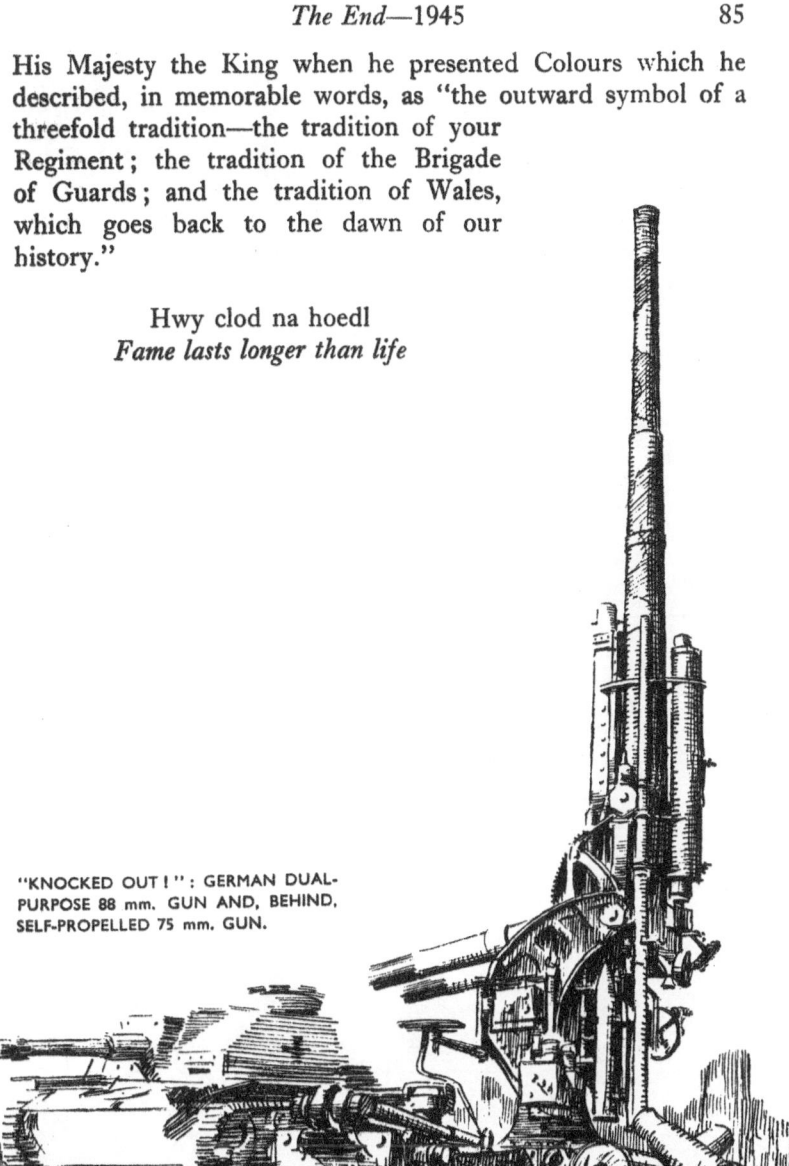

"KNOCKED OUT!": GERMAN DUAL-PURPOSE 88 mm. GUN AND, BEHIND, SELF-PROPELLED 75 mm. GUN.

Part II

THE BATTALIONS IN ACTION

DETAILED ACCOUNTS OF THE PRINCIPAL ACTIONS IN WHICH BATTALIONS OF THE REGIMENT WERE ENGAGED AND OF DEEDS WHICH HELPED TO DECIDE THE ISSUES.

SIGNALLER USING D5. FIELD TELEPHONE (LINE).

ARRAS.

"The enemy's drive westwards through the French positions to the south reached Abbeville on the coast and turned north towards the Channel ports. Not only were our long lines of communication cut and Lord Gort's forces separated from their reserves and supply bases, but there was danger now that they might be attacked from the rear. Accordingly Territorial troops which had been brought to France for labour duties, with some Artillery and Engineers, were used to form a second line running from the sea near Gravelines and facing southwest. To the corridor thus formed Arras was the southern door." (Part I, page 10.)

ARRAS was almost unaffected by war and seemed fuller than usual when the 1st Battalion Welsh Guards marched in on the 17th of May, 1940, against a stream of refugees passing through. Many of the native men-folk were away with the French armies, but in their place were some French troops, for the most part "elderly depot personnel . . . not prepared to help in the defence of the town"; a considerable section of the British General Headquarters—"a vast organisation which spread itself many miles over the area with the Palais St. Vaast at Arras as its main centre"; "Cooke's Squadron of Light Tanks" —a reconnaissance unit from an armoured division not yet at the front; the 61st Chemical Warfare Company of the Royal Engineers; a detachment of Military Police; a company of the Auxiliary Military Pioneer Corps; numerous other ranks back from leave and stranded in the town—to be dubbed "the station Rifles"; and, last, about a company and a half of the 9th Battalion West Yorkshire Regiment (Green Howards)— "oldish men who had come out as aerodrome guards"—under Lieutenant-Colonel R. E. C. Luxmore-Ball, a Welsh Guardsman, who had been with the 1st Battalion at Arras in the last war. The defence of the area was in the hands of Major-General R. L.

Petre, but Lieutenant-Colonel F. A. V. Copland-Griffiths commanding the Welsh Guards, was given command of the garrison of the town itself and Major W. D. C. Greenacre, his Second-in-Command, took temporary command of the 1st Battalion.

The Prince of Wales Company (Captain Sir W. V. Makins) was sent to block the exits of the Doullens road on the west; No. 2 Company (Captain J. E. Gurney) went to the southern perimeter, south of the station, where the Sappers were strengthening the railway as an anti-tank obstacle, with orders to block the roads from Cambrai and Bapaume ; No. 4 Company (Captain M. E. C. Smart) was given the northern approaches to defend and in particular had to block the river bridges at St. Catherine and St. Nicholas ; he had also to send a platoon to Achicourt on the south-western outskirts of the town. Headquarter Company (Captain H. C. L. Dimsdale) held a block on the St. Pol road and for the rest was near Battalion Headquarters in the Palais St. Vaast. Carriers and Mortars were moved as required to meet attacks and the former did patrols in the intervals.

Road blocks were constructed as rapidly as possible ; covering positions in nearby houses were loopholed and sandbagged ; slit trenches were dug and blocks were protected by mines supplied by the Sappers and laid by "rather nervous N.C.Os. supervised by equally nervous officers as the mines were alleged to be extremely sensitive." That night and the next passed quietly and by then road-blocks were effective and defences complete. During the next night (May the 19th) all other troops not required for the defence left the town, including rear General Headquarters, part of which moved to Boulogne and was there when the 2nd Battalion Welsh Guards arrived three days later (see page 97).

On the 19th the enemy started bombing the town in earnest. The station was destroyed, two trains filling with refugees were hit with distressing results, and the Battalion had its first fatal casualty. There were signs that the enemy was drawing near the town and as far as was known there was little to stop him. For General Petre's main force outside Arras was the 23rd Division which had been brought up two days before but had been caught by enemy aircraft when embussed and badly cut up. This Division, "which had joined the B.E.F. for work in rearward areas, consisted of eight Battalions only, with Divisional Engineers, but no Artillery, and Signals and administrative Units in no more than skeleton form. Its armament and transport was on a much reduced scale and training was far from complete."

That day the 1st Battalion were ordered to retire to Aire, fifty miles to the north-west, and the transport under Captain A. T. C. Neave had already got there before news that the order had been cancelled overtook the party. Luckily the Quartermaster (Lieutenant J. C. Buckland) was with him and they returned from Aire with much-needed rations. For in spite of his ingenuity and of raids on the N.A.A.F.I. by the Padre, Rev. C. H. D. Cullingford, described in one diary as "a born thief," feeding the Battalion had become something of a problem. There was more bombing that day and more Battalion casualties, and in the night the French troops departed.

The pace of events quickened on the 20th of May. In the early hours came Commandant Poumier to the Garrison Commander with tears in his eyes. "Mon Colonel, nine Zouaves and I are the last Frenchmen in Arras. The remainder have left and the General in his motor car. I place myself and my Zouaves under your command. We are prepared to die for France." His offer was warmly welcomed and he was given a post of honour on the railway. He is described in one of the diaries as "a good comrade and friend." He wore the British Military Cross.

There followed a number of attempts by the enemy's armoured cars to penetrate the road-blocks. In the first both cars were blown up. In the second they were destroyed by platoon weapons, and when their occupants scattered into nearby houses Sergeant D. H. Griffiths (No. 2 Company) and two Guardsmen hunted them out. Griffiths had one arm in plaster following an accident, but he killed three with grenades and showed great enterprise and courage. Meanwhile, lorryborne infantry approaching St. Nicholas on the north were "seen off" by No. 4 Company, and reconnaissance parties at St. Laurient Blangy on the east and Achicourt in the south-west were dispersed by the mortars under Lieutenant W. G. M.

Worrall. With the help of "Cooke's tanks" a platoon of No. 2 Company under Lieutenant W. H. R. Llewellyn beat off a more determined attack by six tanks south of the railway.

To add to the excitement of this eventful day, bombing increased and the Battalion had serious casualties—six killed and nine wounded of No. 4 Company and thirteen killed of Headquarter Company.

To relieve the growing tension, however, came news that there was to be a counter-attack. British divisions were to attack from the north and the French from the south. Arras was to be a pivotal point in the British plans and to strengthen the position there the 8th Battalion Green Howards and the 6th Battalion Northumberland Fusiliers were added to Lieutenant-Colonel Copland-Griffiths' command. The former were disposed in the Citadel and western exits and the latter on the eastern boundary astride the two railway lines. A battery of 25-pounder guns also arrived and shelled a concentration of tanks which was observed in Achicourt.

Next day the British counter-attack went in. Enemy tanks were put to flight and four hundred prisoners were taken; but there was no corresponding attack by the French from the south and though the enemy were held for the moment the situation was not materially improved. In Arras the only change was that they were shelled by the Germans for the first time!

The Battalion held their ground through another day (the 22nd of May), but their position was now very uncomfortable. Refugee traffic through Arras had died away. The few townspeople who were left lived in the cellars; many of the buildings were shattered; and the streets were deserted and dangerous, for soldiers moving in the town were sniped from houses—whether by members of the Fifth Column or by enemy who had penetrated was not proved. One party of Germans caught trying to get in were made prisoners, but others may have succeeded unnoticed. Two unusual jobs occupied some of Battalion Headquarters personnel who were not required for other duties—the feeding and watering of beasts, left unattended by owners who had departed, and the smashing of wine stocks in the deserted stores, a "depressing and fatiguing task."

The Commander-in-Chief decided to retire from the Arras position, and late on the 23rd Lieutenant-Colonel Copland-Griffiths had orders to withdraw the garrison. A message was circulated to the companies which read : "Wake up, get up, pack up." The Green Howards and the Northumberland Fusiliers were by the Garrison Commander's orders the first to leave; the Welsh Guards began moving out just before daybreak on the 24th, Lieutenant-Colonel Copland-Griffiths resuming command of the Battalion.

Luckily there was a thick ground mist and their move was apparently unnoticed by the enemy. To avoid risk the companies moved independently towards Douai. No. 4 Company got away by side roads, but the transport under the Quartermaster took another route, following the Northumberland Fusiliers. They were about three miles from the town when heavy firing broke out on the road ahead and the column halted. A section of the Carrier Platoon under Lieutenant the Honourable Christopher Furness was with the column and some light tanks, and Furness (who had been wounded earlier that night) told the Quartermaster that he must turn the transport and get away quickly. "I explained that it was impossible to turn quickly, in that narrow road, forty vehicles including 3-tonners. As the mist was rising we should be seen by the enemy and it had been impressed on us that the Germans were not to know that Arras was being evacuated. He replied, 'Don't worry about Jerry. I'll go and shoot him up and keep him busy while you turn and get out.' Then off he went in the direction of the firing."

The Germans were in position on rising ground strongly entrenched behind barbed wire, with a copse and a haystack for cover in rear. To engage them from a distance would not keep them busy enough to distract their attention from the transport. Appreciating the seriousness of the position and in spite of his wounds, Furness decided to attack at close quarters and he advanced with three carriers, supported by the light tanks. "At once the enemy opened up with very heavy fire from small arms and anti-tank guns. The light tanks were put out of action, but Lieutenant Furness continued to advance. He reached the enemy position and circled it several times at close range, inflicting heavy losses. All three carriers were hit and most of their crews killed or wounded. His own carrier was disabled and the driver and Bren gunner killed. He then engaged the enemy in personal hand-to-hand combat until he was killed. His magnificent act of self-sacrifice against hopeless odds, and when already wounded, made the enemy withdraw for the time being and enabled the large column of vehicles to get clear unmolested and covered the evacuation of some of the wounded of his own Carrier Platoon and the light tanks." So reads the citation of the Victoria Cross which was subsequently awarded for this splendid action. The full citation is given on page 314.

And with the record of his courage should go the names of the men who gallantly followed his lead.

No. 1 CARRIER.

Lieutenant the Hon. Christopher Furness	Killed.
Guardsman J. W. Berry (*Driver*)	Killed.
Guardsman J. P. Daley (*Gunner*)	Killed.

No. 2 CARRIER.

Sergeant G. E. Griffin	
Guardsman C. D. Griffiths (*Driver*)	Wounded.
Guardsman G. Roberts (*Gunner*)	Wounded.
Guardsman D. Williams (*Gunner*)	Killed.

No. 3 CARRIER.

Lance-Sergeant A. E. Hall	Taken Prisoner.
Guardsman I. L. Thomas (*Driver*)	Wounded.
Guardsman T. Griffiths (*Gunner*)	Wounded.

The last named—and the last to leave the field—told how this action ended. "We went round the post after Sergeant Griffin. Then we saw his carrier and Mr. Furness's behind one another near the tank. . . . Sergeant Hall shouted to me that the Bren gun wouldn't fire. The bullets had been hitting the plates all this time and one had come through and hit Thomas in the leg, but nothing bad, and another had blown off the Bren gun's tripod legs. . . . We went back down the hill into some dead ground where we were hidden from the post. I jumped out and took the gun off the carrier and put it in working order.... We ran up to the Northumberland Fusiliers ... the Company Commander said he was having trouble from a machine gun to the left of the Jerry post. Thomas stayed behind and I got in front with Sergeant Hall, but we could not find anything, and when we got back the company had gone.... So we went off up the hill again towards the Jerry post.... When we got up to the post we found it had been deserted."

They found a wounded sergeant-major in a nearby ditch, possibly from the Northumberland Fusiliers. "We put the sergeant-major on the tool box and I laid beside him, and two others got into the gunner's seat.... We were crossing a field when they started firing at us out of the wood with an anti-tank gun. I was struck in the behind with a splinter and the next shot went through the back of the carrier. The engine gradually stopped.... I lifted the sergeant-major down on to the grass and put a blanket underneath him. He was moaning and I couldn't do anything for him. So I took my rifle and left him there and went after the others. I could hardly walk myself."

Here, we too leave Arras. The fight of the carriers had not been in vain, for while it was taking place the company of the Fusiliers was extricated and the transport of the 1st Battalion Welsh Guards moved safely to another road.

BREN GUN CARRIER.

BOULOGNE

"Their true role was not as clear to them at the time as it was afterwards, namely to hold German forces round Boulogne while the miscellaneous troops collected there were evacuated and to delay, by that much, the enemy's full concentration against the main British forces farther north." (*Part I, page* 11.)

A NEWLY formed Battalion could hardly have a more shattering introduction to war than the 2nd Battalion Welsh Guards had in May, 1940. They had had a dullish time at the Tower of London from October till March. This had been followed by six weeks of intensive training at Camberley, of the sort that is more directly related to operations in the field and therefore appeals to the imagination of a young Battalion eager to meet the enemy. On the 21st May they were preparing for an "attack" in the pine-clad country near the Staff College. Thirty-six hours later they were fighting for their lives—and the lives of many more—on the outskirts of Boulogne ; and thirty-six hours after landing in France those who could get away were back in England ! The fact that they had done what was asked of them and done it well could hardly soften their disappointment or dispel the sense of futility which deepened their sorrow for comrades who had not returned. Their expedition had a clear purpose and their sacrifice was not fruitless, but they could not then understand the significance of events, they could only judge from appearances.

* * * * *

At half-past eleven on the morning of May the 21st the telephone brought orders that the Battalion would leave Camberley at once for service overseas ; so the exercise in progress was cut short, preparations for the move were put in hand and early that afternoon they left in motor vehicles for Dover. "It was a lovely day and Surrey and Kent looked very peaceful in the spring sunshine. War seemed far away." The other Guards Battalion in the 20th Guards Brigade (the 2nd Irish Guards) was with them and the column reached Dover shortly before

Boulogne 97

midnight, having been delayed by an air-raid *en route*. From there Brigadier W. A. F. L. Fox-Pitt, in command of the Brigade, went ahead on a destroyer while the Battalion followed on the s.s. BIARRITZ and MONA'S QUEEN. "There had been no time to say goodbye to friends or relations—perhaps rather a relief. . . . The sea was luckily dead calm. . . . We soon saw our first glimpse of war—a burning tanker, obviously bombed, a few miles off Boulogne. She was an eerie sight in the half light; the flames spread a deep red glow under a big pall of smoke. Soon we were outside Boulogne; but it seemed to take hours till, after frantic signals from the destroyer and other ships stopped outside, the boom was opened to allow us to enter. A small French fishing-boat was coming out at the same time and I wondered what fish they hoped to catch and land." After further delays the BIARRITZ tied up alongside the quay in the exact spot where Lieutenant-Colonel Sir Alexander Stanier had landed in France, for the first time, in 1918—then a very new Ensign.

The quay was filled by large crowds—"Every kind of soldier and civilian—French, Belgian, Dutch and British. Even some German prisoners of war waiting to be taken off in ships that had brought the Brigade over. In the midst of this very orderly crowd stood three or four men with led horses—the chargers of H.R.H. the Duke of Gloucester and the Commander-in-Chief, Lord Gort. I was sorry for the groom: he was obviously very tired and puzzled as to how he was ever going to get his chargers on board a boat. Later I was told that they were shot on the quayside."

Information was scanty and uncertain. It was believed that some enemy forces were about twenty kilometres away, but all reports were quite vague. French and British soldiers from lines of communication were coming into the town in considerable numbers and the part of General Headquarters which had left Arras on the 19th of May (see page 90) was in the vicinity pending evacuation. The Brigade's orders at that time were to defend Boulogne "to the last man and the last round." The Irish Guards were allotted all ground to the south-west of the harbour and river, the Welsh Guards all to the north-east.

There is high ground all round Boulogne, the city lying on the lower slopes which run down to the water. The main roads enter the town through the sector allotted to the Welsh Guards—a stretch of country which one Battalion of infantry could not possibly occupy effectively. Lieutenant-Colonel Stanier put his companies as far out as he dared at first and found that, even though their front measured six thousand yards, there was still a gap on his left flank; he realised that he would have to shorten

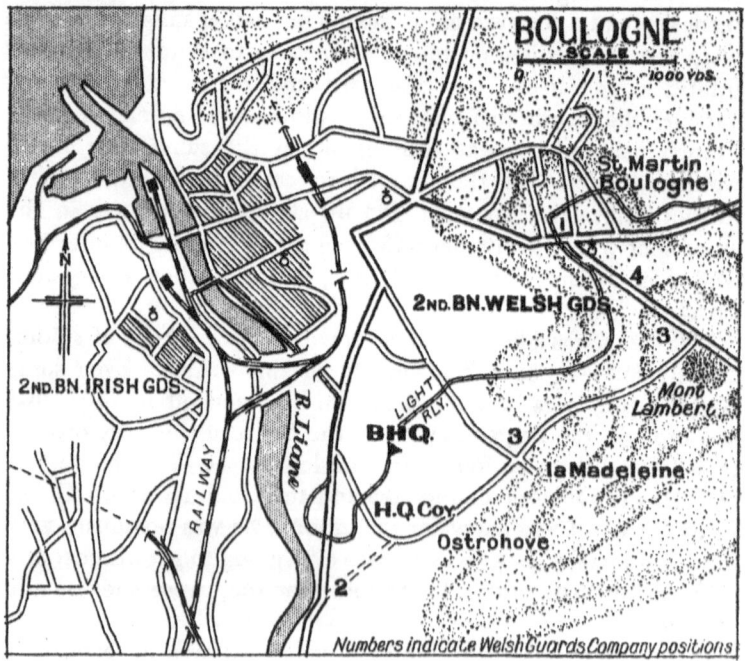

WELSH GUARDS' POSITIONS AT BOULOGNE.

his front if the enemy made a serious effort to take the town. With these considerations in mind he stationed No. 2 Company (Major H. M. C. Jones-Mortimer) between Ostrohove and the river on its right; Headquarters Company (Captain R. B. Hodgkinson) held Ostrohove itself. From there No. 3 Company (Major J. C. Windsor Lewis) continued the front with a platoon at La Madeleine road junction and two more covering road junctions north-west of Mont Lambert; Company Headquarters held a farm on the Boulogne road. No. 4 Company (Captain J. H. V. Higgon) were posted along this road with their left at the church in St. Martin; and this northern flank was continued by No. 1 Company (Captain C. H. R. Heber-Percy) covering the chief roads into the town on that side. As they marched off "the troops began to sing—to the surprise of the fleeing French."

There was comparatively little enemy activity during the first day, though German troops were observed on the Mont Lambert ridge and in the evening tanks approached both No. 3 and No. 4 Companies' positions, but were driven off. Meanwhile the town was shelled for some hours. Shortly afterwards the Commanding Officer was informed that twelve hundred Auxiliary Military Pioneers who had arrived from work on lines of communication were at his disposal. "Old, unorganised, tired but keen, with no food and not much ammunition" they could be of little effective use in the defence of the town and only a small number ever got into position. The remainder were a liability rather than an asset. The same was true of the groups of French and Belgians who were flocking back to the town. Some Royal Engineers, on the other hand, did most valuable work cratering roads and helping the companies to strengthen their positions. It will be easiest to take the companies in turn and tell what happened on each sector of the Battalion's long front.

No. 2 Company, on the right, looked downhill to where the main road crossed a stream and then rose more steeply to the hill before them. Soon after the company were in position an enemy plane machine-gunned them and thereafter they were continuously under artillery and mortar fire, but there was no attack that day and they had a quiet night. Some Royal Engineers helped them to strengthen their position by cratering the road at the stream-crossing. A gas main was set on fire in the process and its flickering light rose and fell on the road-block they had built nearby. Early in the morning shelling started in earnest, with mortar and machine-gun fire, and tanks appeared coming over the hill-top. For about two hours these were held off, but eventually they got the range of the company position and the latter were withdrawn about three hundred yards to the line of the single-track railway. From there they succeeded in dispersing German infantry and drove them back over the crest of the hill opposite. But the German tanks found the new positions and they side-stepped again, to avoid heavy losses.

Meanwhile Headquarter Company at Ostrohove had been attacked but also had succeeded in holding the enemy off, thanks largely to the skilful way in which Lieutenant R. C. Sharples led his platoon. But No. 3 Company with its nose sticking out towards Mont Lambert took a harder punch. Their right platoon under Second-Lieutenant H. H. Hughes was at the cross-roads in the hamlet of La Madeleine and faced the ridge which culminates in Mont Lambert. Early in the morning four tanks came over the ridge. One came down almost to the cross-roads and got behind La Madeleine Cafe and Hughes moved part of his platoon so that he could engage it. But a second tank was covering the position and Hughes was killed while moving. The other tanks worked round their flank, and those of the platoon who were not casualties were ordered to withdraw on Headquarter Company.

At the Mont Lambert cross-roads a platoon under Lieutenant R. C. H. Pilcher was dug-in in positions to cover approach from the enemy direction: road-blocks were formed and an anti-tank rifle was sited in a good position. There was some refugee movement on the road and late at night an innocent-looking furniture van drove up to the block, which had been closed. A German got out from behind with a motor cycle and, taking a hasty look at the road-block, rode back into the night, pursued by rifle fire which missed him in the darkness. Next morning a light tank roared downhill, set the road-block alight and began firing at the company positions from close quarters. Rifle and Bren-gun fire did little damage to it, but the platoon anti-tank rifle and an anti-tank gun under Lieutenant P. Black eventually knocked it out (later in the action Black was himself knocked out after having previously been wounded twice). Then other, heavier tanks appeared, while machine-gun and mortar fire increased as the enemy worked round No. 3 Company's positions. By-passing Pilcher's platoon, they overran the post on the road towards St. Martin which another platoon under Lieutenant A. M. D. Perrins held. Captain W. H.

Carter was badly wounded on the road and Major Lewis's Company Headquarters were almost surrounded. He was cut off from his forward platoons when later in the day the Battalion were ordered to retire to the town and he got away with the platoon near his Headquarters with great difficulty.

At the time when Pilcher's most forward platoon had the signal to withdraw the enemy were between him and Boulogne. They were forced to make a wide detour to the north and Boulogne had been evacuated when, eventually, they reached the coast on May the 25th. There, while he was trying to get food for his men, he was taken prisoner and the men were taken some hours later.

No. 4 Company and No. 1 Company had suffered from mounting enemy fire but had not been heavily attacked before they were withdrawn to the town. A sniper in the church tower caused No. 1 Company much trouble till Captain Heber-Percy had a ramp built and, tipping an anti-tank gun up on it, blew away the sniper and the top of the tower together.

Later in the day the Battalion were ordered to withdraw to the town and block the approaches to the harbour. They got back with some difficulty, for not only was enemy pressure continuous but there was now continual sniping from houses on both sides of the river. Where practicable, houses were searched and some Fifth Columnists were taken, with important papers on them which were afterwards handed in to the War Office. Communication with companies had to be by dispatch riders who, because of the sniping in the streets and the enemy shelling, had a difficult time. It was made more difficult by the absence of maps—for only one useful scale map was available for the whole Battalion throughout these operations! The fact that orders were got round at all was largely due to the only dispatch rider who was unwounded, Guardsman T. F. Potter, who rode fearlessly through fire-swept streets and round the front line and whose tenacity and courage won high praise. There were many others who did heroically that day. The Regimental Quartermaster-Sergeant, F. T. Jones, went forward and under fire removed precious rations from a lorry that was put out of action; then, seeing that the position was in danger, he organised a post with the men under him and helped to stem the penetration of the enemy. Similarly Lance-Corporal B. Booker combined the feeding of his company (plus one hundred and fifty Pioneers) with the manning of a fire position with the company cooks, whenever the enemy attacked.

About six o'clock that night the Battalion were ordered to withdraw to the quay—and all did so except about twenty men of No. 3 Company who remained with Major Lewis, at that time heavily engaged on the defence of a road-block and unable to break off the fight. One of the Company Commanders who had served under Brigadier Fox-Pitt when he commanded the 1st Battalion (and later, the Regiment) wrote in his diary: "As I reached the buildings I saw the Brigadier standing outside, looking as unperturbed as usual, in the deafening noise and chaos round about. He asked me why the hell I was so late; but as he had asked me the same question in the very same voice regularly, during the past ten years, the fact that I had only just received the orders to retire did not make his question seem at all out of place." By now enemy tanks and infantry were in the town and firing was heavy and continuous. Sergeant J. King, the Medical Sergeant, greatly distinguished himself carrying in wounded under heavy fire till he himself collapsed utterly exhausted. Lance-Corporal Booker again showed good leadership here, for he collected many wounded in a lorry and drove them to the quay where, finding he was on the wrong side of the basin, he got a motor boat working, ferried the men across—and went back to his cooking duties.

While these events were happening ships and personnel of the Royal Navy had taken a hand in the proceedings. One after another destroyers had entered and left the harbour, the perils of their task increasing as the enemy's guns got into action from the high ground which surrounded the port and as air bombardment increased. The naval guns were indeed the only effective answer to the enemy's long-range attack, for the army had no artillery to support it. The Navy's heroism on that day made a deep impression on all the troops at Boulogne. They talk still of the destroyer which was hit and set on fire as she entered the harbour. With her hull damaged and a raging furnace, there was grave risk that she would sink in a position which would block the entrance and put an end to all further use of the basin;

yet efforts to deal with the fire were not allowed to slacken for a moment the pace with which her own guns were being served; and eventually she got away, her stern aflame and all her guns still blazing at the enemy. The German *communiqué* claimed that she was sunk, but, in fact by magnificent courage and fine seamanship, she was brought safely home to fight another day.

While parties of Marines blew up bridges and dock installations the remaining troops were collected by the quay, where there was still so great a throng of unorganised personnel waiting to be evacuated that Lieutenant-Colonel Stanier had much difficulty in communicating with his own men. A considerable proportion of the Battalion were taken off, but not all. No. 2 and No. 4 Companies, waiting in a large Customs shed on the quay for orders to re-embark, were wrongly told that the last ship had left. So they decided to try to make their way to the south, hoping to find there another port open. It was after midnight when they left and before they were clear of the streets they came under machine-gun fire and had to take cover for a time in houses; then they started again, but had not gone far when again they were machine-gunned. Second-Lieutenant R. C. Twining and Second-Lieutenant E. G. F. Bedingfeld with a party of men, finding themselves separated from the main body, returned to the harbour and were taken off by the last destroyer to use the port; but the others, not knowing of this ship, decided to occupy buildings and wait till daylight made reconnaissance possible. They had no map. They were very exhausted and needed food and sleep before setting out on a long and difficult march. But when day came the Germans had fully occupied the town and a sortie to get food for the men had meagre results. Any Germans who came near were shot, but being in a side street there was no attack. Several efforts were made to get away in small parties; some were captured almost at once; some got clear of the town and were taken only after several days' journeying across country. The main party could neither get out nor do anything effective where they were. So they just held on—shooting any German who approached. Extracts from a diary may complete their story.

"*May the 25th.*—The men were in great form and we organised quite a decent breakfast and made every man wash and shave and clean his weapons. We replenished ammunition from an abandoned R.A.F. lorry; I found some more for my revolver. The party on the other side of the road shot another German bicyclist and that attracted the heavy tanks. They lumbered incredibly slowly up the road and then with great deliberation started to pump shells into the opposite house. The position was obviously hopeless."

Meanwhile there was another party of Welsh Guardsmen in Boulogne who had also missed the boat. The story of their fight, told in the words of Major Lewis who led it, may form the epilogue to what happened at Boulogne.

"After 'stand to' on the morning of the 24th of May I learned that the Battalion had gone and decided to move as quickly as possible to the quayside with the men I had left. On arrival at the quayside with the remnant of my company, I found the utmost confusion. There were a few men from No. 2 and No. 4 Companies, some Irish Guards, about one hundred and fifty refugees, a hundred and twenty odd French soldiers with two officers, two hundred of the Auxiliary Military Pioneer Corps, one hundred and twenty men of the Royal Engineers and others. I collected this force in the sheds by the station and with Major E. G. M. Burt, who has since died, I went off to find the minesweeper which had just come into the harbour and ask if it would evacuate us to England. The minesweeper, which was French, refused, but I had previously learned that boats were supposed to be returning for us. They never came, and I heard later that they had been sunk in the effort to reach beleaguered Boulogne.

"On recrossing the bridge we were heavily fired upon by machine guns from neighbouring houses, but using cars, etc., for cover we managed to reach the sheds without being hit. These were now very congested with troops and refugees, so I sent off an officer of the Royal Engineers, Lieutenant Kenneth Roscoe, to make a reconnaissance of the station itself and see how best we could defend it and obtain cover there for all. This officer returned shortly after with a comprehensive report and I decided immediately to move the refugees into the shelters underneath the station itself.

"The Germans then began to fire on us in the sheds and

several men were wounded. I immediately began to retire my force into the station. This move was quite easily effected as there was a covered way of approach afforded by a line of railway trucks. The fire from the German tanks was quite severe when we finally abandoned the sheds, which shortly afterwards went up in flames. The Germans then began to fire incendiary bombs into the station and several of these lit up trucks which contained ammunition and inflammable material. I hastily prepared the station for defence by the erection of a sandbagged breastwork in front of the station and on the left flank overlooking the Custom House. The sandbags were already in the station. Many of my command, such as the Pioneer Corps, were unarmed, and while they prepared the position and carried sandbags the Welsh Guards personnel and some French took up positions under cover and in trains, two of which were in the station. All ranks worked very hard and carried out their tasks under fire from enemy tanks and machine guns.

"By midday on the 24th of May we had established as good a defensive position as possible under the circumstances. The position was held by the Welsh Guards and French infantry. These were already thoroughly exhausted and their tenacity and bravery in keeping the enemy at bay for nearly two days without sufficient food and water is worthy of the highest praise.

"Firing from the German tanks, of whom three were in front of our position, continued all day, sometimes intense, at other times mild, and dying down altogether after ten o'clock at night. In the evening of May the 24th, about six o'clock, the Germans made an effort to land from a boat on my right flank. Their party of infantry was a small one and we drove them back to the other side of the harbour with Bren, anti-tank rifle and rifle fire, inflicting losses upon them.

"The troops holding our positions had some rest that night in relays, but early in the morning after 'Stand-to' when the French infantry were holding our front line, the Germans again attacked heavily and we lost several men. At about nine o'clock we could see with binoculars big troop movements taking place on the high ground above Boulogne, which soon turned out to be an enemy force arriving to consolidate the capture of the town. Their artillery, which had begun to fire upon us the previous evening, was increased, a big shed to the right of my position was blown up and my wounded men were knocked about. A reconnaissance was made to our right flank to see if there was any possible way of escape, but the route was covered by two enemy tanks. At noon the enemy, now strongly reinforced, opened up intense fire upon my position and I was compelled to withdraw from the front line of breastworks into the station itself, protected only by glass overhead and by a train on the left flank.

"There was little food and ammunition left and no more water, and after another hour of the greatest discomfort I decided that the position was now quite hopeless and that a massacre would ensue if we did not capitulate. Having an eye to the number of refugees under my care and the big percentage of unarmed men, I decided to surrender.

"My little force had fought most splendidly in the face of heavy odds. Exhausted and without proper nourishment, they never lost heart."

One thing remains to be said. This account only describes the fighting east of the river, the ground for which the Welsh Guards were responsible. On the west the 2nd Battalion Irish Guards had to deal with simultaneous attacks which they too held off, though with difficulty and heavy losses, until they were evacuated.

The *communiqué* of the German High Command dated the 26th of May included the statement that "Boulogne was taken after a grim fight with land and naval forces." As has been shown, all the main forces were evacuated on the 24th.

STRETCHER-BEARERS.

VYFWEG AND WEST CAPPEL

"They were transferred north to hold another threatened flank position south of Bergues." (Part I, page 14.)

THE small but costly rearguard action fought at Vyfweg and West Cappel on the 29th of May, 1940, is a sobering reminder of the price which must be paid by a thin screen of infantry left to protect retiring forces from a thrusting enemy's advance. British infantry have paid that price over and over again and must continue to pay it so long as almost every campaign is begun with inadequate forces. The modern use of swift-moving armour makes the rearguard role of infantry more exacting.

The 1st Battalion had held their ground at Cassel without difficulty through the night of May the 27th and the following morning. Then a report came that the enemy were at Soex (on the flank of the corridor through which the British Expeditionary Force was withdrawing to the coast) and the Battalion were ordered to move to positions east of Soex. They were supported by the light tanks and carriers of the 1st Fife and Forfarshire Yeomanry. They got back through Rexpoede with some difficulty, for the roads were choked by transport (largely French) seeking the coast, while streams of miscellaneous soldiery on foot, all formation broken by the thronging vehicles, eddied in and out and round the columns. Because of the consequent delays, dark was falling when the Battalion reached their destination. The Prince of Wales Company under Captain Sir W. V. Makins were to hold Quaedypre as an advance guard until Vyfweg and West Cappel had been occupied. A German party was there before them when the village was entered, but withdrew when Lieutenant J. R. Martin Smith and a patrol tried to catch them.

The Battalion held a triangle of which the base from Vyfweg to West Cappel faced south-west towards the enemy in Soex and the apex was near the Ratte Ko to the north. After withdrawing

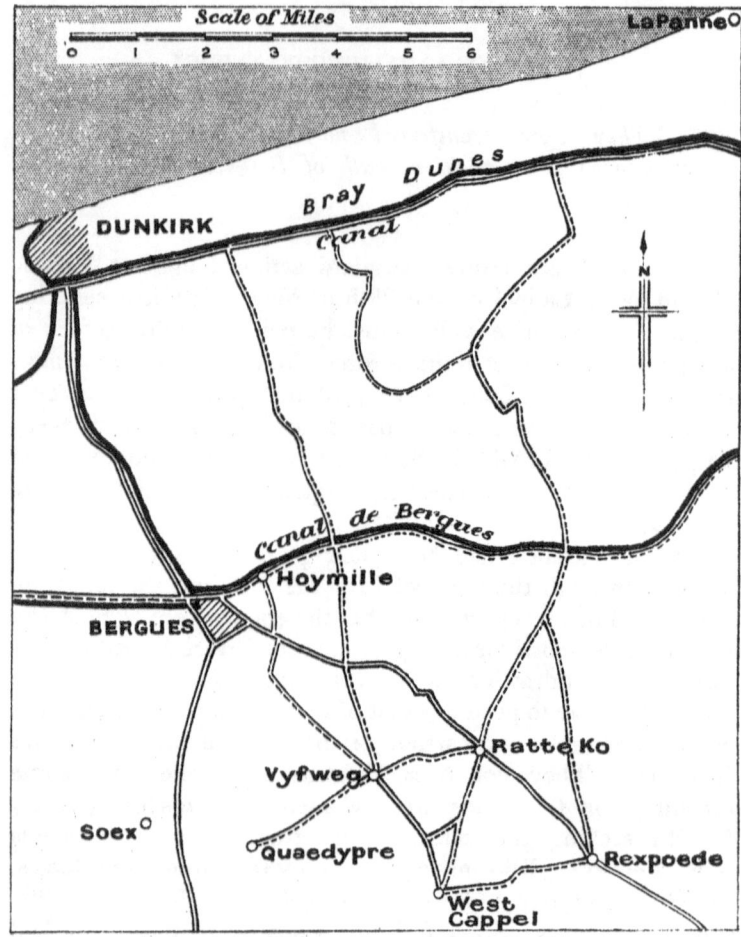

THE WELSH GUARDS' LAST FIGHT IN 1940.

the advance post in Quaedypre, the base of the triangle was extended on the right to the cross-roads near Hoymille, east of Bergues, by a platoon post under Lieutenant J. M. Miller. The 48th Division were on the Battalion's left in the neighbourhood of Rexpoede; but there was a two mile gap between them and West Cappel, the village held by No. 2 Company under Captain J. E. Gurney, and he was a mile away from No. 3 Company's nearest post in the centre of the triangle.

Vyfweg and West Cappel

The night was comparatively quiet, but West Cappel was bombed and there was the sound of rifle and gunfire not far away. It was a dark night following the one wet day in that miraculously fine month, with only the glow of many distant fires to break the surrounding gloom. Next morning (the 29th of May) enemy patrols were seen and in the early afternoon an attack on No. 2 Company, by tanks and infantry, opened from the south-west against the position held by No. 5 Platoon on that side of the village. Lieutenant W. H. R. Llewellyn, in command, and several of the platoon were wounded and it was soon clear that they could not for long hold the forces which were against them; so Captain Gurney withdrew what remained of the platoon to the grounds of the moated chateau which he had made his Company Headquarters. Meanwhile, No. 6 Platoon under Platoon Sergeant-Major H. G. Maisey, posted on the northern outskirts of the village, was attacked and completely cut off from the party in the chateau. For a time the enemy were held off, but in the late afternoon the Company were heavily mortared and tanks entered the village and overran No. 6 Platoon's position. There was close-quarter fighting but the tanks drove over their slit trenches, burying those who were not crushed, and the survivors were taken prisoner. The German officer told them that those in the chateau were very brave but very stupid not to surrender.

Though Captain Gurney did not know it, the position of the Company had been radically changed by the fact that the 48th Division had by now been withdrawn and Rexpoede occupied by the enemy. With Soex and Quaedypre on the west and Rexpoede on the east in German hands, and with the enemy in West Cappel itself, the position of No. 2 Company—now reduced to two depleted platoons—was desperate. An attack from the south-east had begun and after Lieutenant N. M. Daniel and several men of No. 4 Platoon had been wounded, they too were withdrawn to the chateau grounds. One tank got into the grounds and shelled the chateau, which fortunately was well built of stone and stood up to the shelling. As the enemy seemed to be working round to his left Captain Gurney set out to visit No. 4 Platoon's position on that side of the grounds. "I crawled away towards the moat and as I was in the ditch two tanks came into the garden and shot at me. I dived under the moat bridge (see photo on page 317) and there I was, with a tank pounding at the bridge above me; luckily he didn't see the moat, went into it himself and stuck; but his gun was trained on the chateau door. Eventually my servant crawled to me and I decided that we must make the chateau. As we got out of the moat, Daniel and his servant and some of No. 4 Platoon came in. They had a man on a stretcher and I said we must make a dash for it and picked up the front end of the stretcher; Daniel's servant had the other end. As we made for the door of the chateau the tank in the moat fired and caught Daniel's servant and killed him. Daniel tried to grenade the tank but without success." For a time further attacks were held off till more tanks broke into the grounds, when Captain Gurney gathered his small remaining force into the buildings of the house. From there the fight was continued, casualties being carried to the basement to be cared for by Madam Delaplanque (her father owned the chateau), who had retired below with her children when the fighting began. The wounded were grateful for her kindness; there were only thirty-five unwounded in the house at this point. Guardsman I. Davage, a stretcher-bearer, worked fearlessly to bring in the wounded and in the absence of a Medical Officer himself administered first-aid. Many men owe their recovery to his initial care.

Earlier in the day tanks from the direction of West Cappel and Rexpoede attacked No. 3 Company positions and enemy shelling and machine-gun fire developed against Prince of Wales Company and Headquarter Company in Vyfweg; and although, with the help of the 1st Fife and Forfarshire Yeomanry, all attacks were held off, yet casualties mounted.

At one time enemy tanks broke in from the east and reached the road between Vyfweg and Ratte Ko. Brigadier C. W. Norman's Headquarters at the roadside were partly overrun and the Commanding Officer of the Fife and Forfarshire Yeomanry was killed. A battery of Royal Horse Artillery eventually drove off the tanks, but the road between Vyfweg and Ratte Ko remained under enemy fire from infantry and machine gunners who were closing up. This Battery of the Royal Horse Artillery did its gallant best to cover the Battalion's positions to

Vyfweg and West Cappel

the end and, when it was finally ordered to retire to the beach, stayed to fire off its remaining rounds before destroying the guns.

At about six o'clock the Battalion were ordered to move to the coast, where evacuation to England had already begun. No. 3 Company, under increasing fire but not at that time directly attacked, moved off without much difficulty. Prince of Wales Company got away in lorries, the Fife and Forfarshire Yeomanry tanks covering their flank as the German infantry were closing round the position. All through this action the Fife and Forfarshire Yeomanry showed magnificent enterprise and courage. No mission was too hard or too risky for them to undertake. One of the Welsh Guards Company officers expressed the general view when he said, "I reckon they just about saved us." Headquarter Company followed in what transport remained, but there was not enough to take all Battalion Headquarters. Lieutenant H. S. Forbes, the Intelligence Officer, set off across country with a small party, but had hardly left the Vyfweg when they were surrounded and taken prisoner. And before a second party could leave, German infantry rushed the building they were in. Regimental Sergeant-Major E. L. G. Richards was wounded and Captain A. C. W. Noel, the Adjutant, Drill-Sergeant F. Mills and the few men left with them were taken prisoner.

No. 2 Company were by then surrounded and effectively pinned down. Captain Gurney saw that he could not hope to extricate his men until darkness gave them some small chance to get away. So they fought on, with tanks in the grounds and enemy infantry working in closer and closer. At last it was dark enough and they slipped out, one by one, through a hole in the wall and collected in a nearby ditch. Their move was undetected till some of the enemy's infantry approached and they opened fire; then the reply from many directions showed that the grounds were already occupied in some force. In twos and threes, therefore, they crossed the Rexpoede road and reached more open country : but some were hit or lost their way in the darkness and confusion and it was a smaller party still that finally got clear. Even so their troubles were not over, for when they were well off the road Captain Gurney halted them and went to find the Platoon (No. 6) from which he had been cut off

all day; but on approaching the position they had held he heard
only German voices and was met by enemy fire. The same
thing happened again when his small party reached the position
which No. 3 Company Headquarters had occupied before that
company was withdrawn. Here there were further casualties, and
they were reduced to nineteen unwounded and four wounded.
He went back again but could find no more, so decided to go on
to where Battalion Headquarters had been. There he met a
rousing fire and no friends. So they pushed on again, and again
ran into a party of the enemy; but they finally approached a
bridge over the canal and found two Frenchmen who, "on
questioning with a pistol," said the British held the bridge and it
was not yet blown. They got across and as it was nearly three
o'clock in the morning they slept on the floor of an empty
house. At six o'clock they started off across flooded fields.
Some gunners gave them tea and by mid-day they were in the
sand dunes, where they met Lieutenant-Colonel Copland-
Griffiths and reported. They slept in the dunes till evening. Then
they got on an old lifeboat which took them to a trawler, which
took them to a paddle-steamer, which took them to Sheerness.

* * * * *

After No. 2 Company had gone, the enemy made the chateau
of Monsieur Jean Chocqueel their headquarters. The following
extract is translated from an illustrated German paper found in
the chateau some time later.

"In West Cappel stands a chateau, an English Headquarters,
which the English have turned into a small fortress. Slowly
dusk deepens and it looks as if the defences have been
evacuated: but hardly have our first infantry entered the
hamlet than they are met with a murderous fire from all the
houses. Our engineers are called on.

"The barrels of our guns swing on to the fronts of the fortified
houses. Mortars crash their shells into the chateau and tear
pieces from it. The English answer in kind and it is plain their
men are exceptionally well trained, hand-picked men of the
Expeditionary Force. They are skilfully protected by sandbags, in slits as deep as a man's height, dug in the garden, covered
in, almost invisible, with but a small loophole. And they defend

their position to the last. The place is like a witch's bubbling cauldron until at last the engineers reach the middle of the village. The battle only ends late at night; a fight which, in the midst of a furious retreat, stands out as a last desperate action."

That is the German explanation of what held up their advance all day. But "the fortified houses" were ordinary cottages, and the chateau "which the English have turned into a small fortress" was only a naturally strong house, held by a sadly depleted company of Welsh Guardsmen.

GERMAN "MARK IV" TANK KNOCKED OUT.

FONDOUK

"The 6th Armoured Division in which was the 1st Guards Brigade, attacked the Fondouk gap with the object of cutting into the flank of the enemy retreating through Kairouan." (Part I, Page 30.)

AT Fondouk El Okbi the main road from Pichon to Kairouan and the coastal plain up which the Germans were retreating before the 8th Army, runs between two arms of rocky hills. With the southern arm we are not concerned ; the name of the one on the north is Djebel ain el Rhorab. It is a narrow ridge of rock, rising to about 700 feet, and it is divided into two main features. These are not separately named on the map, but for operational purposes the right feature, overlooking the pass, was called "the Djebel" and the left "the Razor-back" ; a mound on the saddle which connects the two was appropriately known as "the Pimple." Through the sandy ground which surrounds El Rhorab the river Marguellil winds its way from the mountains in the west, through the Fondouk gap and out into the Kairouan plain. As with most of the rivers in these parts, the torrent that comes down in winter has cut wide irregular channels through the sand, but much of this winter water-course is dry in summer and a narrower and shallow stream trickles through the sandy banks. About two miles west of El Rhorab it is deflected northwards by some slightly higher ground, and half-way between El Rhorab and this bend the wadi of a stream, the Rhouil, usually dried out in summer, runs into the Marguellil from the north.

On the night of April the 8th, 1943, Battalion Headquarters and all the companies except No. 1 Company were dug in near the higher ground west of the river bend : No. 1 Company was across the river on a knoll, Point 252 on the map, acting as advance-guard to the Battalion. The transport was stuck in the sand some miles back and unable to reach the Battalion. Acting on orders, Captain R. C. Twining, who was commanding No. 1 Company, sent out a small patrol to discover if El Rhorab was occupied by the enemy and when they failed to return he went himself to try to find them. It was a gallant though a fruitless journey. There was the low ground to go through, a number of sandy wadis to cross and an Arab village to skirt before he reached the hillside; his concern for his men must have been great to impel him forward in the darkness and over country he had never seen, up the hill to the point where his body was found next day. "Greater love hath no man than this, that a man lay down his life for his friends."

Next morning the Battalion were awake early and stood-to at five o'clock. At half-past five the Commanding Officer summoned his "O" Group—that is to say, the group of Company Commanders, specialist officers and any other subordinate commanders to whom he wished to give personal orders. Orders were clear. At half-past six the Battalion were to advance and capture the whole El Rhorab feature so that the armour might get through the pass which it overlooks. The companies began to move forward half an hour later, No. 2 Company on the right with No. 4 Company behind it in support; No. 3 Company on the left with No. 1 Company in support. No. 2 Company was to capture the Djebel and the Pimple; No. 3 Company the Razor-back. They started in open order and the leading companies reached their first objective—the Rhouil wadi which crossed their front half-way to the hills—without opposition and the support companies took up positions in front of Point 252. Between the wadi and the hills the ground rises gradually, and when the leading companies advanced again they came under heavy machine-gun and mortar fire. As they pushed on the fire increased and they had many casualties before they were finally stopped in the foothills. Machine-guns and mortars hidden in the hills did unanswerable damage and snipers in the Arab village (see map) had many victims. With every attempt to get forward casualties multiplied. By eight o'clock one section of No. 2 Company under Lieutenant D. A. N. Allen was well up near the top of the final objective, but the rest, sorely depleted, were effectively pinned down in the foothills.

Seeing what had happened from the point he had selected for his Advanced Headquarters (see map), Lieutenant-Colonel D. E. P. Hodgson ordered No. 1 Company (now commanded by

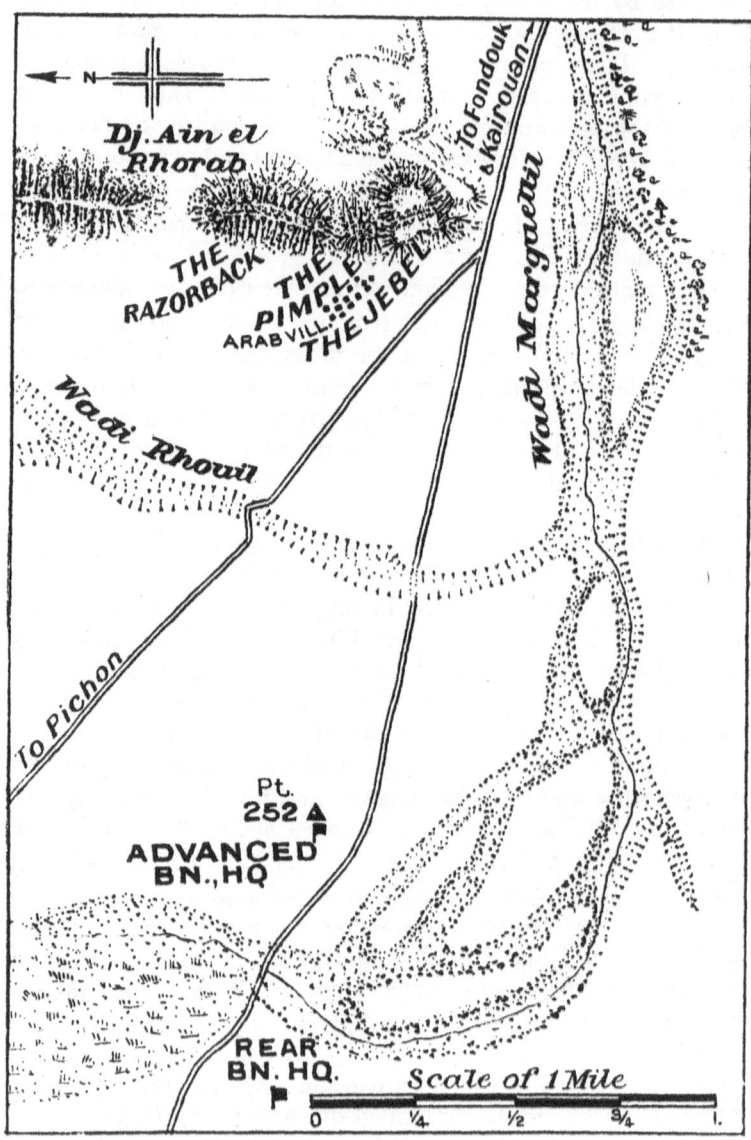

ATTACK AT THE FONDOUK GAP

Lieutenant A. G. Stewart) to support No. 3 by moving round their left flank and attacking the Razor-back from the north. Captain C. A. B. McVittie, commanding the Carrier Platoon moved forward at the same time to protect the left of No. 1 Company. This flanking movement was carried out, but No. 1 Company too encountered heavy fire and were finally stopped about six hundred yards short of the hill, where they found some cover in small wadis and some cactus bushes. About half-past nine owing to a misunderstanding which might have been serious but was in fact fortunate, No. 4 Company went forward in an effort to carry on the attack on the right of No. 2 Company. They too were caught at sorry disadvantage by the enemy shooting down on them and they too were finally pinned down in the foothills. All four companies were now committed and they had had a gruelling experience already. Some further help must be given them to enable them to make a successful attack on the hills. Lieutenant-Colonel Hodgson realised this and leaving Major Sir William Makins his Second-in-Command, in Advanced Headquarters, he went back to Rear Headquarters to arrange for artillery support. There he met Brigadier F. A. V. Copland-Griffiths, who decided to ask not only for additional artillery but also for tanks.

At Advanced Headquarters wireless communication with the companies had practically broken down and the Second-in-Command agreed when the Adjutant, Captain G. D. Rhys-Williams whose father served in the Regiment in the Great War, volunteered to go forward in a carrier and try to find out what was happening. He reached No. 3 Company through heavy fire and learned that the Company had had severe casualties and that Captain C. A. laT. Leatham and Lieutenants B. B. Pugh and R. L. Harrison were all wounded, the Company Commander very seriously. He then tried to reach No. 2 Company, but was turned back by heavy fire. Had he done so he would have found that Captain C. A. St. J. P. Harmsworth had been killed as he was giving a drink of water to Corporal F. S. Cox, who was badly wounded and later died of wounds ; that Lieutenant B. P. R. Goff was wounded and that Lieutenant D. A. N. Allen was somewhere up on the hill. In fact, Allen and his section had put a machine-gun post out of action and had almost reached the hill-top when he too and several of his section were wounded and unable to move. No. 2 and No. 3 Companies were thus without any officers able to lead a further advance. In No. 4 Company Lieutenant F. M. Eastwood had been severely wounded.

When Rhys-Williams got back to Advanced Headquarters the Second-in-Command was completing arrangements for the forthcoming attack with the gunner officer. He had also sent the 3-inch mortars up to support the advance from the forward company areas. Zero hour for the attack was to be one o'clock and it was already just on noon. Time was short and Rhys-Williams suggested that he should go forward again to explain to the companies personally the plan for the new attack, to give them their orders and ensure that they were ready to go forward when the artillery concentration lifted. He went in the Commanding Officer's carrier, fortunately fitted with a wireless set which was to prove invaluable. Major Makins remained at Advanced Headquarters with Captain Parry, the Gunner who was observing not only for his own guns—the 152 Field Regiment —but also for a medium battery under command for the occasion. The tanks (a half squadron of the Lothian and Border Horse from the 26th Armoured Brigade) duly arrived there and Makins decided to go forward with them, leaving the Gunner at Advanced Headquarters. With great skill the tanks eventually manœuvred round the left flank to positions from which they could fire on the reverse slopes of the Razor-back, and their action was very effective in loosening the enemy's hold on the hill. So too was the accurate shooting of the artillery, timed perfectly with the attack. But one thing more was needed and it was supplied by a boy of twenty-one. For it was the young Adjutant, Rhys-Williams, who turned what might still have been a stalemate into a resounding victory.

When Rhys-Williams reached No. 1 Company, fifty minutes or so before the attack was due to start, Stewart's depleted platoons had been in action for about six hours. Fighting in the foothills, they had had little chance to eat : latterly they had been hanging on to their present positions in small groups who had no information as to what was happening elsewhere ; till he arrived they knew nothing of the plans for a new attack on the hills. "From the moment that he came," says Sergeant B.

Garrison, "he seemed to dominate everyone. Besides organising the company, he visited each section in turn, giving words of encouragement and telling them exactly what was to be done." Then he got through to the Gunner at Advanced Headquarters on the wireless set. Stewart wrote afterwards: "He stood in front of the carrier in full view of the enemy and proceeded to direct the artillery on to the objective. He did this with great calmness and so good were his directions that the barrage laid was extremely effective." Then he went off to the other companies. No. 2 and No. 3 Companies, *with all their officers killed or wounded*, had been involved even before No. 1, and had done well to maintain their positions under fire from the hills. He told them the plan of attack, gave them orders to advance when No. 1 Company was seen to move, and made sure that everyone knew what he was to do. He then returned to No. 1 Company and took the rifle and ammunition of Guardsman S. Bezani, his carrier driver, for he had decided that he must lead the attack himself. It was not boyish enthusiasm which induced him to take so unusual a course, but the strong sense of duty and the cool judgment of a good soldier. He had already done much more than is expected of an Adjutant by personally bringing up orders, by directing the artillery preparation, and by seeing that all the companies were ready to play their part. But in doing so he had realised how much was being asked of the men after what they had done and suffered already and how easily, even when the tanks and the gunners had done their best, the final assault on those rocky hills might still fail. Yet he was confident that if they were well led they could succeed, and as the only Captain on the spot he decided that he ought to supply the necessary leadership. It was a brave decision and clearly the right one.

Lance-Sergeant K. G. Summers was in charge of the 3-inch mortars in a wadi near No. 1 Company. "I was told to fire all along the ridge and to keep the enemy occupied till Captain Rhys-Williams reached the foot of the ridge with the company. They had to cross very open ground for about six hundred yards which all the time was being raked by small-arms and mortar fire. I could see Captain Rhys-Williams dashing from one section to another encouraging them on to their objective. He never seemed to tire although he was covering twice as much ground as anyone else by dashing about from one to another. On reaching the bottom of the hill they paused for a few moments and then went on to the final assault. The whole way up the hill I could see Captain Rhys-Williams in the lead." The company, which might well have faltered after all they had already done, responded nobly. Sergeant Garrison was one of the gallant party. "I heard Captain Rhys-Williams all the way on the advance shouting out to the men, 'Keep your distance,' 'Not too fast,' and 'Come on, boys; we can do it.' It went like that till we reached the top of the hill, and then I was ordered to take a section out to the left and that was the last I saw of him." Sergeant W. Davies from Maesteg, who also went up the hill with him, saw the action which crowned his effort. "On the ascent to the top of the objective Captain Rhys-Williams was still in the lead ... having reached the top we were met with a stream of hand grenades which began to cause heavy casualties. Captain Rhys-Williams called to the men near him and immediately went over the top. The stream of grenades ceased and later we found him kneeling in the act of reloading his rifle." He had been shot by a sniper when he crossed over the spine of jagged rock which, sticking up like a wall along the skyline, had sheltered the grenade throwers till he scattered them. So he died, giving his life to ensure a victory which already owed so much to his quick understanding of what was needed, his unhesitating acceptance of responsibility, and his selfless devotion to duty.

For at this point a second platoon under Stewart reached the crest, having attacked the hill by a different route, and the enemy who remained surrendered. The whole of the Razor-back was ours.

The tanks now moved round to support the other companies in the attack on the Djebel but their further help was not needed. Seeing that the Razor-back was lost and that the other companies were moving forward, the enemy on the Djebel came out to surrender. By half-past three in the afternoon the whole of the El Rhorab feature had been occupied. About one hundred prisoners were taken in the action, and among the enemy weapons captured were two anti-tank guns, two 3-inch mortars and thirteen machine-guns. Our own casualties were nine officers and one hundred and five other ranks.

* * * * *

Two footnotes may be added. The first is a description of the final assault on the hills as it was seen by Mr. Alan Moorehead, the writer, from a point of vantage overlooking the battle-ground.

"It was the Welsh Guards I especially remember that day, though there were others in the fighting as well. In a steady, unflinching line the Welshmen went up the last bare slopes on foot, and they faced a withering machine-gun fire all the way up. When a man fell, someone was always there to step in and the line went on until it reached the top."

* * * * *

The second is an afterthought set down by Captain J. F. F. Baron de Rutzen, who commanded No. 4 Company on that day. The verses are quoted from a longer poem which he contributed to the Battalion paper, *The Occasional Leak*.

THE LASTING GLORY

Campaigning—means it only
  That, though the sense be keen
For knowing sudden danger,
  There is little of beauty seen ?
No ! Perception of beauty is quickened,
  And almost every day
There was something I longed to show you
  So many miles away.

I thought of you by Mejerda,
  Banks orange with marigold,
And little flowers on the hillside
  Shut tight against the cold.
Did I tell you a golden eagle
  Soared over Beja Plain,
After the night we climbed the Djebel
  Up in the biting rain ?

Crusaders learned their hunting cries
  From Arabs in years gone by ;
When I heard them call in the mountains,
  At first I wondered why
It struck a chord of memory,
  But then I understood.
Of course ! It's the cry of the second whip
  Hulloing above the wood.

I looked at the faces, strangely grey,
  Of friends who lay so still
Beside the guns they'd silenced
  Up on Rhorab Hill.
But I saw their graves in the sunshine—
  Peace after desperate hours—
By the quicksands of the Marguellil
  Where the oleander flowers.

Poppies and fields of marguerite
  In the hills behind Kournine—
This was the lasting glory
  The eyes of the dead had seen.
Convolvulus in the sunshine,
  Acres of heavenly blue—
They loved them quickly,
  And passed through.

A SELF-PROPELLED 17 Nr. ANTI-TANK GUN (M.10)

HAMMAM LIF

> *On the 7th of May, "armoured cars of the 6th and 7th Armoured Divisions entered Tunis. . . . The 6th turned south-east towards the neck of Cape Bon peninsula. . . . On the 8th the 6th Armoured Division continued south-eastwards and by the afternoon reached the approaches of Hammam Lif." (Part I, page 32).*

THE 6th Armoured Division had harboured for the night about seven miles south of Tunis. At first light on the 8th of May the advance was resumed towards Hammam Lif, the 26th Armoured Brigade in front with the 1st Guards Brigade following. About mid-day as the leading tanks approached the outskirts of the town enemy anti-tank guns opened fire straight down the road and the armour was brought to a standstill. A little way ahead of them the road from Tunis to the Cape Bon Peninsula (on which they were travelling) runs out to the coast to avoid a mountain massif, of which the hill-ridge nearest to the road is called Djebel el Rorouf. There is a gap of less than a thousand yards between this massif and the sea, and in this gap, with the mountains behind and the sea in front, lies the town of Hammam Lif astride their road. On Rorouf the Germans had established a number of machine-gun positions, and from observation posts on its summit they could bring down heavy and accurate shell fire on troops concentrating to attack the town. For in the town itself they had a strong armament of anti-tank and other guns, backed by mortars and *nebelwerfers*. Frontal attack on so concentrated a position was certain to be a desperate venture. The first essential was to capture the dominating ridge and so deny the enemy the advantages it provided.

When the armour was held up soon after mid-day the Welsh Guards were near Madeleine, three miles back. At half-past one they were ordered forward to capture the ridge, and while the Battalion came on in troop-carriers the Commanding Officer and his "O" Group went ahead to reconnoitre the position. From the roadside farm near which they left their cars Rorouf lay on their right, six hundred yards away across slightly rising, open grassland. The hill itself, steep-sided and rocky, rises to about seven hundred and fifty feet, and its sharp crest line is broken by three well-defined hills. The nearest, on the right, they called "Double Hill," from its formation; the one in the centre was "Cave Hill," from a cave mouth showing on the slope below it. Out beyond this, near to the seaward end of the ridge, was "Little Hill."

Lieutenant-Colonel Hodgson decided to assault the right or inland end of the ridge first, using two companies to capture Double Hill and Cave Hill. A third company was to give them covering fire and the fourth to be held in reserve. The mortars and machine guns of Support Company were to cover the attack, which would also have the support of the artillery and of tanks of the Lothians and Border Horse.

Brigadier Lyon Smith, in command of the Divisional Artillery was on the spot and directed the artillery in person.

While orders were being given out the assaulting companies were forming up along hedges and in a grove of olives near the roadside, and those who had field glasses and telescopes studied the hillside in an effort to spot the enemy's positions. Many claims were made and, whether justified or not, the gunners shelled every target pointed out to them with undiscriminating generosity. A heavy shoot was in progress well before the companies moved forward to attack the hill at ten minutes to three in the heat of the afternoon sun.

Captain J. R. Martin Smith led No. 3 Company on the right towards Double Hill, Captain W. N. R. Llewellyn, M.C., with No. 2 Company went towards Cave Hill on the left. Firing from the hill broke out as soon as they moved forward, but the tanks helped them to cross the open ground and they reached a belt of scrub at the foot of the djebel without much loss. Martin Smith chose a gully as the way up and his leading platoon, under Lieutenant O. N. H. M. Smythe, climbed slowly towards the crest. Then the guns had to cease firing at the hill-top and at once enemy machine-gun and mortar fire increased. Martin Smith was himself wounded but went on undeterred, and in spite of thickening fire Smythe and his platoon worked steadily forward, crawling among the loose rocks near the crest. When at last they were able to attack at close quarters the thirteen Germans who manned the post surrendered. So far things were going well. But it was only when this post had been silenced and the leading sections tried to go forward that the strength of the position was fully revealed. The crest is but a yard or two wide and it is bent in a crescent. Double Hill and Cave Hill are more or less in line, but beyond Cave Hill the crest swings back and from Little Hill and the seaward end of the ridge the enemy could sweep the crest and the steep slope on his side of the ridge by close range machine-gun fire. Moreover, a second mountain feature, separated only by a deep and narrow valley, completely dominates that side of Rorouf. Every attempt to cross the ridge resulted in heavy casualties, and a mortar, firing from the direction of Hammam Lif towards Double Hill, caused much damage. Fire still came from Cave Hill, which No. 2 Company had been unable to capture, and until this was silenced No. 3 Company could make no further progress. So Martin Smith kept his remaining men below the crest line to gain the only cover available, leaving a section to hold Double Hill.

There had been no gully to give even partial cover to the leading platoons of No. 2 Company by the route they took and they had severe casualties as they climbed the hill. Both Captain Llewellyn and Lieutenant Sir Hugh Arbuthnot were wounded, and though some reached the crest they were met by heavy fire and those who were not hit were too few to take the Cave Hill position.

Fortunately wireless communication worked admirably on this occasion, but even without it Lieutenant-Colonel Hodgson could see that the attack had not yet succeeded and that neither No. 3 Company, clinging somewhat precariously to Double Hill, nor No. 2 Company on the slopes below Cave Hill could do more. So he ordered forward the two companies which he had kept back for such a need. No. 4 Company under Captain J. D. Gibson-Watt was to pass through No. 3 Company near Double Hill and attack along the far side of the ridge; No. 1 Company under Major H. C. L. Dimsdale to take Cave Hill and from there to attack along the near side. The artillery put down heavy fire on the far end of the ridge and on the feature behind, and a squadron of tanks moved out to help the companies across the open ground. It was after five o'clock when they started forward. Both were fresh, for while the assaulting companies had had a gruelling time in the heat of the afternoon sun they had waited in the shade of an olive grove.

Keeping his company well together, Major Dimsdale climbed to the summit by the gully which No. 3 Company had used and turning left led them forward well below the skyline till they were within assaulting distance of Cave Hill. Then they went in and captured it. Many did well, but it was Guardsman Charles Davies, Dimsdale's servant-orderly, who "did as much as anyone to carry the company forward," and afterwards showed great courage in bringing in wounded men under fire and great energy in getting them safely down the hill. By this time it was growing dark and Dimsdale was ordered to remain on the ground he had captured.

Meanwhile No. 4 Company had been seen to cross the crest, but there they were lost sight of. They had reached the top of the hill without difficulty near Double Hill. Careful reconnaissance showed Gibson-Watt that a short way down the steep slope on the far side thick scrub clothed the hill. So he ordered Lieutenant D. F. Pugh to rush the ridge and drop fifty yards in the scrub below; when this had been done a second platoon under Sergeant Thomas Haydn Evans followed to a position above them; then both turned left and began to advance through the scrub along the side of the ridge. Pugh was wounded and they had about fifteen other casualties, but the remainder made good progress till the scrub ended abruptly where a belt of one hundred yards or so had been cleared from top to bottom of the hill. Beyond the clearing thick scrub began again and from its cover heavy rifle and machine-gun fire opened as soon as No. 4 Company's men attempted to cross the intervening ground. On a steep and rocky slope, across which no one could move quickly under any circumstances, a better defence could hardly have been planned.

Gibson-Watt decided to attack the enemy from a flank and now brought his third platoon over the crest and led them down to the bottom of the hill. He had a number of casualties in doing so and was himself wounded, but with about seventeen men under Sergeant Nelson Rees (a tin-worker from Llanelly before the war) he turned down the valley. As they progressed he found that the hillside dropped more, suddenly at the foot, forming a gully in which they were completely screened and could do nothing to help the men up on the hillside. But in front of them, where the gully runs down to the outskirts of Hammam Lif, they saw a German post with the mortar which had done them so much damage on the top of the hill. It was an entrenched position among the outbuildings of cement works which stand just beyond the mouth of the valley. Working quietly up to close quarters they assaulted without warning, firing as they went in. The surprised enemy fled and the mortar was captured and taken into a forge adjoining the cement works. It was now about seven o'clock in the evening and Gibson-Watt decided that, while he must go back to the company, Sergeant Rees and his men should hold the position they had gained at the back door of Hammam Lif. When he regained the hilltop he found that the Battalion had been ordered to consolidate its present positions.

Enemy fire died away as dusk fell, for the strength of the position was broken. The troublesome mortar had been captured. No. 1 Company had cleared and consolidated the Cave Hill position. Men of No. 3 and No. 4 Companies held the Double Hill sector and Sergeant Rees's party occupied their outpost position in the forge behind the town. No. 2 Company had been withdrawn and lay with Battalion Headquarters, now at the foot of the hill. During the night the Coldstream Guards moved up through our positions and cleared the remainder of the ridge without difficulty. The enemy who remained showed little fight.

The task which had been set the infantry was thus accomplished. An enemy-held Rorouf no longer looked down on the Armoured Brigade when they attacked Hammam Lif next morning, but the other dangers remained. This is not the place to tell of the daring with which the Lothians and Border Horse fought or the enterprise which led them to outflank the enemy by driving their tanks through the sea. They captured Hammam Lif at severe cost, and the fact that in doing so they overcame a defence which included thirty-four anti-tank and dual purpose guns is a yard stick by which their achievement may be measured.

Welsh Guards casualties in this fight were twenty-four killed or died of wounds and fifty wounded, the wounded including five officers and eleven sergeants.

MEMBER OF SIGNAL PLATOON WITH 38 WIRELESS SET.

MONTE CERASOLA

"To the south-east of Cassino British forces had won a foothold across the Garigliano and had captured a series of mountain heights, forming a salient over the river which was later to prove of great value." (Part 1, page 42.)

ON February the 9th, 1944, the 3rd Battalion lay on a shoulder of Monte Furlito, a thousand feet above the Garigliano. Since landing at Naples four days before they had had little time to accustom themselves to surroundings vastly different from those they had left in Algeria. They had been on the move most of the time and they had had a long climb at the end of their journey. (See map overleaf.) They had crossed the river by "Skipton" bridge. At the nearby "Skipton" dump, where the accumulation of rations, ammunition and stores brought up in jeeps was distributed for men and mules to carry up the mountains, they had left the road. From there onwards they had climbed in single file, a long snake of men winding slowly up and down the narrow tracks. The country was strange to them and the Indian porters and mules were strange, but everything was accepted with the philosophy and collective self-confidence which are born of Regimental tradition, nurtured in training and matured in battle—the things that make a good Battalion so much more than the mere sum of its individual members.

Their transport and heavy equipment were coming from Africa by separate ships which had not yet arrived, and the Quartermaster (Lieutenant K. W. Grant) and his staff had had a hectic time in finding sources of supply and drawing what was necessary. It was characteristic of their tireless efforts for the Battalion's well-being that Lance-Sergeant L. J. Barnes pursued them to "Skipton" dump with a N.A.A.F.I. supply of extra cigarettes, chocolate and matches and issued it to the men as they moved off. By the time they reached their first destination behind Furlito they were glad to rest. Because of an insufficiency of porters and mules they had carried not only full

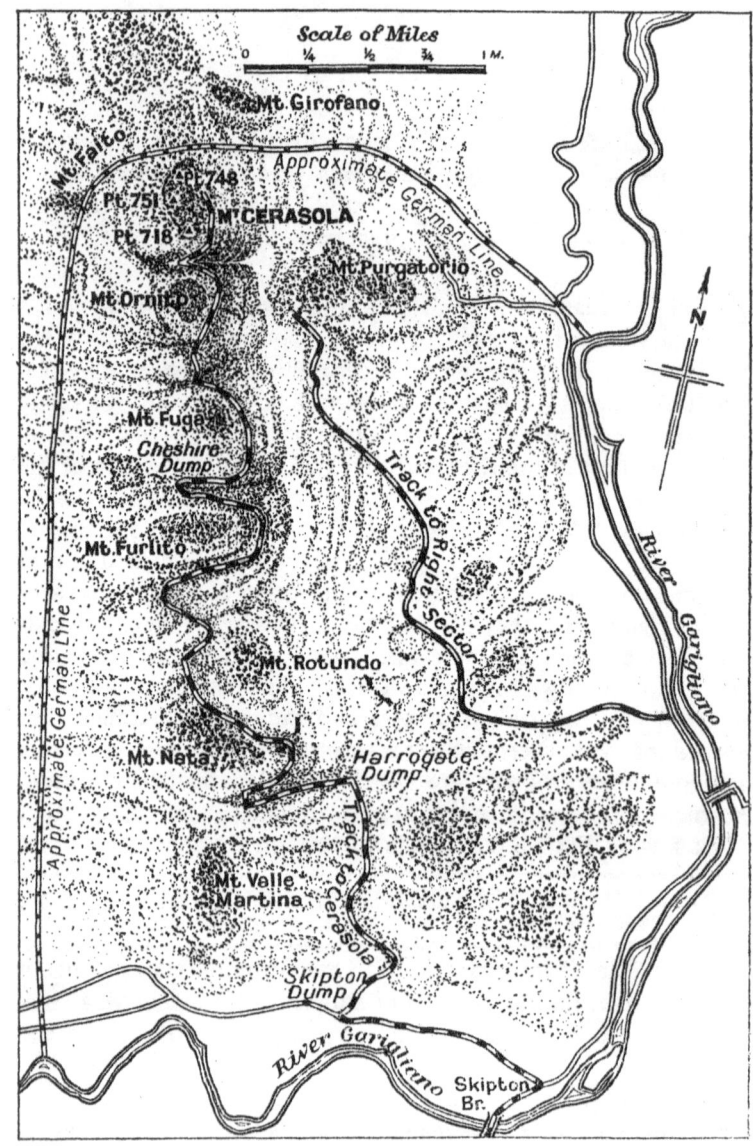

THE MOUNTAIN SALIENT.

(NOTE.—The approximate German line indicates the extent of our salient and does not imply that the enemy in fact had any continuous line.)

Monte Cerasola

equipment with greatcoats and blankets but also considerable loads of rations and ammunition. Yet they were in great form as they dug their slits and improvised bivouacs from ground sheets and blankets, and though it was cold they were old hands at making themselves comfortable and they were tired enough to go quickly to sleep. And then it started to rain as though the very flood-gates of heaven were opened and to blow hard and cold. Water poured down the mountain side and drove into the bivvies. There was no more sleep that night, for there was no shelter from that hard-driven rain and everyone was wet to the skin almost before they were properly awake. When morning came they tried with ill success to dry their sodden clothes and blankets in a wind which froze them stiff between showers that melted them again into a soggy mess.

They had been brought there for an operation which was now cancelled. Instead they were ordered to relieve the 2nd/4th Hampshires, who had been having a bad time on Monte Cerasola, the apex of our mountain salient. The Coldstream Guards had already taken over the neighbouring Monte Ornito.

The relief had to take place in darkness and there was little time for preliminary reconnaissance, so the Commanding Officer, Lieutenant-Colonel Sir William Makins, ordered the Adjutant to bring the companies up later and himself took the Company Commanders forward to find out all they could while it was still light. Led by a guide from the Hampshire Battalion, they went by a precarious path which wound round Monte Furlito, dropped into "Cheshire dump," climbed again round Monte Fuga and passed below the crest of the saddle on to the back of Monte Ornito. They had started to round Ornito's reverse slope when pandemonium broke out ahead, and as they went towards the ravine that separates Ornito from Cerasola the noise of the shelling, machine-gun and rifle fire increased. It looked as if Cerasola and possibly Ornito too was being attacked. At first they were protected by the angle of the mountain side from enemy shells and those that came over burst on the slopes below them. Then two things happened to discomfit them. Mortar shells, aimed at a steeper angle, began to fall around them and it began to snow. While the mortaring continued they were pinned down where they were, but when it eased up they went forward again towards the sound of battle. It seemed a bad time for reconnaissance, but daylight was precious and there was not much left. Here their guide made the mistake of leading through instead of round the head of the ravine and they had an exhausting climb before they emerged at last on to the mountain they were to occupy.

The summit of Cerasola is a confused mass of bare rocks, rising to a crest line bent in a half-circle towards the west. There and on the north it falls steeply to the valleys which separate Cerasola from the heights of Faito and Girofano, both held by the enemy. Behind this crest, on the side that faces the river, the slopes, though still considerable, are less acute and they culminate in a sort of tilted saucer or amphitheatre rimmed by the westerly heights. The Hampshires' Headquarters were on the reverse slope of this rim, but the guide took the Welsh Guards party too far out and the first men they saw were Germans trying to infiltrate the position by working up the easier slopes on the river side. The Commanding Officer had already given the unusual order, " 'O' Group, Load" and at this point Major R. L. Pattinson opened fire with his rifle, killing the leading German and scattering the others. The battle was dying down when they reached Battalion Headquarters and during a lull in the fighting Company Commanders went forward to see the positions they were to hold, while the Commanding Officer and the others with him "took over" at Headquarters and decided where machine guns and mortars should be placed.

As soon as it was clear that Cerasola was being attacked he had sent back orders for the Battalion to move up at once, but it was dark before Captain J. D. Gibson-Watt, the Adjutant, led the head of the long single file on to Cerasola. What followed was a nightmare. There are no tracks—not even bad ones—on the mountain top, only a maze of broken rocks and boulders from which, as it was impossible to dig in, the Hampshires had built low stone sangars. In the darkness these were hard to locate and shell fire and snow which fell intermittently did not make the task easier; and when the companies found them they were very inadequate. The Hampshires were much reduced in numbers: the Welsh Guards were nearly at full strength. The existing sangars were too few for full companies and too small for Guardsmen. Those who arrived early did something to arrange additional protection that night, but in many cases there was little time, for the relief was not completed till four in the morning.

The companies were near points 748, 751 and 718 just below the crest line; the Germans had outposts over the crest on the face of Cerasola which was overlooked from their main position on Faito and Girofano. With the dawn on the 11th February another German attack came in. It was pressed home with great determination, and before daylight had come to give the companies a chance to see their positions clearly for the first time or to grasp the layout of the Battalion the enemy managed to reach the crest, closely following heavy shell fire. The main attack fell on No. 2 Company, in the central position, and when grenades and small-arms fire failed to dislodge the enemy from the rocks in front of them Captain D. P. G. Elliot, in command of the company, ordered a bayonet charge. He was killed leading it, but the crest was cleared of the enemy. Sergeant William Doyle took charge till Lieutenant R. G. Barbour (who was with Advanced Battalion Headquarters as Intelligence Officer) came up to command the company, and then what had already happened was repeated. The enemy again attacked strongly and reached the crest; again rifle fire and grenades failed to dislodge him; again the company cleared the crest at the point of the bayonet and again the officer directing the charge—this time Barbour—was killed. In all twenty-two were killed and forty-nine wounded that morning, and of No. 2 Company only thirty-eight men were left; but the enemy's attack had failed, the Battalion held all its positions and tails were up.

There were no further attacks that day. The companies busily set about strengthening their positions while their wounded were got away. The first to be hit had been Lieutenant D. N. G. Duckham, who had been wounded as they came on to the mountain and had left Headquarters on a stretcher at four in the morning. It took six men to get a stretcher-case down the rough and tortuous track and was a difficult and hazardous task. Sappers were working hard to improve the going, but in many places the path was so narrow and rough that it was hardly

traceable by day. At night, slippery with rain or ice, liable to be
obstructed by a recent fall of stones, it made the carrying of a
Guardsman-laden stretcher a very slow business. It took
thirty-six hours to get Duckham from Cerasola to Skipton
Dump and a jeep ambulance, and although this time was
reduced later it never took less than twelve hours.

Captain O. D. Morris, R.A.M.C., the Battalion's beloved
medical officer, had his Regimental Aid Post on the reverse
slopes of Ornito, the nearest point to Cerasola at which any
cover from shell fire could be got. Even there shells fell un-
pleasantly close to the tent in which he worked, wedged in
between the mountain and the mule track, with the river far
below. There he dealt with the heavy casualties of his own
Battalion, those of the Coldstream Guards' wounded on Ornito
who came down that track, and a number of wounded men
whom the reduced Hampshire Battalion were unable to get
away when they were relieved. Captain Morris never spared
himself in action or out of the line. He served the Welsh
Guards throughout their campaigns in Africa and Italy, refusing
all offers of promotion in order to stay with them. He came
home with them in the end and stayed to see the older men
demobilised. He earned the undying affection and respect of
everyone who served with him in the Regiment.

It continued to be bitterly cold. Alternating rain and snow-
storms swept over the mountains, and a wind which at times
rose to gale force howled an accompanying bass to the whistle of
falling shells. The men had no chance to get really dry or warm
and some were suffering acutely. The Commanding Officer
was so ill that Brigadier J. C. Haydon ordered him to hospital,
and Major D. G. Davies-Scourfield came up to take command of
the Battalion, disguising the fact that he was himself suffering
from a badly poisoned foot.

During the day a German with a Red Cross flag appeared on
the crest behind which our sangars were sited and asked for an
armistice so that they might collect their dead. He was sent under
guard to Battalion Headquarters for the request to be dealt with,
and shortly after a German officer appeared on the crest renewing
the request for an armistice. By then Headquarters' decision
was known. He was told that none would be granted and

moreover that the man who had been sent to Headquarters would be returned, later, across a different sector of the front as he had seen our positions. The German officer accordingly withdrew and shortly after the sangars which had covered him during the parley were fiercely attacked. The attack was beaten off without loss and the balance of advantage remained with us, for the man who was retained gave much useful information about his unit and declined firmly to be returned to duty ! So the first day, February the 11th, passed. After night had returned Indian porters under Captain A. J. S. Cassavetti arrived at Battalion Headquarters with rations, water (there was no water on Cerasola except rain), additional clothing which had been asked for, and the mail. Then out of the darkness ration parties from the companies emerged to bear away their quotas and the porters faded back into the night. In the company sangars rations, stores, water and letters were distributed, news from home was exchanged and more than half the night had passed.

There were two groups who could take no part in these diversions. The men on duty had to concentrate their attention on the ground in front, staring into the darkness to catch the slightest sign of movement. And it took other men to go out on patrol. The undisputed use of no man's land cannot safely be left to the enemy. Active patrolling in front of any position to be held is an integral part of its defence. But it is an unpleasant part. Nerve and resolution—and many kinds of skill—are required in men who leave the shelter of their company position and the support of their comrades and steal away into the darkness to look for the enemy. As they pick their way over strange ground they must strain eyes and ears to distinguish a dim figure or a faint sound of movement. They must prowl with furtive silence, freeze into immobility on a signal, move on again without noise. They must keep direction as they go out and remember the way when they turn back. They know that the enemy is likely to be patrolling too and that at any moment they may be fired on by unseen opponents. Yet night after night all through the campaign men went out. Some came back with "nothing to report," which is often useful information. Some brought only a tale of loss and disappointment. Others returned in triumph having greatly discomfited the enemy. And with every patrol goes luck, good or bad. One may be ruined by a single unaimed shot and another pass unscathed through a sharp fusillade.

On the first night on Cerasola Lance-Corporal D. Beynon and a few men from No. 2 Company made a reconnaissance patrol which brought much useful information. On another night Lieutenant A. E. L. Schuster and a fighting patrol went down into the valley to investigate a deserted cottage. They found it occupied, and in the fight that followed he was mortally wounded. But Guardsman Walter Jones, a miner from Kenfig Hill, Glamorganshire, "whose courage and leadership were of a high order," took command of the men near him, and first leading them against a nearby enemy post which they destroyed, returned and searched, though unsuccessfully, for Lieutenant Schuster before leading the patrol safely back into our lines. Schuster's body was recovered later : Guardsman Jones was subsequently killed in action.

On yet another night Lieutenant B. B. Pugh took out a patrol from No. 3 Company which penetrated to the foot of enemy-held Girofano, destroyed an enemy post, reclimbed the slopes of Cerasola on the face held by the Germans and, coming up behind the line of their sangars, attacked and put one out of action before breaking through to our own lines. It was a very fine performance. Not only had the patrol gained useful information on the enemy's positions and destroyed two posts, but they brought back the pay book of one German killed, which revealed the presence of a unit not before identified on that front.

So the days and nights wore slowly on. A routine was gradually evolved and the men adjusted themselves to life under these strange conditions. Everything possible was done to counteract the cold and wet. Once when there was snow to be melted the Battalion shaved ; but owing to the shortage of water the men were afterwards encouraged to let their beards grow and when they finally left the mountains they looked more like members of an Arctic expedition than a Guards Battalion. Leather jerkins were issued and torn or damaged clothing and boots were renewed daily. The Commanding Officer said afterwards : "Thanks to all who worked on supply, we never failed to get all we asked for while we were on Cerasola." Of the Battalion not only the Quartermaster but Regimental Quartermaster-Sergeant H. P. N. Dunn (with over nineteen years' service as a Welsh Guardsman) was a tower of strength.

None the less a number of men had to be evacuated daily through frost-bite and exhaustion, and shelling and mortar fire took a steady toll—three wounded on the 13th, two on the 15th, two killed and five wounded on the 16th, five wounded on the 17th, three killed and six wounded on the 18th. This constant bombardment had the further result of frequently cutting the telephone lines by which, as well as by wireless, communication between companies, Battalion Headquarters and Brigade was maintained. That they were maintained was due to "the courage of a high order" displayed by the Signal Officer—Lieutenant M. J. B. Chinnery—and the men who worked with him. Lance-Corporal Trevor Easter repeatedly went out under very heavy fire to repair broken wires and "his gallantry, resolution and coolness were responsible for maintaining communications at a critical moment." But there were many others throughout the Battalion who showed fine soldierly qualities—too many to mention here.

An hour before the dawn on the 19th of February the enemy made a last determined effort to surround and capture Cerasola. The frontal attack was not pressed home : the German main force moved round the northern slopes to the easier gradient behind the Battalion's positions and penetrated well into the amphitheatre enclosed by the crest line. Companies were engaged from the rear and Battalion Headquarters was attacked. Captain Gibson-Watt and Drill Sergeant David Davies promptly organised a counter-attack which "resulted in the death or surrender of all the attackers," but Drill Sergeant Davies, "whose cheerfulness and gallantry at all times set a high example" was so severely injured that he died of his wounds. In the course of the fight Lance-Sergeant William Mairs, in charge of the 3-inch mortars nearby, came under fire from the enemy who for a time overlooked his position, yet he did not allow his men to be deflected from their battle task of screening the Battalion front with mortar fire. Without pause he kept up a mortar barrage which did much to prevent the frontal attack from succeeding and killed many of the enemy—"his personal courage and coolness were of a very high order." These and the machine guns which together formed the supporting weapons of the Battalion played a big part in breaking the attack. The personal gallantry and good judgment with which Lieutenant W. K. Buckley commanded them were reflected in the manner in which all the teams fought.

To have penetrated into the very centre of the Battalion positions doubtless encouraged the enemy, but it did not depress the companies. None of their positions had been lost. They were still firmly placed round the rim of the saucer, and as it grew lighter the Germans were caught in the open and overlooked on three sides. The companies had a grand shoot and very few Germans got away. The enemy quickly decided to "eat his leek" and gave in.

Meanwhile the secondary force had tried to get round the southern flank of Cerasola by way of the saddle which joins it to Ornito. They got too near to Ornito for their own good. The Coldstream Guards and a company of the 1st/4th Hampshires who were in a position to cover just that ground also had a good killing before the surrenders started. In all a hundred and twelve were taken prisoner that morning and there were many killed. But in addition to Drill Sergeant Davies there were sad casualties in the Welsh Guards' ranks. Major Pattinson was killed in the heavy preliminary shelling with which the attack opened. Back at main Battalion Headquarters in Cheshire Dump Company Sergeant-Major F. G. Baker and Sergeant A. Evans, the Master Cook, were killed and fourteen others in the course of the action. Lieutenant J. A. G. Wolfers and nineteen men were wounded. But the Germans made no further attempt to recover Cerasola and, later, this and the other salient heights became the jumping-off point from which French forces drove the enemy finally from the mountains which contain the Liri Valley on the south.

On the night of the 19th the Welsh Guards were relieved, among the last to go being Major Davies-Scourfield. He could no longer get a boot on his poisoned foot. It was swathed in sandbags and had been for days. But despite the pain he was suffering and the great difficulty he had in moving over rough ground, he had neither failed to pay personal visits to the companies nor lost grip of the situation. In the words of the Brigadier, he "set a magnificent example of unruffled calm and confidence." Confidence was indeed the feeling which inspired the bearded and bedraggled Battalion as they wound their way down the long track to "Skipton Dump." Their number was reduced by casualties and sickness, but their pride was increased by the knowledge that they had beaten the enemy decisively and more than once, and they were confident that they would beat him again.

GERMAN INFANTRY WITH "*SPANDAU*" MACHINE GUN, "*SCHMEISER*" LIGHT AUTOMATIC AND HAND GRENADES.

CASSINO

"The key to the Liri Valley is Cassino, closely guarded by the almost unscaleable Monastery Hill." (Part I, page 42.)

CASSINO had a unique place in the strategy of the Italian campaign and in public interest throughout the world; it will hold a unique place in the memories of those who fought there. Its military importance has been explained in Part I (page 42). Public interest was captured by the grim story of the four months' fighting there and was sustained by accounts of the Monastery which overlooked the town and by much ill-informed discussion on the rights or wrongs of its destruction. Troops who fought there remember it as the place above all others where the hideous characteristics of war were revealed in naked obscenity.

The Welsh Guards only went there after a third assault had captured about half of the town, only after tons of bombs and uncountable shells had shattered every building, obliterated every road, let loose the waters of the Rapido and sown the ruins with undiscovered death. They went there to hold what had been so dearly won; they made no attack and none was made on them; and yet the weeks they spent there put as hard a strain on them as any similar period in the campaign. Partly this was due to physical conditions—to a troglodyte existence in the gloom of half-underground ruins never left in daylight; partly it was due to the impression on the mind made by this stagnant pool of death. In the country round the sun might shine; it never reached them in the depths of this inferno. In the country round men went about their lawful occasions by day; here they left cellars only when it was dark. "Only the bull-frogs revelled in this scene of horror, croaking and chuckling with delight .... the very atmosphere made one's flesh creep."

But chiefly it was the effort to rise above these conditions—as they did—that made life in Cassino such a strain. For in spite of forced immobility they found plenty to do; in spite of gloomy surroundings they found abundant excuse for humour; in spite of the absence of comfort and good fare they dispensed hospitality to visitors. And in spite of limited opportunity they maintained a spirit of enterprise and aggression and were continually devising means to trouble the enemy.

"To enter Cassino was like stepping into the pages of Edgar Allan Poe's 'Tales of Mystery and Imagination.' There was an atmosphere about the place, if not of evil, at any rate of the fantastic. It was only possible to enter the town at night and the powers and mysteries of darkness lurked round every corner to assail the traveller. We start down a dirt track with high hedges on either side; in peace it must have been quite a pretty little lane. This lane continues for perhaps half a mile and then slides through a dozen ghostly houses and enters 'the abomination of desolation' that surrounds Cassino. All vegetation falls suddenly away and on either hand there is nothing but swamp and marsh caused by the overflow of the river. We are in a world of mists and shadows. Each night the river gives off a fog, which rises perhaps a hundred feet above the floor of the valley. Above it stands the black mass of Monastery Hill; in the moonlight the broken scaffolding of the rope railway can be seen clearly—it looks like a gallows. Impressions crowding one's senses create a weird atmosphere; the roaring frogs with their krark, krark, krark; the pop, pop, pop of the smoke shells; the swirling mist, the tricks of moonlight, the odd bursts of machine-gun fire; and the whistle and crump of mortar bombs breaking the silence of the night."

On reaching the outskirts of the rubble the path was taped and, twisting and turning over fallen masonry, it brought them finally to a jagged bastion which was what remained of the town gaol. This was to be their headquarters. There was only one room with a ceiling and it resembled the Black Hole of Calcutta. All the air outlets, including the small barred window, had been blocked up with masonry and covered with blankets (to prevent bullets coming in or light shining out). The air was thick with tobacco smoke, the room lit by guttering candles and hurricane lamps. In this room were to live the Commanding Officer and his staff, signallers and intelligence personnel. The place became the focal point of the Battalion and often as many as twenty people squeezed into the cell. Throughout the day nothing could be done except constructive work on the ruins such as the improvement of lines of fire, or the revetment of strong-points. The soldiery got what sleep they could and interspersed this with rather unappetising meals, cooked on smokeless fuel lamps. Once it was dark, however, everything was stepped up and feverish activity ensued. Rations brought up by jeep and trailer to the Quarry on the northern outskirts of the town were collected by ration parties. Plans were made and orders issued and patrols sent out to discover the enemy's movements. It was in these hours that they received visits from members of the Brigade Staff.

Brigadier J. C. Haydon came to see them almost nightly and after he had left the Commanding Officer went out to visit one of the companies. The following account of one such visit gives a good picture of what was involved. "Owing to the darkness, the difficult going and the need for silence, it took several hours to get to a Company Headquarters and from there to the various platoon positions. We crept through the blanket-covered mousehole in the gaol, turned sharp left up a steep rubble incline, through another blanket curtain, and then crawled over rough fallen masonry through a small aperture formed by the top of an old arch. Here we moved very slowly and gingerly along the fallen masonry that had once been the walls of the gaol until we reached what had been a road running along the end of the ruins; we manoeuvred round and across one or two big bomb craters and reached what was clearly the remains of another house. This was a Company Headquarters, but we turned left-handed, down some steps to a lower level, and followed a white tape which had been laid to guide parties to positions ahead. This area had probably been an open space before; there were no remains of buildings for about eighty yards, but the whole area was pitted with enormous bomb craters all half-full of smelly stagnant water. By good luck or good management we reached the beginning of the 'houses' again. The first obstacle was a high bank of rubble about thirty foot high which had to be walked up, crossed, and descended again. Then one passed through more ruins into what had once been a small square and after being challenged we slid or slipped down

Cassino
by
L. F. Ellis
(The Gaol ruins, the Castle and the Monastery behind)

a chute into a double blanket screen and so through into a room underground. This room was lit by a couple of hurricane lamps and bodies of sleeping soldiers lay about. This was a platoon, less one section of six men who were in positions either just outside in the rubbish or up on the top of the house in a kind of sangar, built in the rubble. The house, like all the others, was merely a cellar with the rest of the house heaped on top of it and one or two holes created to make entrances. We came in at the bottom, but for a change when we left we climbed up a kind of ramp made from the fallen stones of the house, through a hole at about the original top floor level, where a two-man post covered an approach from the enemy lines and was also used as a snipers' post in daytime. Down this rubble to the ground level again to another house which contained the other section of the platoon just visited. A long, dark trek led to the next platoon of this company, which was rather isolated. The approach was across what presumably was once the town's public park, but the whole place was now waterlogged, full of bomb craters and virtually impassable except along the path we took—probably the remains of some hard-surface walk. This platoon's position was a very unpleasant one as no lights could be allowed after dark ; for there were various openings in the shell of the house which could not be blocked up as they afforded fields of fire to deny the approach of enemy patrols or raiding parties. The return journey took just as long as the outward journey and the party would not get back to the gaol till between two or three in the morning ; dawn came between four and five."

From the start it was the Commanding Officer's policy to harass the Germans, to allow them no peace. For every shell landed in our area we would put back five ; any movement heard or seen by forward companies would be severely dealt with, by the companies themselves or by our 3-inch mortars. Each platoon headquarters had air photos of the town, elaborately marked with numbers on almost every ruined house. It was an easy matter to phone or wireless back the number where a disturbance had been heard and the information was relayed to gunners or mortars. A very high standard was attained by the mortars both in accuracy and speed ; they could guarantee to have bombs on the desired spot within three or four minutes of noise or movement being reported. They were very close to the enemy, at some points within eighty yards. Neither side knew exactly where the other was most of the time, and so as not to give their position away they had to avoid all noise, talking in low voices and laughing softly. To Lieutenant M. J. B. Chinnery, the Signal Officer, it seemed possible that the enemy could intercept wireless messages. "I thought if this was the case we might try a little Welsh. This we did and about twenty-four hours later German propaganda pamphlets were scattered in our area printed in Urdu !"

Platoon commanders spent much time on charting panoramas of ruins in front of their positions. Every nook and cranny was noted and sentries were for ever on the alert for any clue to the enemy's movements. The most effective way to discover their positions was to draw their fire and many ingenious methods were used to do this. One of the most successful was evolved by Lieutenant I. P. Bankier's platoon in No. 2 Company. Someone extracted from the ruins two large portraits of a mid-Victorian Italian soldier and a Guardsman who had considerable artistic skill transformed them into likenesses of Hitler, complete with Iron Cross and Swastika. They were then hoisted in turn over positions where a hidden sniper could take advantage of any reactions. The result was better than had been hoped for. The Germans fired freely and in their anxiety to pierce the Fuehrer's breast gave away their own positions.

The Welsh Guards' first tour of duty in Cassino lasted from April the 7th to April the 23rd, when they were relieved. "The hand over went smoothly and the time eventually came for the Commanding Officer and myself to leave," wrote Lieutenant Chinnery afterwards. "We were none too certain of the way out, especially as now there was no moon to assist us. There was a Gunner in the Command Post at that time who had come up to visit us : he said he would come with us as he knew the way and we set off, very thankful that we were at last to return to civilisation. We knew that it should take about twenty minutes to get back to Rear Headquarters outside the town, and when we had blundered along for about that time we came to the unanimous conclusion that we were off our route. This was an understatement. We were lost. Several times we had to wade through irrigation dykes nearly four feet deep—very cold and most unpleasant. The only directional indication we had was the smoke shells landing in Cassino. Eventually we arrived at what had once been a copse. There we sat down to take stock of our position. We were sunk in gloom: no one said anything: daylight was approaching and with its arrival we might be subjected to unpleasant German attention. Suddenly we all pricked our ears. Amid ruin, death and desolation a nightingale was singing with utter abandon. We listened spellbound and eventually the voice of the Commanding Officer was

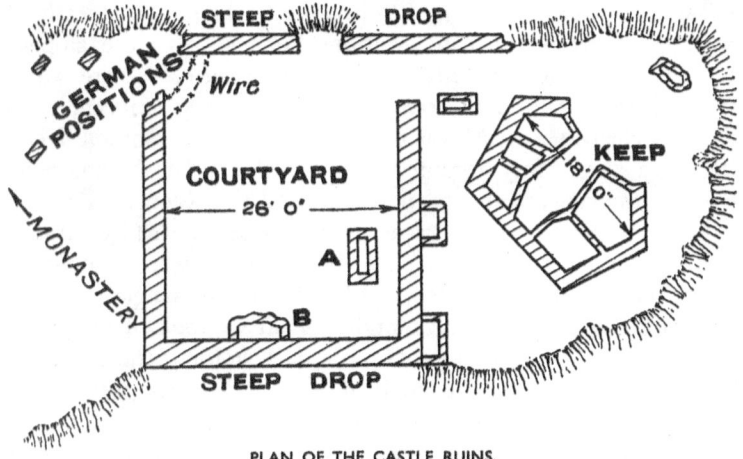

PLAN OF THE CASTLE RUINS.
(For the situation of the Castle see plate facing page 142.)

heard saying sleepily, 'We must be in Berkeley Square.' After that all went well. We happened on the reserve company of the Coldstream Guards, who put us on the right track. Three and a half hours after leaving the gaol we arrived at Brigade Headquarters, very tired and wet. We were given whisky and told that we must have been going round and round in a mined area. We couldn't have cared less."

After resting for twelve days they went back, to hold Cassino till the day that it fell. This time the Castle was added to their responsibilities, though a company of the Coldstream Guards shared with them the duty of holding this most unpleasant of all positions at Cassino. The sketch reproduced on the coloured plate gives a fair idea of the steepness and isolation of Castle Hill but hardly give a true impression of the nearness of the Monastery above or the completeness with which it overlooked the Castle. Captain B. P. R. Goff whose Company (No. 3) held it, can best explain its distinctive characteristics :—"The worst part was getting up to the position ; it was a good twenty-five minutes' hard climb with the aid of ropes in several places and you were in a muck sweat when you reached the top. It was a case of single file all the way as there was only one track ; luckily the Germans never attacked us on the way up. Our own smoke shells often fell near us and made it hard to breathe, and rifle grenades were fired at us from German positions farther down the slopes ; but in the Castle itself life was quiet and eerie. There was a steep drop all round the position, of which the diagram gives a pretty clear idea. 'A' was a cellar in which one platoon lived ; 'B' was a sangar only occupied at night ; the rest of the company lived in the sangars shown in and around the Keep.

"Communication with Battalion Headquarters was by wireless only, and there was no movement by day as we were completely overlooked by the Monastery. We lived in our sangars all day, rations being given out each night. And we took turns with a company of the Coldstream Guards each holding the place for two days at a time. The smell of dead bodies was particularly bad both in the Castle and on the way up, and after Cassino fell and we were finally relieved we counted seventy-four bodies of different regiments and nationalities, all unburied." That was the Castle position. By contrast, it was written by an officer who was at Battalion Headquarters on the morning of May the 18th. "When at last the town fell and we ventured forth in daylight, we found outside the door of the gaol some honeysuckle in full flower and a lovely red rose growing in the rubble."

PICCOLO AND ARCE.

Arce is "a place of some significance, for Route 6 turns sharply south at the town where another road bends northwards through the mountains. It was necessary for the Allies not only to secure the continued passage of Route 6, but also to deny the enemy use of the northern road as an escape route for his withdrawing army. It was also important to capture Arce quickly. But the plans of a commander are liable to be upset by the various and vexing uncertainties of war. (Part I, page 46.)

THERE are some days when nothing seems to go well. May the 26th was one of these. Major-General V. Evelegh, commanding the 6th Armoured Division, was eager to push on rapidly and in particular to clear Arce, the next town on Route 6, as quickly as possible. But first the armour was held up by shell and mortar fire, so the Grenadiers pushed forward on foot ; but the country they had to clear was closely cultivated, and about three o'clock in the afternoon, as they came over a low hill near Coldragone and Le Cese, they too were held and took up position just behind the rise, three and a half miles from Arce. The tanks could not get on again for a bridge, a mile ahead, was blown and the demolition covered by gun-fire ; and as there was no other way forward the whole Division was halted.

The Welsh Guards were a long way back in the divisional column when they were ordered to come up on tanks. They "married" with the Lothians and Border Horse and moved up to an assembly area behind the Grenadiers' positions. They had a tiresome journey. The tracks which had been bull-dozed through farmed lands in the rear were overcrowded with traffic struggling to get forward. There was much congestion and little quick progress. Mounted on the tanks, the companies were separated from the Battalion transport and as a result the men got no hot meal that night and wireless batteries could not be renewed, a fact which had considerable bearing on their subsequent operations.

Company Commanders then joined the Commanding Officer behind the Grenadiers' positions. They could not see beyond the rising ground ahead but their maps told them that Arce lay about six miles from their assembly area and that, two miles before the town is reached, the highway runs through a narrow pass, with Monte Orio on the right and Monte Piccolo and Monte Grande on the left. The Higher Command had received information which led them to believe that Arce was being evacuated and that the hills flanking the pass were not being held. At half-past eight that evening the Commanding Officer received orders ; the Battalion was to march at eleven o'clock and endeavour to occupy the high ground on the far side of Arce.

It was a dark night when the Battalion left the tanks in the assembly area and started on foot up Route 6. They were compelled by the nature of the closely-planted country to keep to the road : they were compelled by military prudence to march with a single file on either side, for the road had been well shelled by day and any closer formation would have been too dangerous. But a Battalion marching this way is strung out over a mile and if opposition were encountered suddenly, in darkness and in unknown country, control of movement would be difficult. With this in mind Lieutenant-Colonel Davies-Scourfield marched at the head of the column.

There was some desultory shelling to the left of the road as they moved over the rise near Coldragone and Le Cese. It was not near enough or heavy enough to trouble them much, but as they drew towards the pass two men of the leading company were wounded by a shell which fell closer to the road.

As the Commanding Officer trudged forward in the darkness, with the Battalion strung out tenuously behind him, the hills overshadowing the pass loomed nearer and nearer. He knew it was not *certain* that the enemy were withdrawing from Arce, and even if they were it seemed to him probable that they would leave rearguards behind them on the hills, to cover their withdrawal. If so these would have the Battalion at their mercy as it passed through the defile into unknown ground behind. He decided that to go on without further information would be to risk disaster and that he must wait till daylight made it possible to prove whether or not the enemy still held the hills which dominate the road. So he ordered the companies to take up positions astride the road and waited for the dawn. It was then about half-past two in the morning and the wisdom of his decision was soon proved. Shortly after daybreak supporting arms and tanks came up and at once it was obvious that the enemy had *not* gone. For as soon as movement on the road became visible he started shelling, and having observation posts which overlooked our positions he shelled them with unpleasant accuracy.

It was now clearly necessary to reconnoitre and if possible to occupy the hills on either side of the pass. No. 4 Company under Major J. R. Martin Smith was ordered to send a fighting patrol to the spur of Monte Orio on the right, while Major R. N. Cobbold's Company—No. 2—was to make a reconnaissance in force of Piccolo on the left. The remainder of the Battalion were to remain in position astride the road till the results of these operations were known.

The patrol sent out from No. 4 Company, twelve strong, was commanded by Lieutenant T. B. Hayley. To reach their objective they had to strike diagonally through the foothills, traversing a number of minor spurs and re-entrants on the way. They made good progress and had nearly reached their objective when the enemy, who had lain low till they were in his net, opened fire from several directions. They were indeed half surrounded and were overlooked from so many points of vantage that their position was hopeless. Three returned to tell the tale; Hayley was killed and the others wounded and taken prisoner.

On this report Major Martin Smith decided to try to reach the top of the hill immediately on his right and from there to work along towards the spur overlooking the pass which had been the patrol's objective. Most of that day was spent in getting through the foothills and up the mountain in face of opposition from snipers and shelling. Lieutenant M. A. Bankier was wounded before they moved off and several others later. Part of this movement was supported by Sherman tanks, and by nightfall the company, now reduced to two platoons and Company Headquarters, was established near the crest of Monte Orio.

The sketch facing page 152 will help to make clear what happened to No. 2 Company, in the meantime. Piccolo is a long, rocky spur at right angles to the road. On the side from which Major Cobbold's Company was approaching, its steep side rises out of a thick belt of trees. Through this, invisible at a distance, a deep lane runs across the lower slope to a biggish white farmhouse and a smaller cottage beyond. Above the lane and above the belt of trees the hillside is terraced for the olive trees which cover it with dusty green; each "step" is two or three feet deep and edged with rocks and boulders. The photo on page 331 does not show the nature of this ground and the slope is far steeper than it appears in the picture. It was a hot May day and men in fighting equipment could only make that arduous climb slowly. As they toiled up the broken ground it was easy for the enemy to cover them from points of vantage on the hillside.

Working their way through the thick foreground, the leading platoon lost direction and got too far to the left. Wireless communication failed so Major Cobbold went after them to lead them on to the true line of advance. Coming into the lane mentioned above they passed the cottage and fifty yards beyond it ran into close-range fire. Major Cobbold and Guardsman C. V. B. Groom, his servant-orderly, were killed. Farther ahead Sergeant William Doyle and several others of the platoon had also been killed, and the remainder of the platoon could get no further in face of the enemy fire. A few got back unaided; more came in later under cover of a smoke-screen which was put down to help them; a few remained on the ground all night and rejoined next day after Piccolo had been taken.

Meanwhile the other two platoons of No. 2 Company were climbing up through the olive trees. In spite of casualties they had nearly reached the top when they came under heavy machine-gun fire from their front and from both flanks. Then began a fight which showed the true mettle of the company. Lieutenant I. P. Bankier (who was now in command) saw that success depended on their ability to put the enemy posts out of action and the platoons pushed on, though men continued to fall from the cruel cross-fire. By now Lieutenant J. H. G. Davies, the only other officer, had been wounded and many of the men with him; though some posts had been silenced, the enemy still held others and there were signs that a movement had been started to outflank their attackers. Bankier realised that they were hopelessly outnumbered and the position too strong to be captured by the small force he had left, so he ordered the withdrawal. Gradually disengaging his men, Davies showed coolness and skill, but he and the men who got away owed much to Bankier who with five men, half surrounded at the highest point reached in the attack, were killed covering the withdrawal of their comrades—a fine example of selfless courage.

Another member of this covering party, Guardsman H. R. Jones, a press operator from Dulas in Anglesey, was severely wounded after firing four magazines, but he fired four more before being satisfied that the men he was covering had got clear and by doing so he lost any chance to get away himself. He was too badly wounded to walk. But having already accomplished so much, he determined not to give in now and he lay still till nightfall enabled him to drag himself to a less exposed position a little way down the hill. He got as far as he could that night and lay quietly through the long, hot day, and once more when night fell he dragged himself farther down the hill. On the third morning he was found in an exhausted condition, having had no food or water all this time. He had been content to stay behind, wounded and alone, in order that his officer and the rest of his platoon might get away, but he was not willing to be taken prisoner; and by his great determination and courage he managed to avoid capture after having inflicted many casualties on the enemy.

When a final count of No. 2 Company was taken there were forty-six men left under Company-Sergeant-Major B. F. Hillier. Of the three officers, two had been killed and the third wounded; and Piccolo remained in enemy hands. It was a sad day for the Battalion, relieved only by great pride in the gallantry which had been displayed. Meanwhile No. 1 and No. 3 Companies, astride the road, had been well shelled, Lieutenant C. A. F. J. Maude and a number of men had been killed, and eventually both companies were moved back to positions near La Cese. No. 4 Company remained on Monte Orio.

When No. 2 Company's "reconnaissance in force" had shown how strongly Piccolo was held, the 1st Guards Brigade was ordered to attack and capture both Monte Piccolo and Monte Grande, the feature on its left. The hill, which a depleted company without artillery support had failed to take, was now attacked by a Battalion of the Coldstream Guards under cover of darkness and after artillery preparation in which the Divisional Artillery and 4-inch mortars and the tanks of the Armoured Brigade shelled the German positions heavily. Following hard behind the barrage, the Coldstream Guards attacked and the company of Scots Guards which at this time formed part of the Battalion reached the summit of Piccolo "without any casualties" and occupied the eastern end of the hill. The enemy had withdrawn from the crest to escape the shelling, but he quickly returned once the shelling stopped and sharp fighting continued throughout the night and the following day while the Germans tried without success to dislodge the Guardsmen. A rocky outcrop and the western spur which commands the road through the pass had not been taken, and late in the afternoon of the 28th No. 1 Company Welsh Guards were ordered to go through the Coldstream Guards' position and capture this vital portion of the hilltop.

After a further artillery preparation Major Gibson-Watt's Company started up the hill just before six o'clock in the evening, duly passed through the Coldstream positions and attacked eastwards along the ridge. The leading platoon was led by Sergeant Elfed Morgan, who gave a text-book demonstration of attack by "fire and movement." The main objective was a peak of rocks in which the enemy had several machine guns. Disregarding his own safety when necessary to give personal orders to his section-commanders, Morgan manoeuvred his platoon steadily forward, "saving many casualties by his calm and determined conduct . . . . His initiative and quick grasp of changing situations were invaluable assets to his company," and it was largely due to his courage and self-discipline that this strong position was captured and held. A second platoon under Sergeant John Meredith Powell also fought extremely well and there were many acts of gallantry by non-commissioned officers and men. Gibson-Watt's ability to maintain a co-ordinated attack was largely assisted that day by a runner of the company, Guardsman John Brindley Davies, who went backwards and forwards over bullet-swept ground with information and orders ; "his personal bravery, intelligence and coolness were of

Piccolo and Arce, *by L. F. Ellis*

an exceptional order." Another Guardsman, T. J. L. Arnold, twice took command of a group of men and "by his coolness under fire and his fine leadership helped to give the necessary punch to the attack" which again resulted in the capture of the position. After the Bren gunner of another section had been wounded, Guardsman Christopher John Keogh, who had formerly been a machine-tool setter in Cardiff, took the gun from him and advanced on the nearest post, firing from the hip. He was himself hit twice, in the face and in the foot, and twice his gun was blown from his hands by the blast of bursting grenades, yet each time he recovered it and reopened fire.

But the supreme example of self-sacrifice and devotion to duty on a day when there were many was given by a young Lance-Sergeant. Frank Goodwin was twenty-five years old. His home was in Cefn, Denbighshire, and before the war he worked as a bus conductor. On this day he commanded the leading section of his platoon in an attack on an enemy machine gun sited in a stone-walled sangar, high among the rocks at the very top of the hill. They had to cross eighty yards of open ground swept by fire from this and three other nearby guns. All were causing casualties, but the one which was posted up in the rocks was the most dangerous and difficult to silence. With his section following, Goodwin advanced across the open, shooting with a Bren gun as he went forward and ignoring the enemy's murderous fire. He reached the foot of the rocks and dropped his gun to throw grenades into the sangar. Then as the enemy gun still fired he scrambled up into the post and it stopped at last. When the men of his section reached the position they found the German gunner dead and Lance-Sergeant Goodwin, also dead, his arms thrown round the gun now silenced by his own shot-riddled body.

Twenty-two men of the two platoons which made this attack were killed or wounded. Both Lieutenants O. N. H. M. Smythe and J. D. S. Nicholl-Carne were wounded: so was Company Sergeant-Major W. Davies. But the fighting ended with the whole of the hilltop ours at last, and any of the enemy who remained on the far slopes made off that night. Monte Grande, which the Germans had held, was also evacuated that night and the enemy pulled back from Arce.

At half-past eight on the morning of May the 29th, No. 3 Company under Captain F. B. Bolton, mounted on tanks of the Lothians and Border Horse, drove through the pass as soon as Sappers had made a diversion round the demolished bridge and entered Arce. Route 6 was again clear, but the three days occupied in overcoming this obstruction had reduced correspondingly the chance to catch the main German forces retreating northwards. And it had cost the 1st Guards Brigade nearly three hundred casualties, of whom one hundred and twelve were Welsh Guardsmen.

BRITISH " PROJECTOR INFANTRY ANTI-TANK " (PIAT).

PERUGIA AND SAN MARCO

> "*Key positions on the approaches to Perugia from the west and south were in our hands and the enemy, to avoid being surrounded, abandoned the town itself and moved back into the hills which overlook it from the north and east. He was quickly pursued.*" (*Part I, page* 50.)

PERUGIA stands on the southern end of a ridge of high ground. The railway station area on the west and some suburban and commercial buildings, modern and unattractive, sprawl round the base of the rock; but the old city above is unspoiled and looks serenely over the valley through which the 1st Guards Brigade had travelled.

By the 19th of June the Grenadiers and the Coldstream had driven in the German outposts in front of Perugia, but the enemy still held the town. The Welsh Guards, in reserve, lay at the little village of San Martino Delfico, two and a half miles south of Perugia—and it poured with rain. Then during the day the 61st Infantry Brigade coming up on the left captured the high ground which dominates the approaches to Perugia from the west and, finding himself threatened from the west and the south, the enemy drew his forces back into the hills as soon as darkness fell to cover their movements. The Grenadiers and the Coldstream at once pushed forward to secure the outskirts of the town and the Welsh Guards were ordered to pass through and occupy the ridge of high ground beyond it which runs away to the north-west, flanked first by shallow valleys and beyond these by higher hills. Two miles from Perugia along this central ridge lies the village of San Marco—or "Tulip" in the code used by the Division for these operations. "Tulip" was the Welsh Guards objective. Two roads, a northern and a southern, lead to it from Perugia and they are linked half-way by a cross-road. The first step was to secure the road junctions at each end of this cross-road and this task was given to No. 1 Company (Major W. T. C. Fogg-Elliot) and No. 2 Company (Captain A. J. S. Cassavetti).

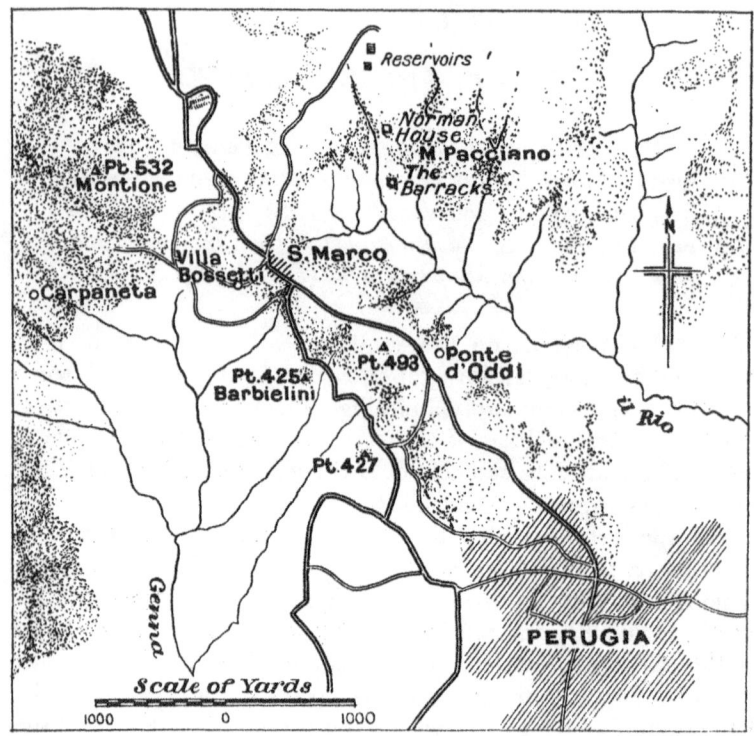

PERUGIA AND SAN MARCO.

   The Coldstream Guards had already occupied the station area of Perugia when Major Fogg-Elliot's company passed through them in the very early hours of June the 20th. It had stopped raining but was very dark, and in darkness they reached the midway road-junction on the southern route and took up positions covering it. So far there was no sign of the enemy, and Captain Cassavetti's company, following hard behind them, secured without opposition the road junction on the northern road to San Marco. The first phase of the operation was thus carried out. The second, which began when No. 3 and No. 4 Companies went through to capture San Marco, was not to be accomplished so easily.
   Daylight had come when Captain B. P. R. Goff led No. 3 Company through No. 1 Company's position near Point 425,

and the enemy started to shell and mortar the road as soon as they moved forward. Tanks of the 16th/5th Lancers which were supporting them had an unpleasant time, but the company deployed on ground to the right and left and the whole force worked steadily forward till they came to a place where the road runs between high banks. The leading platoon had cleared this defile when the platoons deployed behind them came under heavy machine-gun fire from either side. The left was cleared without much difficulty, but Lieutenant P. F. F. Brutton's platoon, with tanks co-operating, had a stiff fight before the high ground on the right was captured. The key to the position was a lone house defended in some strength by infantry with machine guns and supported by an enemy tank. The latter was "seen off" by tanks of the 16th/5th Lancers and Brutton's platoon assaulted the house in two parties. One he led himself, the other was led by Sergeant O. F. Abrams working round a flank. The assault, pushed home forcefully, ended with hand-to-hand fighting in which Brutton claimed two kills and Sergeant Abrams three : one prisoner was taken but the rest got away.

Meanwhile No. 4 Company under Captain F. L. Egerton, who were to advance on the left of No. 3 Company, were late in arriving. They had taken a wrong turning in the station area and soon found themselves in the main square of Perugia in a scene of wild excitement. The Perugians surged around the men whom they regarded as their liberators and the Company had great difficulty in getting along. Flowers, fruit and vino were thrust upon them as they vainly sought for the right road to their objective. The number one of a Bren gun team, temporarily cut off from his section, was seen elbowing his way through the crowd with a wreath of lilies round his steel helmet and a bunch of roses stuck firmly in the muzzle of his gun. But the crowd became less pressing when shots rang out from a few Germans in a top window and Lieutenant J. T. Jerman took his platoon to round them up. He succeeded in eliminating a spandau and its crew, but had considerable difficulty in preventing the crowd from "eliminating" the German prisoners he brought out, for with their courage renewed the Italians were most anxious to lynch them there and then. At length, however, the company, complete with prisoners, freed itself from Perugia and its citizens and found its true road to the scene of action. They had to clear the enemy from another house *en route* before they came up on Captain Goff's left in time to cover his attack on the Villa Bosetti on the southern fringe of San Marco. It stands on rising ground and was held in the usual German fashion by a machine-gun team who waited till it was clear that the attack would be pressed home and then, at the last safe moment, slipped away. On this occasion a trail of blood showed that one at least was wounded before he left.

So it went on. It is not easy to give a coherent account of fighting spread thinly over a considerable area and through many hours. At point after point small but stubborn resistance had to be overcome. Even No. 2 Company, consolidating the position they first occupied on the northern road-junction, were suddenly fired at from a house which overlooked them and the help of the tanks was enlisted to clear it. All that day the tanks of the 16th/5th Lancers gave ready and valuable help. Just before San Marco was reached the leading tank put its nose round the last bend in the road, and Captain Goff was discussing the next move with the tank commander when an anti-tank gun's armour-piercing shell hit it fair and square. The tank at once "brewed up," but neither Goff, who was leaning against it, nor the crew inside were hurt. About this time a factory on the roadside was set on fire by enemy shells. It burned all night and the Germans continued to shell it, to the great satisfaction of those in other houses from which the enemy's attention was thus diverted. By four o'clock in the afternoon San Marco was completely in our hands and the ground between it and Perugia finally cleared of the enemy, with the Battalion's mortars and machine guns sited to cover the ground ahead. But enemy shelling and mortar fire continued and the Intelligence Officer, Lieutenant G. N. Evans, was mortally wounded. Lieutenant-Colonel Gurney was also hit by a number of small splinters, of which the last to be got rid of was extracted by Lance-Corporal H. E. B. John in the Regimental Aid Post three months later.

With Perugia behind it the Battalion faced north-west. The hills on either hand lay back some distance from the central ridge which they had cleared, but those on the left stretched out a long arm across their front, ending in a hill called Montione (Point 532 on the map). It is about a mile from San Marco, and the road from Perugia continuing northwards runs at its foot. Italians reported that the Germans had withdrawn from it and Lieutenant-Colonel Gurney ordered No. 4 Company to occupy the hill.

It was about six o'clock in the evening when Captain Egerton led the company forward and they reached the foot of the hill without difficulty, though they met some machine-gun fire where they had to cross the road. Choosing a shallow gully as the way up, the two leading platoons under Lieutenant Jerman and Sergeant Emrys Davies were well up the hill when they were fired at from a low sangar at the top. They replied with rifles and grenades and continued to climb, and as they reached the crest they saw the Germans running back and speeded them on their way with parting shots. The third platoon under Captain C. Brodie Knight, held in reserve at first, now joined them on the hilltop and the platoons dug in (when they could) or built stone sangars.

Their position was not very comfortable. They were widely separated from the rest of the Battalion and could expect no personal aid from that quarter should they be counter-attacked. They had cleared the Germans from their immediate vicinity, but the hill was but the rump of a long broad hogs-back formation stretching westwards for miles. A whole battalion could easily be deployed on it, and as both the sides and the top of the hill are thickly masked in oak scrub and thickly strewn with loose rocks a whole battalion could easily lie there undetected. A beacon of rock, visible for miles, stuck up a few hundred yards away from their position and Egerton put a standing patrol there while daylight lasted; but he wisely withdrew it when night fell, for it would have been easy to surround and capture it in darkness.

About one o'clock in the morning, in driving rain, a sharp fusilade of rifle and spandau fire suddenly ringed them in the darkness. It was too dark to see more than a few yards from their position, so the company were withdrawn to the hillside to take advantage of the crest-line. At first light Egerton re-formed them and led them up again and they cleared the hilltop and reoccupied their former position. By day this was a comparatively strong one and several attempts by the enemy to raid it were beaten off. Patrols were sent out to ensure that the immediate vicinity was clear, and one of these found a most mysterious but very welcome dump of British Army rations about one hundred and fifty yards from their position! They had been growing anxious about supplies as none had reached them during the night and the only water they had was what was left in their water-bottles. However, they now had rations enough to see them through the day, and before long they had orders by wireless to withdraw as soon as darkness made this possible. For as it was now clear that the enemy still had troops along the ridge of hills there was no point in trying to maintain a company on the final spur.

As soon as darkness fell the sound of enemy movement was heard on three sides of No. 4 Company's position, so Egerton ordered the sections to slip away quietly, one at a time, and to reassemble at the foot of the hill, and the manoeuvre was so well carried out that all were away before the enemy fired a shot. They were back in their old headquarters, a house behind San Marco, by soon after midnight. It was a large house with plenty of room for the whole company. They had a hot meal before turning in and all this acted as a great tonic to the men, who were very exhausted by the end of the operation. "We ate off plates and table cloths again and I had a wonderfully comfortable bed with linen sheets." It was only when they rejoined the Battalion that they learned what had happened in their absence.

Captain Egerton had only taken a skeleton Company Headquarters on to Montione: he had left behind Company Sergeant-Major F. Tremblett and others who could be spared, and during the night Tremblett organised a party to take rations up to the company. Major the Baron de Rutzen led them and they reached the crest of the hill without finding any of No. 4 Company. They heard voices and called to them quietly, but got no answer. So de Rutzen stood up just below the crest and shouted loudly. He was answered promptly by the unmistakable fire of spandaus and realised then that the voices he had heard were German. (Doubtless they came from the force which subsequently attacked No. 4 Company.) There was nothing for the lightly armed and heavily loaded ration-party to do but withdraw, but de Rutzen ordered them to dump the rations they had brought up and this wise decision explains the company's mysterious find.

But it was realised at headquarters that in the morning supplies must be got up to the company; Major Fogg-Elliot, accompanied by Captain J. R. Roberts (observing for the guns of the Ayrshire Yeomanry), and a party which included Company Sergeant-Major F. Tremblett and Sergeant John Essex, set out to make contact with No. 4 Company. To avoid the enemy post which de Rutzen had encountered in the night they chose a wide left-handed approach, and they had reached the foot of the hill when they came upon a German soldier at the back of a farm building and quickly made him prisoner. They were about to question him when others appeared and fire was opened by both sides. This attracted heavier fire from a nearby house and garden. Captain Roberts was wounded but was able to get away. Tremblett and Essex were both too badly wounded to move and there were other casualties. The force which remained was too small to take the position, so Fogg-Elliot withdrew, getting away with difficulty over open ground. As soon as he got back to his company he detailed Lieutenant J. D. S. Nicholl-Carne and his platoon to return with him, and at once they set out to capture the post and bring in the wounded. But when they approached the scene of action the enemy were well prepared; they were greeted by mortar and machine-gun fire; Fogg-Elliot and Nicholl-Carne were both killed and after a vain effort to subdue the enemy's fire the remainder of the platoon withdrew. No. 4 Company were therefore still cut off from the Battalion and the Commanding Officer decided on the withdrawal recorded above. Two days later a Battalion attack by the Grenadier Guards finally cleared this left flank and the hill-top ending in Montione.

Neither this withdrawal of No. 4 Company from an outpost position which it was impossible to support, nor the ill-luck which dogged Fogg-Elliot's attempts to reach them can diminish or obscure the success of the Battalion's action at San Marco. The companies had to capture widely scattered positions, in difficult, undulating country, thickly planted with crops and fruit trees and sprinkled with lone houses well spaced for rearguard defence. They were well led, fought skilfully and achieved all that was asked of them ; and throughout a complicated series of moves Lieutenant-Colonel Gurney directed the action with a sureness of touch that gave confidence.

All reports of this action speak of the gallantry and courage of a set of men whose service is not always recognised—the despatch-riders and company runners on whose work commanders of all ranks are often largely dependent. Despatch-riders on this occasion had to carry messages to Brigade Headquarters and elsewhere by roads which the enemy overlooked from the hills and shelled consistently with notable accuracy ; yet neither on this nor any other occasion did weather conditions or the enemy's action ever deter them. Of Lance-Corporal David Glynn Ruddle it was said that throughout two and a half years of active service with the Battalion he showed dauntless resolve and a cheerfulness which on many occasions infected all ranks. Lance-Corporal Raymond Douglas Porter, with a similarly long record of service, was "an influence for good upon all ranks. . . . The most terrible conditions never checked his intrepid resolution." Of company runners one was killed trying to get back from Montione to Battalion Headquarters with a message from Captain Egerton, but Guardsman Cecil William Sparrow, who volunteered to take the place of a wounded runner in No. 3 Company, crossed and re-crossed open ground swept by machine-gun fire seven times to carry orders and information. "Throughout the battle he was quite fearless." There were many others for whom he must stand as representative.

* * * * *

On June the 22nd the Battalion remained in the positions occupied and apart from intermittent shelling had a quiet day. They moved back on the 24th to rest in billets behind Perugia and that night they suffered another severe personal loss. Captain B. R. T. Greer, the Adjutant, walking in his sleep, fell from the balcony of a house used as Battalion Headquarters and broke his wrist : and the ambulance in which he was taken to hospital had an accident *en route* and then his leg was broken. He had had long service as Adjutant both in the Training Battalion and in Italy, and the 3rd Battalion felt his loss keenly. Captain Egerton was appointed to succeed him as Adjutant; and Major R. C. Sharples came from a Staff appointment to command No. 1 Company after Major Fogg-Elliot had been killed.

* * * * *

The remaining operations which finally cleared the enemy from the vicinity of Perugia need not be told in detail. All battalions of the Brigade were employed, and for the Welsh Guards they involved moves forward into the hills to the northwest of San Marco and the seizure of a succession of key points— two large houses known to the Battalion as "Norman House" and "the Barracks" and finally the reservoirs on which Perugia's water-supply depends. There was little fighting and the Battalion's biggest haul of prisoners was taken at the waterworks. It was already clear that the enemy's main force had been withdrawn, leaving only small rearguards to discourage us from following too quickly. In this he succeeded, for when a small mobile force under Captain F. B. Bolton was pushed boldly forward on June the 30th they covered fifteen miles before finding any serious opposition.

ONE OF THE ANTI-TANK PLATOON'S
6-POUNDER GUNS AND A DESPATCH
RIDER.

THE ARNO VALLEY

"*Little more than a mile to the north of Arezzo the River Arno turns north-west towards Florence sixty miles away. On its western side are the Chianti mountains flanking the road from Arezzo to Florence (Route 69). Across the river, a mile or so to the east, secondary roads connect the little towns and villages in the foothills of the Prato Magna massif, encircled by the great loop of the Arno, and still in enemy hands.*

"*When the 6th Armoured Division renewed their advance, three days after the fall of Arezzo, they moved up Route 69 while other troops converged on Florence. The 1st Guards Brigade were used to clear the right flank of the Divisional front by occupying in turn key places on the secondary roads and by patrolling actively in the foothills of the Prato Magna.*" (Part I, page 59.)

THERE were no battles in the Arno valley. At the outset the 6th Armoured Division, doing right flank guard to the 13th Corps, were not called upon to set the pace but only to see that no counter-attack developed from the Prato Magno mountains and to clear the valley and the foothills as the Division moved in conformity with the Corps advance. The enemy was withdrawing to the Gothic Line and his retiring rearguards were only hustled when, on one or two occasions, they moved too slowly for our convenience. The battalions of the 1st Guards Brigade leap-frogged up the valley, and the battalion in the lead at each stage maintained contact with the enemy by probing into his positions night after night to discover their situation and to give the artillery fresh targets. There were various signs of each impending withdrawal to watch for— the demolition of his bridges, an increase of vehicle movement on roads behind his forward positions, reports of civilians and information extracted from prisoners captured. But only when patrols by the Armoured Brigade or by the infantry established with certainty the fact of a withdrawal was a fresh advance made.

Then "the sappers would repair the main axis and all the minor lateral roads freed by the advance, and behind them the whole apparatus of an Armoured Division—the guns, the rear echelons, the headquarters, the workshops, the medical centres and the supply services—would be stepped up" for the next move forward.

So far as the Welsh Guards are concerned the story begins on the 19th of July and at the southernmost point of the valley. On that day they left Arezzo to occupy Quarata and to guard the bridge across the Arno at Burriano. The latter task was given to the newly joined company of Grenadier Guards, which, under Major D. Willis, was to serve with the Welsh Guards for the next five weeks. (See Part I, page 58.) Five escaped prisoners of war came into their positions one day and many Italians brought in the news of the enemy's movements in the hills. And on one occasion a parish priest from Castiglion Fibrocchi arrived with four German prisoners. A meal was prepared for him, but when confronted with a mug of tea he called for wine in stentorian tones. The atmosphere of cordiality soon created was only disturbed when he was asked to hand over a pistol which he produced from his robes. "He took another draught of morning wine and demanded more ammunition, maintaining stoutly that fifty rounds were insufficient to defend his parish."

Reconnaissance patrols were sent out nightly and on July the 23rd Castiglion was found to be empty, so a platoon of No. 3 Company occupied it as a base for patrols into the country ahead. On the 28th Lieutenant D. F. Pugh penetrated five miles into enemy territory to gather news of their positions and strength. It was one of the innumerable patrols which could be reported in a sentence as a matter of routine needing no comment, for it succeeded in its purpose without any special incident. Yet a few details may be added to show how such projects were organised. There were fourteen in the party. Pugh, Lance-Corporal W. E. Brace and Guardsman J. H. Wildsmith were to get the desired information: they were the advance party Sergeant William James Marshall and eight Guardsmen were a main body on which if need be Pugh's party could fall back. Behind was a group of two signallers with a wireless set and a small covering party. After the main body were in position well forward, the advance party, wearing gym shoes and in dead silence, moved slowly on till they got into the German position. "The silence had gone. Around us were the noises of coughing, stamping of feet and talk in low voices. Then a bare ten yards away sounded the tramp of heavy boots as a section moved along a stony track, talking loudly and shouting for someone named 'Czar.' By now we had a fairly good idea of the German position and very slowly we started to withdraw, checking with difficulty an impulse to run." They were glad when they heard Sergeant Marshall's challenge as they got back to the main body and had great satisfaction when, later, they could use their wireless set to put the guns of the Ayrshire Yeomanry on to the German position.

While the Welsh Guards were based on Quarata, His Majesty the King visited the forward area near Arezzo and a party from the Battalion lined the road to cheer their Colonel-in-Chief as he slowly passed, stopping for a few moments to talk to a group of officers and men. It was here, too, that Brigadier J. C. Haydon, D.S.O., O.B.E., who had commanded the 1st Guards Brigade throughout the whole of its campaign in Italy, handed over his Command to Brigadier C. A. M. D. Scott, D.S.O., another Irish Guardsman.

Other Battalions of the Brigade had by now gone forward, and on the 30th of July the Welsh Guards went to join them near Montevarchi. It was one of their most pleasant staging-places on the banks of the Arno. The weather was lovely, and the country, and they bathed and relaxed in the sunshine. Fruit was abundant, including a plentiful supply of peaches. But after two days they went forward to Renacci (with companies at Faella and Castelfranco) and the usual patrolling began again.

About four miles to the north of Faella is a hamlet called Pian Di Sco. On August the 2nd Lieutenant S. A. Hall, with Lance-Corporal L. A. Hodgson and four Guardsmen, went out from Faella in daylight to find if the hamlet was occupied. It was not; but civilians told them that four Germans were resting in an outlying farm. Hall knew that prisoners would be valuable for intelligence purposes and set out to capture them. He was leading the patrol and had nearly reached the building when fire opened from an undetected position on their flank and Hall and Guardsman H. Thomas were killed.

Lance-Corporal Hodgson, not to be stopped by this mishap, rushed the farmhouse with his remaining men and captured four Germans, though some others in the house ran off. Having got in, however, Hodgson realised that it would be fatal to emerge in daylight, for they were well into the enemy's territory and the house was doubtless being watched. So he drove his prisoners up into an attic and waited with them there till darkness should make it possible to get away. A party of the enemy entered the house soon afterwards, looking for their companions and calling them by name; but they missed the attic and Hodgson and his men saw to it that their prisoners kept quiet. After the Germans had left he made all the party bind their feet in sacking to deaden noise, and when darkness came he got them away through three miles of the enemy's territory "complete with prisoners." On the way back they met Lieutenant D. F. Pugh, who had come out to find them with a fighting patrol. Hodgson had shown a fine sense of duty when he refused to allow the death of his leader to deflect the patrol from its purpose; his resourceful and courageous leadership were alone responsible for the patrol's success.

On August the 4th the Battalion moved forward again. No. 2 (Grenadier) Company with two troops of tanks from the Lothians advanced and captured Torre-a-Monte, a large strongly built villa on a commanding hill from which good observation could be got over a wide stretch of the country ahead. Shortly afterwards Advanced Headquarters was established there with the companies in various positions in the vicinity. Though such a conspicuous landmark was inevitably shelled heavily its walls were stout enough to make it reasonably safe. Active patrolling continued nightly, but it would need a large-scale map and many pages to describe it in detail and there were no outstanding incidents. Here and there they killed a few Germans or made a few prisoners of war. They themselves had some casualties, Lieutenant R. H. Leake of No. 2 (Grenadier) Company being so badly hurt on August the 6th that he died of his wounds. But the country was gradually cleared and on August the 8th they moved forward again. The weather had broken and torrential rain now fell frequently.

One damp morning Guardsman H. H. Hamer of No. 4 Company, returning to his platoon's position after being sent to Company Headquarters, saw a German crouching in an elementary and undignified position behind a pear tree. Oberst Leutnant Egger, commander of the Parachute Regiment which had opposed the Battalion at Cassino, San Marco and Arezzo, was here "caught bending" by a Guardsman, who promptly took him prisoner and marched him off to Headquarters.

On August the 10th the Battalion moved back into Brigade Reserve. Spending one night in a fantastically gaudy palace belonging to an Italian sweet vendor, they went to a comfortable position on the west bank of the Arno near Figline, where they stayed happily for ten days while parties of the more fortunate went on leave to Rome. The final chapter of the Arno story began when, their rest finished, they relieved the Grenadiers at Torre a Monte on August the 24th, and before first light on the 25th No. 4 Company under Major J. R. Martin Smith went forward to seize high ground near Altomena, while No. 3 Company (Captain F. B. Bolton) took the Grille feature further east. Later that day No. 3 Company advanced again and liberated the little town of Pelago. The Germans moved out just before they reached it, but left a host of mines and booby-traps which took a lot of cleaning up and killed and wounded a number of the more impetuous civilians.

The head of the valley had now been reached. The towering heights of the Gothic Line rose before them.

Since a large part of warfare consists in moving from place to place, the accounts which have been given of life on Cerasola or in Cassino need to be supplemented by some detail of times in which the Welsh Guards were not continuously in close proximity to the enemy, of days (and they were many during this long Italian summer) when the weather was not unkind.

In their passage up the Arno valley they lived for the most part in Italian farmhouses or farm buildings. These were usually primitive and stuffy at the best, and where the Germans had used them they were always indescribably filthy; but they provided some shelter and once inside men could move freely and cook without fear of enemy observation. The alternative, in forward positions, was the slit trench with a roofed-in section in which a man could sleep ; or, when they were back in reserve near Figline, two-man bivouacs and ten-men tents, pitched in olive groves or orchards away from the dust of roads. In reserve they did a little training in the morning, firing company weapons, doing run-walks or route marches, or a few simple schemes. In the afternoon they conformed to Mediterranean practice and enjoyed siesta. Early and late they bathed in the cool if yellow waters of the Arno, and in the evenings there were company sing-songs and occasionally visits to a nearby town. To make up for the extreme hardships of mountain warfare in the winter, summer-time soldiering in the valleys was about as comfortable as any active service could be. The worst of it was that they were never long in one place and the continual movement of a modern infantry battalion is a complicated affair.

It is complicated first by the fact that the Battalion is very seldom concentrated in one place or moved as a whole. When it was in action it was normally in at least four places at once ! The rifle companies would be forward and in contact with the enemy ; behind them but as close as was convenient lay Advanced Battalion Headquarters (normally known as "Tactical Headquarters" or for short "Tac H.Q.") A mile or two further back (for reasons of security) was main Battalion Headquarters, and behind this in the Divisional area was what was known in this Battalion as the " 'A' Echelon Transport," described below. Thus when the Battalion moved up to the head of the Arno valley the rifle companies were at Pelago and on the Altomena ridge, "Tac H.Q." at Sant Ellero, Battalion Headquarters at Figline and " 'A' Echelon" at Faella.

A move was complicated in the second place by the variety of men and stores to be moved and properly distributed and by the number and variety of vehicles employed. This can well be illustrated by the layout of the Battalion at the head of the Arno valley.

    I. FORWARD POSITIONS. (Pelago and Altomena ridge.)
        Each of the three companies had with it the Company Commander's jeep and the company carrier, the latter fitted out with wireless and loaded with a reserve of ammunition and certain essential stores. The three

companies therefore had ... ... 6 vehicles.
In close support was Support Company, in which the Carrier Platoon had thirteen carriers, the Mortar Platoon seven carriers, the Pioneer Platoon a White scout car and two jeeps and the Company Commander another jeep. Thus Support Company had ... ... 24 vehicles.

II. ADVANCED BATTALION HEADQUARTERS. (Sant Ellero.)
Here would be the Commanding Officer, the Intelligence Officer, the Signal Officer and the officer commanding Headquarter Company, with detachments of the Intelligence Section and of the Signal Platoon. So far as vehicles went there would be the Commanding Officer's jeep and carrier: the Intelligence Officer's jeep and trailer: the Signal Officer's jeep and a 15-cwt. truck with essential stores of line, etc., and a White scout car fitted with a powerful wireless set tuned in to Brigade Headquarters. The officer commanding Headquarter Company would have a jeep and a 15-cwt. truck for cooks and Headquarter personnel. There would thus be at Advanced Battalion Headquarters ... ... 8 vehicles.

III. MAIN BATTALION HEADQUARTERS. (Figline.)
The Second-in-Command, the Adjutant, the Transport Officer were here, with the Orderly Room staff and the remainder of the Signallers, Pioneers and Intelligence personnel and Police and their heavier stores. And here under charge of the Regimental Sergeant-Major was the reserve ammunition of the Battalion. Finally, each of the forward companies left here two 15-cwt. trucks loaded with company stores and the vehicle built for use as a wireless truck, known universally as "the gin palace" and commonly used as a mobile company office. The transport with this party numbered about ... ... 20 vehicles.

IV. "A" ECHELON TRANSPORT. (Faella.)
The Quartermaster lived here with the Regimental Quartermaster-Sergeant and the Company Quartermaster-Sergeants, the armourers, boot repairers and other tradesmen. And here was all the transport required to draw rations, stores, petrol and water for the Battalion from the Royal Army Service Corps or Royal Army Ordnance Corps at the Divisional Supply Depots, and such of the Company and Battalion transport as was not needed in the forward positions. The detail varied from time to time and place to place, but in the normal way there would be at "A" Echelon something like ... ... 16 vehicles. (Here too would be a Captain in command and any officers left out of battle and waiting to be called forward to their companies.)

Movement orders for even one battalion needed careful writing if every section was to be given clear directions and the move was to take place without confusion.

To complete this picture of Battalion organisation a few details of procedure may be added, again using the last move up the Arno valley as an illustration. When the companies moved forward to the Altomena ridge on the evening of August the 25th their rations for the next day had been issued to them before they started and had been packed into the company carriers to be drawn in the morning. Early the same morning the Quartermaster drew the following day's rations in bulk from the Divisional supply point and, having divided and issued them to the Company Quartermaster-Sergeants, saw them loaded on to company 3-ton lorries and sent them up to officer commanding Headquarter Company with Tac Headquarters at Sant Ellero. There the company carriers had assembled in readiness to take them up to their respective Company Headquarters together with any ammunition or stores which had been called for. The note of their requirements in these respects was handed each morning to the Regimental Sergeant-Major. As far as possible it was met from what was being held at Tac Headquarters, but the Quartermaster was advised of requirements which could not be filled and either he sent it up with the rations from stocks which he held or he drew it from Royal Army Service Corps or Royal Army Ordnance Corps supply depots and sent it forward with the following day's rations. So the companies in action were maintained, and because the men employed at every stage knew their jobs and performed them faithfully it was seldom indeed that the companies were short of anything they needed. And everyone realised that this was due as much to the zeal and efficiency of those who dealt with supply at Brigade and the higher formations as to their own labours within the Battalion.

It was due, too, to the work of another group of men whose service can hardly be over-estimated, namely, the motor transport drivers of the Battalion. In fair weather or foul, in pelting rain or blinding dust, often in darkness and often under fire and nearly always on shockingly bad roads or tracks, these men drove day after day, unfailingly carrying out orders which imposed a heavy nervous and physical strain and demanded "guts" as well as skill. Neither of the three Battalions of the Regiment could have moved or fought successfully if their transport drivers had failed them : but they never did.

MINE DETECTOR USED BY PIONEER PLATOON.

CAGNY AND LE POIRIER

"*At dawn on July the 18th Field-Marshal Montgomery attacked with strong forces of armour and infantry east of Caen, the assault being preceded by the heaviest and most concentrated bombing hitherto used to support a military operation.*" (*Part I, page 54.*)

THREE armoured divisions were employed for Field-Marshal Montgomery's "threat to break out" on the eastern flank of the Normandy bridgehead. The 11th Armoured Division went in first, the Guards Armoured Division next, and last the 7th Armoured Division. The Guards Armoured Division went into action for the first time.

Both the 1st and 2nd Battalions had been lying near Bayeux with the rest of the Division. They left this area in the night of July the 17th-18th, the 2nd Battalion moving off about midnight and the 1st Battalion shortly after. "It was after midnight and very dark. Long lines of vehicles were formed up near the entrance to the field with their engines ticking over and despatch riders sitting astride their machines opening and shutting their throttles. Somewhere the Regimental Sergeant-Major was shouting at someone; we might have been on any exercise in England. Then, suddenly, we were on the move, bumping and swaying out of the field and into narrow lanes, with their tall enveloping hedges dimly moving past on either side. Every road junction we came to was beautifully sign-posted by the Provost Company with illuminated arrows and boards lit by electric torches with directions for 'tracks' and 'wheels' in black type. It was not possible to go wrong and the heat of the engine, combined with the hypnotic winking of the next vehicle's convoy-light, soon sent one into a fitful doze; there is no room for excitement in the coma induced by a night drive in convoy. Sometimes at one of the many halts I would get out to stretch my legs, but without knowledge or curiosity as to where we were, till at last the hedges began to show more clearly and the long jolting columns took shape as the light increased.

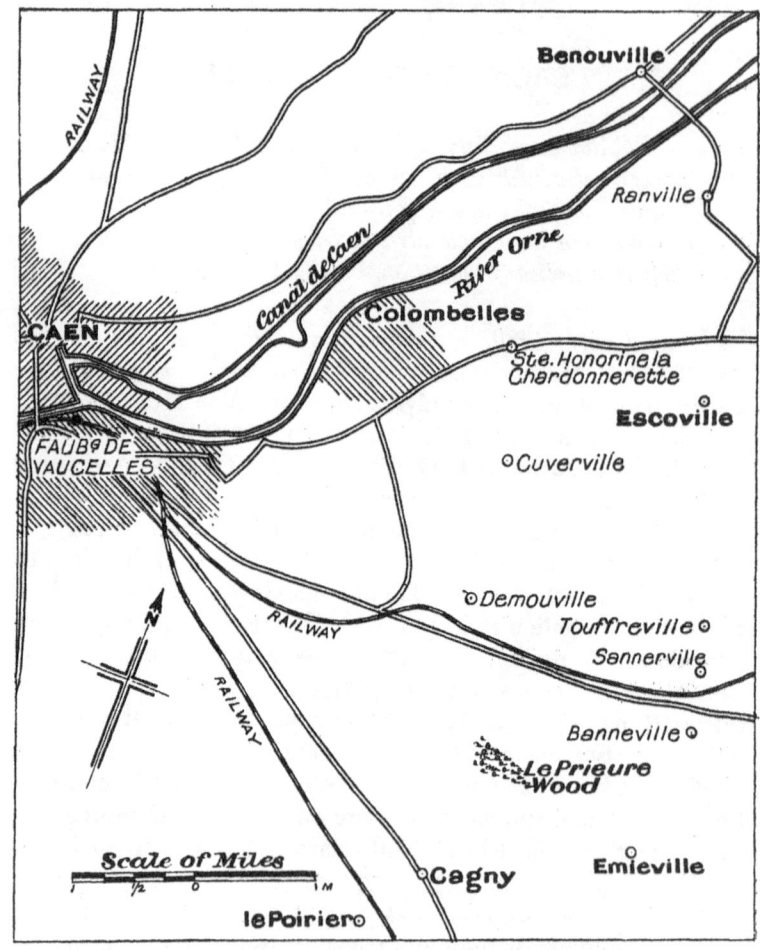

THE SCENE OF OPERATION "GOODWOOD."

"We came to a halt on what seemed to be a long ridge which sloped away gradually into the distance on the right." (They were on the west bank of the Orne near Benouville.) "I got out and found myself on an artificially constructed track with chain netting laid over its bull-dozed surface. Twenty yards to the left was another which I knew from the signposting to be the tank track. On either side of us were cornfields, their tall crops

Cagny and Le Poirier 175

almost ripe. A thin ground mist lay over everything, but apart from one or two wispy clouds the sky was clear and the air cool and very still. It was going to be hot later on. One by one the vehicles shut off their engines. Apart from the drone of a motor cycle diminishing as it passed away up the column and the snoring and coughs of the men in my T.C.V., complete stillness settled on us. Richard and James climbed out of their little car just behind me and the Quartermaster walked back from farther in front. We speculated on our position in hushed voices. It was unbelievably quiet."

"High in the sky and away to our left a faint and steady hum caught our attention and, as we watched, it grew into an insistent throbbing roar and the first aeroplanes appeared high up in the pale sky. Then the whole northern sky was filled with them as far as one could see—wave upon wave, stepped up one above another and spreading out east and west till it seemed there was no room for any more. As the first passed overhead guns began to open up on our right and the wonderful hush of the morning was finally shattered. The bombers flew in majestically and with a dreadful, unalterable dignity, unloaded and made for home; the sun, just coming over the horizon, caught their wings as they wheeled. Now hundreds of little black clouds were puffing round the bombers as they droned inexorably to their targets and occasionally one of them would heel over and plunge smoothly into the huge pall of smoke and dust that was steadily growing in the south. Everyone was out of their vehicles now, staring in awed wonder till the last wave dropped its bombs and turned away. Then the guns took up in a steadily increasing crescendo the work which the bombers had begun."

"Someone produced something to eat from somewhere, and since the sun was now well up in the sky we dragged our valises out of the trucks and lay down to sleep on the edge of a corn-field." Thus one Welsh Guardsman prepared for his first great battle in 1944.

The 2nd Battalion tanks moved again first, at about a quarter past eight, crossing the canal and the Orne by the famous Pegasus bridge which Airborne men took on D Day and had held ever since. Then they drove south, still nose to tail. "It is an amazing contrast to 1940 ! No enemy aircraft—no need to keep vehicle distance—no need to glance at the sky. Three fully equipped armoured divisions in a great punch to the south."

A few miles south of the point at which they crossed the Orne lies what has sometimes been called the Caen plain. It is a narrow belt of open undulating country falling slightly to the south and lying between the Orne on the west and a ridge of wooded hills on the east. There are a few hedges and a number of small copses and although tanks can move freely the uneven ground offers plenty of cover to defending troops. The scattered villages had been targets for the bombers and most of them were now mere ruins. It was to be a day of confused fighting and considerable losses in armour, but neither of the Welsh Guards Battalions was heavily engaged. The 5th Guards Armoured Brigade bore the brunt of the Division's fighting that day and had reached Cagny by late afternoon. They had dealt with the main opposition there when Prince of Wales Company and No. 3 Company of the 1st Battalion, by now concentrated on the north of Cagny, were sent in to clear the village. Both companies made a good bag of prisoners, eager to give themselves up after the morning's heavy bombing ; and truly Cagny was no longer a place for human habitation, though the Welsh Guards occupied it that night.

The 2nd Battalion meanwhile had been responsible for the left flank of the Division and after co-operating with a Grenadier Battalion in the capture of Le Prieure Wood had been screening Emieville, which the enemy still held. Among the casualties in this their first day in battle was Lieutenant Rex Whistler, who was killed while commanding a troop of the 2nd Battalion's tanks. His death was an irreparable loss not only to the Regiment but to England, for in the hearts of his friends and in British art he occupied a unique place.

The diary of No. 1 Squadron (Major A. A. Bushell) illustrates the kind of day they had : "18*th July*. Squadron moved on at 0900 hrs.... Delay in getting through taped gap in minefield.... First heavy fire encountered on line Ste Honorine-Escoville.... Squadron Sergeant-Major W. J. Rodd severely wounded in head.... Nos. 1, 2, and 3 Troops now engaged by anti-tank gunfire from Squadron objective, Le Prieure Wood, and No. 4 Troop with self-propelled guns went up to support them. Situation very confused as a tank unit of another division had attacked unsuccessfully and withdrawn, leaving four tanks burning.... Attack organised in co-operation with a company of Grenadiers.... Attack cleared orchard and houses but had to re-form and mop up again as men were holding out in dug-outs all round the banks of the orchard.... Captain Fisher's tank hit by mortar, caught fire but was extinguished and recovered the next day. Nos. 4 and 5 Troops were pushed forward and encountered three Panther tanks late in the evening, but without conclusive results—one knocked out and the others withdrew.... harboured about 2100 hrs."

Next day the 1st Battalion were ordered to capture the village of Le Poirier to the south of Cagny. The attack started at five o'clock, No. 2 Company under Major M. J. Turnbull and No. 4 Company under Major J. D. A. Syrett leading the attack. They met only light opposition: a few Germans were taken prisoner and a few got away; and the companies dug in on the outskirts of the village. They remained there till the 22nd. Patrols led by Lieutenant V. G. Wallace and Lance-Corporal Eric Fletcher, the successful mortaring of the posts they located, and the shooting down of an enemy plane provided the chief incidents. The weather changed and "a four-day downpour of warm rain turned the clouds of yellow dust into a two-foot deep, creamy mud. We were dug-in in a big potato field where we were subjected by day and night to heavy German mortar and shell fire, and after one particularly bad night of shelling and continuous rain, morale and spirits were low for the first time. 'Stand to' came about 0330 hours and every man was soaked to the skin standing in his trench that was half-full of water. Officers and men alike were feeling pretty miserable for they could not get out of their holes because of the continuous bursts of shells and mortar bombs. Suddenly, flying very low, a Messerschmidt fighter aircraft came skimming over the trees. I'm afraid 'fire control' rather went to the wind; each man seemed to realise that at last here was something they could shoot back at. Every man raised his weapon and as the aeroplane roared overhead it was met by a hail of fire from rifles, Bren guns, Sten guns, revolvers and even Guardsman Bradley on the Piat sent a bomb rocketing into the air after the raider. Believe it or not, a miracle happened; the German engine faltered, stopped and the aircraft crashed two fields away. A wild cheer went up as the men saw it fall. All their unhappiness of the night disappeared. Each man *knew* that it was *his* bullet that had shot the German down and the bedraggled, mudspattered company started singing and laughing as they cleaned their weapons and waited for breakfast to come up." But Major Syrett was killed by shell fire and Captain W. D. D. Evans took command of No. 4 Company.

The 2nd Battalion sent squadrons daily to watch the country between Cagny and Emieville. Here are diary entries for their first and their last days there. "19*th July*. Three patrols under Lieutenant N. S. Kearsley, Sergeant E. F. Mabey and Lieutenant H. W. J. E. Peel to area of Emieville; Peel 'brewed up' one Tiger. 22*nd July*. Three patrols to Emieville. Squadron ordered to cover village from east. All No. 7 Troop tanks bogged about 1300 hrs. within two hundred yards of strong enemy position. One tank abandoned. 1330 hrs., Sergeant John's tank blown up on a mine; his and the Lance-Sergeant's tank both recovered. 1630 hrs., Captain I. M. Stewart's tank 'brewed up' by direct hit from shell—no casualties. 2200 hrs., returned to laager. Losses, three tanks, no personnel. Very lucky day."

The abandoned tank was found next day apparently undisturbed, but in fact the Germans had booby-trapped it in the interval and when the squadron's armoured recovery vehicle went to tow it out it was itself blown up.

In every fighting battalion there is a First Aid Post where the Medical Officer and the men who help him deal with personnel casualties. In every armoured battalion there is also a Light Aid Detachment to deal with wounded tanks. Welsh Guardsmen of the 2nd Armoured Battalion had been carefully trained to do the skilled work necessary to maintain their tanks in good working order and to carry out minor running repairs. But more advanced engineering skill and special plant and equipment were needed to deal with badly damaged tanks and these were supplied by the L.A.D. Captain D. W. J. Harrowell and his staff were members of the Corps which is familiarly known as R.E.M.E., that is The Royal Corps of Electrical and Mechanical Engineers. His chief of staff was Quartermaster-Sergeant A. C. Cook, a man who made a great reputation in the Battalion. Under him were three Staff-Sergeants and twenty-two other ranks. Their plant and equipment consisted of two heavy recovery vehicles fitted with cranes and winches; two three-ton lorries carrying spare parts, materials and stores; a 15-cwt. lorry to carry personnel and another fitted as a wireless truck; an armoured half-track truck (*i.e.*, wheels in front and tracks behind) carrying a welding plant; a White scout car (also armoured), a jeep and two motor-cycle despatch riders. With each squadron there was also a light recovery vehicle, that is a tank without the gun turret, carrying a R.E.M.E. Sergeant and a skilled vehicle mechanic.

Captain Harrowell's scout car was seldom very far behind the scene of fighting, and it was a matter of pride with him and his men that a damaged tank was made fighting fit again as quickly as possible. The casualty would be reported on the wireless by Captain N. M. Daniel the Battalion Technical Adjutant. He would then go forward if it was at all possible and decide whether repair could be done on the spot, or whether the tank must be brought back to the L.A.D. (usually with the Battalion transport) or whether it must go back to hospital—that is the Brigade workshops. If it could be towed back by the squadron's armoured recovery vehicle (which played a part similar to that of stretcher-bearers in an infantry battalion), well and good. If it could not be towed, the heavy recovery vehicle—the ambulance of the tanks—came up to collect it. So skilful and so zealous were these L.A.D. men that many a tank blown up on a mine or hit by shell fire was back in action in a very few days. In the fighting in Normandy they worked not only through the day but often through the night as well, with tank tarpaulins spread over them to hide the light of their lamps. They are among those whose service though essential is apt to be unrecognised except by the Battalion concerned. *They* are not likely to undervalue it, and Captain Harrowell and his men will not be forgotten by Welsh Guardsmen who served in the 2nd Battalion.

On the 23rd of July the Guards Armoured Division was withdrawn into reserve, for the battle known in Orders as "Operation Goodwood" had ended. To those taking part in it it seemed an untidy and inconclusive affair, but as explained elsewhere (see page 54) its principal purpose was achieved. For it engaged the main enemy forces while away in the west the Americans prepared to initiate the real breakout from the bridgehead.

GERMAN "TIGER" (56 TONS) WITH 88 mm. GUN.

FIGHTING IN THE "BOCAGE"

"The Americans attacked on July the 25th and, overcoming the enemy's resistance, broke out of St. Lo and spread rapidly southwards. On July the 30th British armoured and infantry forces launched a major attack on the left flank of the Americans, striking south through Caumont." (Part I, page 55.)

THE fighting which engaged the Welsh Guards Battalions in the first fortnight of August was largely conditioned by the nature of the country in this part of Normandy. The "Bocage" country is a lovely intimate land of hill and valley, richly clad in woods and orchards and starred with little stone-built villages where a few farms and cottages cluster round the church. Roads and lanes run between deeply banked hedges and the streams in its valleys flow happily and unpolluted. For it is purely agricultural. No chimneys of industry disfigure its beauty. Its chief machinery—the unhurried ox-drawn plough—is in perfect harmony with quietly growing crops.

But it is country which is better suited to defence than attack. Woods and hedgerows abound to hide the enemy. Steep banks and close country control the movements of advancing armour and every rise of the road and every bend may hide a lurking Tiger or a deadly 88 mm. gun. In the dry August heat clouds of dust rose to give the enemy good notice of any movement on road or track.

Both Battalions moved southwards to the neighbourhood of St. Martin des Besaces on August the first, and while they lay there the 1st Battalion were ordered to clear St. Denis-Maisoncelles, three miles away to the south. The deployed companies had a hot and tiring day, working slowly through the thick country, but there was little opposition and by the evening they had occupied the ridge on which the village rests. Captain W. D. D. Evans (No. 4 Company) patrolled forward to La Ferriere, where he made contact with the American troops on our right. Lieutenant P. C. Luxmoore-Ball and Sergeant G. P. Hill were killed by mortar fire as they were digging in that night.

Next day the advance of the Division was continued. Both Battalions were involved, but they fought separately and it will be convenient to deal first with the 2nd Battalion. For during the next few days they were to perform for the first time the role for which they had been specially trained—the role of an Armoured Reconnaissance Battalion covering the divisional front.

The squadrons began to move south at first light. They had little to fear on the west as the American drive had freed them from danger on that flank; but in the country east of their road the enemy still held his ground tenaciously. Infantry were to take St. Pierre Tarentaine, but the high ground between Montamy and Montchamp had then to be conquered and beyond that lay more high ground near Estry.

Three reconnaissance tasks were set the Battalion. Part of No. 2 Squadron (Major J. O. Spencer) was to reconnoitre the road from Catheolles towards Montamy; No. 1 Squadron (Major A. A. Bushell) was to reconnoitre the road from Catheolles to Montcharivel; and while these two squadrons probed the enemy's country on the left flank, No. 3 Squadron under Major W. L. Consett was to push boldly south through St. Charles de Percy and try to secure the high ground near Estry.

The squadrons had no difficulty in reaching first Le Tourneur and then Catheolles; and while No. 3 Squadron moved down through St. Charles de Percy we may see what happened to the others when they felt their way into the enemy's positions on their left.

(a) THE ROAD TO MONTAMY.

Lieutenant D. A. Gibbs soon proved that Montamy was firmly held and that the enemy had infantry, tanks and anti-tank guns covering the road to the village. He had nearly crawled into an infantry position and his troop had been shot at by tanks and guns in carrying out this reconnaissance, but he succeeded in withdrawing them to screen St. Pierre till infantry who had already reached the village were reinforced. Then No. 2 Squadron was ordered to withdraw and to follow No. 3 Squadron southwards.

(b) THE ROAD TO MONTCHARIVEL.

The road to Montcharivel runs up a narrow valley. On one side a thickly wooded hill rises steeply, the trees at the foot overhanging the road. Before the hills rise on the other side of the valley a river runs through a belt of marsh-land beside the road. Steep woods on one hand and the river on the other effectively confine advancing armour to the narrow and often blind road. Major Bushell's squadron was of necessity strung out thinly in single file and in spite of some mortaring, sniping from the woods and one attack by infantry at close quarters they made steady if slow progress. Then as the leading tank commanded by Lance-Sergeant Thomas Hughes of Wrexham was approaching Montcharivel over a slight rise of the road it was knocked out by shell fire and burst into flames. The road was effectively blocked and the long column was halted. While they waited for orders Guardsman J. Lewis from the tank that had been knocked out came limping slowly down the road. He had several leg wounds and had been dreadfully burnt about the face, neck and hands while trying vainly to extricate Sergeant Hughes from the burning tank. He had struggled back over a mile to warn the squadron that the gun which had hit them was only fifty yards off the road and was bound to hit any other tank that tried to cross the rise. The great pain he was in did not prevent his thinking first of the safety of his comrades.

It was clear that armour could not proceed by this road. The squadron was ordered to return and in due course they too were to join the other squadrons in the south.

(c) THE RIDGE BY ESTRY.

No. 3 Squadron had shown great enterprise. After reaching St. Charles de Percy they found that Courteil was strongly held as well as Montchamp. Undeterred by this threat to their line of advance, they by-passed both places and pushed on to their objective. There were pockets of enemy well behind them when they reached the country south of La Marvindière and patrols found that Estry was strongly held. But they deployed on the high ground and were able to keep a considerable range of country under observation. Later the other two squadrons

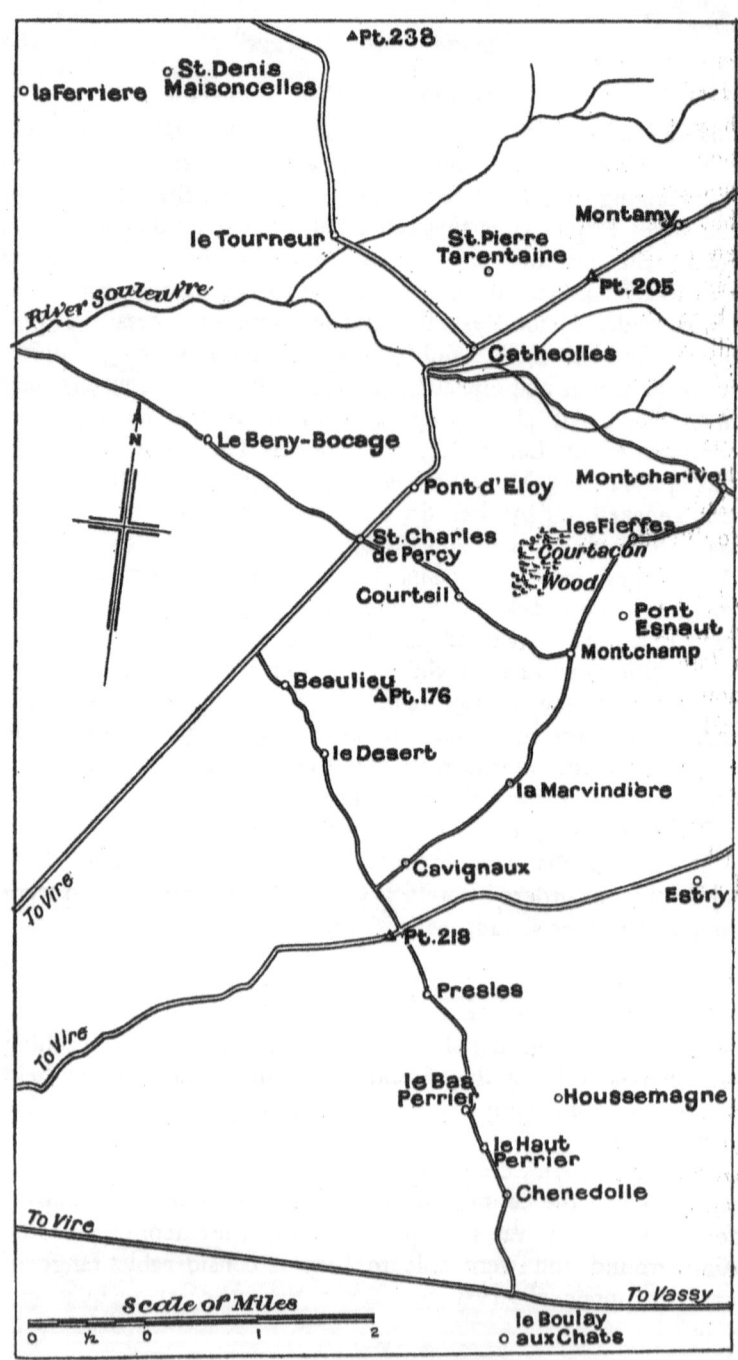

THE "BOCAGE" COUNTRY.

(NOTE.—Minor roads and lanes, of which there are many, are not shown.)

came up to occupy ground near Cavignaux and north-east of La Marvindière. This was August the 2nd and they remained there for forty-eight hours. They had no infantry to support them; they were in enemy territory and they were attacked by infantry and constantly sniped, shelled and mortared. During that night a German patrol armed with a bazooka got within a few yards of one troop and destroyed a tank. Sergeant Thomas Canavan took four men and, leading them through the orchard where the squadron was harboured, dispersed the Germans, killing two and capturing their bazooka. But another tank was hit during that night and the wireless operator very severely wounded. Canavan helped to get him out of the tank, gave him first-aid treatment and nursed him through the night; when the wounded man reached the Regimental Aid Post next day the Medical Officer said that Canavan's care for him had undoubtedly saved his life.

It should perhaps be explained that the German weapon which is referred to as a bazooka was somewhat similar to an American weapon of that name, but was called by the Germans a *Panzerfaust*. Bazooka may be regarded as a popular translation and as such it will be used in these pages, as it was in the daily speech of the Battalion.

Two quotations from a diary show the discomfort of their position.

August the 4th. "No. 3 Squadron were attacked in harbour last night and had a man killed and two wounded, including Lieutenant Hon. A. B. Mildmay (slightly) when his tank was bazooka'd. We (No. 1 Squadron) started this morning at 0530 and immediately ran into trouble in the shape of a Mark IV tank and two Panthers, well concealed in a locality we had been told was held by our side. Ivor Froystad was blasted off the top of his scout car, but unhurt. Lieutenant J. H. Carson's leading tank was knocked out, and the leading tank in Lieutenant A. W. S. Wheatley's troop. . . . Ivor shot and killed the commander of the German Mark IV with his pistol and took another German prisoner, but unfortunately the man escaped in the confusion."

August the 5th. "This has been a most confused day, with any amount of sniping and also some trouble from two Panthers

—one was knocked out but the other hit one of our fitters' vehicles. A man in this vehicle was killed and another wounded. . . . Sergeant E. J. Myddleton (Intelligence Sergeant), who was visiting us with the Commanding Officer and the Intelligence Officer, went to bury the man killed and was mortally wounded in the head by a sniper. Colonel Jim (Lieutenant-Colonel J. C. Windsor Lewis), though under the fire of snipers, dragged him into a trench without any thought of his own safety. There are so many isolated German positions which are giving trouble that 'the fog of war' locally was as complete as yesterday. . . ." Ivor Froystad was a Norwegian officer who was attached to the Battalion. He drove in a scout car, usually ahead of everyone; for he was an enthusiastic soldier and recklessly daring ; his one desire was to get to close quarters with the enemy.

They patrolled aggressively by day and closed in for self-protection at night. They lost several tanks and had some sad casualties. Captain J. C. R. Homfray was killed and Lieutenant R. G. Whiskard and Lieutenant R. D. Stevens ; and there were five others killed and twenty wounded. It was almost impossible at first to get to them and Captain J. S. Gwatkin, taking up water and petrol on the 3rd of August, had an adventurous journey, meeting the enemy well in rear of the squadron. He started by a route through Point 176, but found that it was in enemy hands, so he turned back and made a long detour by Beaulieu and Le Desert. It was late evening when they started. "All went well till the calvary at Le Desert. Here there was a number of little roads and I wasn't sure of the way even with a map. Some 3rd Division men were moving up (the first we knew of their existence in this area) and they advised me that there were German tanks about a mile down the road to the right—the way I should have gone." He tried another way and "after a bend in the lane we came to a sinister avenue of great birch trees, at the end of which through a tunnel of foliage stood a ghostly, deserted chateau. . . . We approached gingerly but nothing appeared and we turned on to the road. Shooting was going on at the end of it about four hundred yards away." He left two guides at the chateau and two at the next cross-roads, reached the squadrons, delivered their supplies and started back. "When we came to pick up the guides at the chateau turning they were not at first to be found, and when they did appear it was to tell us that they had had a skirmish with a German patrol." Finally when he got back to St. Charles de Percy "there was a great deal of shooting. A Bren gunner was in position covering the cross-roads. I stopped to ask him if anything was going on. He said that a German patrol had come into the village a few minutes earlier but that it was now clear." All of which illustrates the confusing conditions of those days when the squadrons were near Estry and the enemy was liable to be found at any point behind them from Le Desert or Point 176 to St. Charles de Percy, five miles in their rear. A further illustration is the fact that on August the 3rd, in his Regimental Aid Post by the roadside, Captain Charles G. Irwin, the Medical Officer of the 2nd Battalion, dealt with sixty-one casualties, from eight different units, in one period of three hours. He was greatly helped by three men who worked with him throughout the campaign ; Lance-Sergeant H. Davies, who in civil life was a mental nurse from Stafford ; Lance-Sergeant J. Mann of the Carmarthenshire Police ; and Lance-Corporal L. E. Parsons, formerly employed in the Birmingham milk trade. Both the Medical Officer and the wounded owed a great deal to the skill and unwearying devotion of these men and to stretcher-bearers who, though referred to later in connection with particular actions, would, if space allowed, find a place in all. The noise of battle came nearer on their last day while the fighting raged at Montchamp and that night they were withdrawn. They had admirably fulfilled their role, sending back valuable information, screening the Divisional front and denying the enemy use of a strong position.

Meanwhile the 1st Battalion was playing another part in the Division's advance.

St. Pierre Tarentaine.

Lieutenant D. A. Gibbs' reconnaissance towards Montamy on August the 2nd has already been told briefly. When the news that he was held up on the Catheolles-Montamy road reached the 1st Battalion they were already embussed and on the road near St. Denis Maisoncelles and prepared to move south. There they waited for the road ahead to be cleared.

Prince of Wales Company had finished digging in near St. Denis Maisoncelles at about midnight. At half past three in the morning they had been ordered to move to high ground on the east of the road (Point 238 on the map). They did this and there dug in again. At half past eight they embussed on the road with the rest of the Battalion and they waited with them till mid-day. Then Major J. M. Miller was ordered to clear some woods near St. Pierre Tarentaine ; to capture the village ; and to seize and hold Point 205 on the road to Montamy. Two troops of tanks of the 1st Armoured Battalion Coldstream Guards were to support them but these were delayed by a variety of causes and the Company had to go forward without waiting for their arrival.

The first wood-clearing operation was easy for the wood contained no enemy ; St. Pierre was no problem for it was not occupied by the Germans but by the King's Company, 1st Battalion Grenadier Guards. But while Major Miller was organising for the advance on Point 205, heavy shell fire came down on St. Pierre and Sergeant Evan Helling (from Thomastown, Glamorganshire) had his section of Company Headquarters wiped out except for one man.

The first step was to secure a road junction about a thousand yards short of the objective and this was done. Then Sergeant A. A. Seamark led No. 3 platoon forward on the left of the road and after making good some scattered houses found the enemy just short of the objective. His platoon held them by frontal fire while Lieutenant D. A. Rogers with No. 2 Platoon attacked the left flank, and the enemy, taken by surprise, abandoned the position. Those who were not shot made off hurriedly. The company had got their objective, but civilians told them that Montamy was strongly occupied ; there had been heavy machine-gun fire from their right and tanks were heard moving in front. They were in fact in a dangerously isolated position and the promised support of our own tanks had not materialised. It was therefore with relief that they received orders to withdraw through St. Pierre and to pass through Catheolles to Le Pont d'Eloy. This was three miles from St. Pierre and it was midnight before they got there. Then they completed an exhausting day by digging in for the third time in twenty-four hours.

Montchamp.

The whole of the 1st Battalion was concentrated near Pont d'Eloy by the night of August the 2nd and remained there till the morning of August the 4th. As the companies dug in it was evident that parties of the enemy were not far off. Two men with a Spandau opened up on Captain Sir R. G. D. Powell from close quarters as he was helping to arrange the lay-out of Prince of Wales Company. He stalked and shot one but the other got away. Next day a water-truck of No. 3 Company took a wrong turning and almost at once found itself on top of an enemy post, which promptly opened fire. The two men on the truck dived for cover and managed to crawl away, and a friendly Frenchman hid them in a nearby farm for twenty-four hours, when they rejoined; the truck was also recovered a few days later in good working order. These stories, especially if they are read in conjunction with the account of the 2nd Battalion's squadrons near Estry, show how difficult it was in this close country to know where the enemy were or to be certain that a particular piece of country had been finally cleared.

On the afternoon of August the 3rd the Battalion was put under the temporary command of the 44th Brigade of the 15th Scottish Division. The Brigade was to attack eastwards astride the high ridge which stretches to the north of Montchamp, and the Welsh Guards were to form the right or southern wing of the attack. Their first task was to clear the large Courtacon wood, and they started at half-past six on the morning of August the 4th after an artillery barrage, laid down on the German forward positions, had done its work well. For when the companies moved forward in the early morning mist they met little opposition. Having captured about twenty prisoners, they reached their objectives on the eastern edge of the wood and No. 3 and No. 4 Company went on to capture Les Fieffes and cut the road running south to Montchamp.

From the hillside above the north-east corner of Courtacon wood, Major Miller looked down on Montchamp (the sketch facing page 190 was done from the place where he sat). With him was Major G. T. Hollebone observing for the artillery. "He has always accompanied the Battalion and has given support beyond all praise," but on this day he was not afforded the chance. He and Miller could see enemy transport going in and out of Montchamp, but they could not get the Brigade's permission to shell it. Instead the enemy shelled the Battalion's positions and five men were killed and a number wounded.

There was one macabre incident which made a deep impression on those who saw it. A platoon of No. 3 Company was dug in behind hedges astride the road which runs downhill from Les Fieffes to Montchamp. A heavy German truck drove up to their position with two men in the front cab and one on the roof. All but the driver had their hands up, and when the truck stopped a Corporal and two Guardsmen covered them and stepped out to take them prisoners. At once the canvas cover in rear was raised and two men with a machine-gun inside opened fire, wounding all three Guardsmen. The Piat was promptly fired at the cab by two men who had remained in the roadside post and grenades were thrown into the body. All the Germans were killed instantly except the man on the cab roof. He knelt, terribly wounded, and swaying backwards and forwards began to sing a weird song, his voice growing fainter and fainter. The spectacle seemed to fascinate the men who, forgetting military caution, left their slits and gathered round to gaze on this strange scene. One, more compassionate, climbed up to help the wounded German down; and at once a machine gun opened from a farmhouse a hundred and fifty yards away, killing him instantly. The others got to cover. But the shots set fire to the truck and the singing was finally subdued as the crackling flames made a funeral pyre for the singer and his comrades.

About three o'clock in the afternoon the Welsh Guards were ordered to turn south and take Montchamp. Lieutenant-Colonel C. H. R. Heber-Percy decided that first he would make sure of his left flank by capturing Pont Esnaut which overlooks the road running east of Montchamp. Captain W. D. D. Evans was ordered to do this with No. 4 Company, and Major G. G. Fowke with No. 3 Company was to occupy ground between Pont Esnaut and Montchamp. This first phase opened at half-past five in the afternoon and was completed without much difficulty. A good bag of prisoners was taken and half an hour later Prince of Wales Company and No. 2 Company (Major

Montchamp, in Normandy
by
L. F. Ellis

M. J. Turnbull) attacked Montchamp. As Prince of Wales Company were leaving their trenches another enemy concentration came down on them and they suffered seventeen casualties before reaching their start line. Moreover they had no time to reorganise, for our own artillery had begun a three-minute shoot on Montchamp and it was important to move in promptly behind it. However, "the men were in good heart and eager to have their revenge for those we had lost during the last hour or two."

No. 2 Company on the right were to take the western half of Montchamp, Prince of Wales Company the left or eastern half. They moved through the fields on the east of the Montchamp–Les Fieffes road and had only gone a few hundred yards when they came upon two tanks—a Mark IV with a Panther behind it. Captain Sir Richard Powell, who was with Prince of Wales Company's leading platoon, crawled forward with a Piat. He could hear the Germans talking inside the Mark IV, which had its turret closed for action, and from within a few yards he "let the tank have it. There was a hole in the side where my shot had hit so I hoped they had been roasted." But the Panther's machine gun opened on him and though he was not hit the Piat was put out of action. (He needed it badly later on.) The Panther then retired hurriedly and Prince of Wales Company pushed on behind it into Montchamp. Both they and No. 2 Company had to deal with some snipers there and both had a little street fighting; but the Germans were running away wherever they could and the companies had soon cleared their areas and moved out to consolidate in the gardens and orchards on the south.

The tanks which were to support them had not yet entered the village and the Battalion anti-tank guns had not yet joined them when a German counter-attack with tanks and infantry came in. No. 2 Company was just lining the hedge of a field when the first tank pushed its gun through the hedge and machine-gun fire opened from several directions. Major Turnbull, almost beside the tank, was killed and the company was cut in half. Part fell back on the village. About fifty who were on the extreme right followed suit later, when the general retirement was ordered. Lieutenant D. M. Lester, who was doing a reconnaissance on the right flank, was killed. Through

Major Maurice Turnbull's death the Regiment lost a valued officer and Wales a great sportsman; he captained Glamorganshire County Cricket Club and was a Welsh International for Rugby football and hockey.

Meanwhile Prince of Wales Company had been over-run by tanks, which got right among them just as they were beginning to dig in, and at the same time German infantry coming up in half-tracks opened machine-gun fire from many points. The Company were ordered to fall back, but while the tanks were among them organised withdrawal as a company was impossible. Lieutenant D. A. Rogers extricated a party of about twenty and others got away in small groups, but casualties were heavy. Major Miller and Powell had been in front giving orders for digging-in when the tanks drove into their position. There was no Piat with them so Powell attacked the nearest with hand grenades and got one in among the crew: but at that moment two more tanks came up to within twenty yards of them. Major Miller, waiting to the last to supervise the withdrawal, succeeded in helping a wounded man to get away, but Powell was less successful. He was looking after Guardsman Raymond Lewis from the Rhondda Valley, who had been hit in both legs and could move but slowly, when Guardsman W. K. Smith from Llanelly saw another tank approaching. "We climbed out of the sunken lane and lay down, trying to hide ourselves in the short grass. The tank came up the lane and to our dismay stopped not four yards from us. Slowly it turned its turret and I looked straight into its long barrel. I had thrown all my grenades. Smith and I were lying as close as two pencils in a box. There came what seemed a colossal explosion. I felt Smith lurch against me. He said, quite calmly, 'I'm afraid they've got me, Sir,' and as he died a second explosion seemed to blow my head off—I don't remember any more." In fact Powell was knocked out and carried off by the Germans while he was unconscious; but he was not badly wounded and after various adventures of which the story would be out of place here he made a most daring escape and rejoined his Battalion some weeks later.

Just before the counter-attack began a sniper in civilian clothes shot Lieutenant-Colonel Heber-Percy as he moved towards Montchamp behind the attacking companies. Luckily the wound was not fatal and the sniper was caught and killed. The Second-in-Command, Major J. F. Gresham, had been left out of the battle on this occasion and Major Fowke took temporary command. When the news that the companies were being over-run by tanks began to come in he ordered them to fall back and consolidate on a line north of the village ; and on getting news that No. 4 Company at Pont Esnaut were being steadily surrounded he ordered Captain Evans to withdraw in conformity with the rest of the Battalion. By steady and skilful leadership at all levels, what might easily have been a disaster was turned to success. At nightfall the Battalion held a well-organised line, with companies in good fighting positions facing Montchamp and with supporting arms covering them. Doubtless realising this, the enemy withdrew in the night and in the morning Montchamp was ours.

The measure of success which the Germans had that day was due to the fact that elements of the 9th S.S. Panzer Division were near enough to counter-attack before the companies could dig in and when no supporting tanks or anti-tank guns were in position to help them ; and it was very fleeting. Though the enemy killed and wounded over a hundred they neither saved Montchamp nor damaged the fighting capacity of the Battalion. For three days later they successfully attacked again.

Le Bas Perrier and Houssemagne.

Two days after Montchamp the 1st Battalion moved to Courteil to take over from the Irish Guards. The 2nd Battalion already lay handy. On August the 9th the 1st Battalion moved southwards again, for the battle had already gone forward and the country which had been seized by the 2nd Battalion while Montchamp was still in enemy hands was now well behind the front.

On the 9th of August the 1st Battalion left Courteil at half-past ten at night and, after passing Cavignaux and crossing the Vire–Estry road at Point 218 (see map), they completed an eight miles march at three o'clock in the morning and took over positions round Le Bas Perrier from the 1st Battalion Herefordshire Regiment. They were very uncomfortable positions. The enemy held Le Haut Perrier in front of them, Houssemagne on their left flank and the long ridge north of Houssemagne which lay well behind them. They took over in darkness and learned from the Herefords that their forward positions were overlooked and liable to be heavily shelled and mortared, and that in some places the enemy were dug in only a few hundred yards away. They spent the rest of the night deepening the slit trenches that were too shallow for Guardsmen and drove off an enemy patrol which approached No. 3 Company's line. Through the next day they were shelled intermittently with an accuracy which underlined the warning that they were overlooked. In the afternoon they received orders for an attack on the following morning with the object of taking Le Haut Perrier and Chenedolle and of pushing south to cut the Vire-Vassy road. A battalion of Coldstream Guards was also to be employed and there would be tank support from a battalion of 5th Guards Armoured Brigade and also from the 6th Guards Armoured Brigade, which was not included in the Guards Armoured Division. Colonel W. D. C. Greenacre, who had been so largely responsible for training the 2nd Battalion Welsh Guards as an armoured battalion, was appointed Brigadier and given command of this Brigade shortly after this action. He commanded the Brigade throughout subsequent campaigns to its triumphant conclusion in Germany. The fight at Le Haut Perrier was, however, the only occasion on which the Brigade fought with the Guards Armoured Division.

The 1st Battalion were given two tasks in the coming fight—namely, (*a*) to continue the attack southwards by capturing Le Haut Perrier, so that the Coldstream Guards could go on to take Chenedolle and, (*b*) to gain "elbow room" on the flank by capturing Houssemagne and the ridge to the north of it. Lieutenant-Colonel J. F. Gresham, who was now commanding the 1st Battalion, gave the former task to No. 2 Company and No. 3 Company and the latter to Prince of Wales Company and No. 4 Company. On this occasion they had ample time for careful preparations. As far as the country allowed, reconnaissance of the line of advance was made before nightfall. There was also a careful tie-up with the armoured squadrons who were to support them and targets for the artillery support were registered. As cooking was not possible in their exposed positions, hot meals in containers were sent up from the rear after dark that night and again just before daybreak next morning.

(a) THE ATTACK SOUTHWARDS.

The attack on Le Haut Perrier opened at half-past six on the morning of August the 11th, and No. 2 Company reached their objective, a line of country away to the left of the village, without meeting serious opposition. No. 3 Company on the other hand, took three and a half hours to advance some four hundred yards and capture what is no more than a tiny hamlet. The reason is not hard to discern. Le Haut Perrier stands on the highest ground in the vicinity, on the road running south, and the Germans had decided to hold it strongly. They had not many infantry there, but there were nine separate machine-gun posts spaced out along the hedges in mutually supporting positions; there were three Panther tanks dug in and three more in support. There was at least one mortar, and the whole was covered by artillery with good observation. They had the use of the few houses and plenty of hedges and orchards to hide their movements.

The enemy replied to our opening barrage with a heavy discharge of mortars which caught No. 3 Company as they were forming up for the attack. They suffered twenty casualties, among the killed being Lieutenant J. E. Reid and "at half-past six the company crossed the start line with cries of 'let's get at the bastards!'" Two fields were made good by No. 7 Platoon on the right of the main road and a machine-gun post was silenced before they were held up by more machine-guns in front and on the flank. The Churchill tanks of the 3rd Scots Guards came up to support them and sprayed the hedges with Besa fire mercilessly. But Lieutenant P. R. Leuchars, who was commanding the company, saw that to tackle the machine guns away on their right would lead them off their objective and he decided to concentrate the company for a left-hand attack on the village. No. 7 Platoon accordingly slipped through the hedges which line the road, leaving only a couple of snipers to watch the right flank.

About half-way to the village a line of hedges crossed their front leading on the left into a sunken lane. No. 7 Platoon now occupied this hedge-line while Leuchars went to contact No. 8 Platoon, who were farther forward on the left of No. 7. They had reached the outskirts of the village and had silenced a machine-gun post when two more opened on them and held them up. One of the Scots Guards tanks supporting them was blown up on a mine, but the crew managed to escape and continued to fight as infantry for the rest of the battle. A dug-in Panther and a mortar were also spotted and Sergeant E. Williams moved his platoon back to the sunken road. Meanwhile Lieutenant D. J. C. Stevenson with Sergeant R. G. Fowles and five Guardsmen had made an eventful sortie from No. 7 Platoon. Recrossing the main road, they had crept forward to the first two houses, knocked out a machine-gun post and killed two snipers. They were about to rejoin their platoon when a nearby Panther sent an armour-piercing shell into the house they had cleared and killed Guardsman W. E. Bowen who was standing with his back to the wall ; the rest got back safely. Shortly after this the enemy put down a mortar concentration mixed with smoke which screened the village and suggested that either a counter-attack or a withdrawal was being covered. While the smoke lasted the company could see little, but the Scots Guards tanks worked out to their flank, spotted three Panthers moving and promptly knocked out all three. The company were loud in praise of the work done by the 3rd Battalion Scots Guards that day—"Even when their tanks were hit (they lost two) they came and joined the infantry. One Lance-Sergeant borrowed No. 7 Platoon's Piat to go and deal with a Panther which had knocked out his tank. He came back with his hand bleeding and the Piat in pieces. He then grabbed a rifle and went back again. That was the last I saw of him. Another driver with both legs blown off was incredibly brave."

When the smoke-screen lifted the company advanced on the village and entered now without much opposition, killing a few Germans who remained and taking nine prisoners. No. 8 Platoon went to the far end of the village and had hardly reached their objective when "the ominous clank of tank tracks was heard on the road and round the corner of a hedge came one more Panther. Its huge gun was swinging from side to side—a monster seeking its prey; the tank commander was looking out of the top and had obviously seen nothing. The first two shots from No. 8 Platoon's Piat missed, but the third hit it squarely beside the driver's seat, a loud explosion occurred and immediately flames burst from the crippled tank. In a very few seconds the fire was raging and ammunition started exploding. Only one of the crew got out and he was promptly 'seen off' by a light machine gun. Nobody was in the mood for taking prisoners. The village was a complete shambles. Among the broken and battered and burning houses and the torn and tattered remnants of apple trees which had been green and peaceful a few hours before lay two Panthers well alight and a third with a neat hole through the turret, its engine still running and its wireless still working; they were part of the Scots Guards bag." By ten in the morning Le Haut Perrier was ours. The Scots Guards tanks went on to Chenedolle to support the Coldstream Guards who had by-passed Le Haut Perrier while the Welsh Guards were fighting for it.

(b) THE FLANK ATTACK.

Prince of Wales Company and No. 4 Company started their move to push back the enemy on the left flank half an hour after the other two companies had launched their attack to the south. After their losses at Montchamp Prince of Wales Company were reduced to sixty-five men, organised in two platoons and Company Headquarters. This small force was set a very hard task in the capture of Houssemagne. After knocking out two machine-gun posts they reached the outskirts of the village, but there met more machine-guns and an 88 mm. anti-tank gun. At one point the company attacked some buildings across an open field, but the opposition when they got there was too much for them and Major Miller ordered them to draw back to the road. While Company Headquarters was doing so Lance-Corporal Frank William Dyke, the company clerk ("he was known as the C.I.G.S. of Prince of Wales Company") realised that Guardsman John Rogers (from Cardiff) who had been company storeman for years and was a much-loved member of the company, was not with them. Dyke ran back to the buildings under heavy fire and reappeared trundling Rogers, who was badly wounded in the leg, in a farm wheel-barrow. His bravery was rewarded, for in spite of being shot at from many angles they made the journey unscathed.

Tanks of the 1st Battalion Irish Guards "supported us magnificently," but the clearance of the village proved very difficult. The Irish Guards lost six tanks that day and Prince of Wales Company had thirty casualties—nearly half their small force. Eventually they consolidated on the south of the village with the remaining tanks covering them.

Meanwhile No. 4 Company attacking the ridge to the north of Houssemagne were heavily shelled as they started off. Lance-Corporal John Llewellyn Roberts (of Bangor), a stretcher-bearer who had already shown outstanding gallantry in other actions, distinguished himself in rescuing the wounded. Major Evans said of him, "he was always an inspiration to the whole company and one of the men I knew during the whole campaign of whom one could say that he knew no fear." Like No. 3 Company, No. 4 had the support of a squadron of Churchills from the 3rd Battalion Scots Guards, and as they went forward over flattish country intersected by banks and thick hedges the tanks sprayed every likely hiding-place with machine-gun fire; "they gave us a great feeling of confidence." Their objective was a sunken lane crossing their front and the leading tank was bazooka'd there at close quarters and caught fire. "The crew baled out with the exception of one man who was killed. Lieutenant Lord Bruce, who lost his leg, was got out with great difficulty by the others, who later continued the fight on foot with their pistols, a most impressive spectacle. . . . never had we had such splendid support."

With the support of the tanks and later of the guns of the Leicestershire Yeomanry, the more immediately troublesome enemy posts were gradually silenced, and an attempt by a party of German infantry to crawl into their position through the standing corn was driven off by grenades in a fight led by Company Quartermaster-Sergeant Urias Davies, acting that day as Company Sergeant-Major. So they held their objective throughout the day.

The Coldstream Guards had taken Chenedolle ("China Doll,"

the soldiers called it) and that evening the Welsh Guards were ordered to consolidate positions on the flank between Chenedolle and Le Haut Perrier. So No. 4 Company and Prince of Wales left the positions they had taken and moved to the south, and another brigade came up to take their place.

There had been one other incident that day which must be recorded. Captain A. Unwin, R.A.M.C., and his staff were busy with casualties in the Regimental Aid Post in a quarry by the roadside when three shells burst directly in it. Unwin and all of his staff except one Guardsman were wounded and seven of the casualties waiting to be evacuated were killed. Two men rose splendidly to the occasion. The Reverend P. F. Payne, C.F. (Padre Payne) had just returned from visiting a forward company: Lance-Corporal Roberts the No. 4 Company stretcher-bearer, whose gallant conduct has been mentioned already, had just brought in a casualty. These two took charge, pressed passing vehicles into service as ambulances, cleared the R.A.P. of dead and wounded and maintained it in action during the whole day with only one Guardsman to help them. Before a new Medical Officer came up in the evening they had evacuated over a hundred casualties. For the Battalion lost that day thirty-five killed and eighty-seven wounded. Lance-Corporal Roberts remained with the new Medical Officer throughout the night and all the following day. "He had himself been wounded in the wrist, but would not even consider leaving his post of duty." It was a fine example of leadership and organising ability in a young non-commissioned officer.

In writing of the Battalion's actions it is easy to concentrate on the rifle companies and omit reference to other essential parts of the Battalion. But the success or failure of the rifle companies in action depended not only on their own prowess or even on the support of artillery and tanks when this was available. Always and in every action the part played by the Support Company was essential since it included the Carrier Platoon, the Anti-tank Platoon, the 3-inch Mortar Platoon and the Assault Pioneer Platoon. The company was commanded at this time by Major H. E. J. Lister and his fine spirit and inexhaustible energy were an inspiration to all who came in contact with him. Nothing defeated him. If the nature of the country prevented carriers or anti-tank guns from reaching forward companies he got a bulldozer and made a "Lister Way." In this action he saw to it that carriers and mortars and anti-tank guns were made full use of and he was busy in so many ways that the Commanding Officer wrote afterwards: "He was a great source of strength to me. His disregard for himself and tireless energy were beyond all praise." His platoon commanders were: Carriers, Lieutenant J. F. R. Burchell; Mortars, Lieutenant Hon. D. R. Rhys (who was wounded next day); Anti-tank Guns, Lieutenant R. H. Mosse; Pioneers, Lieutenant R. P. Hedley-Dent. Burchell's father had been Signal Officer in the 1st Battalion in the 1914-18 war and was now in charge of signal instruction in the Training Battalion at Sandown Park.

In the next few days there was a good deal of active patrolling —Lieutenant T. C. H. Rettalack was wounded on one which destroyed an enemy machine-gun post, and Sergeant Stanley Gough with a section of carriers had a notable exploit on August the 13th. He led a reconnaissance patrol in daylight which penetrated about a mile into the enemy territory and was returning by another route when he came upon signs of the enemy. He explored further and discovered a dug-out with two men in it. Pulling them out, he was making his way back with his prisoners when fire was opened on him and his section from a nearby position. He gradually extricated his section by use of covering fire, returning twice through the bullet-swept area to lead his men to safety. "By his courage, resource and coolness he not only brought back his patrol without loss but managed to extract two prisoners of war in broad daylight under the eyes of their own comrades."

A few extracts from the Battalion's War Diary may close this story of the last fight in Normandy :—*August the* 12*th*. "Daylight showed an impressive amount of knocked-out German tanks and abandoned equipment and it was obvious to any passers-by that the Battalion had given an outstandingly good account of itself. . . ." *August the* 14*th*. "The Battalion area is certainly far from pleasant as its chief amenities consist of dead cows, dead Germans and burnt-out tanks. Thanks to the untiring labours of Padre Payne, all our dead have now had a proper and reverent burial and a small and carefully tended

burial ground has been formed just by Battalion Headquarters."
August the 15th. "It does really look as though the Germans are now pulling out in fact and not in the imagination of the 'I' staff. . . ." *August the 16th.* "The Battalion advanced on to the Vire–Vassy road without meeting resistance and Prince of Wales Company, assisted by a troop of Sappers, advanced right on to Point 227 by the village of Rully." This operation was known as "Operation Swan," and the War Diary adds a useful definition of the term "swanning." "It means roughly to wander over an area known to be a battlefield, in an unspecified and probably unknown direction, for an unnecessary and probably illegal purpose—and it is a term in very general use." The War Diary was written by the Adjutant, Captain J. M. Spencer-Smith.

Both Battalions were rested while the mouth of the Falaise pocket was being closed further east and until the time to advance to the Seine and drive on to Brussels. Much detail of the Welsh Guards' fighting in Normandy has of necessity been omitted from this story, and the parts played by other units have for the most part been left unmentioned. Only a far fuller account could tell of all that occurred in these hectic days, when there was no clearly defined front; when the twisting, dusty roads which cross the wooded hills or wind through narrow valleys were constantly shelled and death contested their use by the complex forces of an army crowding along them; when a detour to avoid one trouble might well lead to another and a route which was safe on one day might be covered by enemy fire the next; when, nevertheless, the Allies drove inexorably southwards and, if there was a temporary hold-up in one place, made good progress elsewhere. A full account would be as confusing to read as the fighting often seemed to those who were involved. By focusing from a distance on one part of the picture, the shape and outcome of the Welsh Guards' actions can be seen fairly clearly, but a closer view would show that their life was yet more crowded with unrecorded incident, tempered by unmentioned danger and rich in untold courage—and that all around them other units were having a similar experience.

THE ADVANCE TO BRUSSELS

"An armoured dash unequalled for speed in this or any other war." (*Part I, page* 66.)

ON the 28th of August both Welsh Guards Battalions left the pleasant country in Normandy, where they had been resting and licking their wounds, and started the long record-breaking advance which with ever-quickening pace led to Brussels. The German armies of Normandy had been everywhere broken and large forces had been annihilated in the Falaise pocket. The remnants were in full flight and after the Guards Armoured Division had crossed the Seine by Bailey bridges near Vernon the Division led the hunt into Belgium.

Friday, September the 1st, 1944, was a memorable day for both Battalions. It was the last occasion on which the 2nd Battalion fulfilled its role of battle reconnaissance in front of the Division. In Normandy the close Bocage country had given them no real chance to show their mettle. This time there was no such difficulty. The hedgeless, open country was not unlike the Yorkshire wolds on which they had trained. The enemy were in retreat and the Battalions' orders were to go as fast and as far as possible, by-passing opposition and sending information back. "Our advance began at dawn with No. 1 Squadron on the left, No. 2 on the right and No. 3 in reserve. Our objective was the Vimy Ridge by Arras and we went by small roads and across country. It soon became apparent that the enemy were completely disorganised. In some villages there was no resistance and quantities of Germans gave themselves up without even waiting for us to open fire. In other cases a token opposition was overcome by a few rounds from our leading tanks. Occasionally the enemy made a more determined attempt to delay us, but we by-passed serious resistance and pushed on as fast as the tanks would go. By eleven o'clock in the morning No. 1 Squadron alone had taken two hundred prisoners, whom we left the local Force Francaise Interieur to deal with. Soon afterwards we had the pleasure of shooting up a large quantity of German transport passing down a main road across our front. Great damage was done to vehicles and personnel. By early afternoon we had attained our objective and had begun moppingup operations in the area. Our advance had been mainly across country and against an exhausted and confused enemy, dependent almost entirely on horses and horse-drawn transport. Our job had been exhilarating and exciting and we had done all that was asked of us in a very short time."

The day was no less memorable for the 1st Battalion for they were the first troops to enter Arras, which they had been the last to leave in 1940. "To those of us who had lived in Arras for seven months in 1940 and who had held it to the last, it was a great event to enter the town again. The reception we had had in every town and village was tremendous. At one place an elderly Frenchman with an even older bugle stood by the road and blew 'Cookhouse at the double' as the Battalion went by. But Arras was the best." Their old friends turned out in full force, and Major Miller recovered most of the kit he had left there four years before, though his suitcase had been cut open by a German officer and his uniform taken out.

They moved on September the 2nd to the outskirts of Douai and there a series of marriages took place. For the Guards Armoured Division was reorganised in regimental groups; each consisted of one armoured and one infantry battalion of the same regiment, the 1st and 2nd Battalions forming the Welsh Guards Group. It was a most happy wedding of infantry and armour: battle experience had taught that neither arm could be fully effective without the support of the other and this linking of battalions of the same regiment secured the closest unity. The inter-battalion friendship which already existed was strengthened by team-work in battle and the spirit and tradition of the Regiment were given full scope.

They had a wonderful honeymoon next day which is vividly described by Lieutenant-Colonel J. C. Windsor Lewis, who commanded the Group. "We had moved that afternoon, Saturday, the 2nd of September, 1944, to an aerodrome near Douai; there, as we thought, to perform maintenance upon our long-suffering vehicles and to rest ourselves. For life this week had been gloriously hectic, with the peak our lightning advance across the Somme on Friday to capture by two o'clock that afternoon the high ground north of Arras, ground that had taken our fathers in an earlier war some years to capture. Vimy Ridge had been our objective, hallowed ground, soaked with the blood of Canadian, British and German soldiery of those far-away days.

"On arrival in the aerodrome at Vitry, near Douai, the Commanding Officer was warned for the Major-General's Order Group that evening. It was pouring with rain as the Brigadiers and Commanding Officers, with their staffs, assembled in the General's tent to receive orders, most of us expected, as to maintenance and the general enemy situation; few could have guessed their sensational character.

"General Adair's 'Intention' paragraph cut through the air like a swishing sword. 'Guards Armoured Division will advance and capture Brussels—and a very good intention, too,' added the General, wearing his most mischievous smile. This was greeted by roars of laughter from the keyed-up and astounded audience. The advance was to be dependent upon airborne droppings at certain key points just after first light; then, when these had been achieved successfully, the armoured advance was to begin. Two roads were to be used and the Division was to advance with two Brigades up. The newly formed Welsh Guards Battle Group was to lead on the right road, which ran to Brussels by way of Douai–St. Amand–Enghien–Hal. The left road, on which the Grenadier Group was to lead, ran along the famous and historical Tournai road to Brussels. If the airborne landings should be cancelled, and there was a chance that they might be, then our advance would begin at first light instead of much later. The distance to Brussels was just short of a hundred miles, and everybody in the Division prayed that these airborne landings would be cancelled, as we needed all of the day, and probably some of the night too, if we were to reach Brussels.

"Orders were given out and everybody went to bed very excited. Excitement rose to fever pitch when a message came through around midnight that the air operations had been cancelled, and that the advance would begin at first light. A stiff wind had risen after darkness and persisted until nearly dawn, but then died down completely. Possibly this wind had been the cause of the abandonment of the air landings; if so, it was not an ill wind.

"The start line was in Douai, and punctually at first light No. 1 Squadron and Prince of Wales Company started up engines and were ready for all and everything that lay ahead. Moving in front of us was a squadron of the 2nd Household Cavalry. It was a glorious day, and when the early morning mist and cold had disappeared, the sun quickly took its place and remained with us until it set with a fiery glow in the evening, what time the Welsh Guards Battle Group was fighting its way into the centre of Belgium's capital. The order was given to go all-out and all-out the leading squadron did go, except when held up by the reconnoitreing cars of the Household Cavalry Squadron. On several occasions during this enthralling advance, the leading squadron was double banking down the road with their armoured cars.

"And what of the enemy? Some weak opposition was reported by the armoured cars, but nothing serious encountered until the leading squadron bumped into a small infantry rear-guard well inside Belgium, at Leuze. This was dispersed in just over an hour by a combined action of infantry and tanks of the leading Squadron/Company Battle Group. It was here that Major M. W. T. Leatham, Commanding No. 1 Squadron, was wounded whilst outside his tank, a most unfortunate occurrence as it prevented him from seeing the finish of this glamorous adventure and set the seal on his fighting career for the war.

"The advance continued, growing faster as the roads grew better and wider. As the column approached each village, crowds of delirious citizens appeared, laughing and crying, throwing fruit and drink at the tank crews and yelling the latest, and what always proved to be extremely unreliable, information as to the enemy's whereabouts. The Maquis were there too, in full force, all with their own stories to tell of the 'Sal Boche' and his headlong, unco-ordinated flight from their country. How was it possible to remain calm and unaffected in this exciting atmosphere? It was certainly a tonic after the grim days of Normandy, with its fierce grappling with the enemy in those thick Bocage orchards.

"The next serious hold-up was at Hal in the middle of the afternoon, and it came at a time when the Battle Group was beginning to think in serious terms about Brussels, looming nearer and nearer with every minute and every kilometre that flashed by. Major N. T. L. Fisher, now commanding No. 1 Squadron, and Major J. M. Miller, Prince of Wales Company, quickly made a plan for their squadron and company to deploy, and in two hours the opposition had been cleared up and the advance resumed at its headlong momentum. The Cromwells were performing miracles of speed and endurance, a triumph for the manufacturers and fitters and drivers. Only once during the day did we pause for a long halt to grease, oil, tighten nuts and fill with petrol. Overhead weaved R.A.F. planes, seeking opportunities to batter and destroy German transport and fighting vehicles. With memories of Normandy, tank crews were quick with their yellow smoke and other recognition signals to signify our identity to the aeroplanes.

"A few enemy were encountered in Enghien, but not sufficient to hinder the speed of the advance. Hordes of prisoners were coming down the road as we approached the suburbs of Brussels through cheering crowds and lanes of burning and destroyed German vehicles. We had reached the outskirts of the city before the first instalment of snipers' bullets whistled over the heads of the leading tank commanders. There had been a complete absence all day of German artillery and mortaring. Hardly a shell whined or whistled during the advance. The Household Cavalry were halted by orders in the suburbs; the Grenadiers leading on the left Centre Line had been held up and were not yet in the city; so it was left to the Welsh Guards Battle Group to be the first to enter, penetrate and liberate Brussels, a proud and never-to-be-forgotten operation.

"Resistance in the city itself came mostly from the eager Belgian crowds. It was difficult for any tank or infantry commander to manoeuvre his vehicle down those streets packed with crowds of liberated citizens who had gone literally mad. Drivers were kissed, commanders were embraced and garlanded, everywhere was noise and chaos abounding. It was quite impossible to transmit a coherent message over the wireless, and in any case the air at that time of evening was extremely bad, as, for some unaccountable reason, it usually was. The column by now had orders to seize key points in the middle of the town and harbour there. This proved a task of immeasurable difficulty,

The Road to Brussels by Sergeant C. Murrell

as it was quite impossible to read a map, hear yourself speak, or get any further order in that babel and pandemonium. The Battle Group did eventually harbour in a tight square in the Boulevard Waterloo ; but even to reach this was to prove the task of a lifetime and we were not in position until after midnight. Crowds of joyous, deliriously excited citizens barred the way to our tanks, swarmed all over them, screamed salutations to us, pressed fruit and drink upon the tired, dusty, hot tank crews. By now what there was left of German resistance in the town was making itself felt ; machine guns, anti-tank guns and snipers barked at us. We barked back, the crowds leapt off the tanks and dived into slit trenches, porches of houses and any other cover that presented itself to them. This gave the scattered column some breathing space, and one was left wondering which was worse—to be kissed, hugged and screamed at by hysterical women whilst trying to give out orders over the wireless and to control the direction of your tank ; or to be free of the crowd and shot at by Germans who did not shoot straight. The opposition was not heavy and was soon overpowered. The crowds emerged excitedly from their slit trenches and over-ran the tanks once again. How I wish we had entered Brussels carrying infantry upon our tanks. There is no room on the platform of a Cromwell for excited citizens *and* tired soldiers. I have a feeling that the soldiers would have won.

"Night was falling, and the column was still split and deployed all over the town, each sub-group trying in vain to reach the destination that had been given it on the large-scale map that afternoon. What Germans there were still left in Brussels must have marvelled at so great a force of tanks milling up and down the streets. For that is the impression that our Battle Group must have given, and the enemy, we hope, was duly deceived as to our size and strength. We made enough noise for two Armoured Brigades as each troop got lost in the city, retraced its steps, roared down another street, shot up some more Germans.

"Eventually, and I shall never quite know why, we all met, infantry and tanks. Only the Adjutant of the 2nd Battalion and two troops of tanks were missing, and the reason was that *they* only of the entire column had reached the correct destination. We couldn't dig in. The ground was too hard. The tanks got into a huddle under the trees in the shadow of the burning Palais de Justice ; and the 1st Battalion looked after the perimeter along the pavements of the streets and at certain cross-roads. We tried to keep the jostling, tireless, excited, liberated crowds out of our strange laager area, but this proved to be quite impossible. The scene resembled a market day and the tired, hot soldiers were the exhibits. Most of us would have slept in any position for we were dog tired after this epic record-breaking operation. The Germans never bombed us that night, which was unaccountably strange for they must have known where we were.

"Just before reveille I was warned for an Order Group at Brigade Headquarters, but how the hell was I going to get there, and where was the Brigade anyway ? I rubbed the sleep and dust from my eyes and wandered up the road to get my Jeep. Fifty yards away from our area lay Brigade Headquarters. They had gone wrong too."

An entry in Lieutenant-Colonel Lewis's personal diary for this date reads : "The last time I had been in Brussels was in July, 1940, as a fugitive escaping from the Germans. On that occasion I had entered the city from the east in a tram. Today I entered it from the west in a tank."

* * * * *

The first tank to enter Brussels was commanded by Lieutenant J. A. W. Dent and driven by Guardsman E. J. James ; Lance-Corporal E. K. Rees was the gunner, Guardsman Robert Beresford the hull gunner and Guardsman Ralph Beresford the wireless operator. They destroyed a busload of Germans by the Avenue des Arts on their way to the Arc de Cinquentaire, where they knocked out a German tank before halting for the night in company with Prince of Wales Company of the 1st Battalion. These men, the crew of the leading tank of No. 3 Troop, No. 1 Squadron, 2nd Armoured Reconnaissance Battalion Welsh Guards, were the first soldiers of the Allied Armies to re-enter the Belgian capital on the 3rd of September, 1944.

* * * * *

The story of the 3rd Battalion's actions in the Arno valley includes an outline of the way in which the transport of an infantry battalion was organised in the Italian Campaign. The 1st Battalion's transport arrangements in Western Europe differed in detail, but the general plan was similar and indeed the principle of grouping transport in echelons, based at different points in the Divisional column, was applied to all infantry battalions. They applied, too, to armoured battalions, but these had a different set of problems to meet and an account of the 2nd Battalion's transport arrangements may well round off this story of a three days' movement which covered nearly two hundred miles.

As with the infantry battalions, the reason for grouping transport in echelon was to keep back as far as was practicable all vehicles not involved in fighting and only to have forward those most likely to be needed. Apart from other considerations there was the vital question of road space to consider, for the hundred and five wheeled vehicles of the 2nd Battalion's transport, travelling as one column at twenty miles an hour, would have occupied at least four miles of road.

"*F2*" *Echelon* was furthest forward, travelling with the Battalion behind the reserve squadron of tanks. It consisted, first, of petrol and ammunition lorries ready to refill the Battalion *at any time* in case of need—for petrol and ammunition are a special problem in an armoured battalion; next, Captain H. T. Close-Smith, the Signals Officer, had a small posse of vehicles carrying signal equipment and spare batteries; and in this echelon there were also various scout cars and jeeps which might be sent off anywhere at a moment's notice; and "although theoretically the Sergeants' Mess truck was supposed to be in the rear with 'B' Echelon it was always in F2, no matter how heavy was the shelling!" A subaltern commanded this echelon, usually Lieutenant D. M. Owen-Edmunds, and a notable figure there was Regimental Sergeant-Major Ivor Roberts. In all there would be about thirty vehicles.

"*A*" *Echelon* came next, comprising the main group of petrol and ammunition lorries, the signal section stores, the technical stores, the squadron cookers. So long as the echelon was near enough to re-supply the Battalion with petrol and ammunition *at night* there was no need for it to be near the Battalion by day. By day the vehicles and personnel of this echelon were liable to be all over the place at any given time. Thus at mid-day it would be normal for the Battalion Technical Quartermaster-Sergeant E. E. C. Collier to be forty miles back getting urgently needed spare parts for the tanks; for Drill-Sergeant A. Rees to be four miles back getting eight petrol lorries filled; for Lance-Sergeant R. P. Hornet, the Battalion butcher, to be on his way to the Battalion with tomorrow's rations; for Drill-Sergeant F. German to be returning with empty lorries after taking ammunition forward; for the Signal Sergeant to be fetching repaired wireless sets from the Division; for the Post Corporal to be taking mail up to Battalion Headquarters; for "A" Echelon commander, Captain J. S. Gwatkin, to be at Headquarters, too, finding out what would be required later; for Squadron Sergeant-Major E. Birch of Headquarters Squadron to be attending an "O" group at Brigade Headquarters, as "A" Echelon came under the Brigade Transport Officer so far as movement orders were concerned. That would leave the Battalion Transport Sergeant G. H. Marchant in charge of what was left of this echelon, which when assembled consisted of about forty-five vehicles.

"*B*" *Echelon* contained the remaining wheeled transport of the Battalion amounting to about thirty vehicles.

For movement "B" Echelon came under the orders of the officer commanding the Divisional Administrative Area where it lived: otherwise it was under the Quartermaster, Captain J. C. Buckland. Here were the stores which the Battalion could do without for a period of days—the clothing not wanted in battle, quartermaster's stores, squadron stores and a few spare petrol and ammunition lorries in case those more forward became casualties. "B" Echelon was at any distance of from ten miles to as much as eighty (on one occasion) behind the leading squadron and in between lay the whole of the Divisional column. The Divisional Administrative Area would move in bounds; in Normandy it might not move for a week, but in great advances it would stay for a day or two at one place and then bound forward for a hundred miles.

In the matter of petrol and ammunition supply the Battalion owed a great deal to the Assistant Quartermaster-General, Lieutenant-Colonel W. M. Sale, "who always estimated accurately the Divisional needs. Thus on the advance to Brussels the emphasis was on petrol and the R.A.S.C. supply lorries carried more petrol and less ammunition; while the reverse was true when fighting was more static and more sticky. The Royal Army Service Corps, too, who filled the petrol, ammunition and ration points from which the Battalion drew supplies were a wonderful team."

"CROMWELL" ADVANCING AT SPEED.

WAVRE.

"A detachment of both Welsh Guards Battalions went to Wavre fifteen miles south-east of Brussels on a report that some German armoured troops there wished to surrender." (Part I, page 67.)

THIS little action was fought outside the Divisional boundary and almost by accident. It was not on the Divisional programme but was an "extra" staged by special request of the Belgian resistance movement. The 4th of September had been spent in tidying up the position in Brussels, still *en fête*; No. 4 Company in particular spent the whole day "guarding" likely points of enemy approach. "Everyone was deliriously excited and pleased with themselves . . . ; we all felt capable of engaging any number of Germans and putting them to flight as we had been doing for hundreds of miles. Every Guardsman was surrounded by a crowd of enthusiastic citizens, hanging on in the hopes of being able to touch the hem of his garment. We did not rejoin the Battalion (now stationed three miles out on the east of the city) till late that night. Again we didn't get much sleep and by next morning we were all suffering from reaction. We kept the men hard at work checking and cleaning kit and we did not relax till mid-day. As soon as we had finished dinners we all flopped down on our beds and most of us were fast asleep in a few seconds. Ten minutes later we were on the move again getting ready for battle."

Representatives of the Belgian Armée Blanche had brought news that a large number of German troops in Wavre wished to surrender—"but only to the British Army." This was understandable, for Wavre had been the centre of the resistance movement and the Germans had recently caught and shot their leader; the citizens of Wavre were in no mood to be kind to prisoners.

It was decided to send a small force under Major G. G. Fowke to receive the surrender, consisting of No. 4 Company (Major W. D. D. Evans) two sections of the Carrier Platoon and one section of the Anti-tank Platoon from Support Company

(Major H. E. J. Lister), and a troop of tanks from No. 3 Squadron of the 2nd Battalion under Captain F. S. Portal. While this force was assembling Lieutenant V. G. Wallace was sent ahead with the Belgian messenger to ascertain the size of the force and make preliminary arrangements. Shots were fired at him when he arrived at Wavre, but a brave old Belgian hoisted a white flag and went off to find the German Commander. He soon came back with a message that "the German Army never surrender." After what had been happening in the past few weeks Wallace knew this to be something of an over-statement! But he was not in a position to dispute it, for he had already seen six troop-carriers full of German infantry, some more in half-tracks, two self-propelled guns and two Panther tanks. He was now only anxious to get back to warn the Welsh Guards party, already well on their way to Wavre. He met them on the road a mile or two away and gave them his news.

On this report they could quite properly have withdrawn, for Wavre was not their responsibility; on the other hand, here was the opportunity to kill or capture more Germans and this was at that date their chief aim in life. They decided that the chance was too good to miss and went forward to attack.

Wavre is a straggling town of about eight thousand inhabitants and about four square miles of built-up area. It is cut in half by a river. The road from Brussels tilts down to the river and rises again on the other side. Important cross-roads on both the northern and the southern slopes are clearly visible to each other and the bridge over the river, which lies between them, had at this time been destroyed.

It was decided that while one platoon of No. 4 Company and the supporting armour cleared the northern half of the town, Major Evans should take the rest of the company round the left flank and attack the southern half from that side. The first part of this plan was successfully carried out by Lieutenant E. Scudamore's platoon (12) after some rather confused street fighting in which they killed a good many Germans and captured twenty-five prisoners. The cross-roads position on this northern side was then occupied by the tanks and anti-tank guns so as to cover Evans' flank attack when it came in. Unfortunately the enemy brought anti-tank guns or tanks to bear on them and before these had been located Portal's tank and both anti-tank guns were knocked out and a number of their crews were killed and wounded. Scudamore's platoon was then sent round the right flank to form a pincer movement with the left flanking platoons under Major Evans. With Lieutenant Wallace to guide them these had meanwhile worked eastwards along the railway till they were behind a large monastery on the outskirts of the town. Then they turned south and in spite of considerable

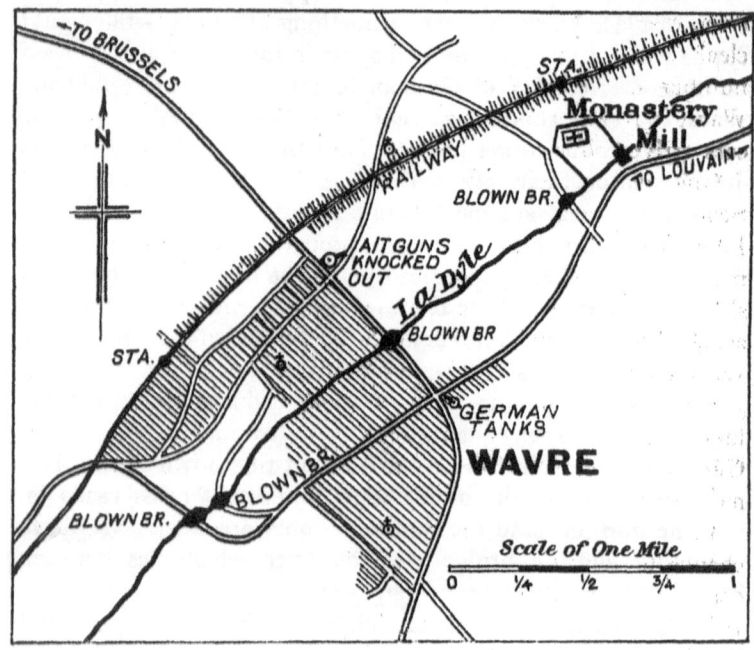

MAIN FEATURES OF WAVRE.

machine-gun fire crossed the monastery grounds and reached a pavilion and outbuildings near the river bank. Here they were heavily fired on by a Panther two hundred yards away on the far bank. Lieutenant A. J. Bland, commanding No. 3 Platoon, was wounded with three Guardsmen; and Lance-Corporal O. H. Hughes of Lieutenant D. N. Brinson's platoon (10), trying to get a shot at the tank with a Piat, was killed. ("He was to have been made up to Lance-Sergeant that day and was probably the most popular man in the Company." Before the war he was a tiler in Holyhead.) At this point Major Evans came up with Company Headquarters. "We picked up a German Sergeant-Major on the way, shot another man and found two more, dead already." Evans found that it was possible to cross the river by a nearby mill, but by the time they were over the tank had gone. However, they continued their flanking movement and eventually reached the cross-roads on the south of the river where they met Scudamore's platoon coming up from the right after wading the river where it was comparatively shallow. Together they had cleared the southern half of the town, killed a considerable number of Germans, taken forty-three prisoners and freed Wavre. It was now dark and when some American armoured cars arrived they handed over and returned to Brussels.

One incident caused a good deal of amusement. As Scudamore's platoon worked its way round the right, Guardsman Lowe spotted a German despatch rider sitting astride of his machine. He took careful aim and fired and being a very good shot he was annoyed when nothing happened. So he fired again and again, but still the German remained quite unmoved. Lowe could not make it out and set off to stalk him. When he got nearer he found that he had been firing at a garage sign—a life-sized dummy on a dummy motor cycle, complete with German uniform and helmet. He was relieved to find that it had five bullet holes through the chest.

In January, 1945, some members of No. 4 Company had a chance to revisit the monastery. "The monks had erected a concrete plaque, on the site where Lance-Corporal Owen Hughes fell, with a white stone cross inlaid in the cement. And Sergeant A. H. G. Phillips (later to win the D.C.M. on the Albert Canal and still later to become a Captain in the Royal Welch Fusiliers) was handed his cap, complete with cap-badge, by one of the monks who recognised him as the man who had lost it in the action on the 5th of September."

BEERINGEN, HELCHTEREN AND HECHTEL

> *"The enemy clearly intended to hold not only the Canal but also the road system behind it, and for the next five days there was hard fighting with the tide of battle gradually receding from Beeringen, Helchteren and Bourg Leopold till only Hechtel remained."* (See Part I, page 68.)

THERE was hard fighting from the Albert Canal to the Escaut Canal over ground shown in the map on page 218. First comes the Albert Canal, bridged only at Beeringen. From there two roads lead, one going south and east to Helchteren, the other north and east to Bourg Leopold. From these two places roads converge on Hechtel and from Hechtel the road continues northwards to the Escaut Canal and into Holland. The Albert Canal must therefore be crossed at Beeringen before the country between the two canals can be entered; then the two routes to Hechtel must be cleared; finally Hechtel itself must be captured.

The Welsh Guards Group was leading when the Guards Armoured Division renewed the advance from Brussels on September the 6th, No. 3 Squadron and Prince of Wales Company being at the head of the column. Through Louvain and Diest they met only cheering crowds, but at Beeringen they were greeted with machine-gun fire and found that the canal bridge was blown though not wholly destroyed. Lieutenant A. F. Q. Shuldham with No. 2 Platoon tried to get over the broken bridge, but it could only be crossed in single file and was too heavily covered by fire for this to be practicable. Plans were therefore made for an assault crossing in boats, covered by No. 3 Squadron tanks; but before it went in a civilian ran over the bridge with the news that the enemy were withdrawing. Lieutenant J. F. R. Burchell, commanding the Carrier Platoon, was the first to cross, with Major Miller leading Prince of Wales Company hard behind. They ran after the retreating Germans, killing about a dozen and capturing twenty. No. 3 Company and No. 4

Company followed over the bridge and they took up positions covering the main exits from the town. At one of these Sergeant Arthur Phillips with a platoon of No. 4 Company destroyed an enemy half-track and a two-ton lorry full of ammunition and drove off, with mortars, the remainder of the column.

Sappers had arrived by then to repair the bridge, but this would take some hours so Miller organised the building of a temporary bridge in the hope of getting company vehicles over, if not tanks. With the men of his Company Headquarters and "a huge party of civilians" nine barges were moved till, side by side, they bridged the canal. The company jeep crossed, but while timber was being brought up to strengthen the "deck" a heavy burst of shell fire came down and the civilians fled. The enemy were infiltrating back into the town. The fighting at Beeringen was only beginning.

While the bridge was still being repaired Major J. O. Spencer's No. 2 Squadron had patrolled to the south and met a company of Hitler Youth, armed with bazookas and other weapons. The tanks opened fire, a horse-drawn cart was driven down by Lieutenant H. W. J. E. Peel—and seventy of the Hitler Youth gave themselves up, many of them with tears of mortification. It was an odd and rather pitiful episode.

Undeterred by increasing shell fire, the Royal Engineers worked on the bridge all night and by four o'clock in the morning it was safe for tanks. The squadrons which had been waiting were glad to get on, for it was a bitterly cold night and rained hard. The Group to lead was No. 1 Squadron under Major N. T. L. Fisher with No. 3 Company under Captain P. M. Beckwith-Smith (whose father, Major-General M. B. Beckwith-Smith, had been a Welsh Guardsman before him). They ran into trouble at once, being sniped in the town, and beyond it they met increasingly stiff opposition. Three self-propelled guns attacked them, but Sergeant H. L. Williams in the leading tank knocked out one with his first shot and No. 3 Company dealt with another by "dismounted action." They met other machine-gun posts and men with bazookas, but they killed some, took some prisoners and got steadily forward. Before reaching Helchteren they suddenly overtook a German battalion forming up on the road and driving past, "shooting and shouting," they practically destroyed it. Some hundreds were killed or wounded, a hundred and fifty prisoners were taken and the vehicles were left blazing. The Group were shot at passing through Helchteren, but pushed on; and they were nearing Hechtel when they were stopped by anti-tank guns which

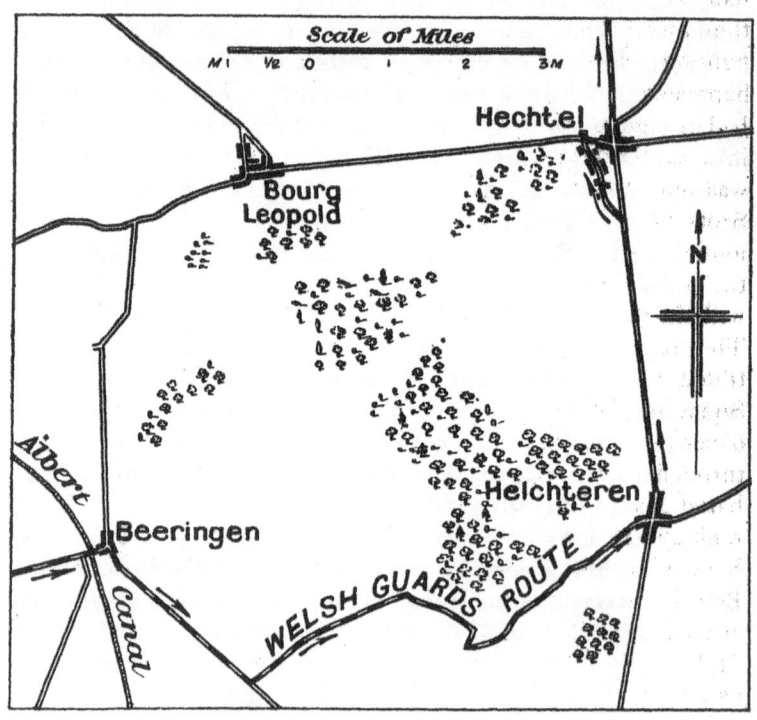

THE BEERINGEN—HECHTEL POSITION.
(NOTE—*Numerous minor roads and lanes omitted.*)

destroyed the first tank by firing down the long straight road. The country hereabouts is mostly flat, well cultivated and cut up by strong hedges and belts of copse and woodland—close country giving no wide field of observation. Ribbon development has put houses straggling along the tree-lined roadside which provide additional cover to defending troops. No. 3 Company deployed and tried to reach the offending gun; but they met numerous machine-gun positions and found the place too strongly held to be taken by one company and a depleted squadron of tanks. Dusk was already falling.

While these events were taking place in front much was happening behind. A second Group consisting of No. 3 Squadron and No. 4 Company had followed to Helchteren and had taken up defensive positions covering the main exits while they awaited the results of the attack on Hechtel ahead and of fighting which had broken out at Beeringen in their rear. What happened at Hechtel we know. At Beeringen the enemy had brought up additional forces and a strong counter-attack came in after the leading Welsh Guards had gone through. There was intermittent street fighting during the day, "X" Company, Scots Guards being heavily engaged for the first time since joining the 1st Battalion. (See page 56.) Late in the afternoon the Irish Guards came up and took over, but they too had to deal with further counter-attacks before they were in turn relieved. The main body of the Welsh Guards Battalions then concentrated near Helchteren, which No. 4 Company and No. 3 Squadron still held. The latter had a quiet night and about ten o'clock the Group which had attacked Hechtel passed back through their positions having been ordered to rejoin their battalions. Getting away was not easy. The squadron lost a tank and the company two trucks to self-propelled guns which hovered on their flank, and there were about a dozen casualties. Before the Regimental Aid Post could move up the casualties evacuated to Helchteren were tended in an aid post set up by "two magnificent Belgian women who did wonderful work for us and for civilian casualties, never resting for three days."

So the night of September the 7th ended with one Group in Helchteren and the rest concentrated just behind the village.

During the morning of the 8th, Prince of Wales and "X" Companies supported by No. 2 Squadron passed through to make a renewed attack on Hechtel. Before following them it will be more convenient to finish the story of what happened at Helchteren. "It was not thought prudent to employ our full strength in the attack on Hechtel owing to a last minute report of a threat to Helchteren where the Battalion was based," a view that was justified by events. For after the Hechtel detachment had passed through, the enemy began a series of counter-attacks on Helchteren which continued all day. Fortunately for the Welsh Guards, they made the mistake of dispersing their forces for a number of separate attacks, all of which were beaten off with heavy loss to the attackers. Two sections of the 3-inch Mortar Platoon under Sergeant T. J. Waters and two sections of the Carrier Platoon under Sergeant Smith put in some effective shooting; Guardsman E. D. Evans gave a distinguished exhibition of long-range rifle shooting and Guardsman J. A. Pearson, with a Bren gun, "had a pile of German dead thirty yards in front of him" after one of these local attacks had been broken. Just before dark the Irish Guards, now freed from Beeringen, came up to relieve the Welsh Guards, who rejoined their Battalions outside the village. The Irish Guards had to deal with further counter-attacks as they had done at Beeringen, but the Welsh Guards Group was now free to concentrate on the capture of Hechtel. The attack made that day had been only partially successful and the position there was confused and uncomfortable.

Prince of Wales Company and "X" Company had attacked not along the main road from Helchteren but astride the crossroads coming in from Bourg Leopold. "X" Company was moving over to the left of the road when three enemy trucks drove rapidly up *from their rear*. Two got past them into Hechtel. The third they shot up and the men who got out were wounded and taken prisoner. Six more vehicles farther back on the road were hastily abandoned by the enemy, who moved off to the north. Working their way through close country, the leading platoons of "X" Company shot up a number of men retreating hurriedly into the village, destroyed one self-propelled gun which they came on suddenly and another at a road junction on the northern outskirts; and established one platoon there and another in the north-eastern corner of the village on the far side of the main road. Their third platoon remained in reserve near the church. Prince of Wales Company on the right of the Bourg Leopold road had to advance over more open country, and after destroying one machine-gun post were stopped by others which swept the open ground. So Major Miller directed them forward by the route which "X" Company had taken till they reached the outskirts of the village, when they moved back to the right flank. Leading platoons reached the main road but were unable to get across it. Lieutenant H. R. E. Mitchley was wounded and there were other casualties. Major J. O. Spencer commanding No. 2 Squadron was with Miller reconnoitring from a house on the main road when it was counter-attacked. The enemy were driven off, but by now it was growing dark and Miller decided to draw back his forward platoons and consolidate on the right of "X" Company's rear platoon.

During the night the enemy made persistent attempts to infiltrate both companies' positions, and although they were driven off they succeeded in re-establishing themselves between "X" Company's forward platoons and the rear position.

No. 2 Squadron's troops had a hard day and had had many tank casualties. In order to rest them Spencer took his own Headquarters up to support the infantry, and during the night he was taking his turn at keeping watch from his tank when he was shot by an enemy patrol which had got to close quarters in the darkness. He was one of the older men who had taken Emergency Commissions and he had proved to be a fine leader. "Younger officers referred to him as Uncle John ... the Squadron loved him."

Next day (September the 9th) No. 3 Company under Captain P. M. Beckwith-Smith attacked on the right of Prince of Wales Company, but were also held in the western outskirts of the village. Two officers of Support Company who were with him were killed: Lieutenant J. A. A. Henderson, wounded at Wavre and back from hospital only the day before, was killed when he went forward to find an observation post for the mortars; and Major H. E. J. Lister was killed trying to help No. 3 Company to take a house which held up the attack. Almost of necessity the War Diaries record casualties without comment, but of Hugh Lister the 1st Battalion Diary says: "His personality and example had been an inspiration to the Battalion. He will be irreplaceable because he was unique. All who served with him will always remember him as a man who was truly great." He was a priest of the Church of England, who thought it his duty to join with other men in fighting the evil of Nazidom and to share the dangers and sufferings which this would involve.

Later in the day the enemy in turn made a strong counter-attack; the forward elements of Prince of Wales and No. 3 Companies were temporarily dislodged and it was largely due to Miller's coolness and determination that the position was restored and the Companies' positions reoccupied.

"X" Company's platoons, which had remained cut off so long, saw the enemy's penetration on the right and wisely retired on the position held by their rear platoon. Lieutenant G. Llewellyn, who commanded one of them (he had been twice wounded), ordered Sergeant M. Dunderdale to withdraw the platoon, which he did with great skill and coolness and a clever use of smoke to cover their movement over open ground. Llewellyn himself stayed with the team of an anti-tank gun which he hoped to get out after dark; but the enemy followed up the withdrawal of the platoons and Llewellyn and the gun team were captured. The second Platoon Commander, Lieutenant N. Thorpe, had been killed. Sergeant Charles McLelland (his Platoon Sergeant) saw a German patrol enter a house from which Thorpe was observing and at once went to his assistance. Three Germans were coming down the stairs and he killed them all, but upstairs he found Thorpe dead and the Guardsman with him severely wounded. The story of these two Scots Guards platoons of "X" Company is a very fine one. Major P. Stewart Fothringham, who commanded the company, had already become "a byword throughout the Division for valour and determination" while his company was attached to the Irish Guards and before it came to form part of the 1st Battalion. "His company regarded him as someone super-human; they knew rightly that he would always be there when dangers and difficulties were greatest and his presence inspired them to the tremendous deeds they have done"; for his company had won three Military Crosses and seven Military Medals in the Normandy fighting. At Hechtel, when for four days his forward platoons were in close contact with the enemy, Fothringham "was continuously in the forefront of this arduous battle, always calm and cheerful"; two enemy counter-attacks supported by tanks were repelled after penetrating his positions and, though twice surrounded and cut off, his forward platoons never gave ground until they were ordered to do so.

Throughout the day following (the 10th) the three companies which were now in the western half of Hechtel tried to work their way forward, but with little success. The enemy had been reinforced and held the place more strongly than at first. They penetrated some of our positions in the darkness, and at one point got into houses on each side of one in which Lance-Corporal Thomas Kennedy had been put in charge of ten prisoners. He was completely isolated from the remainder of the company, but he kept his prisoners quiet, prevented the enemy from entering his house, and at ten o'clock next morning when the company cleared the surrounding area he emerged with his ten prisoners complete. On September the 11th, No. 4 Company attacked from the south and after clearing the houses flanking the main road linked up with No. 3 Company, but could get no further.

It was now decided to lay on a full two-battalion attack with artillery preparation and in the five hours after it was launched Hechtel was taken.

First, all companies were withdrawn during the night and early in the morning of September the 12th. The artillery preparation began at eight o'clock and was accompanied by the 1st Battalion's mortars and machine guns and the Anti-tank Platoon's six-pounders; and the mortars and machine guns of the Royal Northumberland Fusiliers (who supported the Welsh Guards throughout the campaign) fired nine hundred mortar bombs and forty thousand machine-gun rounds. The assault went in at half-past eight. No. 3 and No. 4 Companies attacked from the south, astride the main road with close support of No. 1 and No. 3 Squadrons, who shot up house after house to enable the infantry to get forward. Going was slow, but by noon they were at the main cross-roads in the centre of the village, when Prince of Wales and "X" Company came in from the west. By one o'clock Hechtel as taken and with it the remainder of the garrison who had fought so stubbornly. They belonged mostly to the 1st Battalion Hermann Goering Regiment or the 10th (Grasmel) Parachute Regiment. Of these, one hundred and fifty enemy dead were counted; two hundred and twenty wounded were evacuated; five hundred unwounded prisoners were taken, including Captain Muller, the commander of the force. The equipment captured or destroyed included three tanks; seven self-propelled guns; one half-track with short 75 gun; six anti-tank guns; ten miscellaneous vehicles; and numerous mortars, machine guns and rifles.

The Corps Commander, General Sir R. N. O'Connor, said afterwards when he came with the Divisional Commander and the Brigadier to congratulate the Welsh Guards Group: "It is one thing to gain ground, but it is quite another to destroy a complete enemy battalion."

There was, however, one German at least who did not wait till the end. His diary was picked up by the Welsh Guards after their attack at Hassum in February, 1945. The following are extracts from the entries he had made five months before while he was still in Hechtel.

"5*th Sept.*—All is chaos. Only we go westward. A proud feeling.

"7*th Sept.*—The march goes on to Hechtel. Here we meet Tommy.

"8*th Sept.*—In the night we have our first direct hit. We have been lucky.

"9*th Sept.*—We push forward as an advance post without communication on right and left. Terrorists in the rear. Terrific noise everywhere. English A/T gun 100 metres to our left.

"10*th Sept.*—At 1000 hrs. the enemy starts his attack. We are sure now that we are surrounded.

"11*th Sept.*—In the morning a new attack with increased force. We shoot an English D.R. We put a found mortar in position but do not have the opportunity to fire it. Our light tank is hit, everybody killed. Of 31 men 6 are left and we go to H.Q., which is totally destroyed. We cannot find one of our soldiers there. We decide to break through in daytime. We manage to get out of Hechtel crawling on our stomachs."

So he lived to fight at Hassum—where he lost his diary but may again have saved his life.

There are other personal stories which will be remembered when the story of Hechtel is told. Guardsman Reginald Floyd of "X" Company, Scots Guards, was a carrier driver and when two carriers had already been knocked out he was told to take his casualties out on his carrier and not come back. But he sent another driver and reported that "he wished to see this fight out." He then armed himself with three captured German weapons and "took upon himself the task of keeping the company area a safe place to live in." "...During two days and three nights not a shot was fired into the area but Floyd would be there in a few minutes replying to it with a Spandau, a Schmeisser, or a Luger."

Guardsman Archibald Harley, a company sniper, installed himself in a much-shelled house. Repeated shelling failed to move him and he shot thirteen of the enemy in two days.

Lieutenant D. N. Brinson was in command of the rear platoon of No. 4 Company when the leading platoons were held up by Spandau fire and a self-propelled gun which had knocked out two tanks. He led a group forward under fire and worked through uncleared houses till within twenty yards of the gun. Then standing in the open he directed the fire of the Piat. Two direct hits were made and the crew made off, leaving the gun in our hands and enabling the company to advance.

Three stretcher-bearers of the 2nd Battalion did heroic work at Hechtel—Guardsmen Cecil Lawrie, Thomas Jones and J. V. Evans. Captain C. G. Irwin, the Medical Officer, said of them : "They showed no regard to any danger. In spite of the fact that they were continually sniped at they crossed the main road of the village time and time again and disregarded all personal safety to evacuate the wounded." Similar tributes were paid to all stretcher-bearers of both Battalions. They were among the bravest of men.

This account of Hechtel has referred chiefly to the infantry's part, but the 2nd Battalion's tanks were in close support at each attack and were constantly employed at one point or another throughout the action. The enemy too had tanks and self-propelled guns and there were duels and damage on both sides. It is not possible to tell the story of all these individual actions. Lieutenant W. H. Griffiths' tank, waiting in a wood, let a huge Yag-Panther (easily capable of blasting his tank wide open) pass within a few yards without seeing him and then shot it up from the rear, the gunner being his Troop Sergeant, Ivor Wilcox who had played Rugby in Welsh Trials and for the Army, Lieutenant M. C. Devas (whose father had been Adjutant of th .

1st Battalion during the Great War) saw an enemy gun which had not seen his tank and, finding that he could not lay his gun on it because of an intervening tree and could not start up his engines without giving away his position, sawed quietly through the tree and as it fell shot up the offending gun. Almost every tank had its own adventures, as did each section of the infantry. A book would be needed to tell them all.

GERMAN FIVE-BARRELLED ROCKET MORTAR *NEBELWERFER* OR "MOANING MINNIE."

NIJMEGEN AND "THE ISLAND"

"When they reached Nijmegen on the 19th of September American airborne forces and the Grenadier Guards had captured the bridges intact." Arnhem was only ten miles ahead and its spires could be seen across the low-lying ground which intervened. (Part I, page 69.)

ON the morning after the bridge had been captured the Welsh Guards Group started to cross into "the Island." The Irish Guards were in front of them, the intention being to continue the advance to Arnhem; but the Irish Guards were soon held up. We were beginning to discover the difficulty of crossing this last ten miles. Most of the country in "the Island," as they called this land between the Waal and the Lower Rhine, is dead flat and it is intersected by innumerable ditches which make it unusable by tanks. The only good road, the centre-line of our advance, runs on a causeway raised above the level of the surrounding fields and is bordered by deep dykes. Traffic moving on the road is visible for miles, yet cannot get off the road except at side turnings which are few and far between. The whole country is under observation from the hills at Arnhem and the enemy were in sufficient strength to slow down our advance so long as our reinforcements, bottle-necked by the bridge, could only move up slowly. The difficulty is well illustrated by what happened to the Welsh Guards Group. The leading Squadron (No. 1) was crossing the bridge at one o'clock when the Irish Guards' advance was held up. Major N. T. L. Fisher kept a record of the afternoon.

"1.0 p.m. My tank is just crossing the Waal.
1.15 p.m. We are stationary on the bridge. . . . it is slightly uncomfortable as we are a perfect, silhouetted target for German bombers, if any.
2 p.m. This bridge is not attractive. . . . There is a certain amount of small-arms fire from time to time, but I can't make out quite where from.

2.15 p.m. When I was out of my tank just now a bullet whistled past my nose—literally. Soon after we had a mortar concentration all round us ... now there are a lot of enemy planes over us. One man has been slightly wounded in the Squadron. What a bloody place to be sitting. ... !

2.45 p.m. More German planes over us quite low. This is an unpleasant situation and I shall not forget this bridge for a long time.

3.15 p.m. More shelling and mortaring. Brigade, Division and Corps Commanders have all gone forward in succession to make a plan to deal with the opposition. Meanwhile we stay on this damned bridge.

4.30 p.m. Mortaring every now and again to keep us worried but nothing as close as before ... I hope we shall not have to stay on this bridge all night."

Soon after five o'clock they moved at last. They were ordered to try to find a way round on the left, by a subsidiary road which runs past Fort Lent to Oosterhout.

There was no room for deployment. No. 1 Squadron led with No. 3 Company of the 1st Battalion riding on the tanks of all but the leading troop. They passed Fort Lent (taken previously by U.S. airborne troops) and nosed their way carefully along the winding lane. The leading troop under Lieutenant M. C. Devas encountered three German tanks and knocked them all out in turn, but by then it was growing dark. By then too the Higher Command had decided that before any further advance could be made the bridgehead must be enlarged so that more troops could be brought into the Island. The Welsh Guards were ordered to withdraw to harbour near the bridge.

The 43rd Division came up next day to press forward, and on the twenty-third of September the 1st Battalion Welsh Guards supported by a Squadron of the 2nd Battalion were ordered to enlarge the bridgehead on the right by attacking towards Bemmel. Prince of Wales Company and "X" Company were in front, No. 3 in support. There was no fourth company for No. 4 had been disbanded temporarily after the losses at Hechtel.

The leading companies reached their objectives, each with about ten casualties, and spent a quiet night on the positions won; and in the morning troops of another Division went through them to continue the advance.

It had begun to rain and thereafter it rained heavily if intermittently while they remained in the Island. No doubt the weather and the drab featureless landscape, with the realisation of what the failure to reach Arnhem meant for the gallant airborne troops there, combined to depress their spirits. "We felt that these sad flat lands held no future for us and that we were bogged down indefinitely. No doubt many armies over the centuries have felt equally despondent." Yet as ever they found various forms of diversion. Major P. Stewart Fothringham had "an excellent O.P. from which he could watch Germans and wild duck at the same time, occasionally stalking both"; while Major Sir Richard Powell, "had the undivided attentions of a small white goat which shared a room with him . . ."

No. 3 Squadron lost a tank that day on a mine and the operator was killed. The commander (Lieutenant H. F. R. Homfray), the driver and the gunner "baled out," suffering from burns. The hull gunner was unconscious and trapped in his seat as the hatch was jammed. Lieutenant J. H. Carson saw the tank burning fiercely and heard ammunition exploding inside, but he left his own tank, crossed exposed ground and climbed into the driver's seat. Despite the fire and exploding ammunition he succeeded in manoeuvring the unconscious man out, across the controls and through the driver's hatch and carried him to the shelter of a ditch. There almost overcome by fumes, he administered first aid. One man at least owes his life to Carson's gallantry.

On September the 26th the 1st Battalion were ordered to occupy Aam and to push a company forward. They took over in the village from troops already there and No. 3 Company under Major W. D. D. Evans advanced for nearly two miles with the support of two troops of tanks from No. 1 Squadron of the 2nd Battalion (under Lieutenants Devas and A. W. S. Wheatley) and two anti-tank guns. They reached a willow-clad stretch of the main dyke running east and west in front of Aam and facing Arnhem, from which the remainder of the Airborne Division had by now been withdrawn. The drawing reproduced opposite was made from near Company Headquarters. The old farm buildings in front mark the line of the dyke held by the forward platoons. It was to prove the furthest point reached at this period of the campaign.

Their first night was quiet and they patrolled along the dyke. Next day they were involved in one of the futile and abortive operations which are liable to find a place in every war. The maps showed that half a mile to their right a sizeable bridge crossed the dyke which they were lining. The position would clearly be stronger if this bridge were in our hands so they were ordered to seize it. After artillery and 3-inch mortar concentration they succeeded in fighting their way along the dyke, having a number killed and wounded in the process. But when they reached their objective they found that the bridge no longer existed and, having reported this by wireless, they were ordered to withdraw to their original positions. Only by the help of smoke from the tanks and mortars did they manage to extricate themselves, for the enemy were in some strength and could enfilade them in a long open stretch before the willows were regained.

They were relieved by the Irish Guards that night and moved back, and from then until the 6th of October the 1st Battalion were moved about from place to place to strengthen a part of the line or be ready in case of need where the enemy attacked. For in the days that followed he counter-attacked heavily especially on the dyke, now held by the Irish Guards, in front of Aam. That his efforts failed was entirely due to the tenacity of the infantry of the Guards Armoured Division and the 43rd and 50th Divisions and the high quality of our artillery, which continually broke up enemy efforts to counter-attack. "The artillery on the Island saved us and was of a superlative quality." Meanwhile, as Lieutenant-Colonel J. C. Windsor Lewis put it, "Squadrons were hired out daily to back up or support various Battalions of infantry all trying to drive the Germans away" till they left the Island thankfully on the 30th of September; but they were sent back on the next day on account of an enemy counter-attack. Both Battalions came out at last on October the 6th and went to good billets at Malden.

* * * * *

"In the Island" with Amboyna in the distance, by L. F. Ellis

The Welsh Guards' gloomy memories of the Island are not wholly unconnected with rations. They had grown accustomed to a standard of feeding that can never have been approached in any previous campaign. The "Composite Pack" and the availability of petrol made hot and varied meals possible in any position. The "Compo Pack" in various sizes, designed for anything from two to fourteen men, contained to start with a pound per man of either steak and kidney pudding, Irish stew, stewed steak or meat and vegetables. In addition it included bacon, concentrated soup, margarine, tea, sugar and milk powder, biscuits, a sweet pudding, cheese, chocolate and boiled sweets, salt and cigarettes. The packs varied in detail and there were seven different types; some for instance included one or more of the following: Salmon, sardines, preserved meat, sausages, baked beans, tinned fruit and jam. For cooking each company had petrol cookers and containers in which food kept hot; but a handful of sand drenched in petrol, in a tin or a hole in the ground, cooked any of these things in a very short time. Very often bread, fresh vegetables, fruit, poultry, eggs and other local produce were obtainable to supplement the pack rations, but the calorific value of these alone was 3,950 per man per day.

And beyond these were "N.A.A.F.I. rations," supplied on payment through N.A.A.F.I. These comprised additional cigarettes and tobacco, soap, tooth paste, razor blades, chocolate and many other things, including a limited supply of whisky and gin for messes and canteens.

All these good things did not drop from heaven. Rations were collected from the Divisional Administrative Area; N.A.A.F.I. stores from the nearest N.A.A.F.I. Supply Depot. When the Welsh Guards went into the Island the Divisional Administration Area was stationed away back near Hechtel and the N.A.A.F.I. depot a few miles from Brussels; and shortly after their arrival in the Island the Germans counter-attacked the long corridor behind them and cut the supply route. Thereby hangs a tale. The Quartermaster of the 1st Battalion (Captain W. L. Bray), doubtless disliking the look of the Island, set off back to Brussels to get the N.A.A.F.I. rations. He took a car and a three-ton lorry and had with him four of his most valued and faithful men—

Sergeant Kenneth Turner, Guardsmen Stanley Rossant, Charles Williams and William Tipper—two drivers and his servant. They were held up by traffic on the road just south of Uden when an agitated Dutchman ran up and told him that ten lorry-loads of Germans were debussing nearby. The Quartermaster found a wireless truck and notified Corps Headquarters and before many minutes had passed another Dutchman told him that enemy tanks were in Uden, through which he had just passed. So he moved south as quickly as he could and when he got to Oedenrode he found the Germans attacking the main bridge in the town ! Luckily he knew that the Royal Engineers had built another bridge nearby and, making a detour, he crossed this "at speed" just as the German armour swept over the main bridge and through the town. The road was cut for several days, and more than once, before the corridor was enlarged and made safe, and Bray had to wait for this before he could return to the Battalion. Meanwhile their normal rations had ceased with the cutting of what was then the only supply road to the Island and the Battalion were living on German rations drawn from a huge dump at Oss which had luckily been captured. These were nothing like our own in quality and variety, and in particular the rum was "remarkably inferior both in taste and potency."

The following incident is told of another officer coming back from one of such long journeys in pursuit of stores. It was dark and many miles had been covered in silence ; then :—

OFFICER : "I think we have gone wrong, Corporal Jones ; turn round." (Pause, silence, no action.)

OFFICER (*rather sharply*) : "Corporal Jones. Did you hear what I said ? TURN ROUND !" (Another pause : then—).

CORPORAL JONES : "Sir, *you* are driving, Sir."

* * * *

Casualties in the Island were not heavy, but among those killed was Company Sergeant-Major Fred Beynon of Support Company, "one of the Battalion's finest Warrant Officers," and Guardsman J. A. Harvey, whose father, Sergeant A. E. Harvey of the 2nd Battalion, attended the burial of his own son on the field of battle. It was one of the last of such services conducted by the Reverend P. F. Payne, C.F., who was leaving the 1st Battalion on promotion. He had served with the Regiment almost throughout the war, having been with the 2nd Battalion at Boulogne in 1940 and with the 1st Battalion throughout their fighting in Normandy, Belgium and Holland. The War Diary did not overstate the facts when it put on record, "He will be missed by every officer and man in the Battalion." A true Welshman, he was loved and respected by all ranks and his forthcoming departure seemed to them to involve "a disastrous change."

While they were in the Island Lieutenant-Colonel C. H. R. Heber-Percy, recovered from his wound at Montchamp, rejoined and resumed command of the 1st Battalion, who paid a second visit to Nijmegen when they went back to guard Nijmegen bridge from October the 31st to November the 4th. It had been attacked repeatedly by German planes and one damaged span had had to be made good by the Royal Engineers; it had been damaged by a torpedo fired against one of the piers by frog-men who swam down-stream with their dangerous charge. But it had been successfully protected from serious damage and maintained in full use. At this date it was guarded by infantry and Military Police, anti-aircraft artillery and searchlight units and by Naval guard-boats and river booms above and below the bridge. An elaborate code of precautions was enforced night and day and a complex system of communication between all units and every post ensured prompt action in case of attack. Captain A. G. Graham, the 1st Battalion Signal Officer, and the Signal Platoon had a strenuous time, for they had ninety miles of cable to maintain. They even laid a line on to the river boom for use by guard ships.

Some of them found the bridge "a spooky place," but if there were evil spirits about they kept quiet while the Welsh Guards were there and there were no untoward incidents before they left finally on the 4th of November.

* * * * *

The amount of signal cable used here was of course abnormal, but a Battalion signal exchange was always the hub of an intricate web of lines, wherever conditions allowed the use of telephones. The exchange was anywhere from the room of a house to a slit trench, but in or about it were three groups of signallers. The operators on duty would be at the switchboard, incessantly inserting and removing plugs "after the manner of a cinema organist." They had to be trained and practised to think and act quickly fort he speed and clarity of a call might decide whether, say, artillery or machine-gun fire came down in the right place and in time to save the situation.

Next, there was the cable party. Laying out cable was their first task but its subsequent maintenance their chief worry; shell bursts wrecked it and the ominous crash of a "stonk" was the inevitable signal for the cable party to start putting on their belts and helmets and gathering up pliers and other kit. Perhaps the cable parties of the 3rd Battalion had the hardest task when the Battalion was in the mountains. Rain and snow made cable laying and maintenance a nightmare, lines on occasion being buried feet-deep and frozen to the mountain side; and the mule train could always be relied upon to cut its way through any line it came near if the shells missed it.

Finally there were the wireless operators, all line communications being duplicated by wireless. They sat with headphones on, for ever talking in strange language—"Hullo Uncle Roger Sugar Three—Out to you." "Hullo Queen Dog Fox, hear you strength three"—which was supposed to make for security.

One of the signallers was asked whether he would choose to be a signaller or a rifleman, if he were given his Army career over again. He replied "A signaller, Sir," and gave as his reason that at least one knew what was going on. He was complimented on taking such an interest in the progress of the battle. "Oh, not that, Sir; what I mean is, if you get bored you can always switch over to the B.B.C. and get the news."

— VEHICLES WILL BE DUG-IN AND SANDBAGGED —

VEULEN AND SITTARD

"*They went to hold Veulen, twenty miles to the South (of Nijmegen)." (Part I, page* 70).

ON November the 4th the 1st Battalion were temporarily detached from the Guards Armoured Division and lent to the 11th Armoured Division. They were to relieve an infantry battalion of the duty of holding the line at Veulen and they had to move in after dark as the line was in close contact with the enemy. The companies were fairly near together in the single street of this bedraggled little village, already well shelled and a veritable sea of mud. The Battalion Command Post was in a cellar and Battalion Headquarters some way back. Their role at Veulen was for the first time purely static : no attack was intended and officially nothing important happened while they were there. Yet it was for them a time of strain and discomfort and an idea of their life can be best given in extracts from the War Diary and the account of a few incidents.

"*5th November.*—The Commanding Officer held a conference to consider details of the coming night's patrolling. No less than seven patrols went out on that night, including a reconnaissance patrol under Lieutenant R. W. S. Grimston of 'X' Company to obtain information for a fighting patrol next night. . . .

6th November.—Commanding Officer held a conference, when results of the last night's patrols and plans for tonight were gone into in detail. The most ambitious of these was undertaken by Lieutenant D. J. C. Stevenson and Guardsman Evans. . . ."

On this patrol Stevenson established a standing patrol at a farm building in no-man's-land and then proceeded with Guardsman Evans to explore the enemy's lines. They had got into an empty section of enemy trench when a German officer approached and Stevenson ordered him "*Hande Hoch!*" As he failed to comply Stevenson shot him dead, and when another officer came to investigate Guardsman Evans shot him. A hail of bullets came down round them then and enemy flares went up, so Stevenson and Guardsman Evans returned to the standing patrol they had left. They found these almost surrounded by another party of the enemy and, extricating them only with difficulty, started back. On the way they surprised and dispersed yet another group of Germans busy laying mines in no-man's-land and having got back to the company lines Stevenson contacted the Gunners, who brought down a heavy "stonk" on the place he indicated. Finally he took out a fresh patrol and retook the farm where his standing patrol had been surrounded. He had had, as the War Diary put it, "a remarkably eventful night."

The other patrol of note was the "X" Company fighting patrol under Lieutenant R. W. S. Grimston. "They contacted the enemy and after an exchange of shots brought down a previously arranged 3-inch mortar shoot on the enemy positions. Screams were heard, but it was not possible to find out what casualties had been inflicted."

> "*7th November.*—The Commanding Officer held his usual conference, when details were settled for a raid by Prince of Wales Company on a house known to be occupied by the enemy. A section of the Pioneer Platoon were to go with them to set booby traps in the house. This operation was successfully carried out owing to the gallantry of Lance-Sergeant Webb. . . ."

This raid was made in full daylight. The party, fifteen in all, was commanded by Lieutenant D. Bruce, Lance-Sergeant L. A. R. Webb being in charge of the leading section. The enemy were in force in nearby trenches, but Lance-Sergeant Webb reached his objective near the house in spite of heavy fire. There Bruce had nearly joined him when he was severely wounded. Lance-Sergeant Webb crossed over to him, put on a field dressing under heavy fire and crawled back to his own section. Two stretcher-bearers tried in turn to rescue Bruce, but both were severely wounded in the attempt. Lance-Sergeant Webb then ordered his section to withdraw to the shelter of a wall while he himself stayed behind to cover their movement by fire. When they were in position he again crawled over to Bruce and under heavy fire managed to drag him also to safety, and he went back a third time with a Guardsman and brought in both wounded stretcher-bearers. This highly dangerous task having been accomplished, he led his patrol forward to the house which was their objective and held it while the Pioneer section booby-trapped the building. Their task completed he managed with great skill to extricate the patrol, of whom all but eight were wounded; and finally he got Bruce back almost to the Company lines, taking forty minutes to cover a hundred and twenty yards under continual fire. The last lap was completed with the help of Major Sir Richard Powell, who went out to meet the party and in spite of enemy fire carried Bruce in on his back.

Lance-Sergeant Webb's devotion to duty and power of leadership, joined with courage of the highest order, not only saved Bruce from capture by the enemy but enabled the patrol to carry through the task they had been given. Before joining the Regiment he was a window-cleaner in Swansea.

Major A. H. S. Coombe-Tennant was also slightly wounded that day but returned to duty after one night in hospital. His career too had shown "courage of the highest order." He was taken prisoner at Boulogne in 1940 with others of the 2nd Battalion, thirty-six hours after the last ship had left. He made several unsuccessful attempts to escape and finally succeeded in August, 1942, having been in German hands for over two years. After a long and hazardous journey he reached England, where, after special employment he volunteered to go back to enemy-held territory to help the French resistance movement. Notwithstanding all he had suffered in captivity, he risked recapture and was dropped behind the German lines in France. When the Germans were driven out of France his task was finished so he reported for duty to the 1st Battalion (then in "the Island") and was given command of Prince of Wales Company.

The War Diary for the 7th of November continues :—

> "In the evening a lucky shell landed on the building used by the rifle companies as a cookhouse and set fire to it. A petrol tank exploded, ammunition on the trucks

began to go off and in a few minutes' time the whole place was blazing. By extreme good fortune only two men were wounded, but seven fifteen-hundredweight trucks and their complete contents went up in flames as well as 1,312 rations. . . ."

Losses might have been much greater if the Regimental Sergeant-Major had not been there. Though himself knocked over by the explosion he quickly got carriers organised to tow out what vehicles could be rescued from the fire and his fearless disregard of the exploding ammunition and determination to save transport set a fine example; he drove out two cookers himself. Regimental Sergeant-Major A. R. Baker had already twenty-two years' unbroken service with the 1st Battalion. He had been Regimental Sergeant-Major under six Commanding Officers and his loyalty and devotion to duty were unfailing. With the frame of a giant (he was six foot six) and the heart of a boy he brought a zest to all he did and conditions, however unpleasant, seem powerless to depress his ardour.

"*8th November.*—The Commanding Officer held his usual conference. The road from Veulen to Battalion H.Q. is now almost impassable except for carriers and even they frequently get stuck. During some shelling in the morning Lance-Corporal J. G. Jeffreys and Guardsman M. T. Powell of the Carrier Platoon were unfortunately killed by jumping into a ditch to avoid a shell and thereby setting off a mine. The ditches in this area abound with mines. . .

"*9th November.*—In the evening No. 4 Company sent a fighting patrol to act as flank guard to a patrol of the Herefords (on their right) which was clearing enemy mines. Lance-Sergeant A. Millward of the Carrier Platoon is missing and known to have been wounded and Lance-Sergeant E. T. Williams who tried to find him had a very close call when a Spandau bullet went through his cap and parted his hair for him. Lieutenant D. N. Brinson went out later to look for Sergeant Millward, but was unable to find him. . .

"10th November.—In the morning Major-General Roberts, Commanding the 11th Armoured Division, on his morning visit to the Battalion Command Post was extremely complimentary about the Battalion. . . . After which the Commanding Officer held his conference. Tactics have now been changed and instead of the aggressive policy of the last few days companies are going to keep quiet in the hope that the Germans will think the hand-over has taken place and come to find out who the new occupants are . . ."

But the enemy were not tempted and the Battalion were relieved that night. They had had a hard time. In addition to the numerous nightly patrols—and no attempt has been made to list them here—fifty per cent. of each company were always on duty day or night. There had been much shelling and mortaring, it had rained almost without ceasing and the mud was beyond description.

They went south, now, to the Sittard sector, where they were back with the Guards Armoured Division and had a troop of the 2nd Battalion tanks in support. This was a much more comfortable position. Sittard itself is a typically clean little Dutch town just inside the border. The companies were in fact over the border in two German villages, Millen and Tuddern, with the nearest enemy position about eight hundred yards away. The Dutch population was still living in Sittard and a few elderly peasants and some children had been left in Millen and Tuddern. "Live and let live" was the policy here. "Bar a certain amount of shelling, booby-traps, and some active patrolling on both sides, life has been fairly quiet. The inhabitants of the village have proved themselves un-guerrilla-like in manner and in some cases anxious to fraternise, which of course under GADSO/577/G/Q(MOB) para 4(C) (iii) [sic] is not allowed. However, nearly everybody has taken the chance of liberating a few chickens and pigs. In fact one or two animals go round the place with the name of a squadron or company tied round their necks so that in due course, when they become fat enough, they will get knocked on the head."

Twenty per cent. of the men were allowed to walk out by day
and could attend a cinema in Sittard ! There was, however, one
disconcerting incident. One evening two Guardsmen who were
peacefully cooking chip potatoes in their company billet had a
nasty shock when they turned round and found their room
shared by three German soldiers ! The Germans proceeded to
march them both off, but as they were coming downstairs
Guardsman Lloyd managed to trip and strike one German with
his fist, the only weapon he had, and Guardsman C. Brookes did
the same to another, with the result that both got away, though
Brookes was wounded when the Germans fired after them. The
Battalion had to cover a very wide front and the Germans'
intimate knowledge of their own village made it comparatively
easy for a small patrol to get into the position in darkness;
however vigilant sentries might be they could not be everywhere.

The Welsh Guards side-stepped to Geleen on December the
7th having been in the Sittard position for over three weeks.
They went into the line near Geleen on December the 11th and
were there till the 17th. Plans for an offensive which had kept
Captain Spencer-Smith, the Adjutant, busy were cancelled;
and after he had written in the diary "nothing passes the time
quicker than taking over a part of the line and preparing for a
major operation simultaneously" he made another entry
recording that "the 'change of plans' Committee must have been
working overtime lately" and inscribed in long and complicated
operation orders the arresting if somewhat unusually worded
paragraph : "Reconnaissance parties will probably be required
at a hideously early hour. . . . Orders will be issued separately."

But this was the end of their long period of static warfare.
They had been in the line since November the 4th after the
fighting in "the Island" and the tour of duty on Nijmegen bridge
and they were due for a rest.

CONSUMA AND POMINO

"They had now reached the head of the Arno valley. Here at Pontassieve the Arno turns west to Florence, while Route 70 starts eastwards over the northern spurs of the Prato Magna range to join the Upper Arno and Route 71 at Bibbiena. Another Division was advancing up the latter road and the 1st Guards Brigade spread out to hold Route 70 till their arrival. The Welsh Guards occupied the central position based on Podernuovo and they worked gradually forward over the long finger of high ground running up past Castelnuovo." (Part I, page 60.)

THERE is no need to describe these days at any length, for there was no fighting of note and the procedure followed the lines adopted in the Arno valley. The 3rd Battalion Headquarters were at Podernuovo in a villa known to the Welsh Guards as "Atrocity House." For while they were at Pelago and Podernuovo was still in enemy hands a report had come to them that German soldiers were brutally killing women and children in this villa. It is best to omit the detail of what happened. The fact is that of eighteen women and children who had collected there for safety, nine were wantonly murdered and nine survived the German cruelty only to go to hospital. One of those saved was an Englishwoman.

When the Welsh Guards moved to Podernuovo on August the 30th their patrols found the enemy in posts on Toschi about a mile to the north. On the following day they pushed the enemy off Toschi, killing some and taking some prisoners, and by the 2nd of September they had companies established about a mile farther north still. From there two patrols, out of many, should be recorded.

Just before daylight on the 4th of September Lieutenant R. O. Wrigley with a platoon of No. 4 Company set off quietly along the ridge. He had made a reconnaissance before and had briefed his men carefully overnight. Lance-Sergeant Neville

Pickersgill from Cardiff and two Guardsmen went with him as advance guard. The main body of twelve Guardsmen was under Sergeant F. D. Jones and carried with their other weapons a 2-inch mortar and sixteen rounds. A rearguard of six was commanded by Lance-Corporal Kenneth Culverhouse. Wrigley himself carried two smoke grenades, and he had arranged with the Forward Observation Officer of the Ayrshire Yeomanry that if smoke appeared he would put artillery fire down on it within four minutes.

The patrol had to move slowly and carefully when daylight came, especially when they went beyond the point to which the earlier reconnaissance had been made. It was about ten o'clock in the morning when Lance-Sergeant Pickersgill, who was about fifty yards ahead and on the right, saw a German steel helmet on a tree trunk. After this was reported the advance guard moved with great caution and suddenly Pickersgill came on a German soldier in his slit trench trying to light a cigarette; he seemed "much upset" by the appearance of Pickersgill's tommy-gun and surrendered promptly. Ten yards away they found a bivouac of branches in which a German corporal and two soldiers had slept through this incident; they too were taken prisoner. The main body was now brought up and established in the German position, while the prisoners were sent back under escort. Wrigley had learned from one of them that there was another enemy post two hundred yards along the ridge and he and Lance-Sergeant Pickersgill set off to find them. There is a good deal of cover there and they got to within ten yards of the sentry before he realised that he was covered by two tommy-guns at very close range. He put his hands up and again they found the rest of the post asleep in "bivvies"—one so soundly asleep that he had to be pulled out by his feet and "on waking and finding who had disturbed his slumber he turned a most unpleasant green and became incapable of movement through sheer fright." They learned from this bag of prisoners that the sergeant in command of their platoon was due back from their company headquarters, so sending the prisoners away under guard, Wrigley, with Lance-Corporal Culverhouse and Guardsman L. F. Boston, waited for him. They did not have long to wait. He arrived with a bottle of vino which, alas! he dropped when Wrigley spoke, and he too was sent back under Guardsman Boston's care. Before leaving he disclosed the fact that there was a German observation post under an officer three hundred yards away, so Wrigley and Culverhouse went off to try to collect its occupants. Unfortunately the ground near this post is more open and the sentry on duty was more alert. They were shot at when still a hundred yards away, but when they fired in return the occupants of the post fled down the hillside into the valley. They went on to examine the post, which was empty, and found that the wireless set used for reporting any movement of British troops which was observed, had been left behind and this they wrecked.

Firing now broke out behind them and they returned to find the main body being attacked by a party of Germans who had come to investigate. Wrigley ordered the withdrawal and, remaining with a small covering party till the main body was clear, he threw his smoke grenades and called down artillery fire on the enemy.

The patrol got back soon after one o'clock without a casualty. Their busy and interesting morning's work had produced ten prisoners, put a wireless-equipped observation post out of action and captured two Spandaus, two Schmeisers, two semi-automatic rifles and six ordinary rifles. Two days later when Wrigley led another patrol over the same ground they found recently dug German graves where the artillery fire had come down.

But all patrols were not so successful. On the 6th Lieutenant G. E. Seagar took a fighting patrol to shoot up any enemy found at Cigliano, a hamlet just east of the ridge. They got there and shot up a post of six men, but the whole position was much stronger than had been realised and they found themselves almost surrounded and attacked from several points. Seagar ordered the patrol to fall back to woods behind, but he and seven men were overwhelmed and taken prisoner and it was largely due to the coolness and courage shown by Lance-Sergeant F. E. Williams, a loader from Rhos, that the rest of the party got away.

On the 5th of September a small German patrol succeeded in wounding a corporal in one of No. 4 Company's forward posts, but apart from this the enemy was unaggressive. A trickle of deserters from their lines came in during these days—an odd lot which included Germans from two different regiments, a Frenchman and an Alsacian. And a perfect deluge of rain came down at intervals, greatly to the discomfort of companies living in slit trenches which became water-tanks in a very few minutes.

There is a cryptic entry in the Commanding Officer's personal diary of these days which reads, "Lorna brought wads to No. 1 Company." All soldiers know that a "wad" is a piece of cake or a bun; all who served in the 3rd Battalion in Africa and Italy know that after Captain Twining was killed looking for his lost patrol at Fondouk, Mrs. Lorna Twining went out to minister to the comfort of her husband's battalion and of others in the 1st Guards Brigade. They all know this and bless her. There were many other ladies who served the army in mobile canteens, but there were very few who served with one formation throughout a whole campaign and managed to get so far forward and to arrive with such consistency when "tea and wads" and the other extras she brought were just what were wanted most by men who were having a hard time. Her name will live in the story of the Regiment, as the memory of her gentle kindness will live in the hearts of those who served in the 3rd Battalion. Which accounts for the entry that recurs so often in various diaries, "Lorna arrived with wads."

2-INCH MORTAR USED BY INFANTRY.

BATTAGLIA AND VERRO

After the penetration of the Gothic Line the Allies' advance in the mountains north of Florence made progress, at first, "in face of stiff opposition and all the handicaps of natural conditions and artificial contrivance." But it was slow going even before the winter made movement impracticable. . . . "The Welsh Guards went on to Battaglia on October the 2nd . . . . They remained in this sector till the middle of the following February . . . . Unlike the armies of bygone days, which at this time of year would have retired sensibly to winter quarters, they continued to man what must surely be one of the most fantastic winter lines ever devised for the discomfort of the troops." (Part I, page 63.)

A LARGE-SCALE map of the mountain area in which the Battalion spent that winter shows a confusing and almost unintelligible jumble of contour lines crowding together round the steep crests and ragged ridges, opening only a little in the valleys and gullies which separate one from another. There is no well-defined plan, no central spine. All is confusion as though the earth had boiled and hardened in the process.

On the other hand, the small-scale map which omits detail not only fails to convey a true idea of the country but inevitably gives a somewhat false impression. Places appear to be near together which are in fact separated by heights or depressions that are far more formidable than mere distance. Tracks which appear to traverse but a short mile or two are in fact many times longer than they seem, because of the climbs and descents which they involve. Even the photos reproduced on page 339 give but a poor conception of this country.

After the companies left the road when they went on to Battaglia on the 2nd of October, they started a trek which began at three o'clock in the afternoon and only got them to the positions to be taken over at ten o'clock that night. The ground was reasonably dry then, but the tracks were steep and narrow

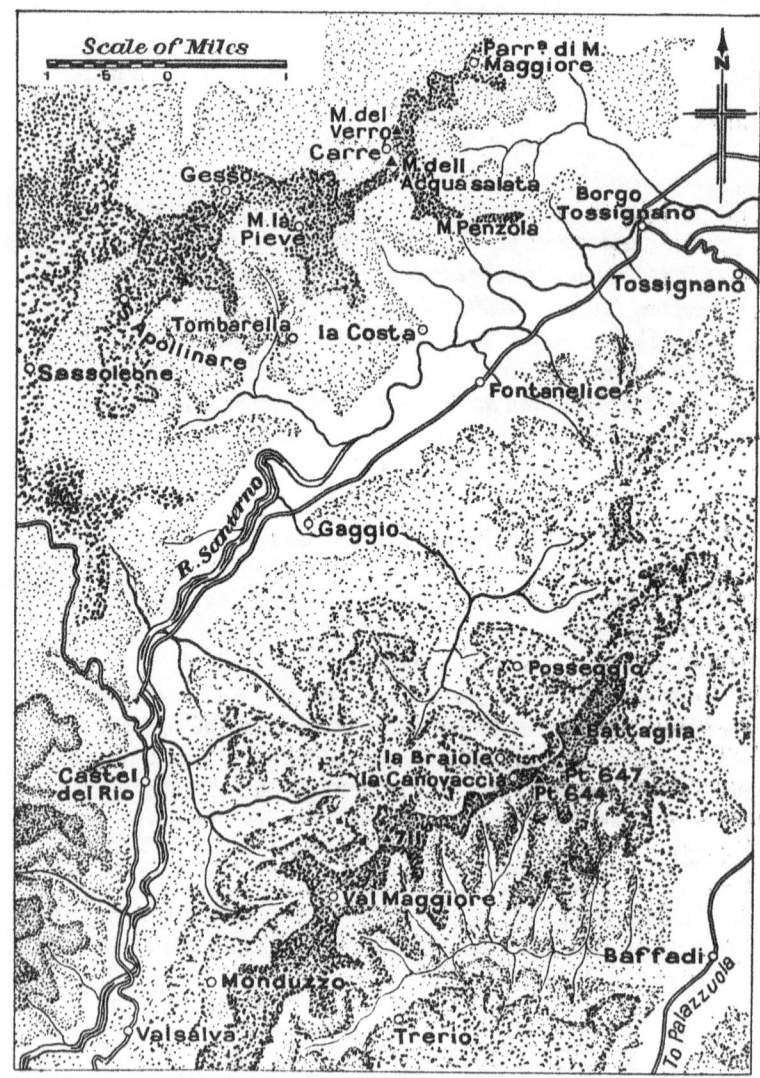

MOUNTAIN POSITIONS HELD IN WINTER OF 1944-5.

and rough, slippery in some places after recent rain and half obliterated in others by loose rocks, and the arms and equipment which the men had to carry made the long climb more testing.

Battaglia is the highest point of a long, twisting ridge. It is crowned by the ruins of an old castle, only to be reached on hands and knees and with the help of ropes suspended from the summit. For a mile or so before this last peak the ridge is a narrow knife-edge from which the mountain-side falls steeply on either hand. The 1st Guards Brigade went there to relieve American troops who so far had held the position against a number of determined counter-attacks; for the Germans were on the extension of the ridge beyond the castle and on other ridges which jutted out from it on either side. On the night of October the 2nd the Welsh Guards took over the causeway defences. On the next night the Coldstream Guards relieved the American troops on the south-east slopes, and on the 4th the Grenadiers took over the castle area.

Unburied dead in both American and German uniforms were evidence of the severe fighting which had taken place, but apart from frequent mortar and shell fire the companies were not greatly troubled by the enemy during their first week there. On the other hand, life was made almost intolerable by rain. The torrential rain that fell was almost unprecedented for Italy at this time of year. "The rain filled the slit-trenches, and a slit-trench was the only place where a man could find shelter from shell fire. He was permanently soaked to the skin, and permanently in danger. He spent his day in the bleak surroundings of stunted, decapitated trees, hundreds of waterlogged shell holes, unburied corpses of American and German soldiers, sopping blankets and discarded ration tins. Night brought him little rest, no relief from rain or shell fire, and the added threat of an enemy raid on either of our open flanks. The lot of the ration parties, which made the nightly journey up the causeway, was almost equally unpleasant. The causeway was the only possible approach to our positions—a veritable knife-edge, so narrow that in places it was only possible to stand with feet astride upon it, registered by enemy mortars and swept by gales of driving rain. But the greatest enemy by far was the mud. The mud could not be cleared. As there was only one track, in use by one hundred and fifty mules and one hundred men night after night, its surface became a knee-deep glutinous morass, which only a month of unbroken sunshine would dry out. Once the surface had been liquefied, a mule's spindly leg, digging deeply in with each step, was a sure way of making the quagmire almost bottomless. It was at its worst after a spell of dry weather, which only dried the mud into a yet stickier consistency and made it necessary with each step to lift the foot out of the ground, instead of merely from it."

Evacuation of casualties was a long and very arduous business. To ease it, small relays of stretcher bearers lived in positions dug in the side of the hill at four hundred yard intervals along the track leading back to the road and by this means the "carry" from the head of the causeway was reduced to three and a half hours; but on the steep and slippery track it was a horrible journey for a wounded man to take. Mercifully casualties in the Battalion were not so numerous as they were on Cerasola.

The companies were spaced along the ridge in some depth, and although they maintained standing patrols in the intervals there was an obvious risk that the enemy, moving up through the gullies on either side, would get between them in the darkness. The Advanced Battalion Headquarters of the Grenadiers were in fact raided on the night of October the 9th and a somewhat comic (and very unwarlike) incident occurred in one of the Welsh Guards' platoon positions on the night of the 10th. The official record says baldly, "Two men of the I/577 G.R. Regiment were taken prisoners." What happened is told by Lieutenant P. A. Carr (No. 4 Company) in a letter home. "At 2 a.m. I was still trying to get to sleep on a stretcher outside my slit trench—trying to sleep lightly enough to hear my field telephone and wondering whether the shelling was coming near enough to make me take cover. Suddenly someone flung himself alongside my stretcher as another shell came over and I, thinking it was my corporal, chided him for being so frightened. On hearing my voice the man jumped up terrified for he had thought I was a protective layer of rock. Another got up behind him, equally frightened, and both flung their arms up and explained that they had wandered from their own lines into ours by mistake. In fact I had captured two Germans!" It was the beginning of an eventful night and Carr's adventures were not yet finished.

At daybreak on the 11th of October the enemy attacked. There is no doubt as to what he intended, for after the action Lieutenant-Colonel Gurney picked up a copy of the German Operation Orders and a marked map. The 1st Battalion 577 G.R. were ordered to "Occupy the enemy maintenance route" to Monte Battaglia and "hold the objectives gained, facing west, south and south-west against enemy counter-attacks." The specific objectives named in the order are (1) Le Braiole, a farm in the gully to the left of the sketch overleaf, (2) Point 647, and (3) La Canovaccia and Point 644. Fortunately our troops were well disposed to defeat just such a plan. The Grenadier Guards held the castle and were astride the ridge immediately on our side of it. No. 1 Company Welsh Guards were astride the ridge farther back and, in particular, a platoon under Lieutenant W. A. O. J. Bell was just below the crest of Point 647. A second platoon had positions on Point 644 and had a standing patrol on the ridge in front during hours of darkness. Then came No. 3 Company, with two platoons: one under Lieutenant J. T. Jerman at La Braiole, and one near Company Headquarters in the farm buildings at La Canovaccia: the Regimental Aid Post and the Advanced Headquarters of the Grenadier Battalion were also there.

According to the evidence of German prisoners their companies were rather late in starting. Two companies moved round the side of Battaglia (where their movements were heard and reported by the Grenadiers), but in approaching their objectives both companies lost direction and became hopelessly intermingled. Captain Cassavetti, commanding No. 4 Company, who had with him Lieutenant Carr and Lance-Corporal J. McGhan, were coming back from a visit to the castle, which they were to take over from the Grenadiers next night. They had just been challenged by the standing patrol in front of Point 647 when they ran into a German party. In the confusion they all got safely in, while four of the Germans were killed by the standing patrol. Just after five o'clock in the morning Germans entered the yard at Canovaccia and were met by fire from a section of No. 3 Company under Lance-Corporal D. F.

Burgess who engaged them point blank and drove them off down the hillside. There an attack was being made on La Braiole. where Jerman's platoon held their fire till the last minute, expecting a standing patrol which they had out under Lance-Sergeant C. Wilcox to come in; but these were apparently over-run for they were missing at the end of the action. One party of Germans also got near to the position, two hundred yards away, occupied by the mortar platoon of the Grenadier Guards, but though the Grenadiers afterwards found three of their men missing both they and Jerman's platoon beat the

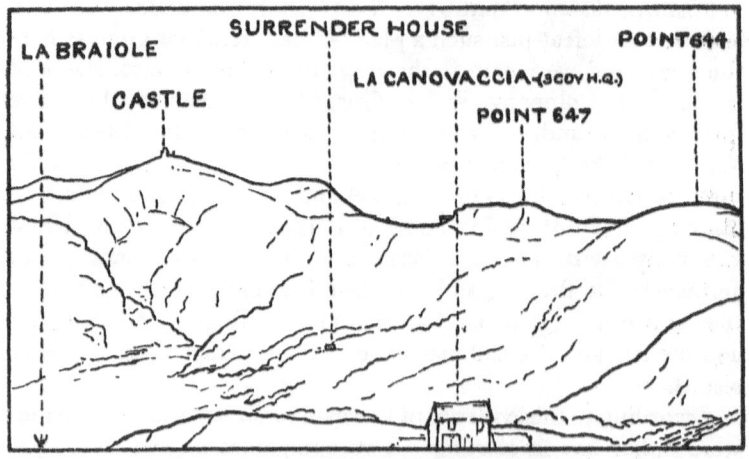

THE BATTAGLIA RIDGE.

enemy off. Our own 3-inch mortars had put down defensive fire in front of No. 3 Company, and machine guns from No. 1 Company were shooting with good effect across No. 3 Company's front. The Germans were in considerable confusion, but shortly afterwards No. 3 Company were able to warn No. 1 Company that an attack was coming in against them. Once again the Germans got very close to the top of the ridge, but the heavy machine-gun and rifle fire which met them again forced them back and they made for cover to a house farther up the valley which is shown in the sketch. This was promptly shot up by mortars, machine guns and small-arms fire from both Welsh

Guards and Grenadiers, and soon a man with a Red Cross flag came up to No. 1 Company and asked for an armistice to enable their wounded to be collected. They were given half an hour, but warned that at the end of that time the house they were in would be obliterated unless the force surrendered. In fact they were given longer, and after three-quarters of an hour a white flag was put out and the officer in command and seventy-four Germans came out with their hands up and surrendered to No. 1 Company.

Apart from the men of the missing standing patrol the Welsh Guards had only three men wounded, but their satisfaction at the outcome of this affair was overshadowed when shortly afterwards a chance shell mortally wounded Major J. F. F. Baron de Rutzen. He had been a senior officer of the Battalion throughout its campaigns in North Africa and Italy and he held a unique place in the affection of officers and men. With a stern sense of duty and discipline he combined a wry wit and a keen sense of fun, and beneath all was a sensitive gentleness which is well illustrated in the lines he wrote after Fondouk. (Page 121.) The whole Battalion felt his death keenly.

That night the Welsh Guards relieved the Grenadiers of responsibility for the castle sector. Sixteen men lived in the ruined keep, and although the walls were thick enough to make it reasonably safe it was a horrid position to occupy. There could be no movement outside by day and the relics of death and destruction inside were unpleasant companions to live with in so small a space. However, the enemy made no further attempts to recapture it and the Battalion were relieved, by companies, on the 14th and 15th, and went back to billets down the valley. Four days later when they came back on to Battaglia their patrols found that the enemy had withdrawn and eventually the castle became a rear position.

The Welsh Guards left the Battaglia sector on October the 24th and on the 25th they crossed the Santerno valley road and went into the mountains on its northern side. Conditions were much the same while they remained there till the end of the month. All supplies reached them on mules and the only entry in the War Diary for October the 25th reads, "Tracks and roads impassable. Continuous rain." There was the usual patrolling, but only No. 4 Company on the ridge which flanks the valley road had any excitement.

One platoon of the Company (No. II) occupied an isolated house on the forward slope of the ridge and could only communicate with Company Headquarters—some way back along the top of the ridge—by telephone. On the 28th of October Lance-Sergeant E. Hart, who was commanding the platoon, was told by an Italian peasant that the Germans were using a house in the hamlet of La Costa, a few hundred yards away in front. He reported this to his Company Commander (Major J. R. Martin Smith) and was told to plan a night raid and submit his proposals later. Before he could do so a heavy burst of shell fire cut the telephone wire, and while Hart was making his plan a mountain mist shrouded the ground ahead. He was quick to realise the opportunity this gave him and decided to make a surprise attack without waiting for darkness or for orders. Leading a small party forward through the mist, they rushed the German sentry and took him and four other German soldiers prisoner. As these came from a regiment which had not till then been identified on that sector of the front their capture was important to our Intelligence Staff. Hart's action was an admirable example of initiative, self-reliance and good leadership in a junior commander.

On the following day Corporal McGhan, who had been promoted to Lance-Sergeant since his escapade on Battaglia, was told to occupy the raided house as it got dark and to hold it through the night. He took a fighting patrol of six Guardsmen, met and dispersed an enemy patrol on the way and duly installed his men. Just before three o'clock in the morning an enemy party of fifteen to twenty men—more than double the number with him—tried to rush the house and succeeded in throwing a grenade in through the window. McGhan and three of his men were wounded by the explosion—one of them seriously. But they kept the enemy out and eventually fought them off, killing and wounding enough to make the party retire. At first light he contrived an improvised stretcher for the badly wounded Guardsman and got his whole party back safely to Company Headquarters. He was in great pain from his own wounded leg and had to be evacuated to hospital, but his determined leadership "not only saved his post from being over-run, after half his section had been wounded, but resulted in the rout of a numerically far superior enemy."

On the 31st of October the Battalion were relieved and moved to billets, first in various places on the Salerno valley road and afterwards round Palazzuola in the Senio valley, which follows a parallel course five miles or so to the south-east. On November the 11th they moved from there and went for the last time into the Battaglia sector, though forward of their old positions for the whole of the ridge was by then in our hands. They had an uneventful week and the War Diary for November the 18th records that "artificial moonlight aided the relief enormously." They were back in their billets in Palazzuola by half-past four in the morning, and at nine o'clock they left in transport for a six-hour drive which ended at Greve, fifteen miles south-west of Florence.

Greve was their salvation in the months that followed. A routine was evolved which limited each tour of duty in the mountains to four or five days and gave them a similar time in Greve before they went back for their next tour. While there they could visit Florence, where they made many friends and received much kindness. So they lived a double life, dividing their time between slit trenches on the barren mountain tops and Florence drawing-rooms and restaurants. "Dates" could be booked for "the next time out." It was like being in London during the season, but having to slip away every five days or so to do some fighting in the Welsh mountains. To repay the hospitality of many Florence hostesses they organised a dance which, if less elaborate then the Duchess of Richmond's in Brussels, was at least done as well as possible with the help of what was euphemistically called the "off-white" market. A number of officers and men were left out of battle each time to give them some relief, and Major J. O. M. Ashton, who was Second-in-Command of the Battalion at this time, alternated with Lieutenant-Colonel Gurney.

It would be tedious to recount in detail their moves backwards and forwards and there is not enough of military interest in this period to give importance to a full record. It was the now familiar round. Positions were occupied and patrolling was organised and when the enemy got tired of being worried, and moved back, our positions were moved forward and the worrying was resumed. Occasionally small-scale actions were fought in order to improve our positions, but the Welsh Guards were not involved except once and then only to a very minor extent. On the 4th of December two platoons of No. 3 Company under Lieutenant J. T. Jerman and Lieutenant B. B. Pugh were employed in a small diversion on the flank of a more serious action in which Monte Penzola was captured by the Coldstream Guards after a stiff fight.

As positions were advanced the way became longer and the mule supply more exhausting. Captain J. J. Gurney, who was in charge of the muling during most of this time, wrote an account of the procedure adopted when mule-base was in the hamlet of Sant Appolinare behind the positions on the northern side of the Salerno valley.

"The available accommodation in what was left of this small village was already taken so we pitched tents in the rain, in a sea of mud. During this operation the enemy put down a fair number of shells, but no damage was done and we were only once again troubled in this respect the whole time we were there. While all this was going on I made contact with the Indian Mule Company who were already established quite near us, and told them the approximate number of mules we should require and the time they were to report. All the kit was ferried forward by jeep and taken over by the mule-base company representatives, who laid everything out by loads in two parallel lines ready for the mules. Each company representative was told how many mules he would be allotted : when they arrived he was to collect this number, lead them between the two parallel lines and load up.

"Zero hour for the mules came, but no stir from the Indians. A full hour passed during which I sent frantic and threatening messages every ten minutes. It was now pitch dark, but at last they arrived—ten mules short and no loading ropes ; luckily we had plenty of signal cable. The Indians made little effort to help, but the Guardsmen worked brilliantly, cutting the wire into lengths and tying up the wet and muddy loads by the light of a few dim torches. All this in pouring rain and bitter cold. At last everyone was ready. An N.C.O. had already reported back from the Battalion to act as guide; he placed himself at the head of the column and we started off. The column consisted of seventy or eighty mules; one Indian to each pair of mules, and three Guardsmen to each company group. I watched the column file by and followed up in rear to see that not too much fell off *en route*. Periodically, despite every care in tying, a bundle of greatcoats or a box of 'Compo' rations would slip its wire and roll off into the darkness and mud. There was really little one could do for if we stopped every time we would never get there. Eventually we arrived at 'Tac. H.Q.' Here guides from each company were waiting and led off their respective mules to their areas. I went into Tac. H.Q. and enjoyed a glass of rum, congratulations for the kit that had arrived, and a 'rocket' for the stuff that had fallen off *en route*. The company mules having delivered their loads returned to Tac. H.Q. When all were present, the party re-formed and started the long walk home. On arriving at mule-base, the Indians and their mules were dismissed with much smiling and gesticulation on all sides. A hot meal and large helpings of rum were waiting for us all.

"Next morning, the first task was to ring up Tac. H.Q. and find out what the companies needed and to let their representatives at mule base know what would have to be provided that night. The next tasks were to telephone the total requirements through to jeep-head at Sassoleone and, finally, to contact the Indians and order twice the number of mules needed an hour earlier than I wanted them. This meant that we got the right amount of mules more or less on time. Meanwhile the Guardsmen were put to improving tents and making fires to dry clothing, etc. In the afternoon there was a compulsory siesta for those going up the hill that evening. There was nothing further to do till teatime when the jeeps arrived with all the kit. This was sorted by the representatives, arranged by loads into parallel lines, loaded on to the mules when they arrived and so up to the Battalion.

"This is a description of a normal day's work, but alas! very few days were normal. On one occasion the jeep track was flooded and I had to organise quickly a second party of mules to ferry the kit from Sassoleone to mule base proper. A worse occasion was when transport failed to get through and I had the humiliation of going round to beg 'Compo' and rum off another unit. I quickly learned to build up a private reserve to cover emergencies. But these difficulties were small compared with getting supplies intact up to the Battalion. The going was often appalling, the hundreds of mules that had to use one track every night quickly churned the mud to an incredibly glutinous mass. Route finding was never easy and guides frequently lost the way. This was not surprising as the tracks all looked much the same even in daylight. It is a miracle that we never took a complete column into the German lines. However, all this was no compensation to the company that last heard of its rations five miles in the wrong direction, and the telephones would get pretty 'warm' in the later hours of the night. In spite of all this, on no occasion was anyone badly let down and no praise could be too great for the Guardsmen who, despite appalling going, obstinate mules and bolshy muleteers, almost invariably got the supplies through."

At the start of the campaign mules supplied to the Battalion were big, strong beasts and all harness was in good condition. Later, when injury and mortality-rates increased and mountain tracks were marked by mule corpses the Battalion had to make do with a smaller and weaker animal known in the mule world as "third class." "The artillery in the mountains were given, very properly, the first-class mules and the Americans, very politely, the second-class. The P.B.I. got what were left." With the advent of frost and snow every slope froze hard and snow caked in the hooves of the mules. At night tracks would be jammed by frantic drivers trying to ease frightened beasts up or down the banks of ice. Poor brutes! There is little wonder they and their Indian drivers liked to hurry back, after delivering their loads, at a pace which left their Guardsmen guides behind and frequently unshipped the light loads of salvage with which they started back. Salvage was important in those days. Lieutenant-Colonel Gurney was an implacable hater of waste and kept the Battalion busy cleaning up the mountains whenever there was salvage to be collected. "Salvage proceeds apace and every evening sees the causeway crowded with enthusiastic Guardsmen picking up petrol cases, mortar boxes, "drawers cellular" and other items of kit, with that charming zeal for hard work which has long been their most endearing characteristic. They sing softly to themselves at their work and from time to time there falls sweetly on the cool night air the enchanted words "——! ——! ——!"

From December to February the companies were at various places, first along the Penzola ridge; next on Monte dell Acqua Salata to the north; and finally, on Boxing-day, on to Monte del Verro, farther north still. For over a month the Battalion had been holding positions in the neighbourhood of this feature and had heard many stories from its tenants. Of the forward company position where no movement could take place by day; of the hazards encountered by the supply train; and of the cramped Command Post in a decrepit hill farm where the Commanding Officer slept in a manger.

By this time the issue of winter clothing had vastly improved, with the result that the cases of frost-bite and trench feet numbered only a small percentage of the total suffered in the south of Italy early in the campaign. Wind suits were issued— outsize hooded canvas garments—string vests, Alpine pattern pullovers, and thick white socks; all of which helped to keep out the cold. But no satisfactory method was ever devised of keeping the thawing snow out of boots.

"In remembering the period that the Battalion spent in these hills, it is not only the weather, the enemy or the supply problems that spring to mind. The pattern of the five-day stays was made of a hundred and one little incidents, few of military importance. One thinks of the clandestine partridge shooting in the reserve company area; of the New Year's Day celebrations when the Germans fired all manner of tracer into the sky in the form of a gigantic 'V' sign, and of our prosaic reply of one round gun-fire from every gun in the Eighth Army."

They went on to Verro for the last time on the night of February the 14th. On the following night there was an unusual amount of enemy shelling and mortar fire, especially on the outpost area held by No. 4 Company under Major J. D. Gibson-Watt. Company Sergeant-Major Thomas Hadyn Evans was killed and eight Guardsmen were wounded, and later two forward platoons under Lieutenant D. G. Cottom were attacked by fifteen to twenty German paratroops. But the company sentries were alert and gave warning of movement before the attack came in. Defensive fire from artillery, mortars and machine guns was called down and when the attackers appeared they were met by a hail of grenades and rifle and Bren gun fire. Their reception was warmer than they had bargained for and after a twenty minutes' fight they withdrew, leaving their dead behind. A few could be seen, but the position of Cottom's platoons was under enemy observation and the ground in front could not be fully examined.

So ended their time on Verro. On the 17th of February, 1945, the Welsh Guards left the mountains of Italy for the last time. They were not in action again until the final battle on this front took them over the Po to victory.

* * * * *

Two months later, on April the 12th Lieutenant-Colonel Gurney left the Battalion which he had commanded for ten strenuous months to take up a Staff appointment. Brigadier C. A. M. D. Scott paid a high tribute both to him and to the Battalion when he wrote: "The high morale and great efficiency of this Battalion, which has been noticed by all who have seen it, is to a very large degree due to Colonel Gurney's example, his refusal to accept anything but the best, and his own considerable personal bravery."

Lieutenant-Colonel R. C. R. Price, D.S.O., was appointed to command the Battalion and Major J. R. Martin Smith acted as Commanding Officer till he arrived on the 22nd. By then the final battle in Italy had reached its climax.

A SCOUT CAR

THE PO AND THE ADIGE

"The doorway to Ferrara—the Argenta gap—had been forced ajar, and on the 19th of April the 6th Armoured Division burst it wide open and struck out into the country beyond." (*Part I, page 77.*)

THERE is a famous story to be told of the heavy fighting in which the fortified defences of the Senio river position were overcome and the Argenta gap was won; but the Welsh Guards had no part in it and so it must be read in other pages. As soon as these positions were won, however, the speed and striking power of an armoured division were needed if the enemy's forces were to be prevented from escaping across the Po. So the privilege of reaping the fruits of that first ten days' fighting was given to the 6th Armoured Division.

During that time the Welsh Guards with the rest of the Division moved up behind the battle, each concentration area more dusty and more deeply scarred than the last. By April the 16th they had reached a little place called Boccaleone (which is not shown on the map on page 260) and saw the extraordinary collection of amphibious and other vehicles which are employed in modern warfare, trundling slowly forward—Buffaloes, Weasels and Dukws, Arks, Crabs and Crocodiles—specimens of what has been aptly called "the ingenious ironmongery of war." Early on the 20th the Division was ordered to break out and the 26th Armoured Brigade advanced, with the Welsh Guards under command. They had hoped for a flying start, but they met stiff opposition after going only four hundred yards and it took the tanks twenty-four hours to win positions that had been reported as already in our hands. During this first phase the Welsh Guards did flank guard to the armour, No. 1 Company being the first to go into action early on the 20th. During the day the other companies were committed in turn and that night the Battalion held positions along the north bank of the Reno river at Traghetto, Malvezzi and Borgo Cortili. There was some fighting in places, but Welsh Guards casualties were

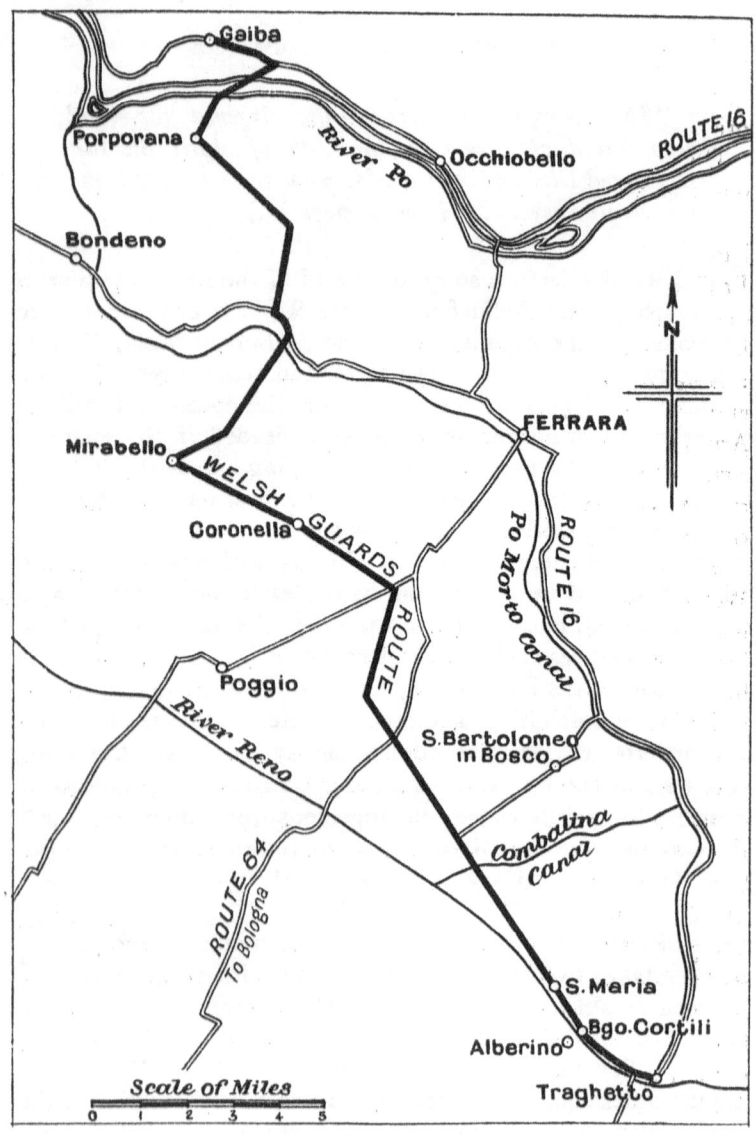

THE ADVANCE TO THE PO.

light and they took about forty prisoners that day. Traghetto had been totally burnt out as a result of our air bombing the day before and Malvezzi was still burning when Battalion Headquarters moved in. On April the 21st nearly a hundred more prisoners were taken.

On that day there was hard fighting for the next water obstacle, the Combalina canal, which the enemy held in some strength. Part of the 1st Battalion of the Welch Regiment (who had taken the place of the Coldstream Guards in the 1st Guards Brigade) made an assault crossing, for the bridges had been destroyed; but before they were across in strength they were heavily counter-attacked by German armour. They were unable to maintain their small bridgehead, but while they engaged the German tanks the 17th/21st Lancers from the Armoured Brigade found an unblown bridge to the narrow strip of ground between the Combalina and the Reno; they rushed the bridge, broke through the forces defending the corridor and poured through, not stopping till they had seized Renalico, five miles behind the enemy who were fighting the Welch Regiment on the Combalina. The Welch Regiment then made a second assault, crossing in strength, and established a firm bridgehead through which the Grenadier Guards passed forward. With the fall of Renalico the Germans were compelled to retreat.

On April the 22nd the Armoured Brigade drove still more deeply into the flank of the enemy, cutting his lines of communication and destroying columns now in full retreat towards the Po. The Brigade had some hard fighting, but reached Mirabello, where the Welsh Guards were called for. Their night in Mirabello was very uncomfortable, for the enemy was still in one part of the town and his mortar bombs fell heavily on the sector held, but when morning came No. 1 Company under Major P. V. Makins cleared up the remaining resistance with the help of a flame-thrower, while the Armoured Brigade again pushed on to capture Bondeno and turn south-west to Finale. A reconnaissance party from the Welsh Guards went forward to be ready should the assistance of infantry be called for, and the scene on the road they took was typical of many during that rapid armoured advance. Dust rose in clouds from passing transport while excited civilians ran frantically about in the high green corn which bordered the road. Already the scattered farmhouses flew white flags, varying in size from a pocket handkerchief to a bed sheet. Here a German half-track stood abandoned on the highway and there a large green and yellow signal lorry lay on its side across the ditch. A nearby ammunition dump exploded fitfully and a dying cow had to be put out of its agony. Several guns were found spiked and the horses which had pulled them into position were in an adjacent shed. Batches of begrimed prisoners marched through the dust and two jeeps came down the road with cherry coloured sheets on their bonnets. These bore Americans from the 5th Army: the two armies had met and the Germans south of the Po were encircled !

Little time was wasted in greetings. Boundaries were agreed and the drive was continued, and soon afterwards came news that the Armoured Brigade had reached the Po. The Welsh Guards party no longer complained of the dust or were impressed by the tracking columns of prisoners: these were now just a part of the after-battle scene. A reconnaissance to the Po was carried out on the 24th and the Grenadiers made a rapid crossing that night, meeting only light opposition. Early next morning the Welsh Guards followed them, "having selected twelve Dukws from an aquarium of amphibious beasts." Major Gibson-Watt with No. 4 Company led and proceeded at once to direct the clearance of a sector of ground which had been allotted to the Company. The country is flat, closely cultivated and for the most part hedgeless, but it is intersected by irrigation ditches and thin rows of slender poplars which mark the boundaries of farms or line the lanes which connect them. For operational purposes key points had been christened with names of a bevy of ladies—Mary, Charlotte, Alice, Juliet, etc.—to be captured by the Guardsmen, and these were chalked on their maps. Among the first away after they landed was Sergeant M. G. G. Chatwin, commanding a platoon of No. 4 Company, and by a combination of skilful leadership and unskilful map reading he managed always to be at least one lady ahead of his named objective. Leading his platoon with great skill and bravery, he directed them in attacks on six in turn and covered a distance of over five miles; and the whole company under Gibson-Watt's energetic command made good a deep wedge of territory. The other companies meanwhile were similarly engaged in enlarging the bridgehead until all had orders to stand fast.

To crown this day of great success, Lieutenant-Colonel Price determined to prepare for another by seizing the bridge at Castel Guglielmo where the Bianco canal crosses their road to the Adige, five miles ahead of the point they had reached, Undeterred by their previous exertions, Sergeant Emrys Davies' platoon volunteered for the task with a troop of the amphibious tanks on which they were mounted. Lieutenant-Colonel Price with Gibson-Watt and Major Grieg of the Ayrshire Yeomanry led the party in jeeps. The road they took was littered with the charred vehicles and dead horses of German transport and many of the houses they passed were half ruined. Italians encountered were surly and suspicious till they realised that these were British troops and that the hated Tedeschi had gone: then their excitement was terrific and their uproarious welcome an embarrassment. But Castel Guglielmo was reached as evening fell and, as one of the party said later, "the place stank from the word go: doors hanging open, dust blowing about the street, no sign of life—all very fishy to anyone who knew anything of war. We stopped short of the bridge and inspected it." It looked all right. Then the Guardsmen who had dropped off the tanks opened fire on a German who ran across the road on the far side and at once a white verey light sailed up from a house beyond. With the platoon deployed to give covering fire, a tank was to cross first. Its engine roared into life and the order to advance was in the troop leader's mouth when there was an appalling explosion and the bridge was no more. Before the smoke cleared the enemy opened fire with spandaus and bazookas. Darkness was falling and with the bridge blown there was no point in continuing the fight. The attempt had nearly, but not quite, succeeded; the party was ordered to rejoin the Battalion, which remained concentrated in the area next day while engineers bridged the canal at another point.

On the 27th the Welsh Guards followed other units of the Division in the drive to the Adige, and while the Welch Regiment went past Lendinara the Welsh Guards were ordered to clear the

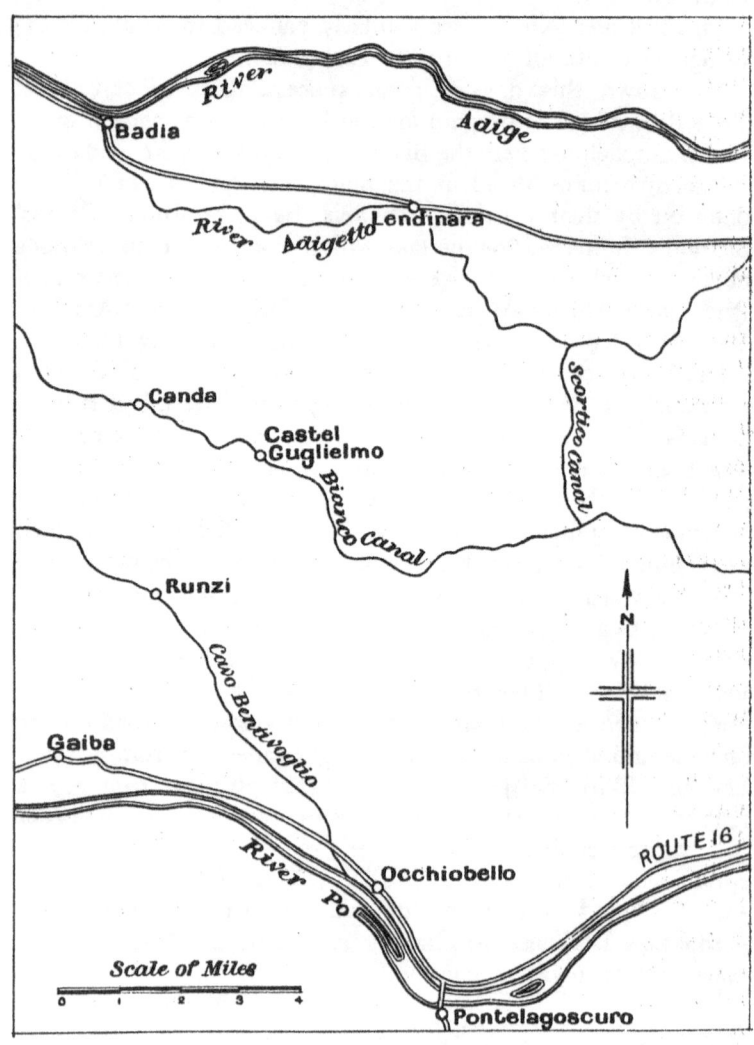

FROM THE PO TO THE ADIGE.

town. The Carrier Platoon under Lieutenant J. J. Hoffman were given this task and in a brisk fight round the cemetery they killed and wounded a number of the enemy, while seventy prisoners of war were taken in the town. They also captured three self-propelled guns : two had been wrecked, but the third was in perfect condition with wireless set still working.

The Battalion were next ordered to cross the Adige and employing tactics which had gained for them the advantages of surprise at the Po crossing, the Commanding Officer directed that no offensive action would be taken against anyone seen on the far bank before the crossing started. But the enemy had no similar reason to lie low and a German sniper, perched high in the tangled steel-work of the blown bridge, narrowly missed the Commanding Officer as he went forward to reconnoitre for the crossing. Then news came that another crossing had been found a few miles away and there was no need to force a crossing here. The order for non-aggression was rescinded and the Welsh Guards snipers took up positions along the south bank of the river. Before long a party of twelve Germans, led by two non-commissioned officers on horseback, moved towards the broken bridge along the far bank of the river. The riders dismounted and the whole party was allowed to climb half-way across the bridge before the Welsh Guards opened fire. One was knocked off and three more were wounded; and making a quick appreciation of their position the whole thirteen surrendered.

These were the last shots fired by the 3rd Battalion Welsh Guards (and by the 1st Guards Brigade) in the war of 1939 to 1945. It was the afternoon of Friday the 27th of April.

But no one realised at that time that there would be no more fighting and the 29th was spent in clearing the area—"Exercise Ferreting"—when the Grenadiers and the Welsh Guards were ordered to "beat" defined areas "in order to liquidate enemy troops and suspicious characters." It was laid down in Brigade orders that "the battalion sending in the biggest bag to Brigade Headquarters will be adjudged the most successful. Entries close 2400 hours on April the 29th." The Grenadiers were the winners with a margin of two marks.

After this the drive north continued, but as the battle had ended so must this account of it end.

THE RHINELAND BATTLE.

"There remained to be cleared the Rhineland territory lying south of Nijmegen between the Roer and the Rhine. . . . The Rhineland battle opened on the 8th of February. . . . In the opening phase of the battle the Guards Armoured Division was one of the reserve divisions of the 30th Corps." (Part I, page 74.)

THE battle had been raging fiercely for nearly a week when the Welsh Guards were called upon. The 1st Battalion moved up on February the 13th and on the 14th they went into action. Their task was to clear a large wood two miles to the south-east of Gennep. There had been heavy fighting at Gennep and the German dead were much in evidence when the Welsh Guards passed through, but in the woods they had to clear thickly planted conifers; they met very little opposition and, following closely a creeping barrage, they reached their objectives and took up positions on the eastern side of the woodland.

A squadron of the 2nd Battalion's tanks (No. 2 Squadron under Major N. M. Daniel) meanwhile supported the Irish Guards in an attack on Hommersum. "The first part of our little operation might have been a demonstration at Aldershot"; the Irish Guards took their objectives and although there was heavy shelling of their position "no one in the squadron was hurt." On the following day (February the 15th) the same squadron went north to the support of a battalion of the Black Watch at Kessel. They had an uneventful time, but on their way back Lieutenant H. W. J. E. Peel was hit by shell fire and subsequently died of wounds. They were near Hommersum at this time and an enemy counter-attack on the village was beginning. Daniel's tank was bogged in soft ground so he ran over to Peel's tank. But Peel was too badly wounded to be moved, and throughout the rest of the action Daniel commanded from the outside of the turret, disregarding a hail of mortar and machine-gun fire and heavy shelling.

On the afternoon of February the 16th No. 1 Squadron (Major N. T. L. Fisher) was ordered to support the Coldstream Guards in an attack on Mull. It was a sorry day for the tanks. Ground which looked sound enough proved to be a squelching quagmire. One by one the tanks were bogged. The tank recovery vehicle which went to their aid was bogged too, as was the Commanding Officer's tank when he went up to visit the Squadron. Out of nineteen tanks in action that day only two under Lieutenant J. W. Dent escaped the morass and were able to go forward with the infantry to the final objective. Major Fisher's own tank was bogged and he was himself wounded by enemy shelling, which was as heavy on that day as on any in the whole campaign. He boarded another tank, but it was blown up on a mine ; luckily the driver was not hurt, although the tank had to be abandoned. The only tanks which could move were helping the infantry so, having been bogged and wounded in one tank and blown up in another, Fisher walked six hundred yards across the open to his second troop and directed the rest of the action on foot.

Similarly Lance-Sergeant Royden Leslie Roberts (from Cardiff), when his tank was bogged took the Bren gun and went into action on foot with the infantry whom his tank would have supported. Thus they did their best to overcome adverse conditions and the Coldstream Guards were duly appreciative.

On that afternoon the 1st Battalion were ordered to make a night attack on Hassum, a large village on the road to Goch. They were to have the help of a considerable barrage, search-lights were to provide "artificial moonlight" and aeroplanes were to bomb the place first. They were still in the positions they had captured on the 14th and as they left the wood the enemy started shelling and two were killed and four wounded. They dug in in front of Hommersum (now held by the Irish Guards) and started forward again at three o'clock in the morning. Everything went well. The "moonlight" enabled them to move quickly, wireless communication worked admirably, the barrage was most effective, and they reached their objective without a casualty. Doubtless the official "Air Notes" were not far wrong when they reported that after eighteen tons of bombs had been dropped there and the artillery programme had been

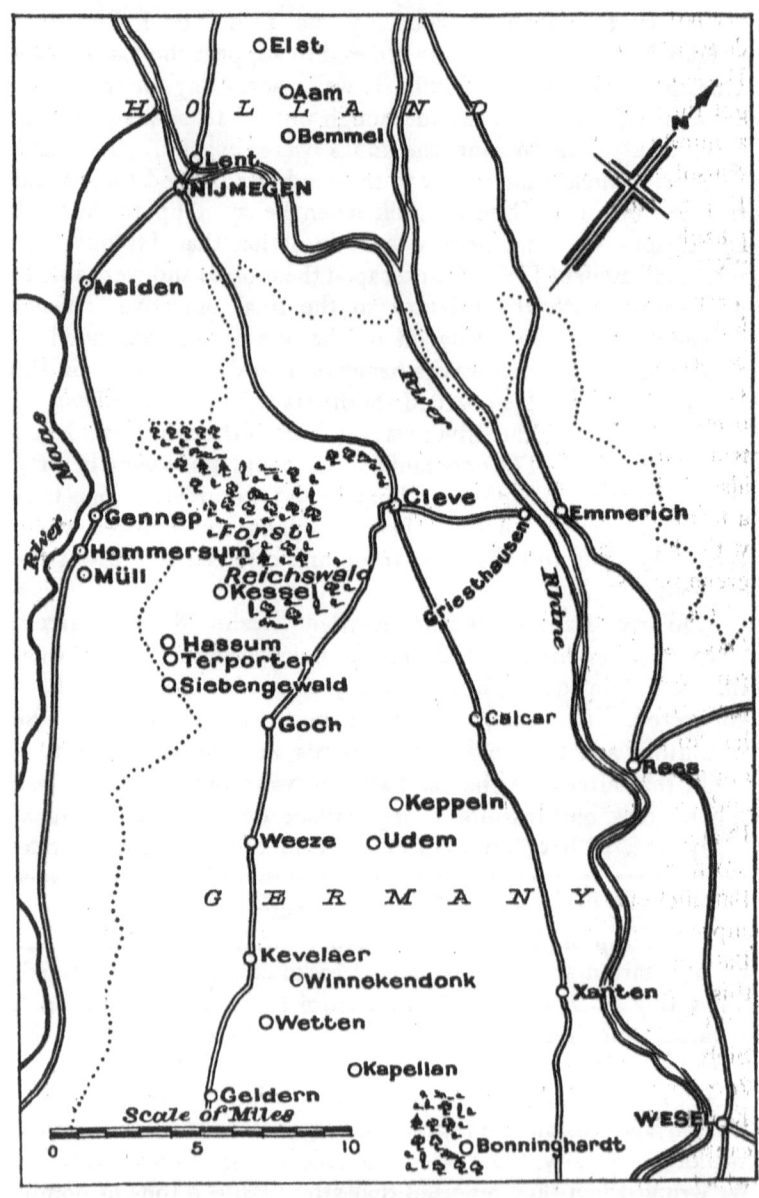

THE RHINELAND.

carried out "the enemy was reduced to negligible strength and, choosing discretion rather than valour, left the remains of Hassum to the Welsh Guards." Certainly Hassum, when they got there, was in utter devastation and only a few prisoners and a number of civilians emerged from the ruins. But as they consolidated the enemy put down heavy shell fire and Lieutenant R. J. S. Howard of "X" Company was wounded. During the day patrols pushed out to gain contact with the enemy. One from "X" Company under Lieutenant E. M. Ling went as far as Terporten, to find the bridge intact and the enemy in position to hold it. Others from the Carrier Platoon under Lieutenant N. L. P. Thomas with Lance-Sergeant N. S. Penrose and Lance-Sergeant D. D. Louden shot some of the enemy and got useful information. Lieutenant J. S. Roberts and a patrol from No. 3 Company came back not only with information but also with eighty-four eggs. Major Sir R. G. D. Powell, entering a farm in no-man's-land, found a German grenadier having tea with the farmer : "Thus ended the war as far as that particular grenadier was concerned."

The 1st Battalion remained in and about Hassum till St. David's Day. They did a lot of patrolling and took a subsidiary part in an attack on Terporten and the bridge there. And their rare run of good luck continued, for while other units engaged had stiff fighting and severe casualties the Welsh Guards met little opposition and their total casualties in ten days were six killed and eighteen wounded. The latter included Major W. D. D. Evans, who had commanded a company with distinction since Normandy—"a terrible blow to No. 4 Company and the Battalion as a whole." In some of these operations they had the support of the Light Reconnaissance Squadron from the 2nd Battalion. The rest of the 2nd Battalion were not employed in this action.

On the 2nd of March the 1st Battalion moved down to Siebengewald, and two days later they "married up" with the 2nd Battalion and went south-east through Goch and Weeze to Kevelaer and Wetten. On the 5th of March came orders for the capture of the woods between Kapellan and Bonninghardt, which involved not only both Battalions but also the 2nd Battalion Scots Guards who had come out from England to relieve the 1st Battalion Welsh Guards. Breakfasts were "at the pleasant hour" of four o'clock on the morning of the 6th and at half-past five they attempted to move off through roads almost solid with traffic. Then there were further Divisional conferences and finally they crossed their start line at eleven o'clock. The Welsh Guards' responsibility was the road running through the wood to Bonninghardt and the southern half of the wood; the Scots Guards were on their left and had to clear the northern half. The Light Reconnaissance Squadron of the 2nd Battalion supported the Welsh Guards and No. 3 Squadron the Scots Guards, and all the attackers were greatly helped by the artillery. The Welsh Guards met various pockets of enemy resistance consisting of fanatical paratroops. Lance-Sergeant Austin Joyce, in command of a leading section, came under fire from a Spandau dug in by the side of a farmhouse, and another opened fire from the house itself against a platoon attacking on his right flank. He led his section forward in a vigorous attack and the first enemy gunner withdrew to the house. Leaving his section to give covering fire, he ran forward and under cover of the house-wall threw a grenade in at the window from which the Spandau was firing. His section then joined him in assaulting the house and surrounding buildings, which were captured, together with twenty-six German paratroops.

With the help of the tanks the companies eventually fought their way through the wood and reached their objectives on the eastern edge by mid-day, having taken nearly a hundred prisoners. Sergeant Albert Edward Kempson, a Cardiff man, with a platoon of Prince of Wales Company had his Bren gun nearly cut in half by a bazooka, and Captain Sir M. G. Beckett, commanding the Light Reconnaissance Squadron, had one tank destroyed by a mine and another by a self-propelled gun and commanded his squadron during the rest of the action riding on the outside of a troop leader's tank. Of the 1st Battalion, Captain E. M. Ling, Lieutenant F. N. H. Widdrington, Lieutenant N. P. G. W. Waite, Company Sergeant-Major Urias Davies and thirty-three more were wounded. Davies had won a great reputation in the Regiment; Neath should be proud of him.

In the Rhineland Battle
by
Sergeant C. Murrell
(An Advanced Dressing Station)

Soon after they had reached their objective Lieutenant-Colonel Heber-Percy ordered a second advance. This time they were to capture Bonninghardt village itself. No. 3 Company on the right was to be supported by No. 3 Squadron of the 2nd Battalion under Captain P. E. G. W. Parish; "X" Company on the left to have the help of the Light Reconnaissance Squadron; No. 4 Company and Prince of Wales Company were to be in support. The leading companies crossed the start line at quarter-past five in the afternoon with a strong artillery support. They had some very open ground to cross and had casualties from enemy shelling and Spandau fire. Captain A. Ritchie commanding "X" Company was wounded and Sergeant T. J. Waters of the Mortar Platoon was killed—a great loss to the 1st Battalion. There was some hand-to-hand fighting in Bonninghardt, and among the prisoners taken was the commander of a German battalion who expressed his satisfaction at having had the honour to be captured by "the Guards Panzers." During the night the town was thoroughly cleared and some fifty Germans were dug out of various hiding places. One got rather the better of Regimental Sergeant-Major A. R. Baker, for on being asked sharply what he was laughing at he replied, "Well, I have finished with the war, which is more than you have."

On the 8th of March No. 4 Company did a flank-guard attack with the Scots Guards, going forward behind a barrage and reaching their objective without loss. But the 2nd Battalion was not so fortunate. No. 2 Squadron under Major N. M. Daniel were in support of the Right Flank Company of the Scots Guards. The attack was started down a steep escarpment in full view of the enemy and its final objective was the apex of a triangle formed by the junction of two railway embankments. The enemy put up stiff opposition and it was dark when the objective was captured. Owing to the nature of the ground and to the fact that the only exit from the battlefield was over a scissors bridge which was blocked by a broken-down tank, No. 2 Squadron formed a close laager and remained there all night. Shelling and mortaring was extremely heavy and Lieutenant P. A. Carter and Lance-Sergeant H. J. Millard were killed during the night. At first light four tanks were knocked out by an enemy self-propelled gun including every tank of the troop commanded by Lieutenant D. A. Gibbs. Between five o'clock on the previous evening and six o'clock that morning No. 2 Squadron lost six tanks knocked out and three bogged.

Other Divisions were now converging on Wesel; the Guards Armoured Division was withdrawn and the 1st Battalion Welsh Guards had fought their last battle of the war.

* * * * *

The story of this series of actions may well leave the reader wondering how the 2nd Battalion could remain effective with such a list of tank casualties day after day. A note on the Light Aid Detachment under Captain D. W. J. Harrowell was given on page 179, but it may be supplemented here by a close-up of Mechanist Quartermaster-Sergeant Frank Roughton's work in this action. On March the 6th two Cromwells were bogged in low ground very near the enemy's forward positions and in full view. Any movement in the vicinity brought down immediate fire. Roughton went down to them after dark with a recovery vehicle, but the enemy realised what he was doing and put down shell and mortar fire. Undeterred by this, Roughton worked on for an hour and a half and got one tank safely away. He then returned for the second and the enemy opened fire again. One of his recovery crew was badly wounded, but Roughton worked on and after another hour brought out the second tank. On March the 8th, as already noted, a tank got stuck on a scissors bridge over a stream, blocking the route for others; the bridge was under heavy fire. This time he had to work on the tank all night, but he got it away in the end, not only saving the tank but reopening a route which was of great importance in the operation. So it went on day after day whenever the 2nd Battalion were fighting—one of the forms of inconspicuous service which are easily forgotten by all except those who depended upon them for their fighting efficiency.

The important part also played by the Forward Delivery Squadron in replenishing the Battalion's tank strength is explained, in connection with a later action, on page 280.

* * * * *

The Rhineland Battle

Throughout their fighting the 1st Battalion had the constant support of a platoon of No. 1 Independent Company, Royal Northumberland Fusiliers, whose machine guns and mortars gave covering fire in every operation. As this was the last occasion on which the 1st Battalion Welsh Guards fought, it is a fitting place to acknowledge their debt to the Northumberland Fusiliers and especially to the platoons which fought with them.

* * * * *

Two entries in the War Diary of the 1st Battalion at this time are illuminating. The first reads: "St. David's Day but nothing much to show for it. Companies have been feeding so well lately that it was difficult to make dinners any better than they would have been in any case"; and the second entry records that at the end of the day on which they captured Bonninghardt "cookers were got up in reasonably good time with the companies' evening meal and blankets also after a considerable delay." Throughout this campaign, thanks to good organisation and mechanical transport, there was seldom if ever a night on which a hot meal and blankets did not reach Welsh Guardsmen who were engaged in actual fighting and the St. David's Day entry shows how well they were fed. It is in such matters, just as much as in good drill, that a high standard of training and discipline is manifest.

GERMAN "PANTHER" TANK.

NORDHORN TO LINGEN

"The 2nd Battalion Welsh Guards crossed the Rhine by pontoon bridges at Rees on the 30th of March. . . . It was hoped that a quick break-through would be made and that they would have another chance to show their paces. But what happened was something very different. . . . Nevertheless in the first ten days of April they advanced over a hundred miles." (*Part I, page* 80.)

THERE are plenty of days in a soldier's life that are empty of incident, but some that are too full. So far as the Welsh Guards were concerned the 2nd of April, 1945, was one of the second sort. The day before had been full enough, starting with Reveille at four o'clock in the morning and ending only after midnight. There had been a lot of hanging about near Enschede while the Coldstream Guards were taking the place and as night was falling they had been sent forward to reconnoitre the nearby airfield. The leading tanks of two troops had been knocked out by anti-tank guns which they had come on unexpectedly in the dusk, and in both cases the troop leader and his crew had been wounded and taken prisoner. When night fell both troops were withdrawn and an attack was planned for the morning.

On April the 2nd Reveille was at five o'clock and two hours later the attack on the airfield was launched by a squadron and a half of tanks (No. 1 Squadron and two troops of No. 3) carrying men of the 2nd Battalion Scots Guards. The enemy had cleared out during the night, leaving the three anti-tank guns which had caused such damage in the dusk of the previous evening and a lot of other equipment. By ten o'clock in the morning the Battalions were on the road again, making now for Oldenzaal. They were crossing a salient of Dutch territory and Oldenzaal, being a Dutch town, gave them a tremendous welcome. Their advance was held up there for some hours while blown bridges were repaired, and Lieutenant A. W. S. Wheatley with a troop from No. 1 Squadron was sent off to shoot up German transport reported moving on roads to the south-east; this he did with considerable success. As soon as a bridge was usable No. 2 Squadron (Major N. M. Daniel) and a company of Scots Guards pushed on to Nordhorn. There are three bridges at Nordhorn and all had been blown, but the tanks managed to work their way across the remaining masonry of one and the group occupied the town without difficulty. Both Battalions were concentrated there when darkness fell.

It is not easy to drive a tank by day; it is usually regarded as impracticable to fight a tank in darkness. As the reader will have already realised the tanks harboured each night, either forming "close laager" (like the hollow square of the old infantry —with any soft vehicles in the centre) so that they were protected on all sides by their own weapons, or less closely concentrated behind a protective screen of infantry. The one thing they did *not* do was to fight in darkness. But rules are made to be broken and Lieutenant-Colonel Lewis got permission to take a big risk in the hope of winning a big prize. Twelve miles ahead, at Lingen, is the Ems river and a few hundred yards beyond is the Dortmund-Ems Canal. The river and canal formed much the strongest line of defence immediately ahead of the Division, and if the vital bridges could be captured quickly the position would lose all value to the enemy. It was decided to try to seize them that night.

Major N. M. Daniel's Squadron (No. 2) was to lead with the Scots Guards Right Flank Company on the tanks of all but the two leading troops; they would be followed first by No. 3 Squadron and then by No. 1 Squadron, also carrying Scots Guards; the Headquarters of both Battalions would move up behind them. This wild and adventurous drive did not start until half-past eleven. It was a black and beastly night with rain falling in torrents when No. 2 Squadron crossed the bridge out of Nordhorn and set off into the darkness. No. 3 Squadron under Major W. L. Consett followed and No. 1 Squadron (Major N. T. L. Fisher) was doing so when Nordhorn bridge collapsed; half of No. 1 Squadron and both Commanding Officers, with the remainder of their Battalions, were left behind. From then on Major Consett took command of the fighting force on the road.

Sergeant Frank Townsend commanding the leading tank had nothing to guide him but the gleam of a wet road and what his map told him of the country; others had only the dim tail lamp of the tank ahead. They drove fast, blazing away with machine guns at any ugly-looking patch of shadow by the road-side; behind the leading troops, spitting luminous tracer bullets at everything they passed, roared the other tanks, with the rifle fire of the infantry they carried adding to the din. The road was not empty, as it might well have been after midnight. They found a lot of good targets; groups of German soldiers walking or driving unconcernedly along the road to Nordhorn; motor cycles, carts, lorries with equipment; and army vehicles whose surprised drivers thought they were snugly parked for the night.

Sergeant Townsend overtook a German recovery vehicle, towing both a Mark IV tank and a broken down self-propelled gun, and he "brewed up" all three; but a well-aimed shot from a bazooka broke the track of his own tank and brought him to a standstill. Lieutenant A. A. Upfill-Brown, his troop commander, found a way round the obstruction across the fields—no mean feat on a dark night—while Sergeant Townsend completed the destruction of the enemy. Most of the Germans were too surprised and too "dozy" to do more than fling a phosphorus grenade or fire a rifle wildly, but by the time the leading tanks reached Schepsdorf (a suburb of Lingen on the west bank of the Ems) the troops there had been fully roused. As tanks roared down the hill to the first bridge "merry hell" was let loose from the buildings on either side of the road. It was about three o'clock, still very dark and raining hard, and though there was a considerable number of German troops these fired wildly and with little effect.

A house which had been set alight by gun fire blazed up fiercely and the tanks on the road, then suddenly illuminated, felt very naked, till the men of Right Flank Company "went through those houses as only Scots Guardsmen would." Meanwhile two platoons worked across the belt of open ground to the river and crossed the bridge in spite of heavy opposition on the far side; and the leading tank was just moving on to their assistance when the bridge went up with a roar. The Scots

Guardsmen managed to clamber back over the ruins, for tanks could make no further progress till the bridge was repaired.

So the gamble did not quite come off; but they had done a lot of damage and had thoroughly rattled those of the enemy they did not destroy. The bridge at Nordhorn was reconstructed during the night and when the rest of the two battalions came up next morning a Scots Guards officer wrote: "The road was lined with charred bodies, at the side of gutted vehicles. Horses and limbers littered the roadside in ghastly confusion. There were some knocked out 88's and trailers and I thought it must be the work of rocket-firing planes till I saw the freshly-killed horses and the trucks still smouldering, which showed it to be the work of the previous night."

Such an advance in darkness, with infantry and tanks working in close co-operation, had not previously been attempted; the enemy were taken completely by surprise and another twelve miles had been gained.

There was no sleep that night. They occupied their position till noon. It rained incessantly and most of them were soaked.

* * * * *

Without a knowledge of the country or close study of a large-scale map it would be impossible to follow the movements of often widely dispersed squadrons through the next few days. Each has its own story and a full account of even one of them would need a long chapter to itself. But extracts from a single squadron-leader's diary will give some idea of the nature of the fighting at this time, provided the reader remembers that in order to form a picture of the whole Battalion's work, even in outline, this one account should be multiplied by three and the work of the Light Squadron and Headquarter Squadron should then be added.

"*6th of April.*—(2 a.m.) Am just going to bed after a long series of 'O' Groups. Our first task is to make a break-out from the Lingen bridgehead and then to go as fast as we can to Bremen, eighty miles away . . . Some task! when letters from home talk of the war being over. (8.15 a.m.) We are off. (9.15 a.m.) Leading tank knocked out on a mine. R.E. are clearing the road. (10 a.m.) Advance resumed. Leading tank fired on from the right—and missed—but the second tank hit and knocked out. Have sent the troop to the right in a flanking movement. (10.30 a.m.) This was successful. (10.45 a.m.) Leading tank of the troop who have taken over the lead has been knocked out by another bazooka and simultaneously hit a mine. There is another road-block in front with bazooka men and anti-tank gun manning it. (10.50 a.m.) A severe stonking ... my scout car was hit and put out of action. (11.15 a.m.) An infantry attack on wooded area to our front is going in—'F' Company Scots Guards, supported by my leading troops and some artillery. This is Bremen in one day—an advance of two miles with three tanks knocked out to show for it ! . . . (1 p.m.) The infantry are having bad casualties . . . David Kemble, commanding 'F' Company has been badly wounded . . . (2 p.m.) Have just heard that David Kemble has died of his wounds. (3.15 p.m.) No. 2 and No. 3 Squadron Groups are to put in a joint attack. (5 p.m.) They have made their attack successfully and are now pushing on, with No. 2 Squadron leading. (5.10 p.m.) Leading tank of No. 2 Squadron reported hit by a self-propelled gun. (6.15 p.m.) No. 2 Squadron report two 88's in their area and our air O.P. reports that at least three more are a little farther on. (6.30 p.m.) Leading troop of No. 2 Squadron have knocked out no less than three of the anti-tank guns. (7 p.m.) They have knocked out a fourth. (10 p.m.) In harbour just off the road. I have been lucky. I was sent for to an 'O' Group ... when I got back I found my own tank had been hit by one of the moaning minnies and my gunner, sitting on my seat, exactly where I would have been, had been very badly wounded." (Two officers nearby were also wounded and the crew of a Scots Guards carrier were killed.)

It was a troop commanded by Lieutenant D. A. Gibbs which knocked out the three anti-tank guns referred to above. Two "kills" were attributable wholly to good shooting, but in the third there was something more. He had spotted the gun, waiting behind a house for any of the tanks to move round into range, and loading his own gun with an armour-piercing shell Gibbs fired through the house. By good luck or good judgment —and probably by both—he knocked out the gun and buried the gunner under falling bricks.

Extracts from the diary entries for one more day will show that April the 6th was not abnormal.

"*7th of April.*—Moved at 7 a.m. No. 2 and No. 3 Squadron Groups are now attacking the woods this side of Lengerich under cover of artillery. (9.15 a.m.) No. 2 Squadron ordered through Lengerich and will continue the advance from there if all goes well. (10.15 a.m.) No. 2 Squadron Group have been committed near the town and their infantry have had fairly heavy casualties . . . (1.15 p.m.) I was ordered to a Battalion 'O' Group to discuss plans for a proper attack on Lengerich by three companies of Scots Guards supported by No. 1 and No. 3 Squadrons . . . and was saved for the second time . . . while I was away my tank was knocked out by a roving self-propelled gun on our left. My acting driver was killed, my operator badly wounded and my gunner slightly wounded. Just before that No. 2 Squadron had two tanks 'brewed up,' also by a self-propelled gun. Upfill-Brown was badly wounded and has lost a leg; his Sergeant may lose his too . . . (4 p.m.) The attack which started at 3.15 p.m. is going well . . . German prisoners are coming back now. (5 p.m.) The attack has been successful. (6 p.m.) On the move again, but leading troops held up by a road-block of very large trees with boggy ground on either side. Have asked for a bulldozer. (7 p.m.) We found a deviation round the road-block (which was mined) and went on . . ."

Armoured columns fighting their way forward along a given route had neither the men nor the time to scour the surrounding countryside; they had to risk the danger it might hold. A well-manoeuvred gun or a small party of determined men coming in behind them from uncleared country could do great damage. On the late afternoon of the 8th Major R. B. Hodgkinson, Second-in-Command of the Battalion, went back with his opposite number in the Scots Guards (Major H. Tweedie) to chose a harbour area for the night. Looking for a suitable place off the main road they ran into a German patrol. All except Major Hodgkinson were killed outright, and he was wounded in the foot but later rescued and evacuated. He was a great loss to the Battalion, having been Second-in-Command throughout the campaign; but he recovered in time to command the 1st Battalion when they again went on service overseas. Major Consett succeeded him in the 2nd Battalion as Second-in-Command.

The fighting went on in this fashion till Menslage had been taken. Since crossing the Rhine they had advanced a hundred miles and were allowed a few days to rest and refit before starting again. Their loss of tanks and tank crews was at this period as heavy as at any time in the war. The valiant efforts of the Light Aid Detachment to recover and repair quickly any damaged tank have already been described, but it must be obvious that many tanks were beyond repair and that crews were continually being reduced by casualties. Such losses in men and tanks were made up from another formation, which has not been mentioned, though without it they could not have got so far. This was known as the Forward Delivery Squadron. It lived and moved with the Divisional Administrative Area and was responsible for supplying the armoured battalions with fresh crews and new tanks needed to replace casualties. Each battalion had its permanent representative with the squadron (at this time Captain I. M. Stewart represented the Welsh Guards); he was responsible for seeing that tanks and crews were not only ready to move up to their battalion at once when they were called for, but that they went up ready to go straight into action if need be. This was of great importance. Often the squadron was some way behind the Battalion, and its demands were not received till the evening. The crews to be sent up might have to drive on crowded roads throughout the night and even so not reach their battalion till three or four in the morning; and they might well find on arrival that the battalion was moving off to battle at first light. So crews could not afford to leave the Forward Delivery Squadron short of any equipment and new tanks had to start correctly stowed with ammunition, food, water and all the kit required to make a Cromwell battle-worthy.

When the 2nd Battalion had finished fighting round Menslage and the Haase Canal so many tanks had been lost that for the first time the Forward Delivery Squadron was unable to make them up to strength; so the Light Reconnaissance Squadron was dispersed and the tanks and tank crews divided among the other squadrons. By these means the 2nd Battalion was made ready to take the road again.

VISSELHOVEDE

"*After a ninety-mile drive they reached Walsrode and there joined the* 12*th Corps. They were to strike northwards now in a wide turning movement designed to loosen the German hold on Bremen and Hamburg.*" (*Part I, page* 82.)

IT has often been argued in jest that Headquarters ought occasionally do their own fighting and let the soldiery have a rest. So a wave of wicked enjoyment swept through the squadrons when the wish came true at Visselhovede. They had taken the town and were quietly holding their allotted positions when they learned that Group Headquarters was fighting for its life ! Now, they felt, they were getting a bit of their own back. Luckily those at Headquarters also saw the humour of the situation, and Lieutenant-Colonel J. C. Windsor Lewis, dodging bullets to fire his pistol through the window, was in his best form. According to his own report, "scenes of the greatest humour (interspersed with moments of fear) were then enacted." So perhaps the affair may be summed up in the well-worn phrase, "A good time was had by all."

* * * * *

On the previous day—April the 18th—the Scots-Welsh Group moved towards Visselhovede from the south, forewarned that they might find it held by German Marines. These Marines had formerly been sailors and although they lacked the trained skill of the parachute divisions they were brave and well disciplined. They had been newly equipped with rifles, bazookas and light machine-guns, but were short of supporting arms. Perhaps this lack of field training and poverty of support may explain the difference between their tactics and those of the paratroops whom the Welsh Guards had fought so often. The paratroops chose the strongest natural positions and there held up the advance till a full-scale attack had to be laid on ; then they retired to fight another day. The Marines, on the other hand, chose to fight delaying actions in towns or villages and there they stayed till they were beaten.

The Welsh Guards encountered Marines for the first time at Kettenburg, a village which stands on high well-wooded ground two miles south of Visselhovede. Three companies of Marines held it, and two companies of Scots Guards, each with a squadron of Welsh Guards tanks, made the attack. There was a bitter fight and the village was taken so late in the afternoon that the attack on Visselhovede was postponed till the following day. Meanwhile the Coldstream Group, moving by a different route, captured Neuenkirchen, six miles away to the north-east.

The attack began next morning soon after dawn. Leaving Neuenkirchen, the Coldstream struck at Visselhovede from the north and captured the northern sector of the town. At the same time the Scots-Welsh Group attacked from the south and, overcoming stubborn opposition at the railway embankment which forms the southern boundary, they fought their way into the town and consolidated in the central and southern sectors. No. 2 Squadron and a company of Scots Guards then moved out on to the high ground on the west, to cover the position on that side. Group Headquarters occupied a house in the main road on the north-west side of the town and other houses down the road, and the preparation of dinners began; two Cromwells were stationed outside Group Headquarters and a tank used by Lieutenant-Colonel Henry Clowes, commanding the Scots Guards, was parked in the side garden. The battle was over and peace reigned in Visselhovede.

Then the fun began. Without any warning Headquarters found themselves surrounded by German Marines attacking at close quarters from all sides. The tanks in front of the house were simultaneously knocked out by bazookas and a hot fire pursued their crews when they baled out; they were lucky to reach the house unhit. No one knew where the attackers had so suddenly appeared from, but in fact there is some dead ground where the Vissel brook winds through a marsh behind Headquarters garden and, a few hundred yards beyond, a thick wood. The Marines had been squeezed out of the town and into this wood when the Coldstream Group attacked from the north and the Scots-Welsh from the south : but they had not wholly withdrawn as was believed (and as the paratroops would have done in similar circumstances). It was from this no-man's-land between the two Groups that they worked their way back through the thickly hedged gardens to houses in the street occupied by Group Headquarters.

It would be untrue to say that the brave men of Headquarters fought back to back ; they were too busy dodging bullets which came in at every window. But replying with pistols or any better weapons they could lay their hands on, they kept the enemy at bay. Great skill is needed to fire a pistol effectively through windows covered by enemy fire. Captain M. A. L. F. Pitt-Rivers in particular showed a knowledge of field-craft not always found in the Adjutant of an armoured battalion and proved to be very quick on the draw. Captain the Hon. N. H. C. Bruce, the Intelligence Officer, lying on his stomach on the floor, tried vainly to notify Brigade that Headquarters would fight to the last man and the last round, but discovered that the snatch-plug on a lead from the wireless set of the tank outside had become disconnected. The gun of Lieutenant-Colonel Clowes' tank was of no help either; it was a commander's tank used to get about in more effectively in action and, to give more elbow-room, the real gun had been replaced by a dummy. Notwithstanding these handicaps, Headquarters kept the fight going briskly and the road was criss-crossed with fire and answering fire. The squadrons had stopped laughing and a welcome breather was afforded to Headquarters when Captain the Hon. A. B. Mildmay's tank from No. 3 Squadron nosed its way out of a side street and blazed off its Besa at the Germans milling round Headquarters. This had a damping effect on their ardour, but Mildmay himself had two narrow escapes. First a bazooka just missed him and burst on the wall beside. A cloud of brick dust and debris hid him from anxious observers in Headquarters, but when it subsided he was still there, his head sticking out of the turret quite unruffled. Next a bullet removed the earpiece of the headphone he had on. As Lieutenant-Colonel Lewis noted, "another inch and it would have removed Mildmay." Meanwhile a troop of tanks under Lieutenant A. W. S. Wheatley from No. 1 Squadron had joined the fray and the Marines soon realised they were beaten and surrendered—four hundred and forty of them with a Brigade Commander and his staff: a few who tried to get back to the woods by the Vissel brook were shot up by tanks of No. 2 Squadron which had closed in from the west.

So Group Headquarters stood down. Officers put their pistols back into holsters and emerged from their stronghold. Prisoners and German wounded were collected and disarmed. Peace and quietness reigned in Visselhovede for the second time.

GERMAN "*PANZERFAUST*," COMMONLY CALLED A "BAZOOKA."

WESTERTIMKE

"They were launched in a westerly direction as part of the movement towards Bremen. Their objective was the stretch of high ground between Zeven and Tarmstedt where, they would meet the 15th Panzer Grenadier Division and would come into the formidable gun area which defended Bremen." (*Part I, page* 83.)

THERE was a Guardsman of the 2nd Battalion who fought at Boulogne in the Company commanded by Major J. C. Windsor Lewis and was taken prisoner with him after the last ship had left the harbour. That was on May the 26th, 1940. On April the 26th, 1945, he was held by the Germans in a large prisoners-of-war camp at Westertimke. The 2nd Battalion, now commanded by his former Company Commander, was only a few miles away at Sittensen.

The 2nd Battalion had been given three days at Sittensen in which to rest and refit after their recent fighting. The village was overflowing with "displaced persons" from the countless millions who had been forced to work for Germany. French, Russians and Poles predominated, but there were also Belgians, Dutch, Latvians and Italians, speaking many tongues but having in common helpless poverty and a longing to be home again in their own lands. Mercifully the Welsh Guards were not responsible for their care, for "Military Government" followed hard on the army's heels to deal with this and other civil problems.

The Scots-Welsh Group left Sittensen at first light on April the 26th, moved through Zeven (which had been taken already by Grenadier and Coldstream Groups) and had a most unpleasant day's fighting, balked by demolitions, opposed by elements of the 15th Panzer Grenadiers and heavily shelled all day. The first check was at Badenstedt where the bridge over a stream had been blown. Lieutenant S. R. Armitage's troop, working with the Scots Guards, found a way round by an unblown railway bridge and so outflanked and overcame the forces covering the road. Engineers then bridged the demolition, but there was much shelling and further fighting before the Group captured Ostertimke. That night they stayed there, and "felt very naked on both flanks, as no one friendly was on either side." On the 27th they set out for Westertimke but first had Kirchtimke to deal with. The first to move were No. 1 and No. 2 Squadrons who, with two Scots Guards Companies, were to make a combined attack; No. 3 Squadron was held in reserve at Ostertimke, in a farm where "chickens killed in the previous day's fighting lay strewn about the yard." The leading squadrons encountered mines and then more mines. After the normal and guileless mines came unexpected and incomprehensible explosions in areas which had been cleared. By hard and dangerous work the Sappers discovered that the enemy had been burying some so deeply that only after a number of heavy vehicles had passed was there pressure enough to send them off; ordinary clearance methods did not reveal their presence. The ground beside the road was soft and soggy with rain and the tanks had a sticky time in more senses than one. Kirchtimke was taken, however, by mid-morning and the Sappers reported the road up to it to be clear. So the reserve Squadron (No. 3) waiting at Ostertimke was ordered forward and told to push on to Westertimke to free the prisoners of war there.

The rather exciting prospect of this mission offset the dreary dampness of the morning, the persistent rain which dripped and dribbled through every crevice of their tanks, the flat expanse of fields that lay sodden, below the road level, the straight thin woods, looking angular and awkward from a soldier's point of view. Major C. A. la T. Leatham commanded No. 3 Squadron and the leading Troop (No. 12) was under Sergeant A. G. Glass. When they neared Kirchtimke they came to the wrecks of tanks and soft vehicles which had been mined in an earlier attack, and as they passed this depressing evidence of the deep-laid mischief there was a heavy explosion and Sergeant Glass's tank lay battered and smoking across the road. Fortunately there were no casualties, though his tank was out and there were some sore heads. It was the third time that Glass had been mined. The Sappers now said that many hours would be needed to search for more deep mines and even then they could not guarantee that the road would be safe. There was no alternate way for armour so the Scots Guards dropped off their tanks and started forward on foot. Kirchtimke at that time was being steadily shelled. "High rockets were flung at us as well as missiles of every other known calibre."

But an overwhelming desire to reach the prisoners of war decided them to risk more mines; No. 3 Squadron resumed its perilous progress and enterprise was rewarded. No more mines were exploded and, having picked up the Scots Guards infantry again, they set off with Lieutenant S. A. Jolly's Troop (No. 11) now in the lead. Threatening-looking woods and higher ground in front of Westertimke necessitated dismounted action by the Scots Guards with artillery cover. Opposition was gradually overcome and about forty prisoners were taken in the process of clearing the woods, but the light was beginning to fade by the time this preliminary action was over.

There was known to be a second camp on the hill leading down to Westertimke, where the S.S. camp guards lived. (Two German officers had come over with a white flag to ask for a ten hours' truce "so that they could evacuate the prisoners of war.") The sound of enemy transport moving was reported by Scots Guards patrols. So our artillery shelled the village and the roads out of it before the tanks entered and all but No. 13 Troop were ordered to take up defensive positions, for it was now dark. No. 13 Troop under Lieutenant I. G. G. Davies carrying Scots Guards, pounded down the hill to the S.S. camp and squirted the huts with Besa fire; the Scots Guards scrambled off the tanks and went through the rooms in their whirlwind fashion; but the Germans had gone and several huts were on fire.

Major Leatham went with No. 15 Troop (Lieutenant R. P. Farrer) into the village. One Pole who was playing cards in a house was wounded: no one but he and his friends remained. And the darkness was only lit by the flaming S.S. huts on the hillside.

Towards two o'clock in the morning the stillness was broken by the sound of hurrahs that were unmistakably British. Soon afterwards No. 13 Troop reported that they had made contact with an outlying part of the camp, housing merchant seamen; and at dawn a Scots Guards patrol returned, tired but elated, to report that all was well in the camp.

Soon after nine o'clock that morning Lieutenant-Colonel Lewis in a tank (for his scout car had been knocked out the day before) drove up to the camp with Major Leatham and met the Guardsman who had been with him at Boulogne five years before. He and eight thousand other prisoners of war were free and the 2nd Battalion had fought their last fight of the war. Lieutenant-Colonel Lewis had been with them in every fight they had, from Boulogne to Westertimke.

They left Westertimke on April the 29th and, passing back through Zeven, turned northwards. On May the 1st they entered Stade and they remained there for a week. After their long and toilsome journeying it was a great relief to rest in this quiet old town, standing at the head of the broad canal which links it with the Elbe below Hamburg. An old brick church dominates the cobbled streets and gabled houses, and the great seventeenth-century warehouses by the quayside have the charm and dignity of old age. In five years the Battalion had grown used to war when nothing seemed permanent and worth was assessed only by military significance. But there was no sign of war in Stade. There they found evidence of enduring peace and a reminder of other values.

"HONEY" LIGHT TANK (10 TON):
BEHIND ARE A HUMBER SCOUT CAR
AND WHITE HALF-TRACK.

EPILOGUE

THE lighter side of life on active service could not well be described either in the general outline of the Welsh Guards' campaigning or in the separate accounts of the actions they fought. Yet the choirs and concerts, the Rugby football matches and sports meetings, and many hours spent happily in other ways or doing nothing in particular, fill a large part of the soldier's life even on active service. A community of men who share a common purpose, face a common danger and are upheld by a common tradition, find also a common satisfaction in the simple and light-hearted enjoyment of nights when they can sleep undisturbed and days when the strain of the front is absent. It is in these times no less than in action that soldiers come to know what Lord Wavell calls "the sense of true comradeship which is the supreme gift of the military life as a whole and of a good unit in especial."

There is an old Welsh saying which runs "Llawer o'r dŵr a â heibio heb wybod i'r melinydd"—"Much water flows past without the miller knowing." Much happens in battle without anyone knowing and the men who have been named are but representative of all those whose joint achievements have been told. The honour belongs to them all.

Equally it is inevitable that of many who gave outstanding service comparatively few can be mentioned individually in a book of this length. The Regiment owes its achievements to men of all ranks, but perhaps especially to the Warrant Officers and Non-Commissioned Officers who were largely responsible for maintaining traditions of self-discipline and devotion to duty, and by patient tuition and personal example inspired a younger generation. The roll of these men is, alas, too long to give here.

Finally, in concentrating on the story of the Welsh Guards' part in the war, the part which others played must be out of focus. The Battalions were proud of their places in the Guards Armoured Division and the 6th Armoured Division. The diaries and reports constantly praise the work of their respective staffs; and of the Artillery, Armour and Royal Engineers, the supply services and medical organisation, and the other battalions who fought with them. The Battalions would be the first to acknowledge how much they owed to others and it is hoped that readers will recognise this too.

At Regimental Headquarters and at the Training Battalion detachments of the A.T.S. worked throughout the war, and their help was valued highly. Ladies and friends of the Regiment under the leadership of Lady Stanier, worked untiringly to ease the difficulties of Guardsmen and their families and to make and distribute large quantities of warm clothing and comforts for men at the front and for prisoners of war.

* * * * *

Eighteen months have passed since the war ended and much has happened during that time. The 1st Battalion is now part of a reconstituted 1st Guards Brigade, and in Palestine. The 2nd Battalion is still with the Guards Division in Germany, but neither the Division nor the Battalion is now "Armoured." The 3rd Battalion was formed only for the war and after two and a half years' continuous service overseas it returned home to be disbanded, rich in honour and with "a reputation earned in action and at rest equal to that of any Battalion in the Brigade of Guards."

The Training Battalion no longer exists, for the five Training Battalions of the Regiments of Foot Guards have given place to two composite Guards Training Battalions, in each of which there is a Welsh Guards Company.

Regimental Headquarters are back in the old offices in Birdcage Walk, which enemy bombs made uninhabitable early in the war. The work of Headquarters was always essential and at times very heavy. It was there that the welfare of the Regiment as a whole was considered and the needs of each Battalion were balanced with resources available. Changes in the appointment of Lieutenant-Colonel Commanding the Regiment have been noted in the story; Colonel Sir Alexander Stanier was appointed Lieutenant-Colonel early in 1945, and visited the 3rd Battalion in Italy, shortly before the final battles, as Colonel Bankier had done earlier in the campaign. Major C. H. Dudley-Ward and

Major the Earl of Lisburne, both of whom had served in the 1st Battalion in the Great War, were in turn Regimental Adjutant, and the Battalions were fortunate to have two such tried friends at Headquarters. Regimental Sergeant-Major J. Copping was there throughout the war as Superintending Clerk, but he and many of all ranks have since been demobilised. There has been much consequent reorganisation and redistribution and there may well be more as the army is adapted to the needs and conditions of a post-war world. Some of the old ways may disappear; but as long as the spirit and traditions of the Regiment remain, Welsh Guardsmen may "view with hopefulness the prospect of incalculable change." A sentence which Dr. Thomas Jones wrote in another connection is quoted at the beginning of this book, with his permission, for it sums up aptly the history of the Brigade of Guards.

"They have sought after excellence and have made no compromise with meanness." It may stand for a summary of the Welsh Guards' record in the war of 1939 to 1945.

* * * * *

Acknowledgments

It only remains to record my personal thanks for the unfailing kindness of all ranks in helping me to write this book, for the patience with which they have answered questions and the generosity with which they have lent private diaries, letters and other personal records. I am specially indebted to those who took me over all the Battalions' battle-grounds in Italy and on the Western Front and helped me, on the spot, to understand what happened there. Captain F. B. Bolton and Captain D. A. Gibbs have given me invaluable help in the detailed work of collecting, sorting and checking information and in many other ways. For all this I am very grateful.

It would be out of place for me to thank Mr. Augustus John for his drawing. He drew it as a tribute to Welsh Guardsmen and all Welsh Guardsmen thank him. Sergeant C. Murrell also made his drawings as a labour of love, and the skill with which he has shown so many of the weapons adds much to the value of this record of how the war was fought. He served throughout as a member of the Intelligence Section of the 1st Battalion, and his many old comrades will be glad to possess these beautiful examples of his art. The maps were all drawn by Mr. W. Brooks in his spare time and for no reason at all that I can discover except the goodness of his heart and his interest as an old soldier; his craftsmanship will be appreciated by all who use the maps.

Finally, I must thank Guardsman D. Roberts, who typed much of the manuscript before he was demobilised, and Guardsman S. Beck, my soldier servant, who learnt how to use a typewriter in order to type and retype every word in this book.

I have had much help from others who are not members of the Regiment and would take this opportunity to thank them all. For any mistakes or inaccuracies I alone am responsible.

L. F. ELLIS.

August, 1946.

BRITISH SELF-PROPELLED 25-POUNDER GUN.

ROLL OF HONOUR

14679834 Gdsn. R. W. P. Abel	2735488 Gdsn. G. W. Bird
4191572 Gdsn. G. Abbotts	2738164 L/Sgt. H. J. Bird
2737000 Gdsn. J. D. Adams	2737925 Gdsn. G. C. Bishop
2734194 C.S.M. E. V. Addis	2737543 Gdsn. F. W. Bistrom
2738824 Gdsn. T. Alcock	2735542 Gdsn. D. Blythin
2734183 L/Sgt. B. Alexander	2735858 Gdsn. R. J. Bond
2737424 Gdsn. E. A. Allen	2737544 Gdsn. S. W. Bond
2733922 Gdsn. J. R. Ambrose	2732548 Gdsn. B. E. Booker, M.M.
2734105 L/Sgt. M. O. L. Amerlinck	2734858 Gdsn. W. W. Bootes
2734502 Sgt. J. D. Ashdown	2737271 Gdsn. W. J. Boulter
2733944 Gdsn. E. T. Ashmore	2734592 L/Cpl. T. L. Bowen
2657510 L/Cpl. A. H. Ashmore	14665196 Gdsn. W. E. Bowen
14362789 Gdsn. C. H. Avery	2735818 Gdsn. D. C. Bowley
2736461 Gdsn. C. T. Baggaley	2738672 Gdsn. R. J. Bowring
2734117 C.S.M. R. G. Bailey	2737186 Gdsn. C. S. Brace
2734322 Gdsn. L. Bailey	2736328 Gdsn. J. J. Bradshaw
2734634 L/Sgt. W. J. Bailey	2736756 Gdsn. G. K. Brassington
2735489 L/Sgt. H. Bailey	2734499 Gdsn. T. J. Bridge
2738652 Gdsn. R. Bailey	3769857 Gdsn. C. A. Bristow
2/Lieut. G. A. H. Baker	2571287 Gdsn. F. F. Bromhall
2733425 C.S.M. F. G. Baker	2732759 L/Sgt. C. T. Brown
2733653 Gdsn. P. G. Baller	2735573 Gdsn. D. T. Brown
Lieut. I. P. Bankier	14584351 Gdsn. R. Bruton
Lieut. R. J. Barbour	2734303 Gdsn. A. Buckley
2735645 Gdsn. R. J. Bartlett	2737189 Gdsn. E. Buckley
2737259 Gdsn. E. T. R. Bartlett	2737274 Gdsn. C. Bunsell
2738629 Gdsn. R. J. Bateman	2733292 Gdsn. D. P. Burge
14592612 Gdsn. H. G. Batterham	2738158 Gdsn. A. J. Burgess
14702388 Gdsn. G. Batteson	2737816 Gdsn. E. Burke
2736895 Gdsn. V. Bayliss	14677236 Gdsn. R. Burns
2735519 Gdsn. A. Beech	2734573 Gdsn. C. Burton
2733644 L/Cpl. W. D. Beer	2736856 Gdsn. W. O. C. Bush
2736155 Gdsn. N. Bellamy	2738213 L/Cpl. K. Butters
2737268 Gdsn. C. F. Bennett	14675371 Gdsn. S. Butterworth
2737269 Gdsn. G. C. Bennett	4190091 L/Sgt. P. Cairns
2737913 Gdsn. W. A. Bennett	2737277 Gdsn. A. H. Cameron
2734210 Gdsn. J. W. Berry	2734790 Gdsn. S. F. Carpenter
2738908 Gdsn. D. Betty	2738982 Gdsn. S. J. Carr
2734301 C.S.M. F. Beynon	Lieut. P. A. Carter
2737183 Gdsn. I. Beynon	2736913 Gdsn. S. Carter
2735895 L/Sgt. F. J. Bint	2735837 Gdsn. A. Cartwright

2737045	Gdsn. R. E. Cawley	2736860	Gdsn. L. Davies
2739144	Gdsn. J. Church	2737191	Gdsn. A. G. Davies
2736759	Gdsn. S. Clark	2737485	Gdsn. S. Davies
2733213	Gdsn. D. G. Clarke	2737718	Gdsn. R. H. Davies
2734358	Gdsn. A. R. Clarke	2738359	Gdsn. L. F. R. Davies
2734389	L/Sgt. E. J. Clarke	2738551	Gdsn. T. Davies
2739029	Gdsn. D. Clarke	2738563	Gdsn. P. G. Davies
2733651	Sgt. W. E. Clayden	2738756	L/Cpl. G. A. Davies
	Major R. N. Cobbold	2739337	Gdsn. D. A. Davies
2733692	Gdsn. J. H. E. Cole	2735989	Gdsn. E. D. Davison
2734418	Gdsn. C. Cole	2736080	Gdsn. E. C. Dean
2739164	Gdsn. A. Coleman		Major J. F. F.
2734910	Gdsn. J. H. Collings		Baron de Rutzen
2735592	Gdsn. D. C. Collins	2730022	Sgt. J. H. Dickman
2738330	Gdsn. M. H. Coombe	2734083	Gdsn. P. Dinneen
4122521	Gdsn. H. L. Copnall	2732779	L/Sgt. W. Dixon
2733663	Gdsn. A. W. Cornelius	2734440	Gdsn. S. J. Doble
2738554	Gdsn. A. D. Cornock	2735999	Gdsn. W. J. Dole
2733450	Gdsn. S. Cornthwaite	2737285	Gdsn. J. W. Dowling
2736676	Gdsn. A. J. Coster	2736909	L/Cpl. J. W. Downes
2735788	Gdsn. F. Cowley	2733448	Sgt. W. Doyle
2736507	L/Cpl. F. S. Cox	2737342	Gdsn. M. J. Drew
2739089	Gdsn. A. G. Cox		Capt. J. Duncan
2738649	Gdsn. J. Crewdson	2737609	Gdsn. W. G. Durrent
	2/Lieut. J. A. L. Crofts	2733248	Sgt. F. B. Eames
2736451	Gdsn. J. J. Crowshaw	2652271	L/Cpl. A. E. Edmonds
2738540	Gdsn. W. A. Cuff	2733455	Sgt. T. H. Edwards
4191299	Gdsn. R. W. Curtis	2736681	Gdsn. R. Edwards
2733668	Gdsn. F. C. Cutler	2736745	L/Cpl. W. F. Edwards
2734576	Gdsn. J. P. Daley	2736864	Gdsn. S. Edwards
2738367	Gdsn. T. J. Daniels	2737056	Gdsn. D. J. Edwards
2738361	Gdsn. A. Darby	2739033	Gdsn. K. J. Edwards
2738409	Gdsn. W. Darby	2734596	L/Cpl. E. E. Elley
2737283	Gdsn. F. H. Davey		Capt. D. P. G. Elliot
2733197	D/Sgt. D. Davies, D.C.M.	2738614	Gdsn. D. F. Emery
			Lieut. G. N. Evans
2733567	L/Sgt. G. H. Davies		Lieut. H. A. Evans
2733791	L/Sgt. A. Davies	2732998	C.S.M. T. H. Evans
2734126	L/Sgt. J. E. Davies	2733359	L/Sgt. C. V. Evans
2734273	Gdsn. B. Davies	2733991	L/Sgt. R. Evans
2734593	Gdsn. M. M. Davies	2734055	Sgt. A. Evans
2734700	Gdsn. J. E. Davies	2734223	L/Sgt. W. E. Evans
2734786	L/Cpl. D. T. Davies	2734252	L/Sgt. R. S. Evans
2736074	Gdsn. J. Davies	2734353	Gdsn. W. H. G. Evans
2736079	L/Cpl. T. Davies	2734556	L/Cpl. J. Evans
2736220	L/Sgt. J. Davies	2734644	Gdsn. B. Evans
2736340	L/Sgt. R. G. Davies	2735038	Gdsn. H. G. Evans

Roll of Honour

2735213 Sgt. C. A. Evans	3778234 Gdsn. G. H. Green
2736083 Gdsn. D. G. Evans	2737989 Gdsn. J. H. Greenhouse
2737827 Gdsn. H. G. Evans	2737557 Gdsn. J. Greening
2737954 Gdsn. F. T. Evans	2733957 L/Sgt. J. C. L. Griffis
2737985 Gdsn. A. Evans	2734026 Sgt. T. G. Griffiths
2738530 L/Cpl. W. C. A. Evans	2734326 Gdsn. W. D. Griffiths
896311 L/Cpl. W. S. Evans	2734580 Gdsn. S. L. Griffiths
14652195 Gdsn. M. Evans	2735162 Gdsn. G. H. Griffiths
2734947 L/Cpl. G. E. Fardoe	2735995 Gdsn. L. A. Griffiths
Major J. E. Fass	2737098 Gdsn. F. Griffiths
2734423 Gdsn. L. Fazackerley	2738512 Gdsn. J. G. Griffiths
2739165 Gdsn. A. Fernihough	2739076 Gdsn. R. E. Griffiths
2739388 Gdsn. J. F. Fernyhough	3976634 Gdsn. W. Griffiths
6145541 Gdsn. C. C. Field	2735424 Gdsn. A. J. Gritton
2734819 L/Sgt. W. Finlay	2732807 Gdsn. C. V. B. Groom
2733023 L/Sgt. A. C. Fletcher	2736283 L/Cpl. W. A. J. Grove
2735937 L/Sgt. E. D. A. Fletcher	2736484 L/Cpl. S. H. Guest
	Lieut. S. A. Hall
2573851 L/Cpl. W. J. A. Foan	2735262 Gdsn. D. E. M. Hall
Major W. T. C. Fogg-Elliot	2737432 Gdsn. A. C. Hall
	2736866 Gdsn. J. A. Hamlington
2735015 Gdsn. W. Forsyth	2733158 Gdsn. W. G. Hancox
4452997 Gdsn. E. Foster	2736536 Gdsn. S. Hantman
2737471 Gdsn. T. Francis	Capt. C. A. St. J. P. Harmsworth
2738589 Gdsn. K. S. Francombe	
14585072 L/Cpl. R. F. Froud	2735907 Gdsn. C. T. Harper
Lieut. Hon. C. Furness, V.C.	2735596 L/Cpl. W. H. Harries
	2736691 Gdsn. K. J. Harrington
14498492 Gdsn. D. Gardiner	2735700 Gdsn. D. Harris
2736349 L/Cpl. R. Garrington	2736479 Gdsn. G. H. Harris
2734598 L/Sgt. E. George	2736480 Gdsn. A. Harris
2738209 Gdsn. A. R. George	Capt. R. L. Harrison
2736470 Gdsn. W. Gething	2737969 Gdsn. L. F. Harry
2734334 Sgt. T. F. Gill	14335554 Gdsn. J. A. Harvey
2732543 L/Cpl. C. Giltinan	2736276 Gdsn. R. E. Hather
2736350 Gdsn. A. Glass	Lieut. T. B. Hayley
2739223 Gdsn. I. G. Glen	5110516 Gdsn. D. W. H. Healey
2737290 L/Cpl. T. H. Glover	2733778 Sgt. W. H. Heap
2734964 Gdsn. J. Godber	2736205 Gdsn. J. H. Heath
2737344 Gdsn. B. Goldstraw	2736799 Gdsn. A. J. Hegarty
2736085 Gdsn. W. Golledge	2733074 L/Sgt. E. Hellings
2735941 Gdsn. A. Goodwin	Capt. J. A. A. Henderson
2737556 L/Sgt. F. Goodwin	2736939 Gdsn. C. Henley
2737364 L/Cpl. W. Greaves	2737563 Gdsn. J. H. Hennah
2737430 L/Cpl. H. L. Green	2739079 Gdsn. A. Higgs
2737474 Gdsn. G. W. Green	2733000 Sgt. G. P. Hill
814103 L/Sgt. W. G. Green	2737388 Gdsn. A. G. Hill

7946643	Gdsn. E. Hill	2735127	Gdsn. D. C. J. C. John
2575668	Gdsn. L. R. Hines	2734177	Gdsn. E. M. Johnson
2736771	L/Cpl. T. Hinkinson	2736777	Gdsn. R. Johnson
2735559	Gdsn. T. Hodder	2040892	Gdsn. J. A. Johnson
2735971	Gdsn. F. Hodgson	2732386	Gdsn. A. Jones
2736166	Gdsn. W. Holden	2733279	L/Sgt. J. Jones
2735073	Gdsn. A. W. Holland	2733817	Gdsn. E. A. Jones
	Capt. J. C. R. Homfray	2733858	Gdsn. H. J. W. Jones
2738372	Gdsn. J. R. Hooson	2734463	L/Sgt. T. Jones
2739345	Gdsn. A. J. Hopkin	2734513	L/Cpl. E. L. Jones
2734042	L/Cpl. I. Hopkins	2734544	Gdsn. D. E. Jones
2737965	L/Cpl. G. Hopkins	2734588	Sgt. R. O. Jones
2734265	L/Sgt. L. C. Hopley	2734911	Gdsn. R. L. Jones
2736269	Gdsn. E. J. G. Horne	2734987	Gdsn. R. F. Jones
2734523	Gdsn. H. G. Hough	2735013	Gdsn. B. J. Jones
2737770	Gdsn. L. Howard	2735068	Gdsn. H. J. Jones
	Lieut. D. W. Howard-Lowe	2735632	L/Cpl. M. S. Jones
		2735662	Gdsn. O. J. Jones
2736664	L/Sgt. D. J. Howells	2736094	L/Sgt. L. Jones
	2/Lieut. H. H. Hughes	2736246	L/Cpl. W. S. Jones
2733768	L/Cpl. E. Hughes	2736407	L/Cpl. E. L. Jones
2734669	Sgt. H. Hughes	2736409	Gdsn. R. L. Jones
2735195	Gdsn. H. Hughes	2736546	Gdsn. L. G. Jones
2735972	L/Cpl. O. H. Hughes	2736622	Gdsn. J. H. Jones
2735991	L/Sgt. T. Hughes	2736700	L/Sgt. W. V. Jones
2736398	Gdsn. L. Hughes	2736969	Gdsn. A. J. Jones
4030198	L/Sgt. A. Hughes	2737008	Gdsn. A. F. Jones
14372843	Gdsn. J. T. Hughes	2737120	Gdsn. T. Jones
2737918	L/Sgt. D. J. Huish	2737974	L/Cpl. R. G. Jones
14513610	Gdsn. G. G. Humpage	2738054	Gdsn. G. Jones
2736088	Gdsn. H. Humphreys	2738087	L/Cpl. B. M. Jones
2739486	Gdsn. D. Humphries	2738136	Gdsn. M. D. Jones
2733856	L/Sgt. J. Humphries	2738921	Gdsn. C. C. Jones
2739000	Gdsn. D. S. Hunter	2738924	Gdsn. S. E. Jones
2737006	Gdsn. T. G. Impey	770548	Gdsn. W. Jones
2736377	Gdsn. E. Ingram	872443	Gdsn. W. J. Jones
2734388	L/Cpl. S. S. Jackson	2564442	Gdsn. L. Jones
2734703	Gdsn. E. W. C. Jackson	2735497	Gdsn. A. J. Jordan
2735010	Gdsn. R. J. James	2737395	Gdsn. F. Jukes
2735426	Gdsn. R. James	2732527	Gdsn. D. Kearns
2738389	L/Cpl. T. Jeavons	2737866	Gdsn. W. A. Kennea
2737920	L/Cpl. J. G. Jeffreys	2737122	Gdsn. J. J. Kervin
2735451	Gdsn. J. A. Jeffries	2736818	Gdsn. G. H. King
2732082	Gdsn. J. Jenkins	2737303	Gdsn. F. J. King
2735429	Gdsn. H. C. Jenkins	2737760	Gdsn. G. R. H. Kinsey
2737007	Gdsn. J. V. Jenkins	2739233	Gdsn. L. L. Kirby
2737105	Gdsn. I. Jenkins	2734421	Gdsn. J. V. Kuner

Roll of Honour

2736904	L/Cpl. F. J. Kynaston		2614106	L/Sgt. H. J. Millard
2731946	C.S.M. C. H. Lang		2732787	L/Sgt. W. H. Moore
2733430	L/Sgt. I. Lawrence		2734136	Gdsn. R. F. Morgan
2735496	L/Cpl. J. Lawton		2734535	L/Sgt. R. Morgan
2734888	L/Cpl. G. E. Lee		2735784	L/Cpl. W. H. Morgan
14295068	Gdsn. A. E. Lemon		2735964	Gdsn. D. H. Morgan
2566049	L/Sgt. C. J. Lentle		2736553	Gdsn. A. Morgan
2737744	Gdsn. R. J. Leonard		2736625	Gdsn. P. L. Morgan
	Lieut. D. M. Lester		2735111	Gdsn. E. E. Morris
	Lieut. J. S. Lewes		2736256	Gdsn. R. J. Morris
2735754	Gdsn. J. E. Lewis		2736782	Gdsn. W. E. Morris
2736001	Gdsn. C. E. Lewis		2735224	Gdsn. D. T. Morton
2736096	Gdsn. G. B. Lewis			Lieut. W. F. Moss
2736702	Gdsn. G. Lewis		2736183	Gdsn. R. W. Munro
2737215	L/Cpl. T. G. Lewis		2735739	L/Sgt. E. J. Myddleton
4073576	L/Cpl. E. F. J. Lewis		2733612	L/Sgt. E. McCarthy
2738175	Gdsn. S. H. Liddiard		2734912	Gdsn. J. A. McCormick
	Major H. E. J. Lister, M.C.		2736310	Gdsn. S. C. McIntyre
			2735510	Gdsn. S. McMullen
2734874	L/Cpl. D. H. Llewellyn		2735522	Gdsn. T. H. McQueen
5334530	Gdsn. I. R. Llewellyn		2737131	Gdsn. P. Neill
2736975	Gdsn. P. Lloyd		2738293	Gdsn. E. Niblett
2735987	Gdsn. E. J. Loveday			Lieut. J. D. S. Nicholl-Carne
829780	Gdsn. W. G. Loveday			
	Lieut. P. C. Luxmoore-Ball		2736185	Gdsn. B. R. Oakley
			2734908	Gdsn. T. P. O'Brien
2737706	Gdsn. W. A. Machin		2733607	Gdsn. G. H. Onions
2733024	L/Cpl. A. V. Main		2737371	Gdsn. C. Openshaw
2739032	Gdsn. A. Male		2732950	Sgt. E. M. Owen
	Lieut. D. H. Marsh		2734393	L/Cpl. W. R. Owen
2735216	Gdsn. C. Martin		2734624	Gdsn. A. Owen
2738514	Gdsn. R. J. Martin		2736296	Gdsn. E. D. Owens
2736780	Gdsn. E. H. Mason		2737842	Gdsn. W. Owens
2733429	C.S.M. W. I. Mathias		2733204	Gdsn. R. H. Parker
	2/Lieut. P. F. Matthews		2735655	Gdsn. J. Parry
	Lieut. C. A. F. J. Maude		2732729	L/Cpl. G. Patrick
3958815	Gdsn. L. C. Maxwell		2735949	Gdsn. J. Partridge
2737310	Gdsn. T. W. May		2737843	L/Sgt. S. W. Partridge
2738421	Gdsn. E. J. Mayhew			Major R. L. Pattinson
2733122	Gdsn. R. A. W. Meechem		2736878	Gdsn. W. Payne
				Capt. A. J. Pearce-Serocold
2733782	Gdsn. E. V. Meese			
2733579	Gdsn. S. C. Melhuish			Lieut. H. W. J. E. Peel
2737494	Gdsn. G. Meredith		2735920	Gdsn. W. Perkins
2734795	L/Sgt. R. G. Meyler		2738729	Gdsn. I. S. Phillips
2733226	Gdsn. C. G. Midwinter		2735477	Gdsn. G. S. Picton
2734697	L/Sgt. A. Millward		2733086	L/Sgt. G. Pincott

2735076	L/Cpl. B. K. Plow	2732946	Gdsn. C. Rock
2733753	Gdsn. R. I. Poole	2734110	C.S.M. W. J. Rodd
2736711	L/Sgt. R. D. Pope	2735031	Gdsn. R. D. Rodgers
2734779	Gdsn. J. R. Powell	2733545	Gdsn. S. G. Rogers
2735354	Gdsn. M. T. Powell	2734427	Gdsn. R. H. Rogers
2737714	Gdsn. F. D. R. Powell	2735604	L/Sgt. G. Rowland
2734736	L/Cpl. J. D. Pratt	2736258	Gdsn. G. Rowlands
2735481	L/Cpl. A. S. Price	2730458	P.S.M. A. J. Sanders
2734413	Gdsn. H. H. Pritchard	2737437	Gdsn. T. C. Sayers
2736051	Gdsn. W. A. Pritchard		Lieut. A. E. L. Schuster
2735371	Gdsn. J. Probart	2737326	Gdsn. D. W. Scott
2738242	L/Cpl. N. L. Prowse	2737504	Gdsn. E. Seare
2733742	Gdsn. G. Pugh	2737153	Gdsn. C. O. Sellick
2735458	Gdsn. B. Pugh	2734287	Gdsn. A. Shaw
2734571	Gdsn. E. J. Pugsley	2735230	Gdsn. D. Sheppard
2738156	Gdsn. D. R. Purchase	2738071	Gdsn. I. G. Sheppard
2732783	L/Cpl. H. Radley	2738749	Gdsn. K. Sherborne
2735921	Gdsn. A. E. C. Radnor	2736268	Gdsn. R. W. Shields
2737678	Gdsn. W. W. Ramsden	2737686	Gdsn. E. R. Short
2733811	L/Sgt. A. D. Randall	2734256	L/Cpl. S. R. Sims
2736150	Gdsn. G. F. Redman	2735438	Gdsn. W. Small
2735705	Gdsn. R. Redmond	2732826	Gdsn. A. Smith
2736423	Gdsn. W. J. Reed	2733121	Gdsn. S. M. Smith
2737733	Gdsn. F. C. Reed	2735153	Gdsn. E. Smith
2735589	Gdsn. D. Rees	2735507	Gdsn. D. E. T. Smith
2735646	Gdsn. W. D. H. Rees	2735633	Gdsn. W. S. Smith
4076380	Gdsn. P. J. Rees	2735661	Gdsn. W. K. Smith
	Lieut. J. E. Reid	2736658	L/Sgt. F. Smith
2733975	Gdsn. J. A. M. Rennett	4032493	L/Cpl. R. H. Smith
	Capt. G. D. Rhys-Williams	14692612	Gdsn. N. T. Smith
		2738948	Gdsn. D. J. Soper
2736562	Gdsn. W. T. Richards	2737848	Gdsn. L. R. Sparkes
2737232	Gdsn. E. B. S. Richards		Major J. O. Spencer
2738050	Gdsn. L. Richardson	2737712	Gdsn. P. R. Spencer
6468155	L/Cpl. C. Richardson	2738350	Gdsn. A. G. Springham
2735119	L/Sgt. S. R. Ridge	4042393	Gdsn. F. W. Sproston
2737929	L/Cpl. W. C. Ridpath	2739031	Gdsn. E. K. Stamp
2733032	Gdsn. J. Roberts	2733036	Gdsn. D. Stanford
2734112	L/Sgt. T. R. E. Roberts	2738976	L/Cpl. J. Stenson
2735850	Gdsn. N. Roberts	2734769	Gdsn. T. Stephenson
2736031	Gdsn. J. Roberts		Lieut. R. D. Stevens
2736294	Gdsn. D. H. Roberts	2738181	Gdsn. D. J. Stock
2736884	Gdsn. H. J. Roberts	2736798	Gdsn. J. R. Stones
2737684	Gdsn. E. W. J. Roberts	2739424	Gdsn. A. F. Street
4191702	L/Sgt. J. L. Roberts, M.M.	2734199	Sgt. I. Sullivan
		2734549	Gdsn. D. G. Sullivan
2735142	Gdsn. H. J. P. Robinson		Major J. D. A. Syrett

Roll of Honour

2734775	Gdsn. T. Talbot		2735121	Gdsn. H. J. Weston
2736115	L/Sgt. L. T. Taylor		2736450	Gdsn. J. Westwood
2736372	Gdsn. W. L. Taylor		2735699	L/Sgt. H. W. Wetherall
2738879	Gdsn. W. H. Taylor		2734038	L/Cpl. E. Wheatley
2733234	Gdsn. W. E. B. Thomas		2734002	Gdsn. H. J. Wheatstone
2734031	Gdsn. G. Thomas		2739402	Gdsn. H. Wheeler
2734350	Gdsn. W. R. Thomas			Lieut. R. G. Whiskard
2734529	Gdsn. A. S. Thomas			Lieut. R. J. Whistler
2734724	Gdsn. T. A. Thomas		2732867	L/Cpl. A. E. White
2735257	Gdsn. D. Thomas		2734144	Gdsn. C. R. White
2735457	Gdsn. T. Thomas		2735564	L/Cpl. F. W. White
2736073	Gdsn. C. Thomas		2737374	Gdsn. H. Whittaker
2736135	Gdsn. D. M. Thomas		2733246	Gdsn. W. Whittle
2736568	Gdsn. W. J. Thomas		2735161	Gdsn. S. Wilkinson
2736992	L/Cpl. H. G. Thomas		2738695	Gdsn. G. Willcocks
2737155	Gdsn. H. J. Thomas		2734403	L/Cpl. H. Williams
2737489	Gdsn. D. S. Thomas		2734417	Gdsn. D. Williams
2738052	Gdsn. W. H. Thomas		2734466	Sgt. H. L. Williams
2738182	Gdsn. G. H. Thomas		2734730	Gdsn. G. Williams
2738322	Gdsn. R. Thomas		2734782	L/Cpl. R. J. Williams
2738575	Gdsn. F. G. Thomas		2734976	Gdsn. G. J. Williams
2738931	Gdsn. H. Thomas		2735080	Gdsn. J. T. Williams
4207862	Gdsn. L. W. Tipton		2735480	Gdsn. W. J. Williams
2734321	L/Sgt. R. J. Topham		2735708	L/Cpl. R. O. Williams
2737587	L/Cpl. F. J. Townley		2735814	Gdsn. K. T. Williams
2738154	Gdsn. F. Trainer		2736125	Gdsn. J. Williams
2734952	L/Sgt. G. A. Trebilcock		2736520	Gdsn. D. Williams
2732329	L/Sgt. D. Tucker		2737157	L/Cpl. T. E. Williams
2735372	L/Sgt. R. F. Tucker		2737210	L/Cpl. S. G. Williams
	Major M. J. Turnbull		2737515	Gdsn. H. Williams
2732391	Sgt. J. E. Turner		2737516	Gdsn. J. E. Williams
2734657	Gdsn. J. R. Turner		2737526	Gdsn. R. T. Williams
	Capt. R. C. Twining		2737653	Gdsn. H. Williams
2734162	Gdsn. J. I. Vaughan		2737854	Gdsn. G. Williams
2735089	Gdsn. W. Vaughan		2738505	Gdsn. W. D. Williams
2734562	L/Cpl. A. H. Veasey		2739181	Gdsn. G. T. Williams
2736892	Gdsn. A. A. A. Villa		1136799	Gdsn. F. Williams
2736464	Gdsn. J. W. Waples			Lieut. C. M. S. Williams-Ellis
2736662	Gdsn. W. H. Wardle			
2734683	L/Cpl. D. J. Waterman		2737699	Gdsn. W. Wills
2737606	Gdsn. H. Waters		3960279	L/Cpl. J. J. Winslade
4076795	Sgt. T. J. Waters		2733892	Sgt. W. Wood
2738129	Gdsn. V. Watkins		2733601	Gdsn. R. Woodage
2737396	Gdsn. A. A. Weals		2736510	L/Cpl. H. Woolrich
14590144	L/Cpl. W. H. Webb		2738160	Gdsn. C. W. Worby
2737884	L/Sgt. A. J. L. Webbon		2733862	Gdsn. A. G. Wright
2736197	Gdsn. G. E. Weetman		2736327	Gdsn. A. W. Wright
2738461	L/Cpl. D. West		2737811	Gdsn. S. C. Wright

HONOURS AND AWARDS

OFFICERS

Name and previous honours	Rank	Decoration Awarded
Allen, D. A. N.	Captain	M.C.
Bailey, H. D.	Major	Mentioned in Despatches.
Bankier, A. M., D.S.O., M.C.	Colonel	O.B.E., Mentioned in Despatches.
Barbour, R. J.	Lieutenant	Mentioned in Despatches.
Bateman, S. O. F.	Major	Mentioned in Despatches.
Beckett, Sir M. G., Bt.	Captain	M.C.
Bedingfeld, Sir E. G. F., Bt.	Major	Mentioned in Despatches.
Bolton, F. B.	Major	M.C.
Bowen-Davies, P. D. F.	Captain	Mentioned in Despatches.
Bray, W. L., D.C.M., M.M.	Major (Q.M.)	M.B.E.
Brinson, D. N.	Captain	M.C.
Browning, G. W.	Lieut.-Colonel	O.B.E.
Brutton, P. F. F.	Lieutenant	Mentioned in Despatches.
Buckeridge, R. G. D.	Captain	Mentioned in Despatches.
Buckland, J. C.	Captain (Q.M.)	M.B.E.
Buckley, W. K.	Captain	Mentioned in Despatches.
Carson, J. H.	Captain	Twice Mentioned in Despatches.
Carter, W. H.	Captain	M.C.
Consett, W. L.	Major	M.C., Mentioned in Despatches.
Coombe-Tennant, A. H. S.	Major	M.C., Mentioned in Despatches.
Copland-Griffiths, F. A. V., M.C.	Brigadier	D.S.O.
Cottom, D. G.	Lieutenant	M.C.
Crosse, W. W. R.	Lieut.-Colonel	Mentioned in Despatches.
Cull, J. K.	Major	Mentioned in Despatches.
Daniel, N. M.	Major	M.C. and Bar, twice Mentioned in Despatches.

Davies, J. H. G.	Lieutenant	Mentioned in Despatches.
Davies-Scourfield, D. G.	Lieut.-Colonel	M.C.
Dent, J. A. W.	Captain	Mentioned in Despatches.
de Rutzen, J. F. F. Baron	Major	Mentioned in Despatches.
Devas, M. C.	Captain	M.C.
Dimsdale, H. C. L.	Major	M.C.
Duncan, A. A.	Major	Chevalier of the Order of Leopold II with Palm, Croix de Guerre with Palm (Belgium).
Eastwood, F. M.	Captain	M.C.
Egerton, F. L.	Captain	M.C.
Evans, A., M.P.	Colonel	Mentioned in Despatches.
Evans, H. A.	Lieutenant	Mentioned in Despatches.
Evans, W. D. D.	Major	M.C., Mentioned in Despatches.
Farrer, R. P.	Captain	M.C.
Fisher, N. T. L.	Major	M.C., Mentioned in Despatches.
Fitzwilliams, R. C. L.	Major	Mentioned in Despatches.
Forbes, H. S.	Major	M.B.E, M.C.
Fowke, G. G.	Major	Mentioned in Despatches, Croix de Guerre with Gilt Star (France).
Fox-Pitt, W. A. F. L., M.V.O, M.C.	Brigadier	D.S.O., Mentioned in Despatches.
Fox-Pitt-Rivers, M. A. L.	Major	Mentioned in Despatches.
Furness, The Hon. C.	Lieutenant	V.C.
Gibbs, B. N.	Major	M.B.E.
Gibbs, D. A.	Captain	Mentioned in Despatches.
Gibbs, P. S.	Lieut.-Colonel	M.B.E.
Gibson-Watt, J. D.	Major	M.C. and two Bars.
Godfrey-Faussett, G. B.	Major	M.B.E.
Goff, B. P. R.	Major	M.C.
Grant, K. W.	Captain (Q.M.)	M.B.E., Mentioned in Despatches.
Gray, E. W.	Captain	M.B.E.

Honours and Awards (Officers)—contd.

Name and previous honours	Rank	Decoration Awarded
Greenacre, W. D. C., M.V.O.	Brigadier	D.S.O., Mentioned in Despatches.
Gresham, J. F.	Lieut.-Colonel	D.S.O.
Griffiths, W. H.	Captain	M.C.
Grogan, M. D. W.	Captain	Mentioned in Despatches.
Gurney, J. E.	Lieut.-Colonel	D.S.O., M.C. and Bar.
Gwatkin, J. S.	Major	Mentioned in Despatches.
Hamborough, B. T. V.	Major	Mentioned in Despatches.
Harrison, R. L.	Captain	Mentioned in Despatches.
Heber-Percy, C. H. R.	Lieut.-Colonel	D.S.O., M.C., Mentioned in Despatches.
Higgon, J. H. V.	Major	O.B.E.
Hodgkinson, R. B.	Lieut.-Colonel	M.C., Mentioned in Despatches.
Hodgson, D. E. P.	Brigadier	O.B.E., Mentioned in Despatches, U.S. Legion of Merit (Degree of Officer).
Homfrey, H. F. R.	Captain	Mentioned in Despatches.
Kearsley, N. S.	Captain	Croix de Guerre with Silver Star (France).
Keith, K. A.	Lieut.-Colonel	Mentioned in Despatches.
Leatham, C. A. la T.	Major	Mentioned in Despatches.
Leuchars, P. R.	Captain	Mentioned in Despatches.
Lewis, J. C. Windsor	Lieut.-Colonel	D.S.O. and Bar, M.C., Mentioned in Despatches, Chevalier of the Order of Leopold II with Palm (Belgium), Croix de Guerre with Palm (Belgium), Knight Officer of the Order of Orange Nassau with Swords (Holland).
Lister, H, E. J.	Major	M.C.
Llewellyn, Sir R., Bt.	Lieut.-Colonel	Mentioned in Despatches.
Llewellyn, W. H. R.	Major	M.C., Mentioned in Despatches.

The Lord Lloyd	Captain	M.B.E.
Makins, Sir W. V., Bt.	Lieut.-Colonel	Mentioned in Despatches.
Mather, D. C. M.	Major	M.C., Mentioned in Despatches.
Mathews, P. F.	Lieutenant	Mentioned in Despatches.
McVittie, C. A. B.	Major	M.B.E, U.S. Bronze Star.
Menzies, K. G., M.C.	Colonel	O.B.E.
Menzies, M.	Major	Mentioned in Despatches.
Mildmay, The Hon. A. B.	Captain	Mentioned in Despatches.
Miller, J. M.	Major	D.S.O., M.C.
Morrice, K. A. S.	Lieut.-Colonel	O.B.E., U.S. Legion of Merit (Degree of Officer).
Moss, W. F.	Lieutenant	Mentioned in Despatches.
Noel, A. C. W.	Major	M.C.
Pattinson, R. L.	Major	Mentioned in Despatches.
Peel, H. W. J. E.	Lieutenant	Mentioned in Despatches, Croix de Guerre with Silver Star (France).
Phillips, The Hon. R. H.	Major	M.B.E, Polonia Restituta IV Class (Poland), U.S. Bronze Star.
Pilcher, R. C. H.	Captain	Mentioned in Despatches.
Powell, Sir R. G. D., Bt.	Major	M.C. and Bar.
Price, R. C. R.	Lieut.-Colonel	D.S.O., Mentioned in Despatches.
Pryce-Jones, D. A.	Captain	Mentioned in Despatches.
Pugh, B. B.	Captain	M.C.
Rees, R. G.	Lieut.-Colonel	Mentioned in Despatches.
Renshaw, M. O. W.	Major	Twice Mentioned in Despatches.
Rhys-Williams, G. D.	Captain	Mentioned in Despatches.
Roberts, I.	Lieutenant (Q.M.)	M.B.E, Mentioned in Despatches.
Robertson, D. L. M.	Major	Mentioned in Despatches.
Sale, R. E. W.	Major	M.C.
Schuster, A. E. L.	Lieutenant	Mentioned in Despatches.

Honours and Awards (Officers)—*contd.*

Name and previous honours	Rank	Decoration Awarded
Sharples, R. C.	Major	M.C., Mentioned in Despatches, U.S. Silver Star.
Smith, J. R. Martin	Major	M.C.
Spencer-Smith, J. M.	Captain	M.C.
Stanier, Sir Alexander B. G., Bt., M.C.	Brigadier	D.S.O. and Bar, Mentioned in Despatches, U.S. Silver Star.
Stevenson, D. J. C.	Captain	M.C.
Stewart, A. G.	Captain	M.C.
Stewart, I. M.	Major	Mentioned in Despatches.
Stewart-Brown, R. D.	Major	Mentioned in Despatches.
Syrett, P. M.	Captain	Mentioned in Despatches.
Tetley, G.	Lieut.-Colonel	Twice Mentioned in Despatches.
Upjohn, G. R.	Brigadier	C.B.E., Mentioned in Despatches.
Vaughan, C. P.	Lieut.-Colonel	D.S.O.
Vaughan-Morgan, J. K.	Lieut.-Colonel	Mentioned in Despatches.
Vigor, G. St. V. J.	Lieut.-Colonel	O.B.E.
Webb, H. H.	Lieutenant (Q.M.)	M.B.E.
Wheatley, A. W. S.	Captain	M.C.
Williams, E. G.	Major	Mentioned in Despatches.
Williams-Wynn, E. W.	Lieut.-Colonel	O.B.E.
Winnington, Sir F. S. W., Bt.	Lieutenant	Mentioned in Despatches.
Worrall, W. G. M.	Major	M.C.

HONOURS AND AWARDS

OTHER RANKS

No.	Name	Rank	Decoration Awarded
2734602	Abrams, O. F.	Sgt.	M.M.
2736599	Andrews, S. J.	L/Sgt.	Mentioned in Despatches.
2656525	Appleby, R. A.	L/Sgt.	M.M., Mentioned in Despatches.
2733454	Arnold, G.	C.S.M.	Croix de Guerre with Silver Star (France).
2737253	Arnold, T. J. L.	L/Cpl.	M.M.
2731403	Baker, A.	R.S.M.	M.B.E.
2737631	Balbiersky, P.	Gdsn.	Mentioned in Despatches.
2734613	Barham, J. A.	C.S.M.	D.C.M.
2736809	Barnes, L. J.	L/Sgt.	B.E.M.
2559572	Barter, A. C.	R.S.M.	M.B.E.
2737129	Beynon, D. W.	L/Cpl.	M.M.
2735059	Blakemore, T.	Gdsn.	Mentioned in Despatches.
2732458	Bond, L. C.	C.S.M.	Mentioned in Despatches.
2732548	Booker, B. E.	Gdsn.	M.M.
2735319	Boswell, A.	Gdsn.	Mentioned in Despatches.
2737190	Burgess, D. F.	L/Cpl.	M.M.
2737643	Burnage, E. J. H.	L/Cpl.	Mentioned in Despatches.
2734573	Burton, C.	Gdsn.	Mentioned in Despatches.
2737545	Bushell, B. R.	Gdsn.	Mentioned in Despatches.
2737451	Cameron, D.	L/Cpl.	Mentioned in Despatches.
2732851	Canavan, T.	Sgt.	Croix de Guerre with Bronze Star (France), Mentioned in Despatches.
2734798	Catherall, J. W.	L/Cpl.	M.M.
2736675	Chatwin, M. G. E.	L/Sgt.	M.M.
2730408	Claydon, H.	R.S.M.	Mentioned in Despatches.
2734543	Cleary, J. J.	L/Cpl.	Mentioned in Despatches.

HONOURS AND AWARDS (OTHER RANKS)—contd.

No.	Name	Rank	Decoration Awarded
2733109	Collum, D. J.	Gdsn.	Mentioned in Despatches.
2734181	Cooke, J. R.	O.R.Q.M.S.	B.E.M.
2734712	Cooper, F.	Gdsn.	Mentioned in Despatches.
2730376	Copping, J.	R.S.M.	M.B.E.
2737520	Cox, R.	L/Sgt.	Mentioned in Despatches.
2736483	Darlington, H. J.	L/Cpl.	B.E.M.
2733705	Davage, I. C.	Gdsn.	M.M.
2734881	David, E. J. L.	L/Cpl.	Mentioned in Despatches.
2733126	Davies, B. J.	Cpl.	M.M.
2733197	Davies, D.	D/Sgt.	D.C.M., Mentioned in Despatches.
2737357	Davies, E.	C.S.M.	Mentioned in Despatches.
2734639	Davies, J. R.	Gdsn.	M.M.
2734842	Davies, K.	Sgt.	Mentioned in Despatches.
4191741	Davies, P. H.	Sgt.	Mentioned in Despatches.
2735156	Davies, S.	L/Sgt.	D.C.M.
2733504	Davies, U.	C.S.M.	Twice Mentioned in Despatches.
2732791	Dodd, F.	R.S.M.	Mentioned in Despatches.
2733448	Doyle, W.	Sgt.	M.B.E.
2731624	Dunn, H. P. N.	R.S.M.	M.B.E.
299370	Dunne, P.	R.S.M.	M.M.
2733442	Easter, T.	L/Cpl.	Mentioned in Despatches.
2736681	Edwards, R.	Gdsn.	Mentioned in Despatches.
2735017	Evans, F.	Sgt.	M.M. and Mentioned in Despatches.
2736347	Evans, G.	L/Cpl.	Mentioned in Despatches.
2734255	Evans, I. M.	C.S.M.	B.E.M.
2733873	Evans, J.	R.Q.M.S.	Mentioned in Despatches.
2732998	Evans, T. H.	C.S.M.	

306

2732825	Fenwick, J.	Gdsn.	B.E.M.
2736917	Greenwood, A.	L/Cpl.	Mentioned in Despatches.
2734250	Griffiths, C. D.	Gdsn.	Mentioned in Despatches.
2734193	Griffiths, D. H.	Sgt.	M.M.
2736688	Griffiths, T. R.	L/Sgt.	Mentioned in Despatches.
2737556	Goodwin, F.	L/Sgt.	Mentioned in Despatches.
2733475	Gough, S.	Sgt.	M.M.
2734347	Gower, L. J.	Sgt.	M.M.
2730577	Hall, A. F.	O.R.Q.M.S.	M.B.E.
2737293	Hansford, C. H.	Sgt.	M.M.
2732479	Harrhy, E. T. P.	Gdsn.	Mentioned in Despatches.
2736473	Hart, E.	C.Q.M.S.	D.C.M.
6083205	Hedditch, F. A.	C.S.M.	Mentioned in Despatches.
2730066	Herd, W.	R.Q.M.S.	B.E.M.
2734685	Hicks, L. A.	Sgt.	Mentioned in Despatches.
2733893	Hillier, B. F.	C.S.M.	D.C.M.
2734818	Hodgson, L. A.	Sgt.	D.C.M.
2738845	Hughes, W. R.	Gdsn.	Mentioned in Despatches.
2735440	Humphreyson, H.	L/Sgt.	Mentioned in Despatches.
2736090	Jenkins, D. V.	C.Q.M.S.	Mentioned in Despatches.
2733395	John, T. H.	D/Sgt.	M.M.
2773603	Jones, A. L.	Sgt.	Mentioned in Despatches.
2733673	Jones, C. S. H.	R.Q.M.S.	Mentioned in Despatches.
2733460	Jones, D. J.	Sgt.	D.C.M.
2732412	Jones, E.	L/Sgt.	D.C.M.
2732572	Jones, F. D.	Sgt.	Mentioned in Despatches.
2732115	Jones, F. T.	R.S.M.	D.C.M.
2738430	Jones, H. R.	Gdsn.	M.M.
4194198	Jones, J. E.	Gdsn.	D.C.M.
2730034	Jones, T.	C.S.M.	M.B.E.

Honours and Awards (Other Ranks)—contd.

No.	Name	Rank	Decoration Awarded
2735182	Jones, T.	Gdsn.	M.M.
2737440	Jones, W.	L/Cpl.	B.E.M.
770548	Jones, W.	Gdsn.	Mentioned in Despatches.
2733952	Jones, W. J.	Sgt.	B.E.M.
4547748	Joyce, A.	L/Sgt.	M.M.
2735135	Keay, D. R.	Gdsn.	Mentioned in Despatches.
2734082	Kempson, A. E.	Sgt.	B.E.M.
2738611	Kennedy, T. L.	Sgt.	M.M.
2738850	Keogh, C. J.	L/Cpl.	M.M.
2733681	King, J.	L/Sgt.	D.C.M.
2731773	Larcombe, E.	C.S.M.	M.M.
2736303	Lawrie, C. G.	Sgt.	M.M.
2735828	Lewis, J. O.	Gdsn.	Mentioned in Despatches.
2734237	Llewellyn, A.	Gdsn.	Mentioned in Despatches.
2733639	Lloyd, C. L.	C.S.M.	Mentioned in Despatches.
2735607	Logan, A. J.	Gdsn.	Mentioned in Despatches.
2733518	Luke, W. E.	L/Sgt.	Mentioned in Despatches.
2734157	Mabey, E. F.	C.S.M.	Order of Bronze Lion (Holland).
2734794	Mairs, W.	C.S.M.	M.M.
2734100	Marsh, D. W.	Sgt.	B.E.M.
2736704	Marshall, R. A.	Sgt.	Mentioned in Despatches.
2733864	Matthews, P. G.	Sgt.	D.C.M.
2737222	McGhan, J. H.	L/Sgt.	M.M.
2734526	Morgan, E.	C.S.M.	M.M.
2735425	Morris, F. B.	Gdsn.	D.C.M.
2737224	Morrison, H.	Gdsn.	Mentioned in Despatches.
2735434	Newell, H. H.	Sgt.	Mentioned in Despatches.

2735174	Nicholson, J. R.	Gdsn.	Mentioned in Despatches.
2737136	Parsons, W. H.	Sgt.	D.C.M.
2736187	Pearson, H. J.	Sgt.	Mentioned in Despatches.
2734495	Phillips, A. H. G.	Sgt.	D.C.M.
2738804	Phillips, M. W.	Sgt.	Mentioned in Despatches.
2736656	Pickard, N.	Gdsn.	Mentioned in Despatches.
2737799	Porter, A. E.	Gdsn.	Mentioned in Despatches.
2737677	Porter, R. D.	L/Cpl.	M.M.
2733284	Potter, T. F.	Gdsn.	M.M.
2734165	Prole, A. H.	C.S.M.	Mentioned in Despatches.
2734220	Rees, N.	Sgt.	M.M.
2731514	Ribton, A. E.	P.S.M.	Mentioned in Despatches.
2730511	Richards, E. L. G.	R.S.M.	M.M., twice Mentioned in Despatches.
2733752	Richardson, H. L.	C.S.M.	D.C.M., Mentioned in Despatches.
4191702	Roberts, J. L.	L/Sgt.	M.M., Mentioned in Despatches.
2732477	Roberts, O. L.	C.Q.M.S.	Mentioned in Despatches.
2735833	Roberts, R. L.	Sgt.	M.M.
552159	Roughton, F.	M.Q.M.S.	M.M., Mentioned in Despatches.
2735101	Ruddle, D. G.	L/Cpl.	M.M., Mentioned in Despatches.
2735585	Sandland, I. G.	Gdsn.	Mentioned in Despatches.
2734436	Semark, A. A.	C.Q.M.S.	D.C.M.
2732564	Shepherdson, R. T.	L/Sgt.	Mentioned in Despatches.
2731799	Sheppard, J. W.	R.S.M.	Mentioned in Despatches.
2733239	Slack, S. J.	R.S.M.	D.C.M.
2734024	Smith, P.	L/Cpl.	Mentioned in Despatches.
2738159	Sparrow, C. N.	L/Cpl.	M.M.
2732706	Stone, C. R.	Gdsn.	M.M.
2734719	Summers, K. G.	Sgt.	Mentioned in Despatches.
2735668	Thomas, D. A.	Gdsn.	Mentioned in Despatches.
2734039	Townsend, F.	Sgt.	M.M.

HONOURS AND AWARDS (OTHER RANKS)—contd.

No.	Name	Rank	Decoration Awarded
2737061	Tumelty, J.	C.Q.M.S.	M.M.
573443	Vale, S. F.	Cpl.	Mentioned in Despatches.
2733185	Vaughan, K.	Sgt.	M.M.
2737851	Waters, J. A.	Sgt.	Mentioned in Despatches.
2732625	Watkins, R. C. A.	L/Cpl.	B.E.M.
2734077	Webb, A. J.	Sgt.	D.C.M.
2735523	Webb, L. A. R.	L/Sgt.	M.M.
2731031	Wedlake, J. M.	D/Sgt.	Mentioned in Despatches.
2736203	Westrop, J.	Sgt.	M.M.
2609500	Whittard, A. G.	D/Major	B.E.M.
2733539	Wilcox, I.	Sgt.	Croix de Guerre 1940 with Palm (Belgium).
2733134	Williams, D. E. G.	C.S.M.	Mentioned in Despatches.
2734166	Williams, E.	C.S.M.	M.M.
1454519	Williams, E.	Gdsn.	Mentioned in Despatches.
2734684	Williams, E. T.	C.Q.M.S.	Mentioned in Despatches.
2735799	Williams, F. E.	L/Sgt.	M.M.
2733819	Williams, F. J.	C.S.M.	Mentioned in Despatches.
2733940	Williams, W. T.	Sgt.	Mentioned in Despatches.

Illustrations and Notes

"CHALLENGER," (OVER 30 TONS) WITH LONG 17-POUNDER GUN.

AT THE TOWER OF LONDON

His Majesty the King, Colonel-in-Chief of the Welsh Guards, with Colonel W. Murray-Threipland, Colonel of the Regiment, shortly before the King presented Colours to the 2nd Battalion. His Majesty's address is reproduced below.

BUCKINGHAM PALACE.

Colonel Sir Alexander Stanier, Officers, Non-Commissioned Officers and Guardsmen of the 2nd Battalion Welsh Guards:

Since your formation last May, I have had no opportunity until today of seeing you on parade. I congratulate you heartily on the smartness of your drill and appearance. I know that you will bring credit to your Regiment, of which I am proud to be Colonel-in-Chief.

The Colours that I have just handed to you are the outward symbol of a threefold tradition—the tradition of your Regiment; the tradition of the Brigade of Guards; and the tradition of Wales, which goes back to the dawn of our history. I am confident that, in the fierce ordeal of war, you will sustain it honourably and loyally.

To the Battalion as a whole, and to every member of it, I wish the best of good luck.

George R.I.
Colonel-in-Chief

14*th February*, 1940.

THE HONOURABLE CHRISTOPHER FURNESS, V.C.

Extract from the Supplement to the "London Gazette"
DATED 7TH FEBRUARY, 1946

The King has been graciously pleased to approve the posthumous award of the VICTORIA CROSS to :—

LIEUTENANT THE HONOURABLE CHRISTOPHER FURNESS
WELSH GUARDS

Lieutenant the Honourable C. Furness was in command of the Carrier Platoon, Welsh Guards, during the period 17th-24th May, 1940, when his Battalion formed part of the garrison of Arras. During this time his Platoon was constantly patrolling in advance of or between the widely dispersed parts of the perimeter, and fought many local actions with the enemy. Lieutenant Furness displayed the highest qualities of leadership and dash on all these occasions and imbued his command with a magnificent offensive spirit.

During the evening of the 23rd May, Lieutenant Furness was wounded when on patrol but he refused to be evacuated. By this time the enemy, considerably reinforced, had encircled the town on three sides and withdrawal to Douai was ordered during the night of 23rd-24th May. Lieutenant Furness's Platoon, together with a small force of light tanks, were ordered to cover the withdrawal of the transport, consisting of over forty vehicles.

About 0230 hours, 24th May, the enemy attacked on both sides of the town. At one point the enemy advanced to the road along which the transport columns were withdrawing, bringing them under very heavy small arms and anti-tank gun fire. Thus the whole column was blocked and placed in serious jeopardy. Immediately Lieutenant Furness, appreciating the seriousness of the situation, and in spite of his wounds, decided to attack the enemy, who were located in a strongly entrenched position behind wire.

Lieutenant Furness advanced with three Carriers, supported by light tanks. At once the enemy opened up with very heavy fire from small arms and anti-tank guns. The light tanks were put out of action, but Lieutenant Furness continued to advance. He reached the enemy position and circled it several times at close range, inflicting heavy losses. All three Carriers were hit and most of their crews killed or wounded. His own Carrier was disabled and the driver and Bren gunner killed. He then engaged the enemy in personal hand-to-hand combat until he was killed. His magnificent act of self-sacrifice against hopeless odds, and when already wounded, made the enemy withdraw for the time being and enabled the large column of vehicles to get clear unmolested and covered the evacuation of some of the wounded of his own Carrier Platoon and the light tanks.

FRANCE, 1940

The upper picture shows part of Boulogne, where the 2nd Battalion fought in 1940. The central quay between the two basins was under fire from the white houses opposite when the last ships sailed. It was here that Major J. C. Windsor Lewis and a small mixed force held out for thirty-six hours when the rest of the town and harbour was occupied by the Germans, and troops and tanks shelled them across the basin. (See page 96.)

The chateau at West Cappel in which No. 2 Company of the 1st Battalion made their last stand under Captain J. E. Gurney, in 1940. On the bank of the moat in the foreground a German tank got stuck but was able to train its gun on the main entrance and on the bridge referred to in the story on page 107.

With the knowledge that both Battalions returned to France in 1944, for the fighting which ended in victory, it is not inappropriate to set beside their story Lord Wavell's description of "the homely but indomitable figure of the British soldier" . . . "who has won so many battles that he never doubts of victory, who has suffered so many defeats and disasters on the way to victory that he is never greatly depressed by defeat: whose humorous endurance of time and chance lasts always to the end."

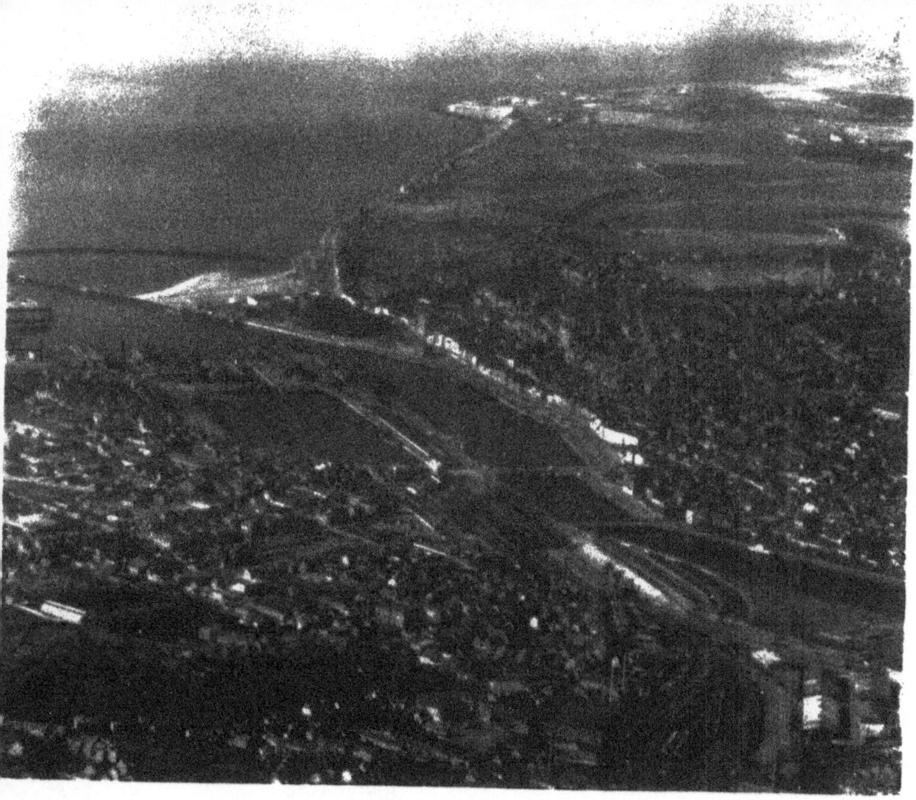

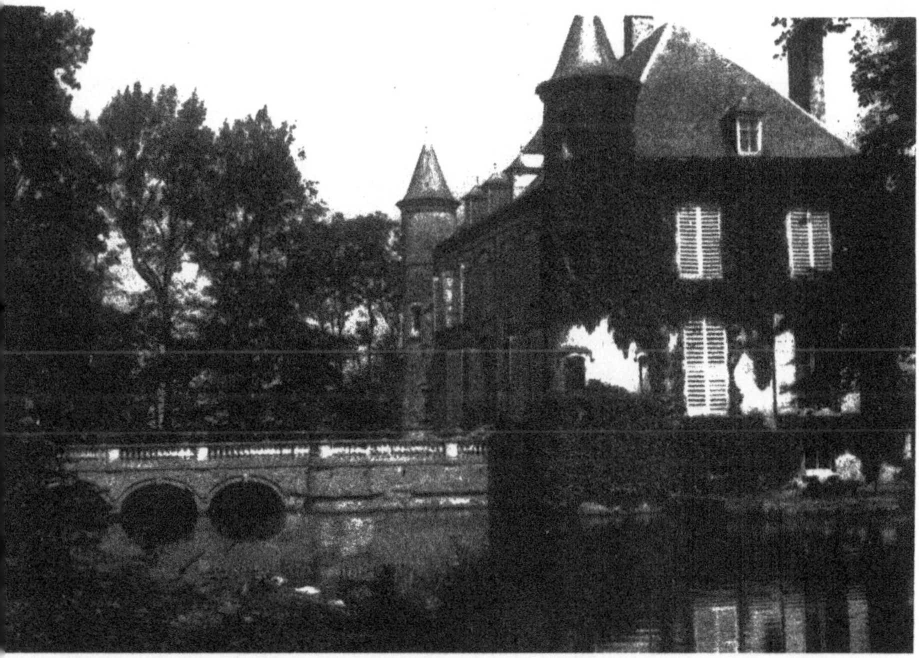

FONDOUK

The top picture shows the El Rhorab feature which the 3rd Battalion captured at Fondouk. The dark ground in the right foreground is point 252 where Advanced Battalion Headquarters was. The white sand of the dry wadi which crossed the Battalion front shows faintly in the middle of the picture: beyond it the ground rises till it reaches the foot of the rocky hills. It was crossing this ground that the companies came under murderous fire from the hills, near the foot of which they were at first pinned down. (See page 114.)

Starting from the left, the hills are "The Razor-back"—or at least the right half of it—"The Pimple," and "The Djebel"; the Fondouk Gap is seen to the right of the last named. No. 1 Company's final assault went up the left-hand slopes of the Razor-back which are not seen in this photo.

The lower picture, taken after the attack, shows a typical German post at the top of the hill. A machine-gun covered the ground in front, firing through a loophole; an assortment of hand grenades was ready to be thrown down on assaulting troops. It is easy to realise the difficulty of dislodging the enemy from such well-prepared and naturally strong positions.

The Welsh Guardsman is wearing Regimental designations and the "Mailed Fist" badge of the 6th Armoured Division.

HAMMAM LIF

These two photographs show the mountain ridge which the 3rd Battalion attacked at Hammam Lif. The two main heights in the top picture are "Double Hill" (right) and "Cave Hill" (left). The orchards from which they started are seen behind the farm building and Battalion Headquarters was near the point where a few taller trees rise in the centre. Above these trees can be seen the gully up which No. 4 Company climbed to capture "Double Hill" after they had crossed the intervening ground, which was swept by fire from the heights above.

The lower picture is taken from a position on this intervening ground, nearer the hills. It is looking down towards the end of the ridge; there it falls steeply to Hammam Lif lying in the half mile or so of level ground between the mountains and the sea. Coldstream Guards cleared this end of the ridge during the night, after the Welsh Guards had captured the ground shown in the top picture.

MONTE CERASOLA

The story of the 3rd Battalion's fight on Cerasola is told on pages 129 to 139. The Welsh Guards had come from North Africa only a few days before, and although, as can be seen, the weather was fine when they went up into the mountains, this was winter; and in fact the weather broke that night. Through the ten days which followed they held the bare mountain-top which is shown in the first picture against enemy attacks, living in a world of driving storms, of snow and ice, or of mist or heavy rain.

In the middle picture they had not yet climbed very high; they had still a long way to go to Cerasola and the roughest part of the journey lay before them.

The men are wearing khaki battledress and leather jerkins: later they normally wore denim overalls when on active operations. They are each carrying a rolled blanket among other things, such as water, rations, ammunition or other stores.

In the bottom picture the Battalion is halted for a rest and the men have taken off their equipment, put down their loads and exchanged berets for steel helmets. The three guns which are being cleaned are medium machine-guns which were carried in two sections of the Carrier Platoon. They fired the same sized bullet as a rifle (.303), the cartridges being fed in on belts. They could fire six hundred and fifty rounds a minute and had an effective range of three to four thousand yards.

The men standing are (reading from left to right), Sergeant D. Thomas, in charge of the machine guns, Lance-Corporal W. J. Rasbridge, Sergeant J. Tumelty and Lance-Sergeant T. Anzani.

CASSINO

This remarkable air photo, taken with other pictures of Cassino, shows how the monastery dominated the castle (marked by a white square) and the town.

The black shadow thrown by Castle Hill in the right-hand bottom corner shows how steep were its sides. The hair-pin bend in the road, just above the castle ruins was in enemy hands and they had posts between there and the castle. The nearest British troops were down below in the ruins of Cassino. The company which held the castle were thus isolated and overlooked.

The photograph was taken in March, 1944, on the day before formations under command of Lieutenant-General Sir Bernard Freyberg, V.C., launched the attack in which Castle Hill was captured by men of the New Zealand Division. The attack began from the air and two thousand tons of bombs were dropped, mostly in the town. Parts of the town, including the station area in the south, were captured and it was to relieve the troops who had carried out this attack that the Welsh Guards first took over a sector in the station area and afterwards held positions in the northern part of the town and on Castle Hill.

CASSINO

This view of Cassino being bombed was taken fairly early in the long struggle to capture the town. Monastery Hill is hidden by the smoke : Castle Hill is just visible in a rift to the right of the picture. Many of the houses were still standing.

The second photo was taken much later. In the background are the ruins of the castle ; in the foreground, a fair sample of the condition to which Cassino was reduced in the end. No houses are left. Those that were built on the lower slopes of Castle Hill have been swept away, and of one of the main streets in the foreground nothing remains but fragments of buildings, rubble and stagnant pools. It is not difficult to imagine the difficulty, discomfort and danger faced by the company which had to climb Castle Hill in the darkness and to hold the ruins, with the enemy just outside and the monastery (not visible in the picture) looking down on them. The conditions in the town itself were hardly better.

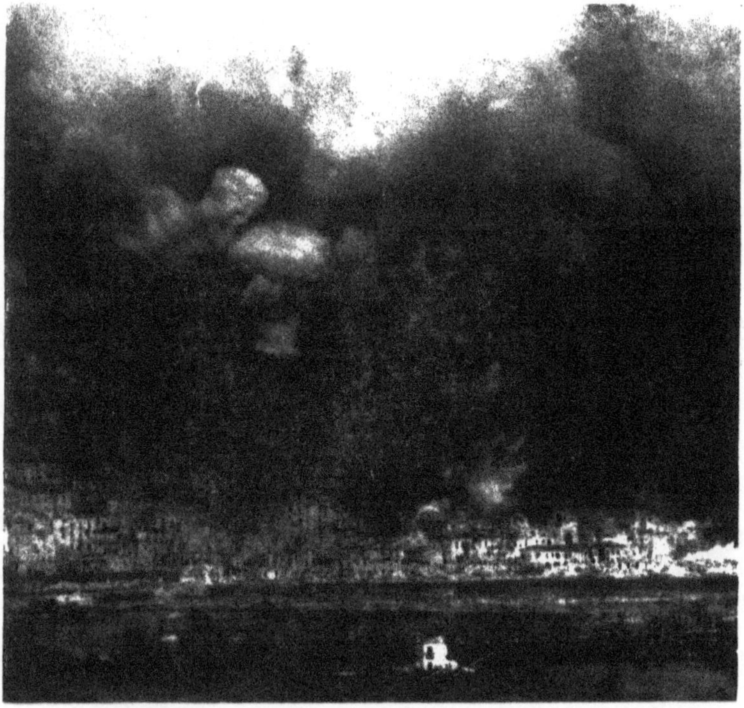

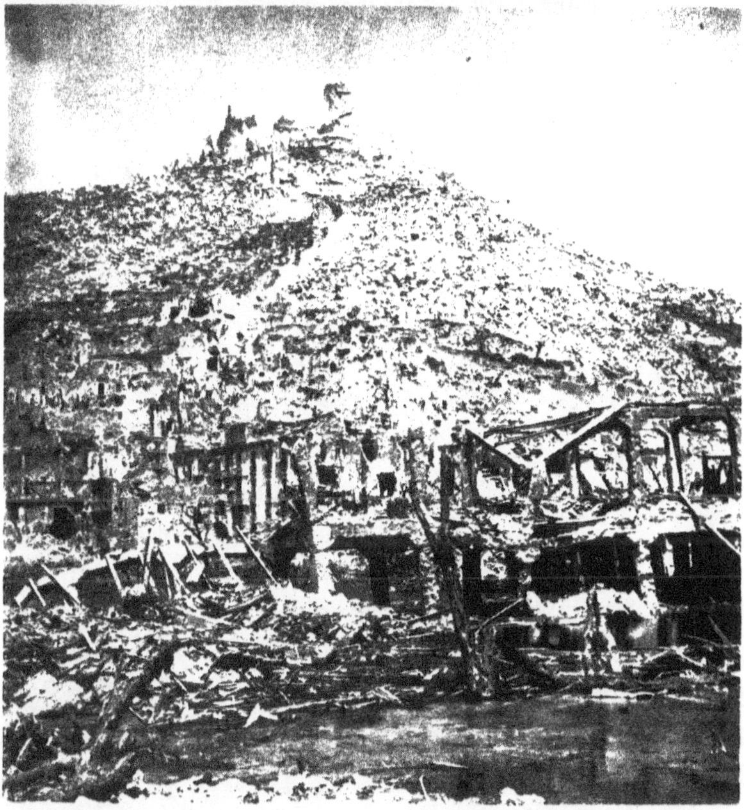

CASSINO

In this view the main town of Cassino with Castle Hill and Monastery Hill are out of sight to the right of the picture. Monte Trocchio in the distance, facing Cassino, was in our hands and the Gunners had their observation posts there. The Welsh Guards used to enter the town by a route past the trees seen on the left, and some of the positions they held were in the ruins from which the remains of a tower stand up. The men seen moving along the right bank of the stream are taking the route by which ration parties went to a quarry on the northern exit from Cassino. There they collected rations which the Quartermaster brought up to the quarry by jeep.

The drawing facing page 142 is taken from a point to the left of this photograph and shows the same bare trees and the same jagged ruins, but from another angle.

THE LIRI VALLEY

Looking back down the Liri valley through which the 3rd Battalion had come from Cassino. The lower slopes of Monte Orio are on the left, the foreground is Monte Piccolo, and Route 6 disappears as it enters the narrow pass between them on its way to Arce and to Rome. The round hill between the road and the mountains is near le Cesse, from which the sketch facing page 152 was made. Above this hill, at the extreme right end of the mountain range, is Monastery Hill, behind which at the hill foot lies Cassino. The cloud-topped mountain in the centre of the picture is Monte Cairo, and Monte Trocchio is very faintly seen under the clouds on the right of the picture.

This view was taken from a point near the top of Piccolo where there is a patch of clear and cultivated ground, but below this patch the hill falls steeply and the ground is terraced with loose rocks and stones. It was on these steeper slopes that No. 2 Company suffered so heavily. Behind the camera the hill rises to much rougher and rockier ground, of which the outcrop seen in the picture is a small sample; cultivation ceases then and the olive trees give place to tangled scrub. See "Piccolo and Arce," page 147.

ARCE

The Germans, having lost Piccolo and Monte Grande, had withdrawn from Arce and a column of tanks and infantry entered the city. The picture shows a Sherman tank—of the 2nd Lothians and Border Horse—with men of No. 2 Company, 3rd Battalion Welsh Guards riding on it.

The 2nd Lothians and Border Horse and the 17th/21st Lancers formed the 26th Armoured Brigade of the 6th Armoured Division and fought side by side with the 1st Guards Brigade in the Tunisian and Italian Campaigns.

AREZZO

Men of No. 1 Company, 3rd Battalion Welsh Guards resting during the battle for Arezzo. It was the height of the Italian summer and the men were in the fighting order worn in hot weather—canvas trousers, American pattern shirts, cap comforters and, in most cases, camouflage smocks.

The Non-Commissioned Officers include Sergeant G. A. James, Lance-Sergeant R. Davies and Lance-Corporal H. Lewis.

The rifles are the old pattern which carries the old long bayonet; it was superseded during the war in most of the army by the Mark IV rifle and short bayonet, which were used by the 1st Battalion in the campaign on the Western Front.

SAN MARCO

San Marco, which the 3rd Battalion captured on June the 20th, 1944, as part of the operations at Perugia. At the end of that day advanced Battalion Headquarters was established in the big white house on the left of the picture. The hill in the middle distance is Montione, on which No. 4 Company spent the night. There is a shallow valley between Montione and the higher ground at San Marco, and it was in this valley away behind the white house that the fight took place in which Major Fogg-Elliot was killed. (See "Perugia and San Marco," page 155.)

THE POMINO RIDGE

This is the country which the 3rd Battalion reached after they had come up the Arno valley, shown overleaf, and were approaching the Gothic Line. Pelago and "Atrocity House" lie behind the photographer. In the right of the picture are the lower slopes of Monte Toschi : away to the left stretches the Pomino ridge. Companies of the 3rd Battalion held positions on the two nearest hills (in shadows) and it was along the ridge, out beyond the left of the photograph, that Lieutenant R. D. Wrigley and his party went on the patrol described on page 241. The picture shows clearly the nature of the country in this part of Italy.

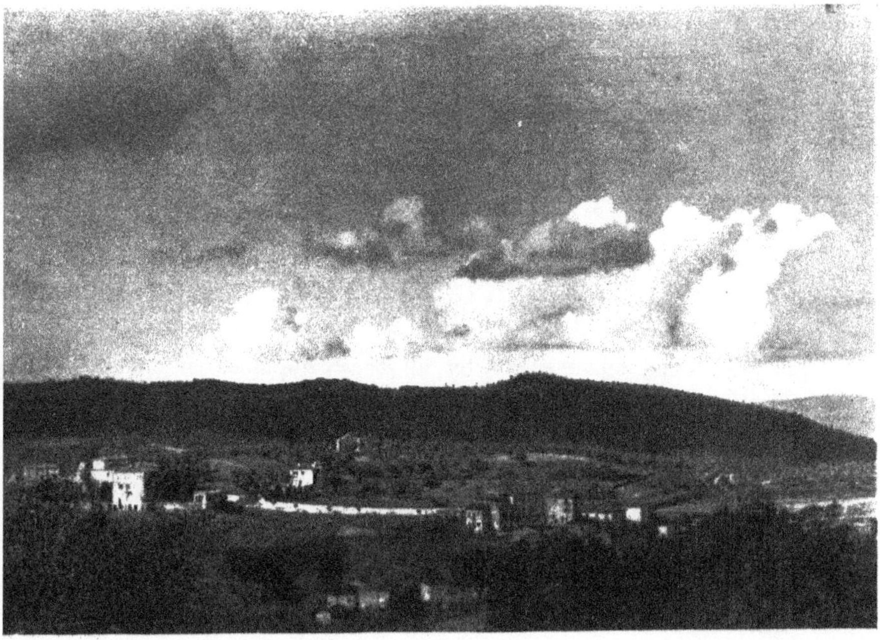

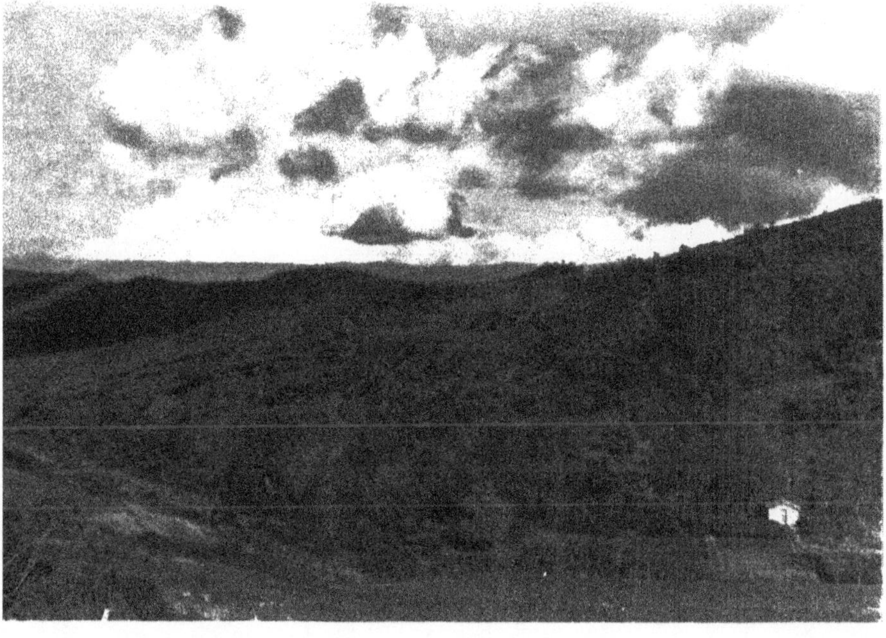

IN THE ARNO VALLEY

This photo was taken from the house at Torre a Monte which was used as Battalion Headquarters during operations in the Arno valley. (See page 164.) The dark ridge in the foreground was patrolled successively by all the companies of the 3rd Battalion. The road in the extreme left corner runs beside the Arno. Lieutenant R. H. Leeke from No. 2 (Grenadier Guards) Company was killed on patrol to the white house above the road. Other patrols went to Merrow Farm, the white house in the foreground on the right.

The second ridge in the left half of the picture is the Altomena-Grille feature, which No. 3 and No. 4 Companies occupied later without opposition. Behind this again is the Diacceto ridge which runs northwards up into the mountains. In the mountains in the centre lie Podernuovo, "Atrocity House" and Consuma. Vallambrosa is behind the shoulder of the slope on the right of the picture.

The picture gives a fair impression of the country through which the 3rd Battalion was fighting in September, 1944.

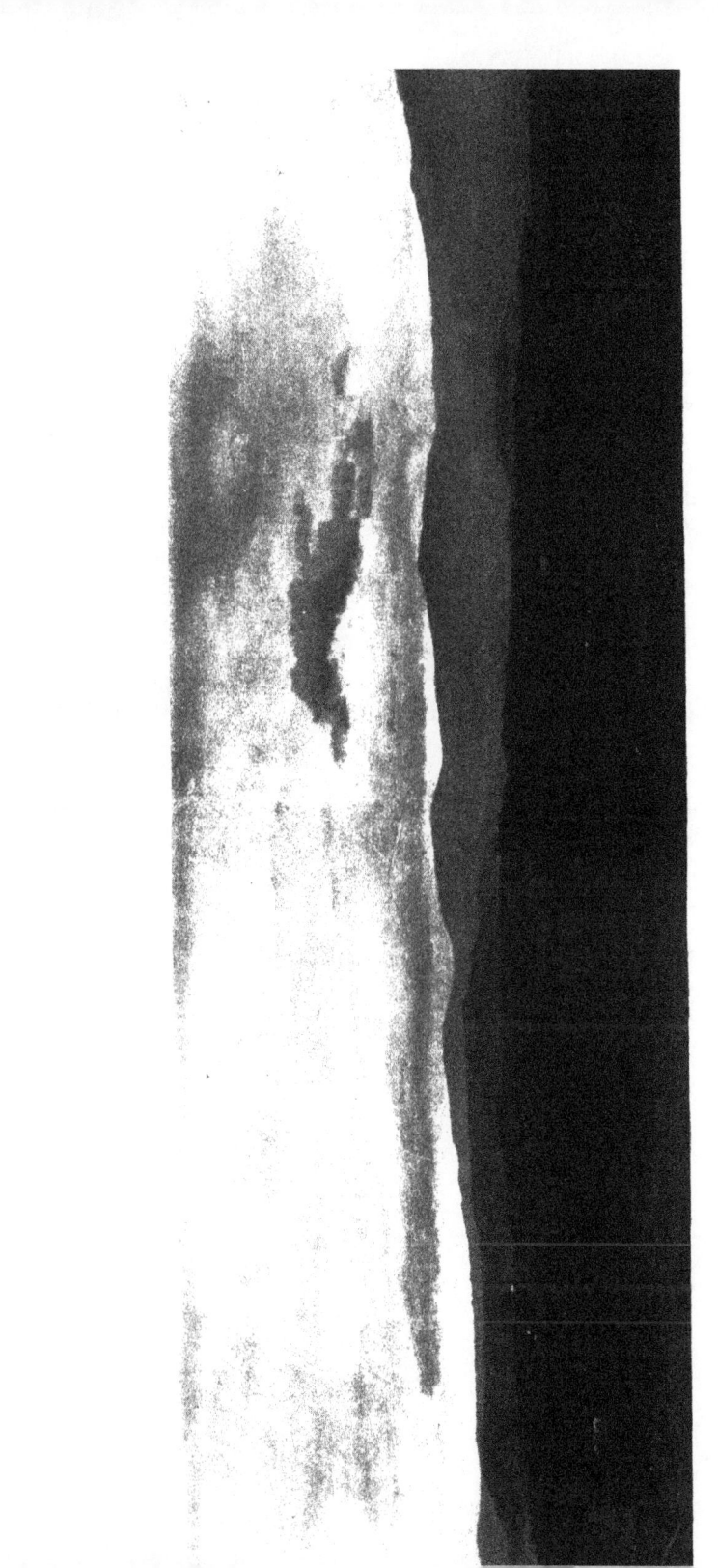

MONTE BATTAGLIA

The castle on Monte Battaglia was battered by every German gun within range and especially by one, known to the 3rd Battalion as "Bologna Bess," which did a "hate" every evening and frequently achieved direct hits. Mercifully the walls which remained standing were very thick.

The sergeant in the picture is dressed for muling. Mule guides and escorts carried arms, but nothing else except the inevitable stick used by nearly everyone in the mountains. His legs are wrapped in the sleeves of an old gas-cape to keep out the mud. When the photo was taken the track on the left was only ankle deep, but in other places men and mules sank almost to their knees and it was usual (and wise) to swathe legs in anything available.

The view from the castle looking back down the ridge on which companies were deployed. The knife-edge character of the ridge can be seen and it is not hard to imagine the difficulty of bringing up mules at night or of carrying out stretcher cases, when strong winds blew and the track was slippery with mud or ice. The Santerno valley lies off the picture to the right : in the distance the Apennines continue, ridge after ridge, towards Rimini and the Adriatic Sea.

WINTER IN ITALY

The top picture shows, on the sky-line, advanced Battalion Headquarters at Carre when the 3rd Battalion held positions in the Monte del Verro section of the Apennines. Shelters in which the defence platoon lived can just be distinguished against the hillside; as they were not in view of the enemy the men in this position did not wear protective snow clothing. The three figures on the right are setting out to visit a company on Acqua Salata: they will come into view of the enemy and so are wearing snow suits—or at least two of them are. Major J. O. M. Ashton, the Second-in-Command, who is the third figure, would never wear one.

The second picture shows Carre from the front. It was "a really luxurious Headquarters." The part lived in did not leak and was proof against driving snow, and there was a perfectly good manger for the Commanding Officer to sleep in. Company Commanders would come a long way from their own less eligible shelters ostensibly to make reports but in truth enjoy the warmth and amenities of this place. The enemy's machine gun could not pierce its walls and his artillery never hit it while the Welsh Guards were there.

The third picture shows a typical villa at Greve, a few miles south of Florence in the Chianti hills. This was Battalion Headquarters when they came off the mountains, and the companies were in similar if smaller villas in the neighbourhood. After living for four or five days at Carre and in mountain-side shelters they stayed here for the next four or five days and then went back on to the mountains. Two houses could hardly be more strongly contrasted nor two stretches of country—the one a primitive and half-ruined hill farm whose shelter was a luxury on the bleak mountain top; the other a house of beauty, designed for fine living and set in the rich, well-cultivated wine lands of central Italy. The view is towards Florence.

TRAINING IN ENGLAND

When the first tanks went into action on the Somme in 1916 they owed their existence to Mr. Churchill. While he was First Lord of the Admiralty his fertile mind conceived the idea of armoured land ships, and with the courage of his convictions he promoted the experimental construction of the first tanks. He is seen in the picture on a visit to the Guards Armoured Division during their final training, discussing the points of a Cromwell tank with Major J. O. Spencer, who commanded No. 2 Squadron of the 2nd Battalion Welsh Guards until he was killed in action at Hechtel.

Behind Mr. Churchill's right shoulder is the wireless aerial. The knobs on the revolving gun turret rivet heavy armour plates to the steel shell inside. Three prongs in front of Major Spencer are sighting vanes to guide him on to the target when firing the gun. This is a 75 mm. high velocity gun, with a muzzle brake fitted to reduce recoil when it is fired. Below, half hidden in shadow, is the Besa machine gun which remains to cover the front when the turret above it revolves. The hull gunner sits unseen behind the Besa; and on his right, looking out through the open visor, is Sergeant T. W. Dredge, the driver.

Each of the signs in front has its significance. On the left a white 45 on a blue and green background is an army sign, meaning that the tank belongs to an armoured reconnaissance battalion. A yellow 26 on a black background is a bridge sign. All bridges were classified and numbered to show what load they could carry safely; a vehicle numbered 26 must not use any bridge marked with a lower number. The white square is a Battalion sign, showing that the tank belongs to No. 2 Squadron, and the A means that it is the Squadron leader's tank. Last comes the Divisional sign, the ever-open eye on a shield painted in the blue and red colours of the Brigade of Guards. It was a famous sign even before the Guards Armoured Division adopted it, for it was first borne by the Guards Division in the Great War of 1914-1918.

The lower picture shows the Training Battalion on parade at Sandown Park, Esher.

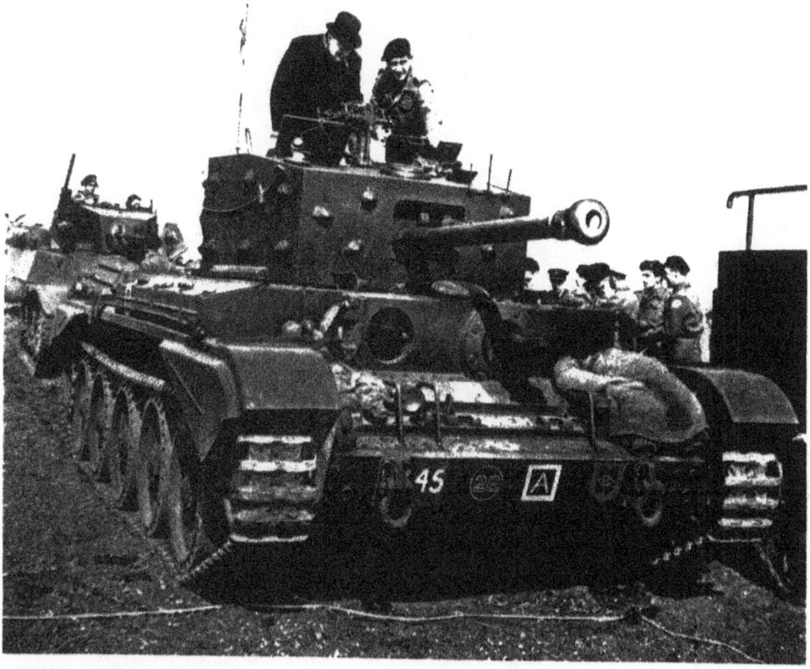
45
A

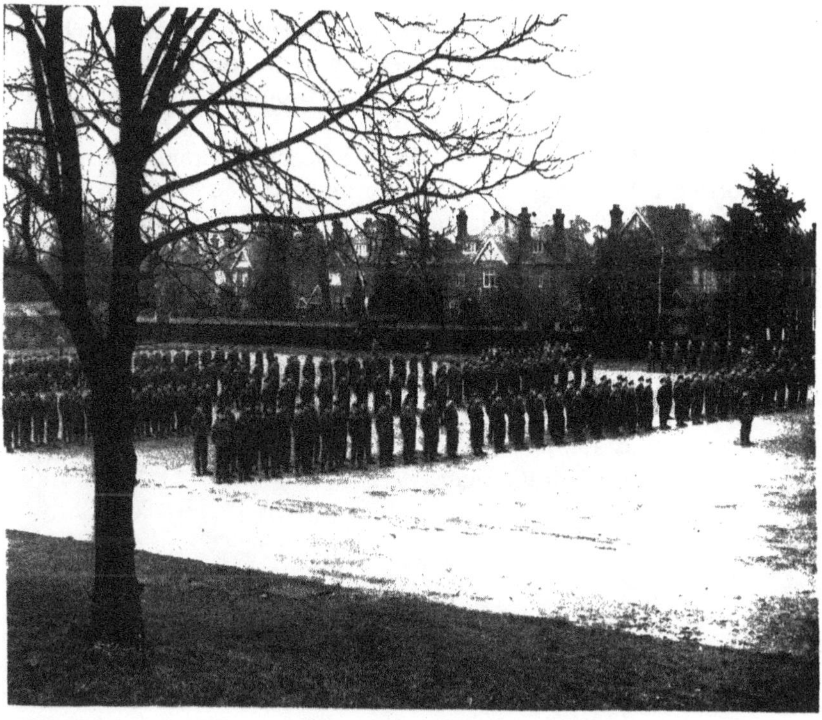

LANDING IN NORMANDY

A Cromwell tank is seen wading ashore at Arromanches, having just left the L.S.T. The "Landing Ship, Tank" was an American boat with a flat bottom and very shallow draft. When about a quarter of a mile from the shore an anchor was dropped and the ship made speed towards the shore until she grounded at high tide. When the tide had ebbed sufficiently the bows opened like two doors and a ramp was lowered to the sand. An L.S.T. could hold thirty tanks in three rows of ten on the lower deck and an internal hydraulic lift took wheeled vehicles on to the top deck. The anchor put out astern was used to haul the ship off the beach at a subsequent high tide.

All tanks were waterproofed to wade in salt water, up to the height of the turret if necessary.

The picture shows a typical scene near the landing beach at Arromanches in Normandy. Leading up the road is a Cromwell tank, followed by a Sherman, another Cromwell and a three-ton lorry.

Waterproofing materials on the leading Cromwell to be noticed are the big chute coming up from the exhausts at the back, the built-up cupola for the commander, through which air for the engine was drawn, waterproof sheeting around the gun mantle and the tow rope raised around the turret.

The two largest vessels in the background are L.S.Ts.; nearer the shore and painted white are a number of smaller L.C.Ts. (Landing *Craft*, Tank) whose load was ten tanks. Anti-aircraft balloons were attached to many of the ships : one flying low is seen on the left and others are very faintly visible away out to sea on the right.

CAEN

From the day of our first landings in Normandy until the day when the town was taken, July the 8th, 1944, it was evident that the enemy continued to regard the defence of Caen as the matter of greatest importance, and seven hundred of his available nine hundred tanks were located in this sector, facing the British Second Army.

In General Eisenhower's report *On the Operations in Europe* he says, the enemy "committed all his available armour and a considerable part of his infantry to the battle in the Caen sector, thus rendering easier the task of Allied troops in the west.... The resulting struggle round Caen, which seemed to cost so much blood for such small territorial gains, was thus an essential factor in ensuring our ultimate success.... Every foot of ground the enemy lost at Caen was like losing ten miles anywhere else. At Caen we held him with our left while we delivered the blow toward Cherbourg with our right.

"The assault on July the 8th was preceded by an air bombardment of nearly five hundred heavy bombers of the Royal Air Force, supplemented by effective naval fire from H.M.S. *Rodney*, *Roberts* and *Belfast* and by artillery.... The result was to paralyse the enemy, who broke before our attack."

Caen was only captured after long and bitter fighting. The extent of the damage can be gathered from this photograph. Of the lower parts of the town, the centre of industrial activity, little was left standing. The more generally residential neighbourhood, on the higher ground to the east, was by comparison little damaged.

The capture of Caen, in which the Guards Armoured Division was not employed, was the necessary preliminary to the battle in which they were engaged ten days later. The story of the Welsh Guards' part in that battle is on page 173.

1st AND 2nd BATTALIONS MOVING UP

Moving up to the front. The soldier looking back on these moves will remember them for their interminable length and boredom, dust and discomfort, exasperation and amusement. As can be imagined, there were very few roads in Normandy to serve the vast concentration of troops within the bridgehead area, and a journey of only five or six miles might easily last an hour or two. It was usual to travel in bounds. There would be a halt of perhaps five or ten minutes ; then just when it seemed that there would be time to brew up some tea the column would once again start moving. Cooking fires were hastily extinguished, drivers of tanks and trucks were shouted orders to get their vehicles started, agonised faces of men would be seen trying to drink boiling hot tea too quickly, and men leaping into already moving vehicles brandishing cookers, dixies, jerrycans and mugs would be a common sight. And having got on the move, the column would be halted again a few hundred yards down the road !

Yet, thanks to good staff work, the marking and signposting of routes, and good traffic control, they got there in due course.

INTO BATTLE

The top picture shows the tanks going into the battle east of Caen, described on page 173. It was the dawn of July 18th, 1944.

Below, the 1st Battalion Welsh Guards moving up towards the front line by one of the countless dusty lanes in Normandy. As was always the case near the front, at a time when we had complete mastery of the air, the road is packed with vehicles. In the extreme right, with a white star painted on the door, is a limber for a 25-pounder gun.

In the centre nearest the camera is a view of the back of a 3-inch mortar carrier with the cardboard cartons for carrying the ammunition strewn all over it.

The jeep behind this belongs to the Royal Corps of Signals, as can be seen by the number 17 which is painted on a blue and white background. In the back of the jeep can be seen a large drum of telephone cable, and the man sitting beside the driver has apparently looted a German forage cap.

Through the back window of the jeep can be seen the number 63, which shows that the carrier drawn up behind belongs to the 1st Battalion Welsh Guards.

On the left of the picture two White half-tracks are drawn up; these sturdy, reliable vehicles had a fine cross-country and road performance and were used for a variety of jobs such as wireless control stations, front-line ambulances (for they were armoured) and for carrying tank fitters.

Men of the 1st Battalion are seen worming their way forward on foot. The leading officer trying to get past the mortar carrier is Lieutenant A. J. Bland; immediately behind him is Lance-Sergeant H. C. W. Brawn. This is No. 4 Company and they are wearing the camouflaged steel helmets and denim overalls, which the 1st Battalion wore normally when in action.

ATTACK NEAR CAGNY

Major J. D. A. Syrett, commanding No. 4 Company of the 1st Battalion in the action near Cagny (see page 173), is seen giving directions to Sergeant J. A. Veysey, in charge of 3-inch mortars—probably pointing out a target to him. On the man nearest the camera, Guardsman G. S. Kitchen, can be seen the rolled gas cape, and a pick-helve. On the other men the following items of equipment can be picked out : rifles, entrenching tools, pick-helve and pick-head, water bottle, gas mask, rolled groundsheets and gas capes, steel helmets with camouflage netting and a Bren gun in the firing position.

Major Syrett was killed in action a few days later.

IN NORMANDY

In the top photograph a squadron of 2nd Battalion tanks is moving uphill across country. The "Bocage" country was rich in little hedges and good pasture land. The red soil became very dusty in hot weather and covered everyone's face in a thin red layer, giving them the appearance of "Red Indians"! With the aid of netting and branches taken off nearby trees it took a short time to blend the squat bulk of a tank into the nearest hedge or thicket, and this camouflaging would be done automatically as soon as the tanks halted for any length of time.

The lower picture shows Captain Sir E. G. F. Bedingfeld's Company Headquarters at one time after the action near Le Bas Perrier, in August, 1944. A slit trench has been dug on his right in the hedge-bottom, covered with a sheet of corrugated iron and camouflaged with straw.

A patrol has just come in and is making its report. The weather then was very hot and except in actual fighting as little clothing as was necessary was worn and equipment was dispensed with whenever possible.

BURNING ENEMY TRANSPORT

During the great advance from Normandy to Brussels and beyond such scenes as the two that are shown here were frequently witnessed.

German transport on the run, their vehicles crammed with soldiers, equipment or loot, were invariably grossly overloaded and did not move very fast if they did not break down altogether. Overtaken and surprised by a column of British tanks, they were a perfect target for a Besa machine-gun. The tracer bullets, a high proportion of which were in every belt of ammunition, soon set fire to the German vehicles; and as shown in the pictures they would be left where they stood, burning fiercely, or dragged just off the road.

The very clever drawing by Sergeant Murrell which is reproduced in the plate facing page 206 gives an artist's impression of the road as seen from the front of a fifteen-hundredweight truck.

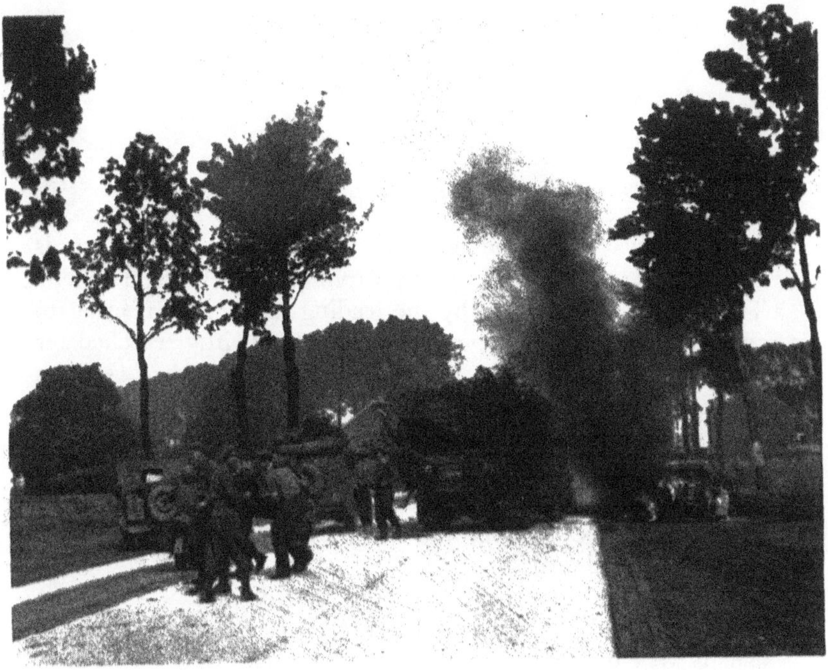

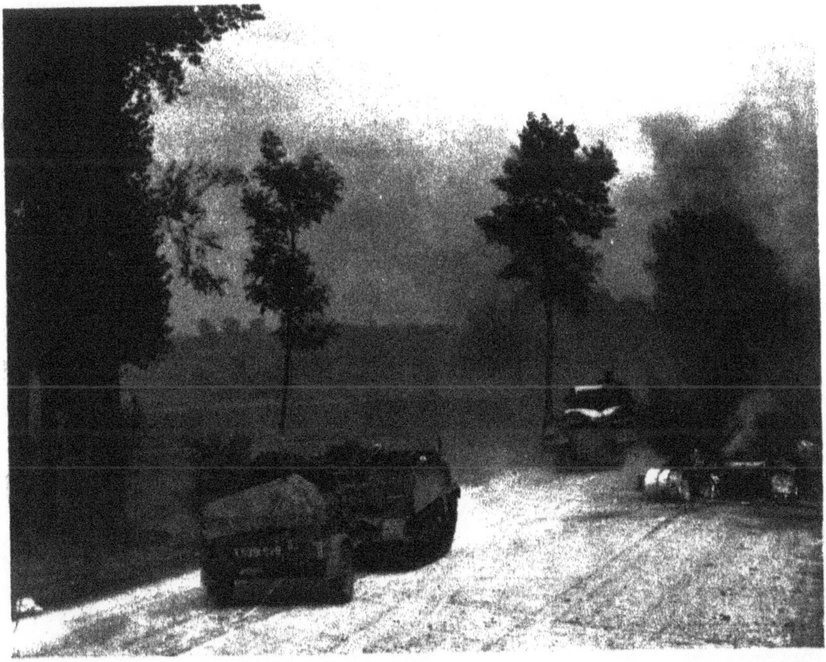

ADVANCE TO BRUSSELS

All the way from the Seine to Brussels the Welsh Guards Group had to cope with greatly varying numbers of prisoners. They would first be met by the leading tanks, and in order to avoid as much delay as possible they were swiftly searched for any weapons, while an officer found out to what German formation they belonged. This information was relayed back over the wireless and the prisoners themselves were told to march back down the road up which the advance was leading until they came to the first prisoner-of-war cage; this would in all probability be a square marked out by barbed wire in a field on the side of the road.

Sometimes owing to the large numbers of prisoners taken it was not possible to provide an escort for them, but they were usually very docile and gave no trouble. On the day on which the 2nd Battalion reached Vimy Ridge and the 1st Battalion entered Arras they took over two thousand prisoners. The Germans were picked up all over the country, sleeping in ditches, sitting in the back of broken-down vehicles, marching in dirty bedraggled columns, in towns and villages or near farms out in the countryside. The top picture shows 2nd Battalion tanks on Vimy Ridge. In the lower picture they are halted on the roadside.

The French Forces of the Interior played a big part in the proceedings. They ranged in age from fifteen to seventy and travelled about packed into captured German vehicles or ancient French cars. Column after column of German prisoners, with only a couple of the F.F.I. men to shepherd them, passed the Welsh Guards during these days.

And at one place an elderly Frenchman with an even older bugle stood by the road-side and blew "Cookhouse at the double" as the Battalions passed.

INTO BELGIUM

The three pictures opposite show scenes which were of frequent occurrence between the River Seine and Brussels.

The top picture shows men from the Motor Transport column of the 1st Battalion taking cover in a ditch by the side of the road; it may have been because of shelling or air attack, both of which are very unpleasant for men travelling in an unprotected lorry which may easily be loaded with petrol or ammunition. Captain S. G. Holland is in the foreground on the bank.

The centre picture speaks for itself. The difference between a Welsh Guardsman and one of the Herrenvolk is obvious.

At the bottom of the page Welsh Guardsmen are seen watching the flank while their company are halted. The man in the centre has a 2-inch mortar.

THE LIBERATION OF BRUSSELS

Scenes in Brussels on the 3rd of September, 1944—the day of its liberation by the Guards Armoured Division. These photographs show how difficult it was to control a tank, let alone a column, while wildly excited Belgians swarmed aboard it. On the Cromwell in the foreground, passing a tram, thirty-six civilians can be counted, and the worried expression on the face of one man at the back may be explained by the fact that his foot is over the very hot exhaust !

The happy tableau in the top picture is made up of (reading from left to right) Sergeant T. E. Williams, Lance-Corporal R. Gibson, a Belgian girl, Guardsman R. T. Pedgeon, Lance-Corporal H. Thomas and Sergeant G. H. Greenstock, who commanded the tank, all from No. 6 Troop of No. 2 Squadron, 2nd Battalion Welsh Guards.

The tow-rope always carried on the tank consists of four strong steel hawsers ; when damage or a break-down makes it necessary to tow the tank it is attached to the two towing lugs, just visible at the bottom of the picture, by specially designed quick-release hooks. The drum of wire just in front of the round driving visor is for removing mines ; a length could be quickly unwound and attached to a mine ; then the tank with all visors shut would reverse and pull the mine clear. Two camouflage nets are rolled up to the right of the hull gunner's Besa machine gun, and above these, apparently holding the dog's attention, are two smoke generators. These could be ignited by the driver from inside in order to provide a smoke-screen to cover the movement of the crew if the tank had to be abandoned.

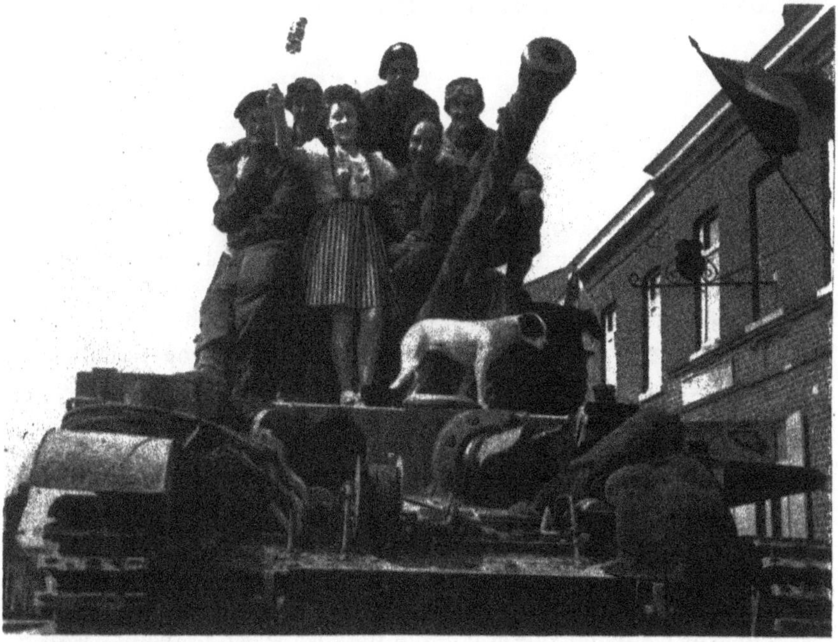

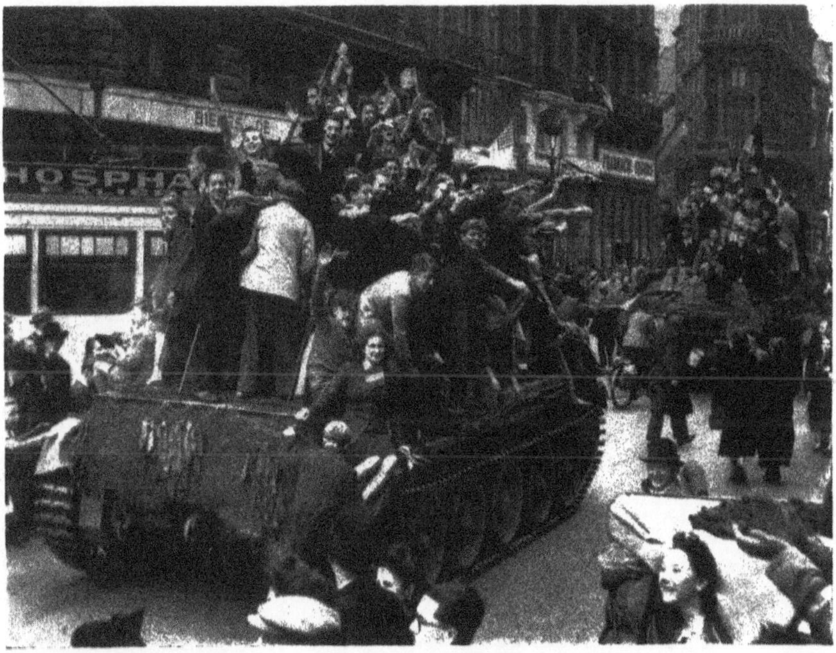

TWO VIEWS OF HECHTEL

In the campaign on the Western front the 1st and 2nd Battalions, forming the Welsh Guards Group, had their stiffest and most protracted fight at Hechtel. It started on the 7th of September and only ended in victory on the 12th. These photos, taken at the end of the action, show the buildings damaged by shell fire from guns and tanks, especially round the road junction which was the centre of the fighting.

In the top picture carriers of the 1st Battalion are seen and Padre Payne in beret and greatcoat walking towards the one at the corner.

In the lower picture a party of German prisoners is being brought in by men of the 1st Battalion; of those who were killed or wounded, one still lies in the road ahead of them. In all over eight hundred and seventy were killed or taken prisoner. They came mostly from either the 1st Battalion The Hermann Goering Regiment or the 10th Parachute Regiment and fought with great stubbornness.

The story of this action and some of the deeds of men who fought it is told on page 216.

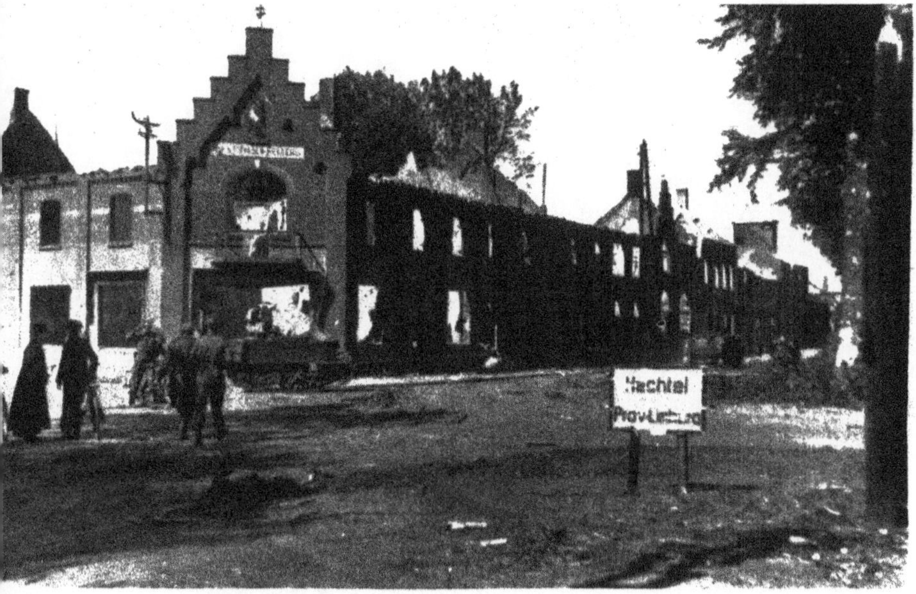
Hechtel

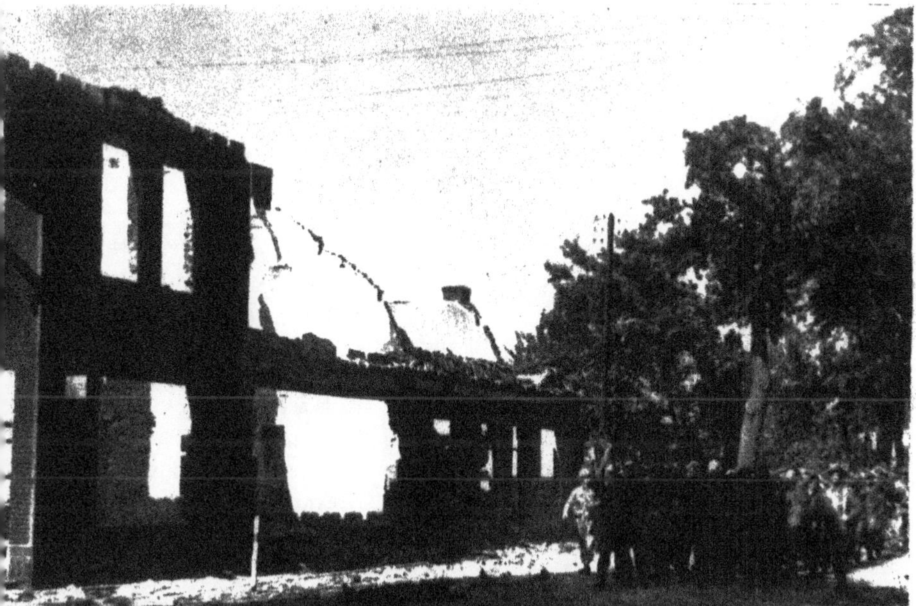

PRISONERS OF WAR

A typical incident which might take place at any time of the day during the big drive from France to Holland. Four German soldiers are lined up against the wall of a house with their hands on top of their heads, a position in which they had to remain until they reached their prisoner-of-war cage. The non-commissioned officer and Guardsmen who face them are about to search for hidden arms or ammunition.

On the left the Rev. P. F. Payne, Chaplain to the 1st Battalion, is watching them.

SALVAGE

Sergeant Hitchcock, who has salvaged a German ham, commanded the anti-aircraft troop of Crusader tanks fitted with twin Oerlikon guns which was only included in the 2nd Battalion for the fighting in Normandy.

He is wearing a "tank suit." This was a special suit issued to all tank crews to counteract the extreme cold suffered from sitting cramped up for long periods in a very draughty vehicle. It was in the form of overalls, made up into three layers of material; the outside was waterproof and the inside was cloth, and there was a thin layer of oilskin in between. A hood of the same triple material was attached to the back of the collar by press studs and would pull up right over the head. There were no external buttons on the suit when it was closed up; two parallel zips which can be seen in the photograph ran from under the collar at the top to the bottom of each leg, and the panel between them, rolled down in the picture, closed up to the neck. Large pockets closed with press studs were on each breast and on the trousers; as shown in the picture, the left breast pocket had slots made in it to take pencils for map marking. It was a first-class suit in every way and was much appreciated by the crews who wore it.

VALKENSWAARD

This small Dutch town lies on the road between Hechtel and Eindhoven about seven miles inside Holland. The Welsh Guards Group left the main road here with orders to test the possibility of another route to Nijmegen via Helmond. But it was found to be strongly held and the Divisional advance was concentrated on the direct road. The picture shows a lorry convoy halted in the town. On the left can be seen a fifteen-hundredweight truck belonging to No. 3 Squadron (shown by the white circle) of the 2nd Battalion Welsh Guards (marked 45).

The large white star surrounded by a circle was painted on the top surface of all Allied vehicles as an aid to aircraft recognition.

The truck in the foreground bears the Eagle sign of the 43rd Infantry Division.

NIJMEGEN BRIDGE

This is the famous 6,000-foot bridge which spans the Waal (a branch of the Rhine) at Nijmegen. The photograph shows the view looking towards Arnhem, twelve miles away. In the foreground is a tank from the 2nd Battalion; the white triangle which can just be seen on the back of the Cromwell shows that it belongs to No. 1 Squadron.

The road level is high above the surrounding country. It was at first under heavy fire for several weeks and it was shelled intermittently for several months, but was never put out of action. It was described by General Eisenhower as "a valuable prize," since without it the river would have been a formidable obstacle. Its capture is recorded on page 227.

IN GERMANY

The code word "Magnum" was given over the wireless when it was decided to mount infantry on to the tanks prior to going in to an attack.

Normally infantry were carried in troop-carrying lorries behind the tanks, but in forming up for an attack, and until the fight was over, the lorries were left behind; over any distances to be covered from then on tanks carried the infantry.

A complete infantry section was carried on one Cromwell; a platoon of three sections would work with and fight with a troop of three tanks.

In this picture the infantry are the 2nd Battalion Scots Guards, who joined with the 2nd Battalion Welsh Guards to make the Scots-Welsh Group after the 1st Battalion had been ordered home.

In the advance from Zeven to liberate the prisoner-of-war camp at Westertimke a number of tanks were knocked out by mines, as is told on page 285. These can be seen in this picture, which was taken on the road between Ostertimke and Kirchtimke. The second tank has had its track broken in the centre and the two middle bogie wheels are badly damaged. A spare bogie wheel which was carried by all tanks is slung on the turret. The tank nearest the camera belonged to No. 2 Troop in No. 1 Squadron. Boxes seen attached to the back of the turret and side of the tank were used for carrying the crew's kit. A case for the powerful binoculars which every tank commander carried is slung over the side of the turret.

The white tape stretched along the edge of the road is to warn traffic that the verges are mined.

AFTER THE WAR

The first picture shows the Guards Armoured Division coming back to Brussels after fighting had ended, to receive the city's thanks for its liberation.

The second picture shows the tanks of the 2nd Battalion on the day when the Guards Armoured Division paraded for their "Farewell to Armour." Before parting with their tanks the Division was reviewed by Field-Marshal Montgomery (now Viscount Montgomery), who in his address said :—

"From Alamein to the Baltic I have had many formations and units under my command. I want to say, here and now, that in the sphere of armoured warfare the Guards have set a standard that it will be difficult for those that come after to reach. . . . The Guards have shown that whatever they are asked to do—whatever they take on—they do well ; maintaining always the highest standards and giving a lead to all others." Speaking as an infantry soldier, he welcomed the Guards' return to their traditional role. "We need you in the infantry ; we need your high standards, your great efficiency in all matters and your old traditions of duty and service." He also paid high tribute to Major-General Alan Adair, who trained the Division and led it from Normandy to Cuxhaven. All in the Division, not least the Welsh Guards Battalions, realise their debt to "General Alan."

The picture overleaf is a fitting close to this record. It shows men of the 1st Battalion training in Scotland before setting out again for service in Palestine. The officers, reading from left, are : Lieutenant-Colonel C. H. R. Heber-Percy, D.S.O., M.C. ; Captain J. M. Spencer-Smith, M.C. ; Colonel the Earl of Gowrie, V.C., P.C., G.C.M.G., C.B., D.S.O., Colonel of the Regiment. Behind the latter speaking to a Guardsman is Colonel Sir Alexander Stanier, Bart., D.S.O., M.C., Lieutenant-Colonel Commanding the Regiment, and on Lord Gowrie's left is Major Sir Richard Powell, Bart., M.C.

Campaign Maps

OF

NORTH AFRICA
ITALY
FRANCE AND GERMANY

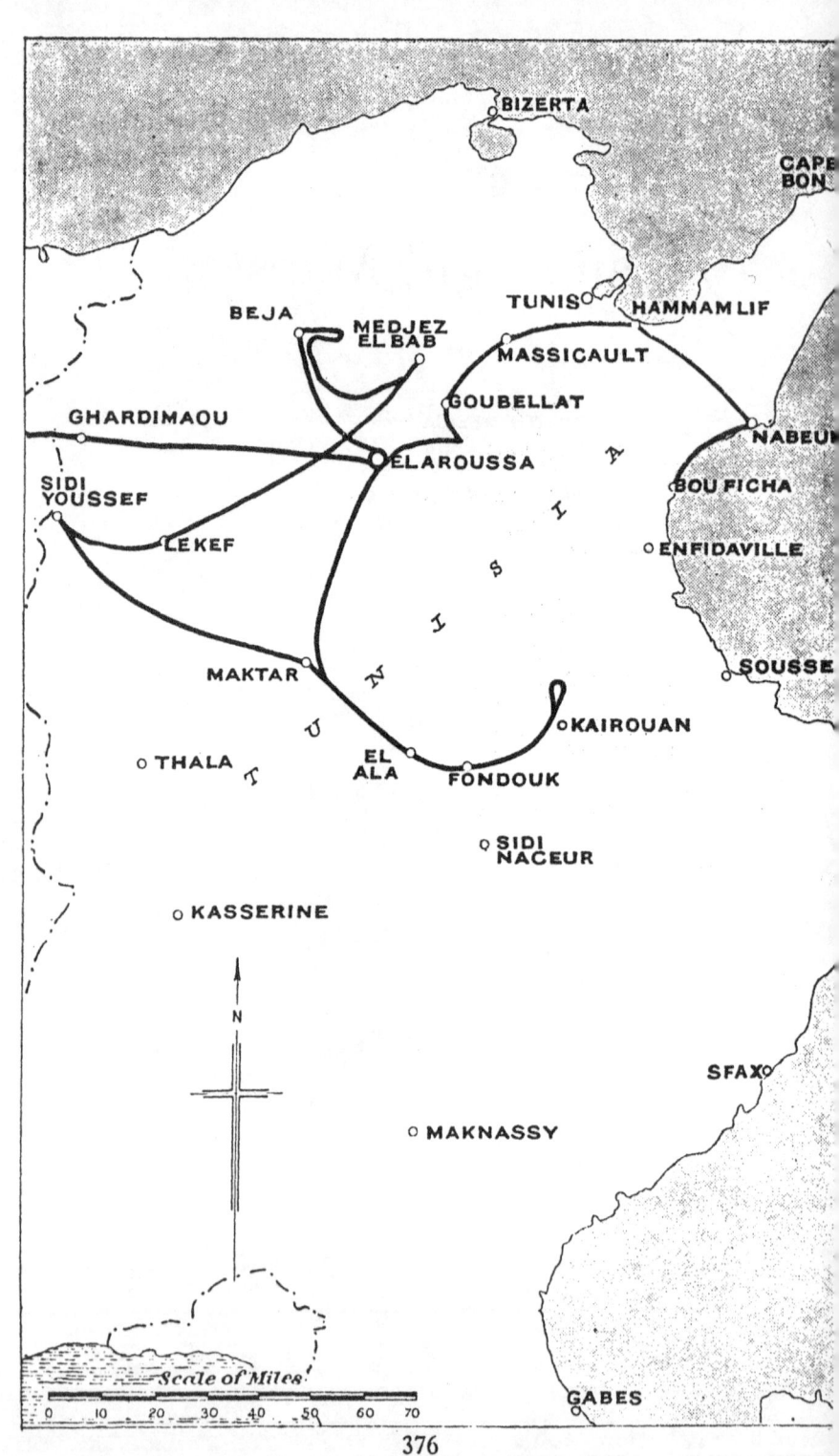

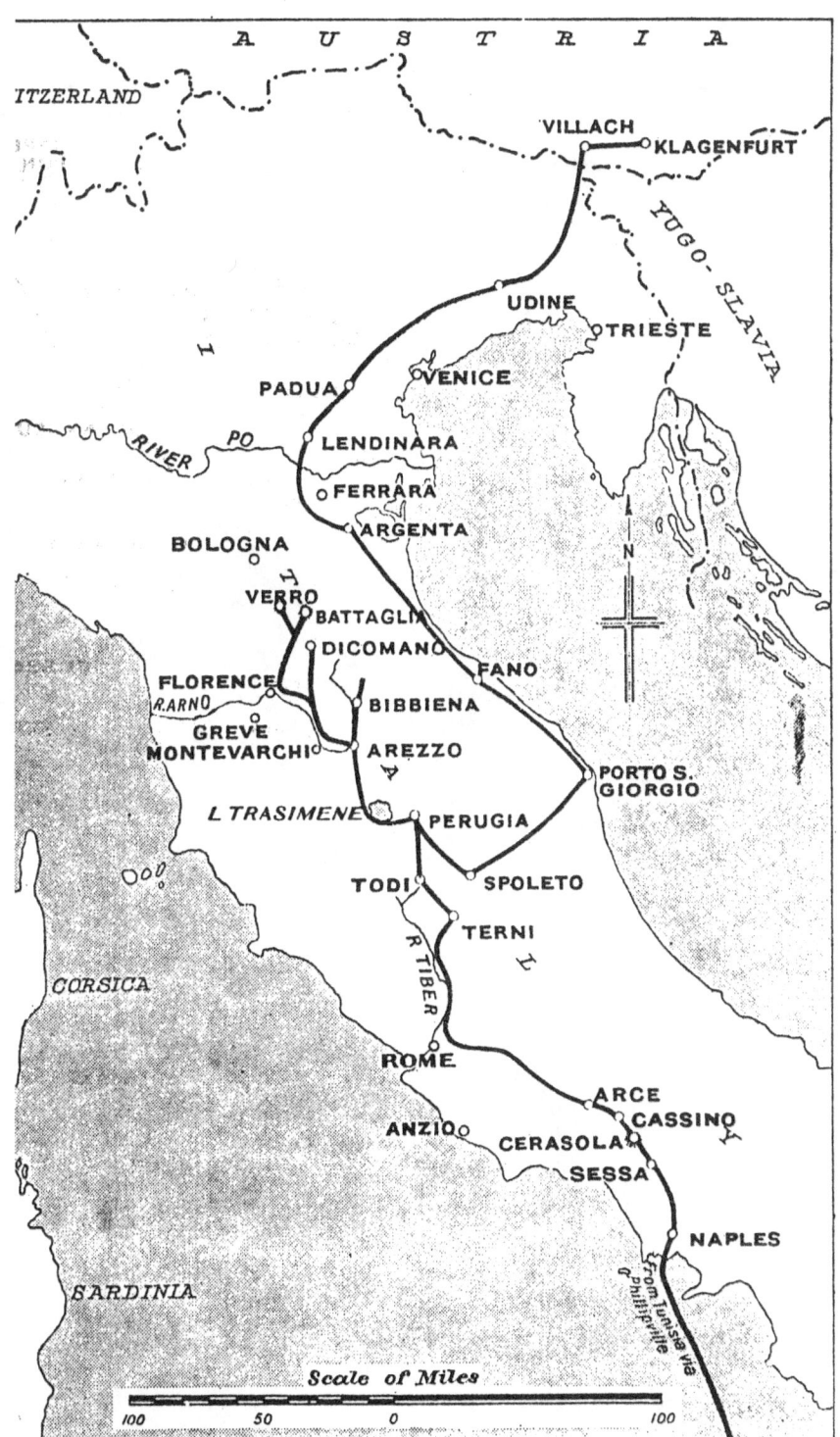

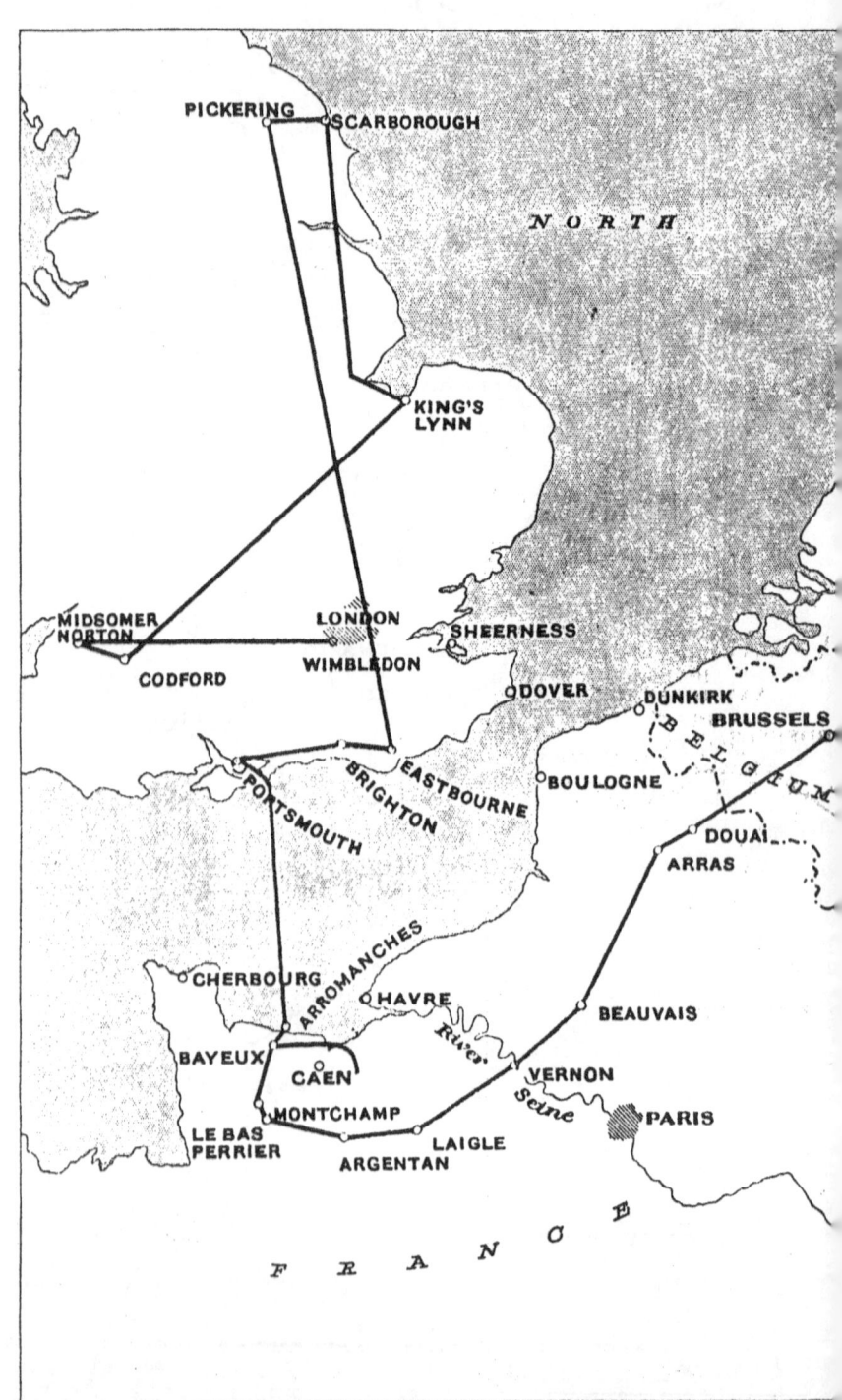

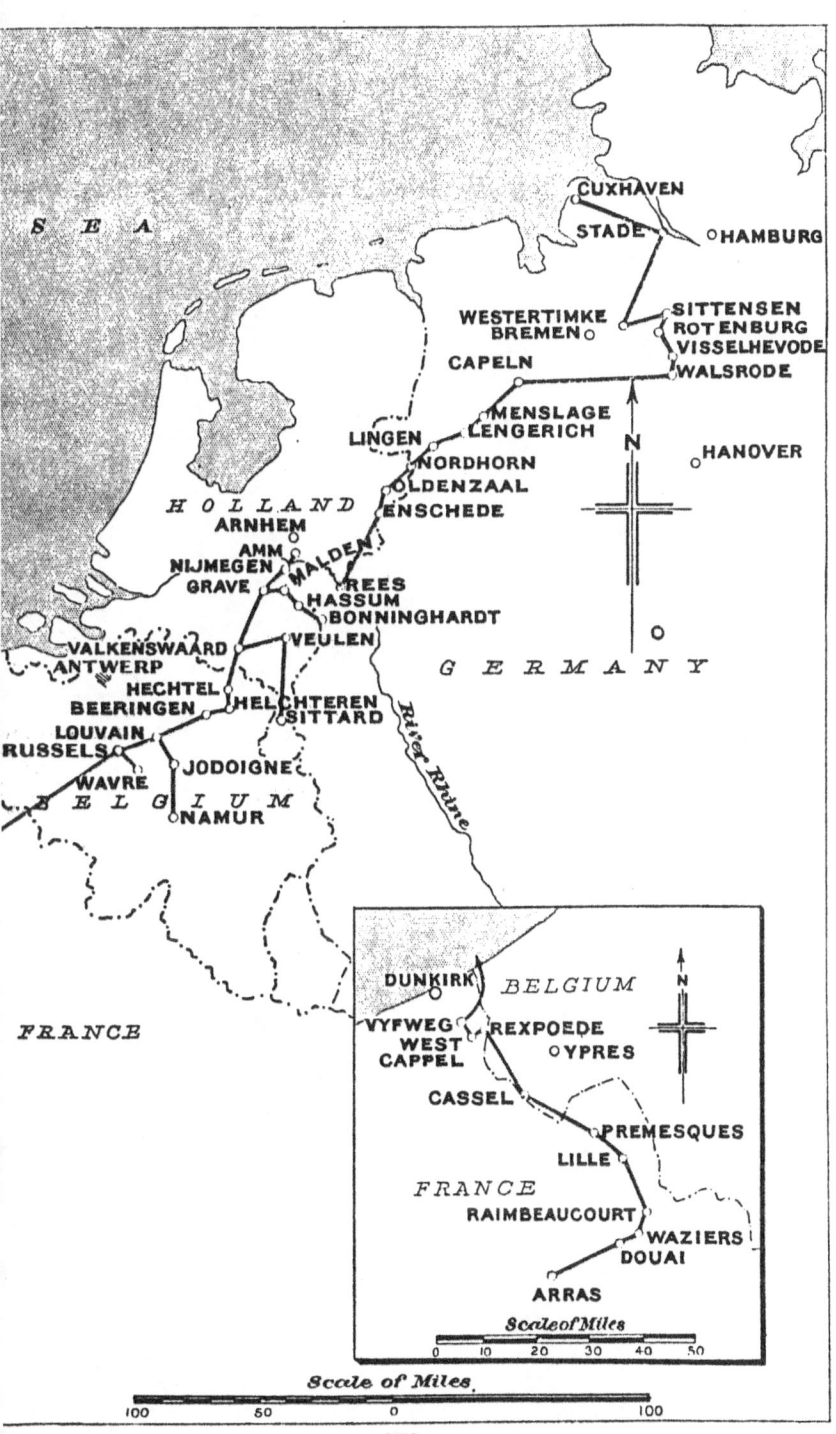

Index

INDEX TO PERSONAL NAMES

Abrams, O. F., 157
Adair, Maj.-Gen. A., 75, 204
Alexander, Field-Marshal The Viscount, 27, 30, 31, 32, 41, 42, 58, 61, 76
Allen, D. A. N., 115, 117
Arbuthnot, Sir H. F., Bt., 125
Armitage, S. R., 285
Arnold, T. J. L., 153
Ashton, J. O. M., 253

Baker, A. R., 238, 271
Baker, F. G., 138
Bankier, A. M., 20, 22, 290
Bankier, I. P., 144, 150, 151
Bankier, M. A., 149
Barbour, R. G., 133
Barnes, L. J., 129
Barter, A. C., 27
Beck, S., 292
Beckett, Sir M. G., Bt., 270
Beckwith-Smith, Maj.-Gen. M. B., 217
Beckwith-Smith, P. M., 217, 221
Bedingfeld, Sir E. G. F., Bt., 103
Bell, W. A. O. J., 249
Beresford, Ralph, 208
Beresford, Robert, 208
Berry, J. W., 94
Beynon, D., 136
Beynon, F., 232
Bezani, S., 119
Birch, E., 210
Black, P., 100
Bland, A. J., 214
Bolton, F. B., 154, 163, 168, 291
Booker, B., 102
Boston, L. F., 242, 243
Bowen, W. E., 196
Brace, W. E., 165
Bradley, Gdsn., 178
Bray, W. L., 231, 232
Brinson, D. N., 214, 225, 238
Brodie Knight, C., 159
Brookes, C., 240
Brookes, W., 292
Browning, G. W., 22, 24, 39, 54
Bruce, Lord, 198
Bruce, D., 236, 237
Bruce, The Hon. N. H. C., 283
Brutton, P. F. F., 157
Buckland, J. C., 14, 91, 210

Buckley, W. K., 138
Burchell, J. F. R., 200, 216
Burgess, D. F., 250
Burt, E. G. M., 104
Bushell, A. A., 176, 182, 183
Bye, R., 2

Canavan, T., 185
Carr, P. A., 248, 249
Carson, J. H., 185, 229
Carter, P. A., 271
Carter, W. H., 100
Cassavetti, A. J. S., 135, 155, 156
Chatwin, M. G. G., 262
Chinnery, M. J. B., 137, 144
Churchill, Rt. Hon. Winston, 22
Clark, General M. W., 76
Close-Smith, H. T., 209
Clowes, Lieut.-Col. H. N., 282, 283
Cobbold, R. N., 149, 150
Collier, E. E. C., 210
Consett, W. L., 182, 275, 280
Cook, A. C., 179
Coombe-Tennant, A. H. S., 237
Copland-Griffiths, F. A. V., 11, 14, 17, 26, 30, 90, 92, 93, 112, 117
Copping, J., 291
Cottom, D. G., 257, 258
Cox, F. S., 117
Cullingford, C. H. D., The Rev., 91
Culverhouse, K., 242, 243

Daley, J. P., 94
Daniel, N. M., 109, 110, 179, 266, 271, 275
Davage, I., 110
Davies, C., 126
Davies, D., 137, 138
Davies, E., 159, 263
Davies, H., 187
Davies, I. G. G., 287
Davies, J. B., 152
Davies, J. H. G., 150, 151
Davies, U. 198, 270
Davies, W., 120, 153
Davies-Scourfield, D. G., 43, 49, 134, 138, 148
Delaplanque, Madam, 110
Dent, J. A. W., 208, 267
de Rutzen, J. F. F., Baron, 121, 160, 161, 251
Devas, M. C., 225, 228, 229

383

Dimsdale, H. C. L., 90, 125, 126
Doyle, W., 133, 150
Duckham, D. N. G., 133, 134
Dudley-Ward, C. H., 290
Dunderdale, M., 222
Dunn, H. P. N., 137
Dyke, F. W., 197

Easter, T., 137
Eastwood, F. M., 118
Egerton, F. L., 157, 159, 160, 162, 163
Eisenhower, General, 24, 27, 74, 75
Elliot, D. P. G., 133
Essex, J., 161
Evans, A., 138
Evans, E. D., 220
Evans, G. N., 158
Evans, J. V., 225
Evans, T. H., 126, 257
Evans, W. D. D., 178, 181, 190, 193, 198, 212, 213, 214, 215, 229, 269
Evans, Gdsn., 235, 236
Evelegh, Major-General V., 147

Farrer, R. P., 287
Fass, J. E., 54
Fisher, N. T. L., 177, 206, 217, 227, 267, 275
Fletcher, E., 177
Floyd, R., 224, 225
Fogg-Elliot, W. T. C., 155, 156, 161, 163
Forbes, H. S., 111
Forster, Brigadier S. A., 30
Fothringham, P. Stewart, 222, 229
Fowke, G. G., 190, 193, 212
Fowles, R. G., 196
Fox-Pitt, W. A. F. L., 11, 97, 102
Froystad, I., 185, 186
Furness, The Hon. C., 12, 93, 94

Garrison, B., 119, 120
George V, H.M. The King, 3
George VI, H.M. The King, 6, 8, 20, 70, 84, 166
German, F., 210
Gibbs, D. A., 182, 187, 272, 278, 291
Gibson-Watt, J. D., 125, 126, 132, 137, 152, 257, 262, 263
Glanusk, The Lord, 6, 18, 22
Glass, A. G., 286
Goff, B. P. R., 117, 146, 156, 158
Goodwin, F., 153
Gort, General The Viscount, 7, 8, 10, 11, 13, 15
Gough, S., 200
Graham, A. G., 233

Grant, K. W., 129
Greenacre, W. D. C., 11, 14, 20, 21, 39, 90, 194
Greer, B. R. T., 162
Gresham, J. F., 55, 193, 194
Grieg, D., 263
Griffin, G. E., 94
Griffiths, C. D., 94
Griffiths, D. H., 91
Griffiths, T., 94
Griffiths, W. H., 225
Grimston, R. W. S., 235, 236
Groom, C. V. B., 150
Gurney, J. E., 49, 58, 90, 108, 109, 110, 111, 158, 159, 162, 249, 253, 256, 258
Gurney, J. J., 254
Gwatkin, J. S., 186, 210

Hall, A. E., 94, 95
Hall, S. A., 166, 167
Hamer, H. H., 168
Harley, A., 225
Harmsworth, C. A. St. J. P., 117
Harrison, R. L., 117
Harrowell, D. W. J., 179, 272
Hart, E., 252
Harvey, A. E., 232
Harvey, J. A., 232
Haydon, Brigadier J. C., 9, 134, 142, 166
Hayley, T. B., 149
Heber-Percy, C. H. R., 9, 54, 55, 99, 101, 190, 192, 233, 271
Hedley-Dent, R. P., 200
Helling, E., 188
Henderson, J. A. A., 221
Higgon, J. H. V., 99
Hill, G. P., 182
Hillier, B. F., 151
Hodgkinson, R. B., 98, 279
Hodgson, D. E. P., 24, 115, 117, 124, 125
Hodgson, L. A., 166, 167
Hoffman, J. J., 265
Hollebone, G. T., 189
Homfray, H. F. R., 229
Homfray, J. C. R. 186
Hornet, R. P., 210
Howard, R. J. S., 269
Hughes, H. H., 100
Hughes, O. H., 214, 215
Hughes, T., 183

Irwin, C. G., 187, 225

James, E. J., 208
Jefferson, J., 17, 21

Index

Jeffreys, J. G., 238
Jerman, J. T., 157, 159, 249, 250, 254
John, Augustus, 291
John, H. E. B., 158
John, F. G., 178
Jolly, S. A., 287
Jones, F. D., 242
Jones, F. T., 101
Jones, H. R., 151
Jones, T., 225
Jones, Dr. Thomas, 291
Jones, W., 136
Jones-Mortimer, H. M. C., 98
Joyce, A., 270

Kearsley, N. S., 178
Kemble, D. H. A., 278
Kempson, A. E., 270
Kennedy, T., 223
Keogh, C. J., 153
King, J., 102

Lawrie, C., 225
Leake, R. H., 167
Leatham, C. A. la T., 117, 286, 287, 288
Leatham, M. W. T., 205
Leatham, R. E. K., 21, 22
Leese, General Sir Oliver, Bt., 7, 11
Lester, D. M., 191
Leuchars, P. R., 195, 196
Lewis, J., 183
Lewis, J. C., Windsor, 12, 39, 98, 101, 102, 104, 186, 203, 208, 230, 275, 281, 283, 285, 288
Lewis, R., 192
Ling, E. M., 269, 270
Lisburne, Earl of, 291
Lister, H. E. J., 199, 213, 221
Llewellyn, G., 222
Llewellyn, W. H. R., 92, 109, 124, 125
Lloyd, Gdsn., 240
Louden, D. D., 269
Lowe, Gdsn., 215
Luxmoore-Ball, R. E. C., 89
Luxmoore-Ball, P. C., 182

Mabey, E. F., 178
Mairs, W., 137
Maisey, H. G., 109
Makins, Sir W. V., Bt., 42, 43, 90, 107, 117, 118, 131
Makins, P. V., 261
Mann, J., 187
Marchant, G. H., 210
Marshall, W. J., 165, 166

Martin-Smith, J. R., 107, 124, 125, 149, 168, 252, 258
Maude, C. A. F. J., 151
McCreery, Lieut.-General Sir R. L., 77
McGhan, J., 249, 252
McLelland, C., 222
McVittie, C. A. B., 117
Mildmay, The Hon. A. B., 185, 283
Millard, H. J., 271
Miller, J. M., 108, 188, 189, 190, 192, 197, 203, 206, 216, 217, 220, 221, 222
Mills, F., 111
Millward, A., 238
Mitchley, H. R. E., 221
Montgomery, Field-Marshal the Viscount, 27, 54, 56, 65, 67, 75, 76, 83, 173
Moorehead, Alan, 121
Morgan, E., 152
Morris, O. D., 134
Mosse, R. H., 200
Murray, Major-General, H., 79
Murrell, C., 291
Myddleton, E. J., 186

Neave, Sir A. T. C., Bt., 91
Nicholl-Carne, J. D. S., 153, 161
Noel, A. C. W., 111
Norman, Brigadier, C. W., 110

Oakshott, T. A., 22
O'Connor, General Sir R. N., 224
Owen Edmunds, D. M., 209

Parry, Capt., 118
Parish, P. E. G. W., 281
Parsons, L. E., 187
Pattinson, R. L., 132, 138
Payne, Rev. P. F., 199, 200, 233
Pearson, J. A., 220
Peel, H. W. J. E., 178, 217, 266
Penrose, N. S., 269
Perrins, A. M. D., 100
Petre, R. L., Major-General, 89, 90
Phillips, A. H. G., 215, 217
Pickersgill, N., 242
Pilcher, R. C. H., 100, 101
Pitt-Rivers, M. A. L. F., 283
Portal, F. S., 213, 214
Porter, R. D., 162
Potter, T. F., 101
Poumier, Commandant, 91
Powell, J. M., 152

Powell, M. T., 238
Powell, Sir R. G D., Bt., 189, 191, 192, 229, 237, 269
Price, R. C. R., 79, 258, 263
Pugh, B. B., 117, 136, 254
Pugh, D. F., 126, 165, 167

Rees, A., 210
Rees, E. K., 208
Rees, N., 127
Reid, J. E., 195
Retallack, T. C. H., 200
Rhys, the Hon. D. R., 200
Rhys-Williams, G. D., 117, 118, 119, 120
Rice, H. T., 6
Richards, E. L. G., 111
Ritchie, A., 271
Roberts, D. H., 292
Roberts, G., 94
Roberts, Major-General G. P. B., 239
Roberts, I., 209
Roberts, J. L., 198, 199
Roberts, J. R., 161
Roberts, J. S., 269
Roberts, R. L. 267
Rodd, W. J., 176
Rogers, D. A., 188, 192
Rogers, J., 197, 198
Roscoe, K., 104
Rossant, S., 232
Roughton, F., 272
Ruddle, D. G., 162

Sale, Colonel W. M., 210
Schuster, A. E. L., 136
Scott, Brigadier C. A. M. D., 166, 258
Scudamore, E., 213, 214, 215
Seagar, G. E., 243
Seamark, A. A., 188
Sharples, R. C., 100, 163
Shuldham, A. F. Q., 216
Smart, M. E. C., 54, 90
Smith, Brigadier Lyon, 124
Smith, W. K., 192
Smythe, O. N. H. M., 124, 153
Sparrow, C. W., 162
Spencer, J. O., 182, 217, 221
Spencer-Smith, J. M., 201, 240
Stanier, Sir Alexander, Bt., 6, 9, 11, 17, 52, 66, 97, 98, 103, 290

Stanier, Lady, 290
Stevens, R. D., 186
Stevenson, D. J. C., 196, 235, 236
Stewart, A. G., 117, 118, 119, 120
Stewart, I. M., 178, 280
Summers, K. G., 119
Syrett, J. D. A., 177, 178

Thomas, H., 167
Thomas, I. L., 94
Thomas, N. L. P., 269
Thorpe, N., 222
Threipland, W. Murray, 6
Tipper, W., 232
Townsend, F., 276
Tremblett, F., 160, 161
Truscott, L. K., Lieut.-General, 77
Turnbull, M. J., 177, 191, 192
Turner, K., 232
Tweedie, H., 279
Twining, R. C., 103, 114, 244
Twining, Mrs., 244

Unwin, A., 198
Upfill Brown, A. A., 276

Vigor, G. St. V. J., 9, 17, 21, 39

Waite, N. P. G. W., 270
Wallace, V. G., 177, 213, 214
Waters, T. J., 220, 271
Wavell, Field-Marshal The Viscount, 22, 289
Webb, L. A. R., 236, 237
Wheatley, A. W. S., 185, 229, 274, 283
Whiskard, R. G., 186
Whistler, Rex, 176
Widdrington, F. N. H., 270
Wilcox, C., 250
Wilcox, I., 225
Wildsmith, J. H., 165
Williams, C, 232
Williams, D., 94
Williams, E., 196
Williams, E. T., 238
Williams, F. E., 243
Williams, H. L., 217
Willis, D., 165
Windsor, H.R.H. The Duke of, 8
Wolfers, J. A. G., 138
Worrall, W. G. M., 92
Wrigley, R. O., 241, 242, 243

www.ingramcontent.com/pod-product-compliance
Lightning Source LLC
Chambersburg PA
CBHW021955160426
43197CB00007B/146